Elementary Children's Literature

THE BASICS FOR TEACHERS AND PARENTS

Nancy A. Anderson

University of South Florida

Allyn and Bacon

Boston ▪ *London* ▪ *Toronto* ▪ *Sydney* ▪ *Tokyo* ▪ *Singapore*

Series Editor: Aurora Martínez Ramos
Series Editorial Assistant: Beth Slater
Executive Marketing Manager: Amy Cronin
Editorial-Production Service: Omegatype Typography, Inc.
Composition and Prepress Buyer: Linda Cox
Manufacturing Buyer: Julie McNeill
Interior Text Design: Carol Somberg
Cover Administrator: Linda Knowles
Electronic Composition and Art: Omegatype Typography, Inc.

Library of Congress Cataloging-in-Publication Data

Anderson, Nancy A.
    Elementary children's literature : the basics for teachers and parents / Nancy A.
Anderson.
      p.   cm.
    Includes bibliographical references and index.
    ISBN 0-321-04914-4
    1. Children's literature—History and criticism.   2. Children's literature—
Study and teaching (Elementary) I. Title.

PN1009.A1 A464 2002
809'.89282—dc21

                                   2001034340

Printed in the United States of America
10 9 8 7 6 5 4 3 2 1   06 05 04 03 02 01

Credits are found on pp. 385–386, which constitute an extension of the copyright page.

To William Oscar Anderson
and Marguerite Cogorno Radencich

I love and miss you both

Contents

Part Two   The Boundless World of Fiction   112

Part Three   Discovering the World through Nonfiction   263

chapter 10
Biography and Autobiography   263

chapter 11
Informational Books   283

chapter 12
Poetry and Verse   303

chapter 13
Tying It Together   323

Preface

I first taught children's literature in 1980, when I was a graduate assistant at the University of Southern Mississippi, home of the extensive de Grummond collection of children's books. Through the years I have searched for just the right textbook to teach children's literature. I wanted one that was brief, so my students could spend most of their reading time with children's books; and I wanted one that was limited to preschool and elementary literature, because a brief text could not adequately cover that realm and young adult literature as well. I also wanted a textbook that integrated pedagogy and applications my students could explore in class. I never found the elusive "just right" textbook, so I spent many years collecting books, information, and resources for my students. When offered the opportunity to develop my class into a Web-delivered course, I decided to pull all my books, information, and resources into a "just right" textbook, which would be appropriate for both traditional instruction and distance teaching through computer technology.

Elementary Children's Literature: The Basics for Teachers and Parents is designed as an introductory text for preservice teachers of elementary, early childhood, and special education. It is also appropriate for noneducation majors who are taking children's literature as a liberal arts requirement. Most of my noneducation students either are, or intend to be, parents, and I believe they will be more purposefully involved in their children's learning after reading this text. In writing this book, I did not assume readers had prior knowledge of contemporary children's literature or were fluent in "educationese." To further optimize readability, I wrote in a conversational tone, speaking directly to readers.

Several features of this text make it especially appropriate for teachers and parents of preschool and elementary children.

- Only books suitable for children through age 13 are included.
- A full chapter features illustration and early childhood picture books.
- Picture books are integrated with juvenile novels and chapter books throughout each chapter.
- Examples of book illustrations are included in each chapter.
- A full chapter is dedicated to animal fantasy.

This textbook is organized around genres and includes a complete chapter on each major genre plus the subgenres of fiction. Each genre chapter contains extensive bibliographies of books in print (as well as a few exceptional out-of-print books that are available in libraries). Also, for each genre there is a list of evaluation criteria. In addition to discussions of books about minorities in each chapter, there is a separate chapter on multicultural and international literature that features works *by* minority authors and illustrators, rather than just books *about* minorities.

Instructional and curriculum tie-ins are woven within the text and also appear in literature response boxes at strategic places in the chapters (rather than in end-of-chapter information, which—if not overlooked entirely—prevents readers from making immediate connections with the text). The final chapter, Tying It Together, is a pedagogical overview of how students can apply their knowledge of literature to help children grow in their language and reading abilities. Included in this chapter are annotated lists of resources, along with their World Wide Web addresses (URLs) and information on how to access the direct links to these sites.

Another unique feature of this book is the overview of the Dewey decimal system in the first chapter. In addition, brief directions for locating books (of a particular genre) are provided at the beginning of each genre chapter.

In summary, this book was especially written to meet the needs of educators who want a concise literature methods text. Such instructors want students to spend most of their reading time with children's books, yet they need a text that presents the basic course content so they may devote more class time to exploring books and related activities. Features of this book include:

- student-friendly text
- relevance to both teachers and parents
- exclusive chapter on animal fantasy
- chapter on multicultural literature, featuring works *by* minority authors and illustrators
- information on Dewey decimal system of classification
- extensive, up-to-date bibliographies with annotations
- annotated Web addresses of literature-related sites and direct links
- scope restricted to preschool and elementary
- chapter on teaching reading through literature
- strands of multicultural literature, picture books, and pedagogy throughout

Supplements for Students

A Companion Website (**www.ablongman.com/anderson**) that includes direct links for referenced Internet sites, an interactive activity, a self test, and essay assignments for each chapter as well as an extensive glossary.

The following activities are available on the companion website: Genre Characters (p. 26), Character Continuum (p. 27), Story Mapping (p. 32), Cultural Literacy on Mythology (p. 85), Harry Potter Wizardspeak (p. 138), Readers Theater (p. 155), Mystery Clues (p. 219), Character Mapping (p. 254), Biography Timeline (p. 265), KWL Chart (p. 292), Pattern Verse (p. 308), and Question Levels (p. 326).

Acknowledgments

Many people contributed to the development of this book, and I want to acknowledge and thank them in order of appearance. I thank Bradley Pottoff who inspired me to undertake this project and who lent his critical guidance in the formative stage. I also appreciate Paul Solaqua, whose encouragement kept me on track in the early stages.

I am very grateful to Virginia Blanford, my acquisitions editor, who brought me to this publisher and who procured the best contract an author could ever wish for. Her revision of my prospectus helped me shape my vision for the book. I sorely missed Virginia when she transferred to another division.

I am eternally grateful to Christine Miranda, my development editor, who—more than anyone else—contributed to the substance of this book. She worked with me from the first draft of the prospectus to the preparation of the final manuscript. Not only did she point out errors I made in preparing the manuscript (e.g., *The Wizard of Ox*); she also helped me recast sentences and whole sections to improve readability. Additionally, she pointed out areas that were incomplete and caused me to reconsider concepts, such as multiculturalism, that needed improvement.

I must also acknowledge and thank my husband, Rodney Crowley, for allowing me to ignore him for long periods of time while I worked at my computer and for taking up the slack on all the work pertaining to our household, which I also ignored for a couple of years.

Some of my esteemed colleagues wrote segments on their areas of expertise for this book, and I gratefully acknowledge them: Sabrina A. Brinson, University of Memphis; Gloria Houston, Western Carolina University; Jerry Michel, Skokie, Illinois, School District; Dan Ouzts, The Citadel; and Jenifer Jasinski Schneider, University of South Florida.

I thank Aurora Martínez, my acquisitions editor, for guiding me through the final stages, and I gratefully acknowledge the skill and thoroughness with which Anne Rogers and the team at Omegatype Typography, Inc., has converted a complex manuscript into the finished book you hold today. I would also like to thank the following reviewers for their helpful ideas on how to improve this book: Rebecca S. Compton, East Central University; Terrance Flaherty, Mankato State University; Darwin L. Henderson, University of Cincinnati; David Levande, Southern Connecticut State University; Louise Stearns, Southern Illinois University; and Suzanne Stringer, Auburn University Montgomery.

—Nancy A. Anderson
anderson@coedu.usf.edu

Alice meets the Cheshire Cat.

Alice's Adventures in Wonderland Written by Lewis Carroll and illustrated by Sir John Tenniel.

Introduction to the World of Children's Literature

c h a p t e r

1

One of my warmest childhood memories is of my mother reading *Miss Pickerell Goes to Mars* (MacGregor 1951) to my older sister and me. We were in elementary school and quite capable of reading it ourselves, but we had grown accustomed to having our mother read to us each night before bedtime. Stories sounded so much better when she read them. Another happy memory is of my sixth-grade teacher, Mr. Conway, reading a chapter a day from *The Adventures of Tom Sawyer* (Twain 1876). The books he read that year helped pass the afternoons in the hot portable classroom. Each day we begged him to read one more chapter or even just two more pages because we could not wait to find out what happened next.

Do you have similar memories of your parents' and teachers' reading to you? Because you are reading this book, you are most likely a teacher or a parent, or you intend to become a teacher or parent. This book will introduce you to the vast and wonderful world of children's literature, so you will be prepared to create such memories for the children in your classroom or your home. In this textbook, when I talk about *your children,* I am referring both to students and to your own children.

Within these pages I will acquaint you with numerous books appropriate for children from birth through age 13—the preschool and elementary school years. This textbook is intentionally brief; after all, most of your reading should be children's books—not a book *about* children's books. Therefore, I will not attempt to cover the many fabulous books available for middle school and high school students; several other good textbooks do focus on literature especially for adolescents and young adults (e.g., Donelson & Nilsen 1997 and Brown & Stephens 1995).

Defining Literature for Children

A few definitions will help outline the scope of this book. You might think *children's literature* could be easily defined as "books for kids." However, there are many different definitions of children's literature and even varying definitions for *literature* and *children!*

What is literature? Are all books literature? Are only stories considered literature? One definition of literature requires that the work be of good quality (Hillman 1999). Hillman describes some signs of poor quality—stodgy writing, plots that are too predictable, too illogical, or too much didacticism. However, there is little agreement on what constitutes good quality. For example, the first time I taught an undergraduate multicultural literature course, I assigned *Ishi, Last of His Tribe* (Kroeber 1964) for the biography reading. I selected it because the book had affected me deeply, moving me to tears when the last members of Ishi's family died. However, my students were nearly unanimous in their reaction to the book: "It stinks!" I learned that quality is in the eyes of the beholder.

I consider all books written for children to be literature—excluding works such as comic books, joke books, cartoon books, and nonfiction works that are not intended to be read from front to back, such as dictionaries, encyclopedias, and other reference material. Obviously, some books are of better quality than others, but each reader must make that determination. In this text, I recommend books I believe are high quality—and hope you do not think any of them stink.

Some people consider children's literature to span the age group of birth through 18. However, no junior high or high school students I know consider themselves children. Therefore, I define literature for youth ages 13 to 18 as adolescent or young adult literature, and literature for youth from birth through age 13 as children's literature. Traditional elementary schools enroll children through sixth grade, and typically children are 12 or 13 years old when they complete elementary school.

It is easy to distinguish between a kid in elementary school and one in middle or junior high school; it is even easy to distinguish between a 13-year-old and a 14-year-old, simply by asking them. But it is not so easy to distinguish between children's and adolescent literature. The definitions and dividing line are arbitrary at best, and sometimes children will surprise you when they cross over these lines with their reading selections.

When my adult students ask me how to determine what age or grade level a book would be suited for, I usually tell them that any book a reader likes is appropriate for that reader. When they do not accept that answer (which is most of the time), I tell them that one rule of thumb (also known as the "quick and dirty" rule) is that the author often makes the main character the age of the intended audience. Like most quick and dirty rules, this one is not always true. For example, the best-selling book *Shane* (Schaefer 1949) is narrated by a young boy. However, the book's subject matter and readability are suited for young adults, and there was a great motion picture made about the book in the 1950s that appealed to all ages.

Some book publishers print an approximate reading level somewhere in their books. For example, Bantam indicates the level in the upper section of the copyright page, and Scholastic puts it on the lower portion of the back cover. In either case, look for the letters RL (Reading Level) followed by a numeral. For example, RL2 indicates a second-grade reading level. The level is written in this code so not to turn away a child in an older grade who might wish to read the book.

Keep in mind that reading levels are approximations determined by readability formulas that take into account only average lengths of words and sentences. Because the formulas cannot measure readers' prior knowledge of the content or interest in the subject, they are often invalid. For example, after my graduate students read *The Devil's Arithmetic* (Yolen 1988), a book about the Holocaust, they engaged in a heated discussion about how early to introduce the book. Some argued sixth grade, but others said definitely not before eighth grade. Then one of the students raised her hand and said, "I read it in third grade." That was the end of that discussion.

I used to think that although some children were not able to read on their grade level, their interest level would be the same as that of their peers. One summer I took a group of preservice teachers to an inner-city school to tutor children in summer school. For the first session, tutors were to read aloud to the children, so I told my students to take four books on different reading levels and let the children choose which book they wanted to hear. When we collected the children from their classrooms, one stood out from the rest. He was about 12, and taller than his tutor; he looked like he might soon be able to play halfback for the Tampa Bay Buccaneers. "I hope his tutor brought some sports books," I thought to myself. But I later discovered that the book he picked for his tutor to read was Arnold Lobel's *Days with Frog and Toad* (1979)!

Therefore, in this text I do not attempt to pigeonhole books by assigning them to grade levels. The elementary children I have encountered like a wide range of books, from picture books to young adult novels. Assigning grade levels to books actually discourages children from reading many fine books. As mentioned, children are reluctant to select a book that has been labeled for a lower grade level. Worse, if children learn they are able to read only books designated for lower grade levels, their self-esteem is damaged, especially when their classmates find out. Often these children choose not to read at all rather than read a book on the primary level. When given varied choices, such as they find in a school or public library, children will select books appropriate to their interests and reading abilities. Read to your children from books that you like and from books they request. You will soon find out if the topic is not interesting because it is too babyish (or too sophisticated), and you can make another selection.

The Birth of Modern Children's Literature

Some schools of library science offer graduate courses on the history of children's literature. In one such school, a sage professor told me, "I don't know why they offer that course. I don't think children's literature has any history!" I laughed, but I did wonder why she said it. After all, every children's literature textbook I had read contained a chapter on history. When I asked the professor, she replied that children's literature as we know it today began in 1865 when Charles Dodgson (under the pen name of Lewis Carroll) wrote *Alice's Adventures in Wonderland*. It was the first novel written especially for children that was purely entertaining with no instructional purpose. The book has a dreamlike quality: Alice follows a white rabbit down a rabbit hole and finds herself in a fantasyland where animals speak, objects come alive, and people change sizes.

What did children read before the publication of *Alice?* Children have always listened to and enjoyed folklore, and after the development of the printing press in the late 1400s, they were able to read folk literature. Because traditional literature is presented in Chapter 4, I will reserve the discussion of its history for that chapter, and briefly discuss the development of children's novels here.

Before 1865, children in the English-speaking world read and enjoyed adult novels such as *Robinson Crusoe* (Defoe 1719), *Gulliver's Travels* (Swift 1726), *The Swiss Family Robinson* (Wyss 1812), *A Christmas Carol* (Dickens 1843), and *Journey to the Center of the Earth* (Verne 1864). If you review the unabridged versions of these works, you will find them very advanced reading, so I think these books must have been read by older, more capable children who perhaps shared them with their younger siblings.

The earliest books written for children were entirely religious, instructional, or for the improvement of their morals and manners. In the latter half of the eighteenth century, however, an English publisher named John Newbery published books for children to *enjoy*. One such book, *The History of Little Goody Two Shoes* (Newbery 1765), is considered the first novel written especially for children. Newbery's books were also highly moralistic, but at least someone had recognized that children needed to be entertained as well as indoctrinated. Young children read and enjoyed these books, of course, because there was little else for them to read. However, those early books would not entertain children today. When I reviewed some of them, I found them to contain all the flaws of "nonliterature" identified by Hillman: "stodgy writing, plots that are either too predictable or too illogical, and socially conscious themes that outweigh the slender story that supports them" (1999, p. 3).

Imagine the delight of children when they first read *Alice's Adventures in Wonderland*. "What made this story absolutely unique for its time was that it contained not a trace of a lesson or a moral. It was really made purely for enjoyment . . . " (Huck, Hepler, Hickman, & Kiefer 1997, p. 96). Charles Dodgson was a mathematics lecturer and ordained deacon at Christ Church College of Oxford University in England. He often entertained the young daughter (Alice Liddell) of the dean of his college by telling stories about Wonderland. Later he published the stories under the pseudonym of Lewis Carroll in *Alice's Adventures in Wonderland* and the sequel *Through the Looking-Glass and What Alice Found There* (1871).

Alice was the **prototype**—the first of its kind—of modern children's literature. Other good books that were widely read by children also appeared during the remainder of the nineteenth century. Not all were specifically intended for children, and certainly not all were free from moralism. (Even today, a common criticism of children's literature is that too many books are moralistic, with implicit lessons built in.) However, these books were primarily entertaining, and most contained child characters. Box 1.1 presents a partial list of the books considered children's classics—not because they were all written for children, but because the children of the nineteenth century read and treasured them. It is interesting to note that the novel *Little Women* (Alcott 1868) was commissioned by the publisher to be written for girls. However, adults read and loved *Little Women* as well—a reversal from the previous century, when children had to read adult books for entertainment.

 Responding to Literature

Comparing Book and Movie Versions of a Classic

Read one of the children's classics, and list the elements of the story that might have attracted children in the nineteenth century. Most of the classics have been made into movies (some several times). View a video of the story and compare it to the book. Make a Venn diagram (see Chapter 11, Figure 11.5) showing the similarities and differences. Determine whether the book or the movie would be most appealing to children today, and explain why.

Because of their age, all the classic books are in the public domain, meaning they are not protected by copyright laws. Therefore, you need to be cautious when you check them out of the library or purchase them because there are many poorly adapted or condensed editions on the market.

Box 1.1

Children's Classics of the Nineteenth Century

1812	*The Swiss Family Robinson* by Johann Wyss
1843	*A Christmas Carol* by Charles Dickens
1864	*Journey to the Center of the Earth* by Jules Verne
1865	*Alice's Adventures in Wonderland* by Lewis Carroll (Charles Dodgson)
1865	*Hans Brinker or the Silver Skates* by Mary Mapes Dodge
1868	*Little Women* by Louisa May Alcott
1869	*Twenty Thousand Leagues under the Sea* by Jules Verne
1871	*Through the Looking-Glass* by Lewis Carroll (Charles Dodgson)
1872	*Around the World in Eighty Days* by Jules Verne
1876	*The Adventures of Tom Sawyer* by Mark Twain (Samuel Clemens)
1877	*Black Beauty* by Anna Sewell
1883	*Treasure Island* by Robert Louis Stevenson
1883	*The Adventures of Pinocchio* by Carlo Collodi (Carlo Lorenzini)
1884	*Heidi* by Johanna Spyri
1886	*Kidnapped* by Robert Louis Stevenson
1886	*Little Lord Fauntleroy* by Frances H. Burnett
1894	*The Jungle Book* by Rudyard Kipling
1900	*The Wonderful Wizard of Oz* by L. Frank Baum

The development of illustrated books for children is also an interesting story. Children's books were usually illustrated with crude woodcuts, if at all, until Sir John Tenniel delightfully illustrated *Alice* in pen and ink in 1865. That same year, a talented English printer named Edmund Evans perfected the photographic engraving process and solicited gifted artists to create the first colored illustrations for children's books. Among the artists he encouraged and supported were Walter Crane, Randolph Caldecott, and Kate Greenaway. The types of books they illustrated included traditional literature, verse, and alphabet books. As you can imagine, Evans's beautiful books were tremendously popular, and they ushered in the modern era of color illustrations in children's books, something we take for granted today.

Kate Greenaway was perhaps the most popular of the three artists, judging by the sheer volume of books sold. Her scenes of happy children in peaceful landscapes charmed the public. (See her illustration at the beginning of Chapter 2.) Greenaway was so popular that dressmakers began styling children's clothing to emulate the dress of the children in her pictures. However, Randolph Caldecott, with his unique way of depicting humor and lively characters in action, is often recognized as the most talented of the three artists.

The nineteenth century produced some lovely illustrated books; however, the pictures served only as decorations. The modern picture storybook did not emerge until the beginning of the twentieth century in England. Six publishers rejected Beatrix

Mrs. Rabbit sends her children to play. From *The Tale of Peter Rabbit,* written and illustrated by Beatrix Potter.

Potter's manuscript of *The Tale of Peter Rabbit,* but she was determined to see her illustrated story made into "a little book for little hands." In 1901 Potter withdrew her own savings of 11 pounds and printed 450 copies of the book, which became the prototype of modern picture storybooks. One of the unique qualities of this book was created when Potter matched her illustrations with the text, using the pictures to share in the storytelling process. You probably remember the main character, Peter, the errant young rabbit who—against his mother's admonition—goes to eat in Mr. McGregor's garden and is nearly caught and eaten himself.

The copies Potter had printed quickly sold and gained the attention of Frederick Warne & Company, who published the second and many subsequent printings. In *Peter Rabbit* and in her twenty-two other books that followed, Potter used clear watercolors to illustrate woodland animals dressed as ordinary country folk. Her union of enchanting stories with expertly drawn pictures became models for the authors and illustrators of the numerous picture storybooks that followed.

 Responding to Literature

Analyzing Potter's Illustrations

Compare photographs of real rabbits with Potter's illustrations in *The Tale of Peter Rabbit.* Read a biography of Potter, such as *At Home with Beatrix Potter* (Denyer 2000), and discover why she was able to draw the animals with such anatomical accuracy.

The Genres of Literature

Many thousands of good children's books are available from libraries, stores, and book clubs, so people often do not know how to begin learning about literature. Literature is best studied if it is organized into categories called **genres** (zhän'rəz). Genres are groupings of books with similar style, form, or content. The term *genres* also applies to other types of media, such as music, movies, plays, television shows, and artwork.

Although one can classify and study literature according to genres, not all books fit into one and only one category. Some books fit well in two categories, and some books fit into none! For example, I am never sure whether to shelve my copy of *The Very Hungry Caterpillar* (Carle 1969) with animal fantasy or counting books. And my copy of *Miss Nelson Is Missing* (Allard 1977) has been moved several times because it has aspects of both realistic fiction and fantasy.

Not everyone organizes literature genres in exactly the same way, but a common organization is outlined in Box 1.2 along with the chapters in which the genres are presented in this textbook. I have categorized literature into six major genres: early childhood books, traditional literature, fiction, biography and autobiography, informational books, and poetry and verse. Notice that some of the genres have subcategories. Four chapters of this textbook are devoted to the subcategories of fiction, and the remaining five genres are covered in one chapter each.

Box 1.2

Literary Genres of Children's Literature

Early Childhood Books	Chapter 3	**Fiction**	
Concept		Fantasy	Chapter 5
Alphabet		Animal fantasy	Chapter 6
Counting		Contemporary fiction	Chapter 8
General		Historical fiction	Chapter 9
Pattern picture books			
Wordless picture books		**Biography and Autobiography**	Chapter 10
		Informational Books	Chapter 11
Traditional Literature	Chapter 4		
Myths		**Poetry and Verse**	Chapter 12
Fables			
Ballads and folk songs			
Legends			
Tall tales			
Fairy tales (Märchen)			
Traditional rhymes and riddles			

The Dewey Decimal System

Libraries also use genres to organize books on shelves so people can easily find them. Although nearly all university and other large libraries now use the Library of Congress classification system, most school and public libraries still use the **Dewey decimal system.** It was named after the Columbia University librarian Melvil Dewey, who in 1876 pioneered this practical system to facilitate classification of books.

Have you ever been frustrated because you made a thorough card catalogue or computerized search, only to find that the book you wanted was not on the shelf? By learning the simple Dewey decimal system, you can walk to the appropriate section and see what books are available. For example, if you need a children's biography of Dr. Martin Luther King Jr., you can walk to the section of the library where the biographies for children are shelved—J920. Then you can quickly scan the books until you get to the *K*s, where books about King are located.

A short overview of the Dewey decimal system follows, and more specific information is provided at the beginning of each genre chapter.

Fiction

The first basic rule of the Dewey decimal system is that nonfiction books are shelved in the numbered sections of the library, and fiction books are in the unnumbered section. All the categories of fiction—fantasy, science fiction, animal fantasy, contemporary realistic fiction, and historical fiction—are shelved together and arranged alphabetically by authors' last names.

Picture books are found in a special section. The **spine** of a picture book—the part you see when it is on the shelf—usually has an *E* with the first letters of the author's last name underneath. (*E* is supposed to stand for *Easy*, but it should really stand for *Everyone* because everyone can enjoy picture books.) The books are typically arranged alphabetically by the author's last name. In busy public libraries, however, you may encounter the picture books in bins, one for each letter of the alphabet. Be aware that young children are sometimes quite fickle with picture books, pulling out one to inspect it and then tossing it back, not necessarily where they found it. Therefore, you may find books in the wrong bins. Even in the most meticulous school libraries, where books are lined up neatly on the shelves, I have heard librarians groan about the hours they spend reshelving misplaced books.

Storybooks or **juvenile novels** are shelved separately from the picture books, and they generally have a *J* (Juvenile) on the spine with the first letters of the author's last name underneath. (A few libraries use *F* for Fiction.) Because they are shelved alphabetically, you can easily browse through other books the author has written. This is especially helpful if the one you were looking for is not available.

 Literature Activity: Locating Library Books

Using what you now know about library organization, visit a school library or the children's section of a public library and locate one novel by each of the following authors: C. S. Lewis, Gary

Paulsen, and Laura Ingalls Wilder. Locate one picture book by each of the following author–illustrators: Tomie dePaola, Beatrix Potter, and Maurice Sendak. ∎

Nonfiction

The Dewey decimal system gets its name because nonfiction books are shelved by subjects that are grouped into ten main classes. See Box 1.3 for the Dewey decimal system of classification. Each class has ten subdivisions, and each subdivision may be broken down further by adding a decimal point and more numbers. This allows very

---

Box 1.3

Dewey Decimal System of Classification for Nonfiction

000–099   General Works
Computers, encyclopedias, reference books, periodicals

100–199   Philosophy and Psychology
Personal improvement

200–299   Religion and Mythology
Mythology, Christianity, Judaism, Islam, Bible stories

300–399   Social Sciences
Traditional literature, family, government, community life, conservation, transportation, law, holidays, costumes, etiquette

400–499   Language
Dictionaries, English language, other languages

500–599   Natural Sciences and Mathematics
Mathematics, astronomy, physics, chemistry, earth science, dinosaurs and prehistoric life, trees, flowers, animals

600–699   Applied Sciences, Useful Arts, and Technology
Medicine, health, diseases, human body, safety, machines and inventions, space and aeronautics, gardening, manufacturing, building, pets, sewing

700–799   Fine Arts, Sports, and Recreations
Architecture, coins, pottery, drawing, handicrafts, painting, photography, music, hobbies, games, sports, magic, "how to do it" books

800–899   Literature
Poetry, plays

900–999   History, Geography, Biography, and Travel
Biography, travel, atlases, United States history, world history, geography

specific subjects to be shelved together. The following example (Pasco County) illustrates this very well:

973	United States History
973.7	Civil War
973.73	Battles of the Civil War
973.738	Appomattox

You will notice that Box 1.3 lists some categories that are not commonly considered nonfiction, such as traditional literature, mythology, and poetry. To librarians, fiction and nonfiction are dichotomous terms. That is, anything that does not meet the definition of fiction (make-believe stories with an identifiable author, designed to entertain) is considered nonfiction. Therefore, if a work is not fiction, it will be shelved in the appropriate numbered section. The majority of the books in the numbered sections are informational books, with the exception of traditional literature, mythology, poetry, biography, and reference books. (Remember that reference books are not considered literature.)

Book Formats

Genre has to do with the content of a book—what it is about—but there are other ways to categorize and compare books. One example is **book format**—the way a book is put together or the way it looks. I have already used several terms that refer to format; for example, *picture book*. What is the difference between a picture book and a storybook? And is there such a thing as a picture storybook?

Picture Books

Norton (1999) explained that "most children's books are illustrated, but not all illustrated children's books are picture books" (p. 214). What makes a picture book distinctive is that it conveys its message through a series of pictures with only a small amount of text (or none at all). The illustrations are as important as—or more important than—the text in conveying the message. Books that have no text at all are called *wordless picture books* or textless books. Picture books for young children, including wordless books, are presented in Chapter 3, which deals with early childhood books such as concept books and pattern books.

Picture storybooks are picture books with a plot, with the text and illustrations equally conveying the story line. "In a picture storybook, pictures must help to tell the story, showing the action and expressions of the characters, the changing settings, and the development of the plot" (Huck et al. 1997, p. 198). Most people simply call these picture books as well, not drawing a distinction as to whether the text conveys a story. In fact, the umbrella term *picture book* is commonly used to refer to any book that has more illustrations than text.

Picture books of all kinds are easy to recognize because of their size and length. They are usually larger than storybooks, and their shapes are varied. The number of pages is fairly uniform. The majority of picture books (excluding unusual formats such as board books or pop-up books) are thirty-two pages, counting both sides of the leaves and including all the pages that come before and after the story. Books of this length typically do not have page numbers. Longer picture books are forty-eight or sixty-four pages. The length of all books is usually a multiple of sixteen because of the way presses print the paper.

Some children's literature specialists combine all picture books in a separate genre and study them as one vast group. However, when people refer to a picture book, they are usually referring to its format. It looks so distinctively different that I could hold up a picture book and a juvenile novel across the room, and you could easily distinguish between the two without looking inside either one. Though all picture books have a distinctive format, they have content as well, and the content can be categorized by genre. In recent years there has been an explosion in the publication of picture books that are appealing to children of all ages. To do justice to this vast and appealing group, I present a selection of picture books in each of the genre chapters.

Easy-to-Read Books

If you selected a hundred picture storybooks at random and reviewed each for the length and complexity of its sentences, and the difficulty and number of syllables of its words, you would see that most of these books are intended to be read *to* rather than *by* young children (Chamberlain & Leal 1999). However, a relatively new format is specifically designed to give beginning readers successful independent reading experiences. The generic name is **easy-to-read books,** but publishers have their own trademarked names for their easy-to-read series—for example, "I Can Read" and "Ready to Read" books.

The uniqueness of easy-to-read books makes them simple to recognize. First, because they are read independently by children, the books are smaller than regular picture books. In addition, the pages look very different. The illustrations are designed to give clues to the meaning of the words, but the pictures are smaller and less profuse, allowing the text to take up a greater proportion of each page. There is a liberal amount of white space that is achieved by larger print, more space between lines, and lines that end with the phrase rather than running flush to the right margin. Perhaps the most significant characteristic of easy-to-read books is the restricted vocabulary. Usually fewer than 250 different words appear in a book, and these are arranged in short simple sentences, often with word patterns, repeated text, and even rhyming lines to make decoding new words easier. The difficulty of the vocabulary is also controlled, with the majority of the words having only one syllable.

Beginning readers tire easily, and their comprehension is taxed when they have to remember the plot of a book that they are not reading straight through. Authors of many easy-to-read books take this into consideration and break their books into separate stories or short episodic chapters. These books have a table of contents with the title of each story or chapter. Young children gain experience in using a table of contents, and they feel accomplishment in reading a book with "chapters." Young readers often call these "chapter books," though they are more aptly called transitional books because they are a bridge between picture books and storybooks.

The relatively short history of this format is interesting. After twenty years of publishing picture storybooks for children, Theodore Seuss Geisel (Dr. Seuss) published the first easy-to-read book, *The Cat in the Hat,* in 1957. Else Holmelund Minarik's *Little Bear* (1957) immediately followed. Both authors wrote several sequels to those early books. Other authors who have enjoyed great success with this format include Arnold Lobel with *Frog and Toad Are Friends* (1970) and Cynthia Rylant with *Henry and Mudge: The First Book of Their Adventures* (1987). Both of these books were also followed by popular sequels.

The majority of the early easy-to-read books were animal fantasy, but they are now available in all genres. Good stories, simple text, and well-matched illustrations make these books appealing to beginning readers of all ages. Remember the 12-year-old halfback from earlier in this chapter? At the beginning of the summer, he read at the primer level; by the end of the summer, he could independently read the Frog and Toad book he picked out the first day.

Illustrated Books

As children grow from infancy to adolescence, they will notice that the books targeted for them have increasingly fewer illustrations. Books for very young children are primarily illustrations with little or no text (picture books). As children develop, books made for them have illustrations that convey part of the message, but the text is needed for the complete story line (picture storybooks). As they begin to read independently, their books have illustrations that add to the story, but there are fewer of them, and the text itself could stand alone. These books are called illustrated books. Though the illustrations depict what is happening in the story, they do not provide new information. The text is clearly more important than the illustrations (Glazer 1997).

Chapter Books

As children approach adolescence, the books targeted for them become longer and have even fewer illustrations. Sometimes the only illustration is the picture on the book jacket or cover. This format is commonly referred to as the *juvenile novel* or junior novel. Of course, children do not restrict their reading to fiction novels. They also read nonfiction works such as biography and informational books and I call nonfiction books in this category **chapter books**. This term connotes that they are lengthy enough for the author to divide into chapters. Lynch-Brown and Tomlinson (1999) describe the nonfiction chapter book as a format that features a large amount of text organized into chapters. In the more recent nonfiction chapter books, graphics and illustrations are common but are still less important than the text. Almost all biographies, with the exception of picture book biographies, appear in this format.

Hardcover Books

So far, I have primarily discussed the format of books in terms of size, shape, ratio of illustrations to text, and difficulty of text. Format also refers to aspects of the physical makeup of a book such as the quality of binding and paper. The publishers' hardcover editions are the highest-quality books. Covers are usually constructed of heavy-duty cardboard covered with quality glossy paper. The pages of the book are sewn together, and they are held inside the cover by sturdy **endpapers** that are glued to the inside of the front and back covers. Designs that pertain to the book's subject or **motif** (theme) colorfully decorate the endpapers of many hardcover picture books.

Hardcover books are durable, and the high-quality paper ensures the best color reproduction of illustrations. This is the best format for books that are going to be read repeatedly, such as picture books. When I reviewed the list of all-time best-selling hardcover children's books that *Publishers Weekly* (1995a) compiles periodically (Anderson 1998), I discovered that nearly all the top-selling hardcover books were indeed picture books. However, hardcover books are expensive, and it is a major loss if classroom copies become misplaced or "permanently borrowed." Also, from a teacher's practical point of view, they are heavy to carry and take up a lot of shelf space.

Paperback Books

Most books are first issued in hardcover and later are issued in paperback to reach a new market of buyers looking for less costly books. Usually the pages of softcover books are made of somewhat lower-quality paper. Instead of being sewn, the pages are glued together and then glued to a stiff paper cover. Quality paperback books can be identified because they have a spine. That is, when you place them on the shelf, you can see the back edge of the book where the title and names of author, illustrator, and publisher are printed. Paperback editions can have their shelf life extended with Mylar book tape that holds the binding together. Paperback is probably the best format for juvenile novels and chapter books that most children read only once. Predictably, the *Publishers Weekly* (1995b) list of all-time best-selling paperback books consists primarily of juvenile novels.

Several popular book clubs, such as Carnival, Scholastic, Troll, and Trumpet, are marketed in schools nationwide. Teachers distribute order forms to their pupils and then collect and tally the orders. The ordering process can be time-consuming, but the companies are liberal with free books for the teachers. Because of this, many teachers have built large classroom libraries without ever purchasing a book. Book club books are the least costly because they are mass-produced. Quality of paper diminishes with the price, and the colors in illustrations are not always true to the originals. Picture books are usually stapled in the center, rather than being glued with a spine; juvenile novels and chapter books are often smaller in size, which results in smaller print. However, book clubs have made great literature available and affordable for all children. An added bonus is that some new books appear in a book club edition long before the bookstores get them in the paperback edition because hardcover rights, paperback rights, and book club rights are sold separately to publishers.

Grocery Store Books

One year I taught in a paraprofessional training program at a community college. All the students were in their 20s or 30s, and most had children. One of their early assignments was to select a children's book, read it to the class, and ask appropriate questions. One by one the students stood up and read books that were about cartoon, comic book, TV, and movie characters. Not one student had selected a quality children's book—what kids often call "library books." I realized they would need guidance in selecting appropriate children's books to use in classrooms.

These future paraprofessionals had selected **grocery store books,** which incidentally can now be found in drugstores and large discount chain stores as well. They are much less likely to be found in libraries or bookstores. A large portion of these books are called **merchandise books** in the publishing trade because their primary purpose is to sell something—movie tickets, dolls and toys, backpacks, admission to theme parks, and countless other things. Merchandise books are so ubiquitous that a majority of parents surveyed in twenty-two states said these were the type of books they read to their preschool children on a regular basis (Warren, Prater & Griswold 1990). Books about Care Bears, Smurfs, and Star Wars were often named in the survey.

There is no doubt these books are popular. Golden Press (publishers of Little Golden Books) published four of the top five books on the list of all-time best-selling children's hardcover books (*Publishers Weekly* 1995a). These best-sellers are *The Poky Little Puppy* (Lowrey 1942), *Tootle* (Crampton 1945), *Saggy Baggy Elephant* (Jackson & Jackson 1947), and *Scuffy the Tugboat* (Crampton 1946). Perhaps you remember reading these books as a child. They represent some of the better stories that are published by Golden Press. They do not have cartoon characters, and their purpose is to entertain rather than to sell something (other than books, of course). When I was a child, my mother bought these books at the grocery store for twenty-five cents. They cost much more than that now, but when you compare their format to that of a regular hardcover book, you can see the differences in quality. The edges of the cardboard cover are exposed, and the cover is stapled to the pages, rather than being sewn and attached by endpapers. More importantly, I hope you will notice the differences in the quality of story and illustrations as you begin to read the books introduced to you in this textbook.

Why do these grocery store books, including merchandise books, sell so well? Perhaps it is because they are readily accessible; most families include someone who goes to the grocery store each week. In addition, these books are relatively inexpensive—partly because of the way they are constructed, but also because of the mediocre quality of the content. There is no doubt they appeal to young children, especially when their characters are familiar faces from Saturday morning cartoon shows or the latest Disney movie.

May (1980) provides a harsh criticism of Disney books. She believes that

> Disney's greatest contributions to American popular culture lie in his use of total merchandising techniques to promote cute, stereotyped characters, his use of familiar children's literature titles, and his misuse of those books' plots, themes, and characterization in order to create a product. . . . (p. 213)

My adult students often complain when I tell them they cannot use grocery store books for their assignments in my literature or reading courses. To help them understand my reasoning, I use the following analogy.

Imagine that when you were a young child, every evening after supper (or dinner, if you lived in the South), your parents gave you a chocolate cupcake with white frosting that they bought at the grocery store. It was delicious! Each evening, you could hardly wait to finish your peas and carrots so you could get your cupcake. It was something you could count on 365 days a year, and you loved those chocolate cupcakes with white frosting.

Now imagine that when you started school, you went to the cafeteria to get your lunch on the first day, and when you got your tray, you found spice cake for dessert. Every day there was something different. One day it was banana pudding and another day cherry pie. Once, when your class went on a field trip to the mall, you visited a bakery. This bakery sold carrot cake with cream cheese frosting, German chocolate cake with pecan and coconut frosting, beautifully decorated white cakes, cheesecake, key lime pie, apple pie, and numerous little pastries with a variety of fillings and toppings. The teacher let you go in the store and buy whatever you wanted.

That grocery store cupcake satisfied you before you knew there were other desserts to be had, but after you found out about the abundance and variety of freshly baked cakes and pies and pastries, the grocery store cupcake was never quite as satisfying again.

By the same token, I believe that after you indulge yourself in quality literature, you will never be satisfied with grocery store books again. I must add one disclaimer. In recent years I have seen some grocery stores, drugstores, and large discount chain stores carry regular books along with merchandise books that tie in to cartoons, comic books, TV shows, and movies. As your knowledge of quality literature grows, you will be able to distinguish the good from the mediocre or poor, and you might pick up some great bargains in the discount stores.

Series Books

Have you ever read a book that was so good you felt disappointed when you were finished because you wanted to know what would happen next to the characters? That is why authors write **sequels.** When a sequel to a sequel is written, it makes a **trilogy.** If the author writes a fourth related book, it becomes a **series.** All the books in a series will have some unifying element, such as characters or theme. Series also exist among nonfiction books, such as the biographies published by Crowell. Some series are delightful and of high literary quality, among them Beverly Cleary's Ramona series and Madeleine L'Engle's series about Meg Murry and her siblings. Most series, however, are written according to a formula and vary only slightly from one book to the next.

Formula books are often found for sale with the grocery store books. Perhaps that can partially explain their enormous success—they are readily accessible to parents and children. Formula series include Nancy Drew (Stratemeyer), Hardy Boys (Stratemeyer), Babysitters Club (Scholastic), Sweet Valley Twins (Bantam), Sweet Valley High (Bantam), American Girl (Pleasant), Animorphs (Scholastic), Goosebumps (Scholastic), and Fear Street (Archway) books. Despite their poor literary quality, formula books tend to have uplifting themes (with the exception of the last two, which are horror stories). These books may help reluctant readers discover pleasure in reading—that is, if the books are actually *read*. There is indication that some children merely collect series books as they would Barbie dolls or "any other childhood collectible—amassed for the sheer joy of having the latest one, counting them up, or trading them" (Mesmer 1998, p. 108).

However, educators and concerned parents want their children to read books that are entertaining *and* enlightening, and often series books are only entertaining (Hillman 1999). Perhaps the best way to teach children to be discriminating readers is to read good literature to them and help them select books from the library, rather than from a grocery store. Generate discussion comparing a strong central character in a quality book to a flat one that shows no growth or change throughout the series, such as Kristy Thomas in the Babysitters Club or Nancy Drew in the long-running mystery series. Eventually, most young readers will become saturated with the predictability of the series and move on to other books. But in the meantime children miss a lot of wonderful literature and, depending on their age when they outgrow the series books, they may then feel that the great books seem too childish.

Responding to Literature

Analyzing Series Books

Read two books from any of the popular children's series. Describe the formula used by the author. List the elements of the books that children would find appealing. Then list several elements or characteristics that might cause literature critics to say the books are of poor literary quality.

The Value of Children's Literature

You now have a basic understanding of children's literature. As you begin to read the children's books that are discussed in this textbook, I believe you will find most of them enjoyable for children and adults alike. Children are never too young to be read to. In fact, some mothers start reading to their children before they are born. What is remarkable is that research indicates unborn babies hear their mothers and react to their voices (see DeCasper, Lecanuet, Busnel, & Granier-Deferre 1994). In addition to building a bond between parent and child, daily reading to preschool children may be the single most important thing parents can do to improve their children's chances for success in school. Children's book editor Janet Schulman (1998) described the educational and emotional benefits of reading to children with her metaphor that "books help give children a leg up on the ladder of life" (p. vi). Of course, nurturing parents should continue to read to their children after they start school and for as long as they will listen—which, if all goes well, will be throughout the elementary school years.

Children are never too old to be read to either. I remember working with a talented student teacher who was placed in a challenging classroom of sixth graders, all of whom had been identified as being at risk of failing or dropping out of school. The student teacher did an excellent job with them, though they were often rowdy. One day when the classroom teacher was out, I walked into the classroom, and the first thing I noticed was that I could hear only *one* voice, and the kids were all awake! In fact, they had their eyes glued on the student teacher, who was reading them *Stone Soup* (Brown 1989), a picture book fairy tale.

Unfortunately, not all parents read to their children on a regular basis. First, not all parents read. Also, some parents must work more than one job, leaving little time to read to their children. Others have the time and ability to read aloud, yet do not see the advantages—both affective and cognitive—of reading to children. Some parents are eager to read to their children but do not know where to start, so they resort to grocery store books. I recommend reviewing *Best Books for Beginning Readers* (Gunning 1998) and *Read to Me: Raising Kids Who Love to Read* (Cullinan 1992). These books and others at your library or bookstore will not only provide descriptions of numerous quality children's books, but also tell you how to maximize your reading time.

Children acquire vocabulary, syntax, story and text structures, ideas, concepts, and pleasure from reading and listening to books. Each book helps children widen their horizons as they vicariously learn about the world and gain new vocabulary. Reading to children can stimulate their imaginations while stretching their attention spans. Also, it nourishes their emotional development and strengthens the bond between child and adult.

Some educators teach reading through trade books—children's literature—instead of using the reading textbooks known as **basal readers** (see Chapter 13). In such classrooms, all the children may read the same book, or they may select their own literature to read. Some teachers provide a list of books from which children can choose. Children's literature is surely more interesting to read than basal readers, which typically contain only excerpts of books or picture book stories minus most of the pictures, and children's literature is definitely more interesting than the basal reading programs' workbooks, worksheets, and board work (read bored work). Children learn to read by reading, and what better thing is there for children to read than the literature created just for them?

CHILDREN'S BOOKS CITED IN CHAPTER 1

Alcott, Louisa May. *Little Women*. Scholastic, 1868/1995.

Allard, Harry. *Miss Nelson Is Missing*. Illus. James Marshall. Houghton Mifflin, 1977.

Baum, L. Frank. *The Wonderful Wizard of Oz*. TAB Books, 1900/1958.

Brown, Marcia. *Stone Soup*. Atheneum, 1989.

Burnett, Francis H. *Little Lord Fauntleroy*. Buccaneer, 1886/1981.

Carle, Eric. *The Very Hungry Caterpillar*. Philomel, 1969.

Carroll, Lewis. *Alice's Adventures in Wonderland*. Illus. John Tenniel. BHB International, 1865/1998.

———. *Through the Looking-Glass and What Alice Found There*. Illus. John Tenniel. Morrow, 1871/1993.

Collodi, Carlo. *The Adventures of Pinocchio*. Philomel, 1891/1996.

Crampton, Gertrude. *Tootle.* Illus. Tibor Gergely. Golden Books, 1945.

———. *Scuffy the Tugboat.* Illus. Tibor Gergely. Western, 1946.

Defoe, Daniel. *Robinson Crusoe.* Knopf, 1719/1992.

Denyer, Susan. *At Home with Beatrix Potter: The Creator of Peter Rabbit.* Abrams, 2000.

Dickens, Charles. *A Christmas Carol.* Creative Edition, 1843/1995.

Dodge, Mary Mapes. *Hans Brinker or the Silver Skates.* Amereon, 1865/1940.

Jackson, K., & B. Jackson. *Saggy Baggy Elephant.* Western, 1947.

Kipling, Rudyard. *The Jungle Book.* Illus. Jerry Pinkney. Morrow, 1894/1995.

Kroeber, Theodora. *Ishi, Last of His Tribe.* Houghton Mifflin, 1964.

Lobel, Arnold. *Frog and Toad Are Friends.* HarperTrophy, 1970.

———. *Days with Frog and Toad.* HarperTrophy, 1979.

Lowrey, Janette Sebring. *The Poky Little Puppy.* Golden Books, 1942.

MacGregor, Ellen. *Miss Pickerell Goes to Mars.* Whittlesey, 1951.

Minarik, Else Holmelund. *Little Bear.* Illus. Maurice Sendak. Harper & Row, 1957.

Newbery, John. *The History of Little Goody Two Shoes.* Newbery, 1765.

Potter, Beatrix. *The Tale of Peter Rabbit.* Frederick Warne, 1902.

Rylant, Cynthia. *Henry and Mudge: The First Book of Their Adventures.* Illus. Suçie Stevenson. Aladdin, 1987.

Schaefer, Jack. *Shane.* Houghton Mifflin, 1949.

Seuss, Dr. *The Cat in the Hat.* Random House, 1957.

Sewell, Anna. *Black Beauty.* Grammercy, 1877/1998.

Spyri, Johanna. *Heidi.* Grammercy, 1884/1998.

Stevenson, Robert Louis. *Treasure Island.* Everyman's Library, 1883/1992.

———. *Kidnapped.* Random House, 1886/1989.

Swift, Jonathan. *Gulliver's Travels.* Price Stern Sloan, 1726/1989.

Twain, Mark. *The Adventures of Tom Sawyer.* Courage, 1876/1991.

Verne, Jules. *Journey to the Center of the Earth.* Reader's Digest, 1864/1999.

———. *Twenty Thousand Leagues under the Sea.* Indiana University Press, 1869/1992.

———. *Around the World in Eighty Days.* Amereon, 1872/1987.

Wyss, Johann. *The Swiss Family Robinson.* Price Stern Sloan, 1812/1977.

Yolen, Jane. *The Devil's Arithmetic.* Viking Penguin, 1988.

KEY TERMS

 Explore the E-Glossary at **www.ablongman.com/anderson**

basal readers (p. 18)
book format (p. 11)
chapter book (p. 13)
children's classics (p. 5)
children's literature (p. 3)
Dewey decimal system (p. 9)
easy-to-read book (p. 12)
endpapers (p. 14)
formula books (p. 16)
genre (p. 8)
grocery store books (p. 15)
juvenile novel (p. 9)

merchandise books (p. 15)
motif (p. 14)
picture book (p. 9)
picture storybook (p. 11)
prototype (p. 5)
public domain (p. 5)
sequel (p. 16)
series books (p. 16)
spine (p. 9)
trilogy (p. 16)
young adult literature (p. 3)

SCHOOL is over,
   Oh, what fun !
Lessons finished,—
   Play begun.
Who 'll run fastest,
   You or I ?
Who 'll laugh loudest ?—
   Let us try.

K.G.

chapter

2

Finding and
Enjoying the Best
in Literature

literary elements.

There are literally thousands of good children's books in print. Some are obviously better than others, but how do you find the best? This chapter will explore different ways to identify and appreciate excellent children's literature. For example, one way is to choose an outstanding author or illustrator and read some of her or his books. Another way is to review the books that some knowledgeable people believe to be superior—so superior that they deserve an award.

Book Awards

Award-winning authors and books are a good place to start, so let me introduce you to the most prestigious awards. Some are given for a specific book, and others are awarded to authors and illustrators for their complete works.

Newbery Medal

In 1921 Frederick G. Melcher, editor of *Publishers Weekly*, proposed a way to honor distinguished contributions to children's literature. The Association for Library Service to Children (ALSC) of the American Library Association agreed to judge and award a medal named after John Newbery, the English publisher who first made books that were both instructional and entertaining available to young people. The Newbery Medal is the oldest of many book awards given today and therefore is the best known and most prestigious in the United States. This award is given to the author of the most distinguished contribution to literature for children published in the United States during the preceding year. Additional guidelines stipulate that the author must be a citizen or permanent resident of the United States.

In 1922 the first Newbery Medal was awarded to Hendrik Willem van Loon for *The Story of Mankind* (1921), an informational book. Additionally, five noteworthy books were given a Newbery Honor, which is much like a "runner-up" award. Each year since, one author has been awarded a gold Newbery Medal, and usually several silver honor medals have also been awarded. (There is no set number.) Often you can distinguish Newbery books by the foil or printed medallion on the book jacket or cover. Remember that the gold medallion is for the Newbery winner, and the silver is for an honor book. However, not all copies of Newbery-winning books will be so designated. None of the books printed and sold in the first year will have the medallions because the award is not bestowed until the year following publication. In addition, book jackets—where the foil medallions are usually placed—are often missing from books.

Caldecott Medal

Sixteen years after the first Newbery Medal was awarded, Frederick G. Melcher established the first award for book illustration. It was named after Randolph Caldecott, an English artist who was one of the first to create color illustrations in children's books. Like the Newbery, the Caldecott Medal is awarded by the ALSC. The first gold Caldecott Medal was awarded in 1938 to Dorothy Lathrop for her illustrations in *Animals of the Bible* (Fish 1937). Two honor books were also named the first year, and one or more honor books have been recognized each year since. The guidelines for the Caldecott winner also require that the book be published in the United States in the preceding year and that the illustrator be a citizen or permanent resident of the United States. However, the illustrator need not be the author of the book. Gold foil or printed medallions also adorn the book jackets or covers of Caldecott winners, and silver medallions indicate honor books. Look for the words "Caldecott Medal" to distinguish this award from the Newbery Medal because the medallions are similar.

To date, several hundred books have won Newbery, Caldecott, and honor book awards—too many to name in a brief textbook. Many of the early winners would not appeal to children today. Additionally, some recent Newbery winners are geared more for adolescents than for children. Therefore, I have included the names of award-winning books that would appeal to elementary school children in the appropriate genre chapters. For the names of more award-winning books, ask your school or public librarian for the various book lists of award-winning and other recommended books for children.

Laura Ingalls Wilder Medal

In 1954 Laura Ingalls Wilder was the first recipient of the award that bears her name. Wilder authored the series of books based on her life in the American frontier known as the "Little House" books. This award is given to an author or illustrator who, like Wilder, has made a lasting contribution to children's literature through her or his body of work. The ALSC also sponsors this award. After 1954 the Wilder Medal was given every five years until 1980, when the interval was changed to every three years. The winners of this award follow.

- Laura Ingalls Wilder (1954)
- Clara Ingram Judson (1960)
- Ruth Sawyer (1965)
- E. B. White (1970)
- Beverly Cleary (1975)
- Theodor Seuss Geisel (Dr. Seuss) (1980)
- Maurice Sendak (1983)
- Jean Fritz (1986)
- Elizabeth George Speare (1989)
- Marcia Brown (1992)
- Virginia Hamilton (1995)
- Russell Freedman (1998)
- Milton Meltzer (2001)

Hans Christian Andersen Award

Perhaps the most prestigious award is the one international prize, the Hans Christian Andersen Award, named after a Danish cobbler's son who became a storyteller and later the author of the first literary fairy tales. (More is said about Andersen's accomplishments in Chapter 5.) Like the Wilder Award, the Andersen Award is given in recognition of individuals whose complete bodies of works have made an outstanding and lasting contribution to children's literature. Since 1956 the Hans Christian Andersen Award has been given to a living author every two years by the International Board on Books for Young People. Since 1966 an award has also been given to a living illustrator. Queen Margrethe II of Denmark is the patron of these biennial awards, but the panel of five judges is composed of individuals from five different countries.

Since the first awards were given in 1956, only the following five authors and one illustrator from the United States have won this highest international distinction:

- Meindert DeJong (1962)
- Maurice Sendak (1970)
- Scott O'Dell (1972)
- Paula Fox (1978)
- Virginia Hamilton (1992)
- Katherine Paterson (1998)

Sendak is the only U.S. illustrator to win this award. In addition, note that Sendak and Hamilton were also honored with the Laura Ingalls Wilder Award, which—like the Hans Christian Andersen Award—is given for a person's life work.

Coretta Scott King Award

Another noteworthy award is named after Coretta Scott King, widow of the late Dr. Martin Luther King Jr., a Nobel Peace Prize winner. The award was designed to commemorate the life and foster the ideas of Dr. King and to honor Mrs. King for her courage and determination in continuing the fight for racial equity and universal peace. The Coretta Scott King Task Force of the American Library Association's Social Responsibilities Roundtable sponsors the award. Since 1970 the award has been given annually to an African American author for his or her outstanding inspirational and educational book published in the previous year. The book must promote understanding and appreciation of the cultures of all people. Since 1979 an award has also been given to an African American illustrator. It was fitting that the first book to receive this award was Lillie Patterson's biography, *Martin Luther King, Jr.: Man of Peace* (1969).

Adults select the recipients of all the awards named thus far. There is no doubt that these selections are outstanding books produced by talented authors and illustrators, but do children like the same books that adults do? Do they read and enjoy the books that adults believe are the best? These questions led me to analyze the lists of all-time best-selling hardcover and paperback books (*Publishers Weekly* 1995a, 1995b). Within the first hundred titles on both lists, I discovered that fewer than 7 percent of Newbery and Caldecott Award books were named (not including honor books). I concluded that these must be truly outstanding books—to receive coveted awards *and* attain best-seller status. The list of these books is presented in Box 2.1. They would be an excellent start for a personal collection.

Make Way for Ducklings by Robert McCloskey (1941)
Johnny Tremain by Esther Forbes (1943)
The Witch of Blackbird Pond by Elizabeth George Speare (1958)
Island of the Blue Dolphins by Scott O'Dell (1960)
A Wrinkle in Time by Madeleine L'Engle (1962)
Where the Wild Things Are by Maurice Sendak (1963)
From the Mixed-up Files of Mrs. Basil E. Frankweiler by E. L. Konigsburg (1967)
Sounder by William H. Armstrong (1969)
Julie of the Wolves by Jean Craighead George (1972)
Roll of Thunder, Hear My Cry by Mildred D. Taylor (1976)
Bridge to Terabithia by Katherine Paterson (1977)
The Polar Express by Chris Van Allsburg (1985)
Sarah Plain and Tall by Patricia MacLachlan (1985)

I interviewed fifth-grade teacher Jerry Michel about how book awards influence the reading preferences of his children, and his responses are recorded in Box 2.2.

Children's Choices and Teachers' Choices

Some lists of outstanding books are selected by children. In 1975 the Children's Choices list became the first such recognition. The International Reading Association (IRA) and the Children's Book Council (CBC) cosponsor this project. Each year, publishers select the books to be evaluated from their titles published in the previous year. The number of books selected can be as many as 700. The books are grouped into five reading levels and then all are sent to five review teams of educators located in different regions of the United States. Each team is responsible for getting the books to 2,000 children in elementary school classrooms; therefore, throughout the school year, the books are read to or by approximately 10,000 children. These children vote for their favorites, and the top 100 titles are announced at the IRA's annual conference. The list is also published each year in the October issue of the journal *The Reading Teacher*.

Since 1989 the IRA's Teachers' Choices list has spotlighted outstanding books that teachers find to be exceptionally useful in the curriculum. Approximately 30 titles are selected from more than 300 recently published books. Books are field tested throughout the United States, with each book read by at least six teachers or librarians in each of seven regions. The educators then vote for the books they believe have the highest literary quality plus potential for use across the curriculum. The list of top books is published each year in the November issue of *The Reading Teacher*.

In addition to general awards given to authors and illustrators, there are several awards that are genre specific, such as the Orbis Pictus Award for nonfiction. Genre-specific awards are described in the appropriate genre chapters of this text. For a

Box 2.2

Interview with Jerry Michel, Fifth-Grade Teacher

Me: Jerry, you have a background in the whole-sale paperback book industry, a graduate degree in children's literature, and experience as a classroom teacher. Can you tell me, Do children read Newbery Award books?

Jerry: Newbery to my kids translates to: "This is a book that teachers/adults really like and want me to read." Kids don't always return to Newberys as they might to a favorite author or particular genre.

Me: Do your children read the books by Katherine Paterson, who is the most recent U.S. winner of the Hans Christian Andersen Award?

Jerry: I have read *Bridge to Terabithia* with my fifth graders for two years now. This year's class is a great bunch of readers. Although they enjoy this book, they are not prone to select other works she has written. At this age, children are just beginning to have the patience to read a novel that doesn't jump with action on every page. Paterson's slow buildups take time to appreciate. Children sometimes still need a little hand-holding in order to slow down and see the points the author is trying to make. To help, we begin the year by reading class novels together, modeling techniques to be used in the literature circles students will participate in as the year progresses.

Me: What are your children's favorite books?

Jerry: Many times their favorite book is the one most recently read. I find many children are continually updating their favorite books list.

Children need the opportunity to talk about the books they read with their peers. In this fashion, they can find books that speak to them honestly.

Me: What do you do to help children select quality books to read?

Jerry: In our classroom, we make a big deal of connecting books to readers for the sake of enjoyment. In the end, we often find that the process of making connections between our reading selves and the books we choose is more important than the books themselves. By cultural design, our educational system values the objective and factual over the subjective and emotional. Making and sharing personal connections to literature provide powerful opportunities to bring positive and natural recognition to the "self" in each class member. These opportunities are like little treasures in our days together and help define our sense of classroom community. With this in mind, we look for award-winning books, yes, but we also try to match writing styles with reader personalities. My efforts to make personal connections with my students' reading is a powerful motivator for many of them, especially once they realize I am not promoting a book because it is "worthy" but because it matters to me that they connect to it as a reader and human being. It does not take long to have a roomful of kids seeking out and making recommendations on what should be read next.

comprehensive directory of book awards and lists of winners through 1990, see *Children's Book Awards International* (Smith 1992).

 ## Literary Elements

Reading books by award-winning authors and illustrators is one way of discovering some of the best books available. However, there is a multitude of children's books in print, and more than 4,000 new ones are published each year. The list of award-winning books is minuscule compared to what is available. How can you select the best from this mountain of possibilities? One way to assess the literary merit of fiction books is to analyze and evaluate the literary elements or various parts of a fiction story: characters, point of view, setting, plot, theme, style, and tone.

Characters

Characters are *who the story is about,* and the action revolves around them. Brown and Stephens (1995) believe that "the effective development of the main character may be the single most important element of the work" (p. 170). Authors develop characters primarily from three sources: (1) from the narrator's description of characters' physical appearance and personality; (2) from other characters—what others think of characters and what others' actions are toward them; and (3) from the characters themselves—what they think, what they say, and what they do. Expect the latter to be the most revealing. "Actions, we all know, speak louder than words, and it is through actions that the most convincing evidence about character is revealed" (Russell 1997, p. 61).

Main characters, especially the central character or **protagonist,** must be fully developed; that is, the readers should learn of the characters' many traits—their strengths as well as their weaknesses. These complex characters are called **round characters.** It is essential that the reader relate to them; and when an author has created a well-developed character, the reader can imagine what might happen to her or him if the book continued (Glazer 1997). "The main characters in an excellent work of fiction for children are rounded, fully developed characters who undergo change in response to life-altering events" (Lynch-Brown & Tomlinson 1999, p. 29). This capacity for change defines such characters as **dynamic.**

Supporting characters are less well developed than the main characters; only a few of their traits may be revealed. Sometimes they are **flat characters** who exhibit only one side of their personality. Flat characters are often **stereotypes** who possess only the traits considered typical of their particular group. Flat characters are usually **static,** undergoing no change in personality throughout the book.

 Literature Activity: **Genre Characters**

What the main characters are often dictates the genre of the story. Match the following types of characters to the genre in which they would most likely appear, selecting from the list at the bottom of this box: (1) realistic boy of today, (2) stereotyped beautiful daughter, (3) talking doll, (4) high-tech robot, (5) realistic girl from the past, and (6) bear living in a condominium.

Genres: fairy tale, fantasy, science fiction, animal fantasy, contemporary fiction, historical fiction. Answers are available at **www.ablongman.com/anderson.** ■

Rothlein and Meinbach (1996) provide a dozen excellent activities for learning about characterization. One of these, the *character continuum,* appears in Box 2.3.

Box 2.3

Character Continuum

Title of Book: _____

Name of Character: _____

friendly ——————————————————————————— unfriendly

happy ——————————————————————————— sad

wise ——————————————————————————— foolish

adventurous ——————————————————————— cautious

outgoing ——————————————————————————— shy

unselfish ——————————————————————— selfish

honest ——————————————————————————— dishonest

brave ——————————————————————————— fearful

leader——————————————————————————— follower

mature——————————————————————————— childish

Instructions: Analyze the inner qualities of this character using the pairs of opposite words. Place an **X** on the line where you think the character falls on each dimension. Most characters will fall somewhere between the two extremes.

Source: Adapted from Liz Rothlein and Anita Meyer Meinbach, _Legacies: Using Children's Literature in the Classroom._ New York: HarperCollins, 1996.

To help children gain a deeper understanding of a particular character, encourage them to analyze the inner qualities of the character as they determine where on the character continuum he or she would fall. With the exception of stereotyped characters (such as are found in traditional literature), most characters should fall somewhere between the continuum's two extremes.

• Point of View

A book's **point of view** is the perspective from which an author presents a story—a perspective shaped by _who is telling the story_ and how much this narrator knows. Though the author writes the book, the story is not typically told from the author's point of view. Before the author begins writing, he or she must determine what point of view to use, because it will permeate the entire book. In a good book the point of view can usually be determined in the first page or two, and the author is consistent in using this point of view throughout.

First Person. When the narrator is one of the characters in the story and refers to himself or herself as _I_ and _me_, the author is employing the **first-person point of view.**

With this point of view, the reader will see events unfold through the eyes and thoughts of the narrator, and only of the narrator. Therefore, the reader cannot learn what other characters are doing or saying if they are not in sight of the narrator. Because the reader can never learn what is in the minds of other characters, an author using the first-person point of view might contrive for the narrator to do a bit of eavesdropping. Through this kind of device, the author can reveal essential information through other characters as well. For example, a child might be able to hear the adults in her family talking when she climbs out her bedroom window to the porch and listens outside the living room window. In this way, the author can move the story line along without changing narrators.

Readers of realistic fiction will find first person the primary point of view for that genre. However, when a story is told only through events the narrator has experienced, the reader should expect the narration to be quite subjective. A good example of a book using this point of view is *Are You There God? It's Me, Margaret.* (Blume 1970), which is told through the eyes of a young girl. An interesting way for the first-person narrator to reveal a realistic story is through letters and diaries. Some good examples are *Dear Mr. Henshaw* (Cleary 1983) and *Absolutely Normal Chaos* (Creech 1990).

Alternating Point of View. Sometimes an author will write a story that is told in first person accounts by two or more characters, called **alternating point of view**. Often, the author shifts narrators each chapter, and a single incident is sometimes told from two or more points of view. Katherine Applegate used this style in *Animorphs: The Andalite's Gift* (1997). The main characters are five children—one of whom has permanently "morphed" (become transformed) into a falcon—who are fighting evil aliens, and each chapter is the first-person account of one of these main characters.

Omniscient. The omniscient and all other points of view are told in third-person narrative, in which the narrator refers to all characters as *he, she, it,* or *they.* The narrator with an **omniscient point of view** is not a book character but rather an all-knowing and all-seeing voice that can relate events that are occurring simultaneously. In this point of view, readers are able to learn what all the characters are doing and thinking, what has happened in the past, and even what will occur in the future. A classic example of a book using an omniscient point of view is *Charlotte's Web* (White 1952).

Limited Omniscient. When a story is narrated through a **limited omniscient point of view**, the story unfolds through the viewpoint of only one of the characters. However, the story is told not *by* the character but by the omniscient narrator, who enters the mind of this character and reveals her or his experiences, actions, speech, thoughts, and history. The reader knows only what that particular character can see and understand. An example is Cassie Logan in *Roll of Thunder, Hear My Cry* (Taylor 1976).

Objective. In the **objective point of view**, the reader learns about characters only through their actions and speech. The narrator does not enter the minds of any of the characters, but rather takes a reporter's view, presenting only the facts. The narrator tells but does not comment on or interpret what is happening in the story. The reader learns nothing about characters when they are not in the author's narrative or dialogue. Their actions must speak for themselves as they unfold in the story. *Frog and Toad All Year* (Lobel 1976) is an example of a book using the objective point of view.

Some nuances of point of view can even be revealed though illustration. In *Why Mosquitoes Buzz in People's Ears* (Aardema 1975), artists Leo and Diane Dillon show the frightened monkey leaping through trees to warn the other animals. A dead limb breaks and falls, killing an owlet. However, four pages later, when Mother Owl (who did not witness the accident) gives her account, the illustrations depict a vicious killer monkey standing on the nest, clutching the baby owl, and beating it with a stick! This book is a great vehicle for showing children how the retelling of a real-life experience changes when it is told by more than one person.

 ## Responding to Literature

Changing Point of View

Read your children a book with several characters. Have the children select a particularly interesting or exciting incident. Ask them to write a letter or journal entry describing the incident from the viewpoint of different characters. You might first want to read them *The True Story of the 3 Little Pigs* (Scieszka 1989) and *The Pain and the Great One* (Blume 1974) to show how different points of view can change stories dramatically.

Setting

Setting is *where and when the story takes place*. Every story occurs in some time period at some geographical location(s). Setting can include topography, climate, and weather when these are integral to the story. Setting "may play a significant role that has an impact on every other aspect of the book, it may be inconsequential and barely mentioned, or it may not be mentioned at all" (Brown & Stephens 1995, p. 175). Setting can be a realistic time and place that the reader recognizes, such as the New Jersey suburb in *Are You There God? It's Me, Margaret.* (Blume 1970). Settings can also be quite abstract, perhaps in an imaginary world with a time period that does not correspond to earth time, as in *The Lion, the Witch and the Wardrobe* (Lewis 1950). The story could cover a time span of only one day, as in *Finding Buck McHenry* (Slote 1991); or it could span decades, as in *The Rifle* (Paulsen 1995). When the title of a book names its setting, expect the setting to be a major element of the story, as in *Little House on the Prairie* (Wilder 1935). In addition, the setting serves a major function in survival stories, in which the conflict is person against nature, as in *Hatchet* (Paulsen 1987).

Setting is more important in some stories than others; therefore, there are two types of settings—backdrop and integral. The **backdrop setting** is relatively unimportant to the story. The name is derived from traditional theater where flat, nondescript painted scenery was dropped from the ceiling at the back of the stage. This is the type of setting often found in traditional literature that begins with a literal or implied "once upon a time." Traditional literature is nearly always set in an indeterminate past time and in an unspecified place, such as a queen's castle, a peasant's hut, a dark forest, or a barnyard. It is not surprising that fantasy, which has it origins in traditional literature, also employs the backdrop setting frequently, as in *Frog and Toad Together* (Lobel 1971). Some authors deliberately leave time and place vague in order to emphasize the universality of their stories (Glazer 1997).

The **integral setting** is essential to the story, meaning that the story could not have taken place anywhere but in the setting specified by the author. According to Lukens (1999), "We say a story has an *integral setting* when action, character, or theme are influenced by the time and place . . ." (p. 155). The integral setting is most often used in realistic fiction, especially historical fiction, as in *Johnny Tremain* (Forbes 1943). Perhaps the most difficult setting for authors to write about is a time before they were born. Both the author and the illustrator of historical fiction must undertake painstaking research in order to present an authentic setting. However, authors can go overboard in developing the setting. Settings should be introduced to the reader subtly, through things the characters see, say, and do within the story. They should not rely on multiple pages of tedious description.

Responding to Literature

Finding Picture and Text Clues

Select a historical fiction picture book such as *Uncle Jed's Barbershop* (Mitchell 1993) or *The Year of the Perfect Christmas Tree* (Houston 1988). Tell your children to look in the illustrations for clues that show the events took place in the past. Read the book aloud and ask the children to tell you the clues they saw in the illustrations. Next, tell them to listen for clues in the story, and read the book again. Make a chart of all the visual and verbal clues that were found.

•Plot

"**Plot** is the sequence of events showing characters in action" (Lukens 1999, p. 103). In other words, it is *what happens in a story*. In order to keep readers involved, the plot must tell a good story; so the lives of the characters in a book should be more exciting or more interesting than the readers' lives. There are four primary types of plots: cumulative, linear, episodic, and circular.

Cumulative. **Cumulative plots** are most often found in traditional literature and pattern books. In cumulative plots there is repetition of phrases, sentences, or events with one new aspect added with each repetition. "The Gingerbread Man" is a good example of a story with a cumulative plot. Young children love to join in on the refrain.

Linear. **Linear plots** are popular in realistic fiction and fantasy, as in *Swimmy* (Lionni 1963). The plot should be constructed logically; that is, events should happen logically and not by coincidence. There are three major parts to a progressive linear plot:

1. In the *beginning*, the characters and setting are introduced, and the central problem of the story is revealed. Usually the main character sets a goal to overcome the problem.
2. In the *middle*, the main character attempts to overcome the problem and usually meets with obstacles, or the main character participates in a series of events that lead to a solution of the problem.
3. In the *end*, either the problem is resolved or the main character learns to cope with it.

Episodic. Episodic plots are most often used in easy-to-read books or transitional books, such as *Frog and Toad All Year* (Lobel 1976). Although the characters and setting are usually the same throughout, there is no central problem that permeates the book. Rather, each chapter has a miniplot complete with introduction, problem, events, and resolution. Books with episodic plots are good for children with short attention spans or for children with limited reading ability. In either case, if children listen to or read only one chapter a day, they do not have to remember what was read the day before to enjoy the book.

Circular. Circular plots have the same components as linear plots, but the resolution or end of the story shows that the characters are in the same situation as when the story started. For example, in *Once a Mouse . . .* (Brown 1961), a hermit's pet mouse is successively changed from a mouse to a cat to a dog to a tiger—and then, because of his vanity, back to a mouse. In *Ox-Cart Man* (Hall 1979), the pioneer family works hard all year to grow and make things for the father to take to a distant market in the oxcart he built. Once at the market, the man sells everything, including the cart and the ox. He returns home with the necessities and gifts he has purchased with the money earned, and the family begins to make and grow the things to be sold at next year's market.

Naming the components of plot, or **story mapping**, is an activity that will help children follow and understand the structure of a story. It can be done while children are reading a book or, with shorter books, after they finish. Figure 2.1 is an example of a story map of the chapter titled "Cookies" from the episodic book *Frog and Toad Together* (Lobel 1971).

Two elements that can be used to move a plot along are flashback and exposition. In a **flashback** the narrator recounts an earlier event to "give the reader background information that adds clarity or perspective to the plot, but does not fit into the chronological flow of the plotline" (Brown & Stephens 1995, p. 173). Flashbacks that explain important relationships or the past history of a character will keep the reader from getting bogged down in detailed descriptions or history at the beginning of the book. A device similar to flashback is **exposition**—passages in which the narrator briefly tells (rather than recreates in scenes) what has happened before the story opens. The opposite of flashback is **foreshadowing**—passages in which a

Title: "Cookies" from *Frog and Toad Together*   Author: Arnold Lobel

Beginning

Main characters:	Toad and his friend Frog
Setting—Place:	Frog's house in a garden
—Time:	Summertime in the present day
Problem:	Frog and Toad cannot stop eating the cookies Toad baked.
Goal:	They want to have willpower to stop eating cookies.

Middle   ⇩

Events/attempts to reach the goal:

1. They put the cookies in a box.
2. They tie the box with string.
3. They put the box up on a high shelf.

End   ⇩

Resolution: Frog takes the cookies off the shelf and gives them to the birds.

FIGURE 2.1   Story Map

---

forthcoming event is hinted at. The author gives these clues to the readers to prepare them for a coming event in the story.

Conflict is the interaction of plot and character or the opposition of two forces. Tension is a necessary result of conflict. Without sufficient conflict and tension, a book is dull; but with well-developed conflict, the story will create **suspense,** a sense of anxiety, because the reader is uncertain of the outcome. There are four primary types of conflict:

- Character against self (e.g., *Wringer* by Jerry Spinelli)
- Character against another character (e.g., *Harry Potter and the Sorcerer's Stone* by J. K. Rowling)
- Character against society (e.g., *The Giver* by Lois Lowry)
- Character against nature (e.g., *Hatchet* by Gary Paulsen)

One outcome of a good plot is that children are better able to understand their own problems and conflicts by reading about the conflicts of the characters.

• Theme

The **theme** of a book is its central idea, the underlying message the author is conveying to the reader. Other definitions include a significant truth, a value-laden statement, a broad and powerful idea that has universal application, or, more simply, the moral of the story. Sometimes the theme is explicit or stated directly by the narrator or a story character. For example, in *Knee-Knock Rise,* Uncle Anson says that "if your mind is made up, all the facts in the world won't make the slightest difference" (Babbitt 1970, p. 111). More often, the theme is implicit. Readers have to infer the meaning from what happens in the story. I find theme to be the most obscure and elusive of the literary elements. To complicate this, some books have a secondary theme or even multiple themes, and others have themes that are so vague they are difficult to express in words.

A theme is more easily understood if it is stated in a complete sentence. For example, *"remember"* is a word. *"Important to remember"* is a phrase that adds a little more meaning. However, *"It is important to remember the history of your culture"* is a sentence and thus a complete thought. It is also the theme of *The Devil's Arithmetic* (Yolen 1988).

To determine the theme of a book, ask yourself these questions:

- What is the underlying meaning or significance of this story?
- What was the author's purpose in writing the story?
- What did the author say to me through the story?
- What are the comments the author makes about beliefs, fundamental truths, human nature, life, society, human conditions, or values?
- What is the common idea that ties the story together?

Responding to Literature

Determining the Themes of Lionni's Books

To gain a better understanding of theme and how to determine it, read picture books by Leo Lionni, for example, *Frederick* (1967). Lionni's themes are usually morals and are easy to detect. Write the theme of each book in a complete sentence.

Style and Tone

There are two related elements of literature that are both somewhat abstract—style and tone. Because they cannot be isolated from the words of the story, they are often challenging to detect. Style is the manner in which a writer expresses his or her ideas to convey a story. It permeates every sentence of the work and sets the mood of the story. Style has to do with the *writing* as opposed to the *content* of a book. It is *how* an author says something as opposed to *what* she or he says. Authors have many ways to use words to express their ideas. Some of these are tone (discussed next), use of imagery, figurative language, allusion, irony, selection of vocabulary, grammatical structure, symbolism, and dialect—as well as the devices of comparison, sound, and rhythm.

Children often select multiple books by the same author because they like the author's distinctive style, such as the style of Judy Blume and Gary Paulsen. However, most authors will vary their style when writing for different age groups or when they feel a certain story warrants it. Style is truly the author's personal choice, depending on the characters, setting, and plot of the story.

To determine the style an author used in a book, ask yourself these questions:

- What kinds of words and sentences did the author choose to tell the story?
- Was there any distinctive language, choice of words, or sentence construction? What mood did this create?
- What effect might the author be trying to achieve?

Tone involves the author's attitude toward the book's subject, characters, and readers. However, tone is often quite subtle and may not be easy to pinpoint. In addition, an author may change the tone one or more times as the main character or the supporting characters change. Some examples of tones used in books for children include serious, humorous, moralistic, hopeful, sympathetic, wondrous, longing, loving, satirical, and nostalgic.

Russell (1997) named several tones that he deemed inappropriate for child readers. These include:

- *condescending:* talking down to the reader as an inferior
- *sensational:* horror laden or thrill seeking
- *sentimental:* overly emotional, conveying an overly sweetened view of the world
- *didactic:* preachy and moralistic

Children's literature is particularly likely to have a didactic tone. The literary elements truly suffer when the story has been created around a message instead of having a message flow naturally from the story.

Like style, tone is developed through the author's choice of words and through the way all the elements of the story work together. Because tone influences the meaning of a story, it is important for children to grasp it in order to comprehend the story. For example, consider the misconceptions that would arise if a child read a tall tale such as the story of Paul Bunyan and believed the author's tone was serious rather than humorous.

Responding to Literature

Not all children love books. I remember Carla, a fifth grader who transferred to my classroom at midsemester. When she first made the weekly trip to the library with my class, I noticed she was the only one who did not check out a book. I inquired why and she exclaimed, "Because I *hate* book reports!" Apparently, the only time Carla had read a library book was to do an assignment, so she associated books with work.

There are so many ways to respond to and extend literature that I hope teachers are not still requiring their pupils to do written book reports. An alternative is to have a child show some of the illustrations and briefly describe the book to other children in the class or in a small group. This is called a **book talk,** and it is a good way to get children interested in reading a variety of books. (Book talks are explained in more detail in Chapter 13.) A great resource for teachers is *Book Talk and Beyond: Children and Teachers Respond to Literature* (Roser & Martinez 1995). This book contains information on a variety of activities, such as focus units, language charts, webbing, grand conversations, literature circles, dramatizing, and literature journals. These and other activities are introduced throughout this text.

Gloria Houston, the author of several historical fiction books, has studied reader response theory for many years. Her explanation and application of reader response follows.

Reader Response Theory

by Gloria Houston

Louise Rosenblatt (1995) is arguably the best known theorist of **reader response,** and is certainly the most influential in the contemporary field of teaching children's literature. Her transactional theory is grounded in the belief that meaning is not inherent in the text; rather, the reader/listener creates meaning in an active mental process when the reader and text converge.

In this constructivist theory, a response to literature is a private inner reaction that is not observable by an outsider. The reader's response begins during the act of reading and may continue well after the reading is finished because reading is an active creative experience. Rosenblatt named two categories of reader response—efferent and aesthetic. An **efferent** (from the Latin *efferre*—to carry away) **stance** is appropriate when a reader's attention is focused on information, facts, or instructions that will be retained after the reading. Therefore, it is the stance of choice for reading nonfiction, such as textbooks, reference books, informational books, and biographies.

An **aesthetic stance** is the appropriate stance for reading fiction. It is more difficult to define because the most important goal of the aesthetic stance is to have a lived-through experience—which Rosenblatt calls an **evocation.** The aesthetic stance may be extended across an entire continuum of responses, from reliving the reading experience to imagining or picturing characters, settings, or events from the story. With aesthetic responses, the reader interacts with the emotions and ideas that the text evokes to create an individual experience. In essence, the reader is living through the experience with the story—an evocation.

Teachers and parents should not assume that young readers will automatically adopt the appropriate stance for a particular text, especially for fiction. Because everything else in the curriculum requires an efferent stance, readers often take that stance when reading fiction as well, even when they are not faced with end-of-chapter questions! Students have been taught the efferent stance so long (both by implication and through experience) that if we do not introduce the aesthetic stance and the concept of reading for pleasure, many will never get it. In a way, we must unteach the efferent stance to unsophisticated readers if many of them are ever to understand the aesthetic stance.

Rosenblatt suggests that, beyond the socially agreed-upon meanings of words (e.g., a *cow* is not an *airplane*), *there is no one right way to know what a text means.*

Because responses are personal, a wide range of responses should be both accepted and encouraged. This theory, according to Rosenblatt, suggests that all interpretations of the meaning of a work are valid meanings. *Meaning* is not in text, and meaning is certainly not in teachers. Meaning is in *readers*. The teacher cannot know what a scene in a book may evoke in the reader's imagination, because the teacher is not privy to the reader's background and emotions. A text will not be the same experience for any two readers, and the meaning of a particular text may change even for the same reader when the work is reread at a later time.

Responses do not need to be active or overt, such as discussing, writing, dramatizing, or drawing. With literature, the most fundamental response is the reader's emotional interaction with the characters and events of the book. One way to enhance this interaction is to engage children with questions during and after reading. (Some sample questions are presented in Box 2.4.)

Although it is acceptable to discuss the story while it is being read, any serious analysis needs to come only after the reader has had time to mentally live through the experience or evocation. Evocation and analysis cannot occur at the same time. Therefore, it is essential for adults to wait for children to internalize the story before formally analyzing it or its elements to avoid the risk of imposing their own or someone else's analysis of the story. During this time for internalizing, I suggest the teacher do something different with the story; for example, reading something else that relates to the story or connecting the story to another subject area such as social studies by talking about the setting. After a minimum of one day, teachers can return to the book. At that time, children should be able to analyze the book informally and spontaneously.

Box 2.4

Story Questions

Questions to Ask While You Read

1. What do you think this character might be thinking? What clues help you to know?
2. How do you think this character feels? What clues help you?
3. Why did _____ finally decide to _____?
4. What was the reason for _____?
5. What do you think might happen next? Why do you think so?

Questions to Ask After You Read

1. Which of your predictions were true?
2. What caused the problem of the main character?

3. What words describe the personalities of the characters?
4. What did the main character learn at the end? What did the other characters learn?
5. What do you think is the most important thing the author might want you to remember about this story?
6. What does the title of the story mean to you now?

One way for the teacher to initiate analysis is to ask children to draw a scene as they visualize it while hearing a passage or after they read. This is a most productive activity for all ages, because much will be revealed that the teacher could learn in no other way. Asking children to tell you about their drawings will help them verbalize their personal meanings. Once the drawings and verbalizations have occurred, then small or large group discussions will allow readers to share their various meanings. This sharing allows readers to learn to respect the opinions of others, to ask questions for clarification, and to extend their individual meanings if they so choose. It is usually necessary for the teacher to model for children how to show respect for the interpretations and opinions of others, but this can be done only if the teacher genuinely accepts diverse opinions.

Promoting Pleasure or Displeasure

There are, unfortunately, a variety of ways to induce children's dislike for literature, one of which was mentioned at the beginning of this section with the story of Carla and the book reports. Perry Nodelman, in *The Pleasures of Children's Literature* (1996), identified several techniques that induce children's dislike for literature and should be *avoided:*

1. **Requiring readers to accurately pronounce every word on the printed page, and spending time with decoding strategies (like phonics) when they are unable to do so.** Once children learn to read independently, most of their reading time should be spent in silent reading. Never should they be required to spend an entire reading period listening to other children haltingly read from a text, one paragraph at a time. Most people read faster and with greater comprehension (and enjoyment) when they read silently. When they do read aloud, give help only when it is solicited, or when substitutions significantly alter the meaning of the author.

2. **Requiring readers to read *everything* closely and analytically.** A child reading from the aesthetic stance often goes at a pace more rapid than when he or she is reading from the efferent stance. For example, a storybook would most likely be read at a faster pace than an informational book the child plans on using for a report. Too often, children take the efferent stance for everything they read, because they expect to be grilled on the content.

3. **Requiring readers to find the hidden messages or morals from the author.** Regrettably, much of children's literature is moralistic, to the point that some adults expect *all* literature to teach a lesson or moral. However, good literature is primarily intended to be pleasurable. Not all authors implant hidden messages in their stories, and even when an author does convey a message, it should not be the focal point of the child's response. From reading broadly, children gain vicarious experience about life, and important truths will be gradually revealed.

4. **Requiring readers to express the same interpretations of a given book as other people do.** Responses are personal and will vary according to a reader's background experience. If children are expected to parrot what the teacher or (worse) the

teacher's manual or guidebook says, they will be trying to guess what the "right answers" are, rather than responding with the personal evocation they experienced with the book.

5. **Requiring readers to respond by participating in entertaining activities loosely based on the book.** Tying other curricular activities to literature is fine, as long as these activities do not supplant the literature experience and are not the only responses children are allowed to make. The primary responses of readers are their own internal thoughts. Discussing their thoughts with others who have experienced the book will allow children to construct new meanings.

Literature Circles

Now that you have read what adults should *not* do with literature, let me introduce some things you can do that will turn kids on to books, allowing them to respond to what they read by sharing their thoughts with others. **Literature circles** are small temporary discussion groups that have chosen to read the same book. More is said about literature circles in Chapter 13, but here I offer a brief outline based on *Literature Circles: Voice and Choice in the Student-Centered Classroom* (Daniels 1994):

- Students choose their own reading materials.
- Small temporary groups are formed, based on book choices.
- Different groups read different books.
- Groups meet on a regular schedule to discuss their reading.
- Students use notes to guide both their reading and discussion.
- Discussion topics come from the students.
- Group meetings aim to be open, natural conversations generated through personal connections, digressions, and open-ended questions about books.
- In newly formed groups, students play a rotating assortment of task roles.
- The teacher serves as a *facilitator*, not as a group member or instructor.

Prereading Schema Building

Current reading comprehension theory is in harmony with Rosenblatt's theory of transactional reader response. That is, in order to interact with text, the reader must bring something to the reading process. This something is called a **schema**, "a system of cognitive structures stored in memory that are abstract representations of events, objects, and relationships in the world" (Harris & Hodges 1995, p. 227). **Schemata** (the plural of *schema*) are more generally referred to as background experience or prior knowledge. In order to comprehend (and therefore fully enjoy) a book, readers must be able to integrate or connect new information in the text with their network of prior knowledge. Reading then becomes an active process of constructing meaning.

If children have little or no prior knowledge of the subject of a book, comprehension and enjoyment are impaired. Perhaps you can relate to the following story.

My eighth-grade English teacher assigned the class to read *Ivanhoe* (Scott), a book with a medieval setting first published in 1820. My library copy had no illustrations— not even on the cover! While slowly reading the first page, I asked myself, "What the heck are they talking about?" I reread the first page. I knew the meanings of nearly all the words, but I could not decipher the sentences. I looked at the back and saw the book was 352 pages! In tears, I went to my older (and smarter) sister and said, "I can't understand this! " She gave me a brief description of the plot and told me to reread the first page once more. This time, when I started reading, I knew where and when the story took place and who the main characters were, and things began to make sense. When I finally finished the book, I actually liked it!

The Process of Schema Building

I had been overwhelmed because my English teacher had failed to help her students build a schema to enable them to read *Ivanhoe*. Fortunately, I had an older sister to collaborate with, but not all the kids in my class had someone to help them. Teaching readers to construct their own schema before reading is a quick and easy thing to do, and I suggest you use it for all the books you read to your children. Most importantly, I hope you will teach this process to your children and encourage them to use it each time they read a new book. It is probably the single most important thing you can do to enhance children's understanding and appreciation of a fiction book. I call it the **prereading schema-building process**, and it can be used with either picture books or juvenile novels. The purpose is to activate the reader's prior knowledge as well as to build a scaffold for new knowledge such as vocabulary and historical or cultural setting.

I. Begin at the End. Please, do not read the end of the book first! However, look at the last page of the text to see how many pages there are and the size of print (small, medium, large) to judge how long it will take you to read the book. Then, starting with the last text page, look at each page until you reach the back cover. These last pages often contain critical information for understanding the book, such as glossaries, maps, or afterwords that will provide helpful information you can refer to while reading. You also may find information about the author. Usually books do not mention that these aids are provided at the end. I have had students who struggled to read a work of historical fiction that contained many foreign words, such as *Ishi, Last of His Tribe* (Kroeber 1964), only to discover the glossary after finishing the book.

II. Cover the Cover. Sometimes information such as a brief biographical sketch of the author is printed on the inside back cover of a paperback book, so always look. If there is nothing there, turn the book over and look at the back cover. Most paperbacks will have a short synopsis of the story there. The ending is not revealed, but information such as the name and age of the main character, and where and when the story takes place, is usually provided. Sometimes there are excerpts from reviews, and these may add a bit of additional information, such as the theme. (On hardcover books, the synopsis and reviews are on the inside flaps of the book jacket. Information about the author and illustrator are also provided there.)

Next, look at the front cover. On a paperback book, or on the jacket of a hardcover book, you should find an illustration. If the book jacket is missing, turn to the first illustration in the book. Think like a detective and look for clues as to what the story might be about. Some questions that will help you make predictions are:

- What clues can you find that tell about the setting of this story—where and when it happened?
- What do you think the characters might be doing?
- What does the title tell you about the story? Predict what kind of story it might be (fantasy, realistic, humorous).
- What do you think might happen in this story? Why do you think so?
- What do you think the illustrations or designs on the colored endpapers or title page mean? What additional information about the story can be found in these illustrations?
- What other books have you read by this author?

III. Finish at the Front. The final stage of building a story schema is reviewing all the front matter—the pages that precede the first text page. Locate the title page with the title, author, and publisher. On the back of this page is publication information, including the copyright date. (In a few picture books, the copyright page is at the end.) There may be more than one edition of the book, so look for the year of original publication. This gives you an idea of when the author wrote the story. It is sometimes important to know the decade in which a book was written—particularly in the case of contemporary fiction, which may not seem contemporary to readers who are younger than the book. Look for a dedication or acknowledgment that might contain clues about the author. Some authors include a foreword that provides information to help readers understand and enjoy the book.

The information you gain by previewing the end pages, the back and front covers, and the front matter should give you enough background to allow your full enjoyment of the book. After reading the first few pages, stop and confirm or disprove your earlier predictions.

Modeling the Process

The following is an example of a think-aloud activity in which you can teach the process of previewing a book for comprehension. Using the paperback edition of *The Voyage of the Frog* (Paulsen 1989), I describe here my thoughts as I preview the book.

> The name of this book is *The Voyage of the Frog*. It sounds like an animal fantasy story where a frog takes a trip. The last text page is numbered 141, but the size of the print is medium, so this won't take too long to read. Following the last page of text is a map. This is probably where the story takes place. The map shows the Pacific Ocean off the coast of Lower California and Mexico, and it outlines the route of the voyage. That's a long way for a frog to swim! There's a lot of detail and notes

The *Frog* encounters a storm. From *The Voyage of the Frog,* written by Gary Paulsen.

on the map, but I'll skip it now and look back at it while I read the book to follow where all the events happen.

On the inside of the back cover is a photograph, probably of the author. He looks a little like my father with his beard and jacket and baseball cap (except he is holding a dog, and my father doesn't like dogs). The author must really like dogs to have one in his picture. Underneath the photograph I see the author's name—Gary Paulsen. The paragraph under the picture says he has won lots of awards. It also lists the names of some of his other books. I've read *Hatchet!* It was great. I hope this book is just as good. The paragraph says he has homes in New Mexico and on the Pacific. The map showed the Pacific area, so he must be writing about one of the places where he lives.

On the back cover of the book, I see an excerpt from the story, a short summary, and some excerpts of reviews. Reading the back cover gives me a lot of information. The main character is named David Alspeth, and he is 14 years old. The *Frog* is the name of a sailboat—not a character. There is a storm at sea, and David is stranded with little food and water and no radio. (He should have taken a cell phone with him.) One of the reviewers said this is a survival book. *Hatchet* was a survival book also, so I think I'm really going to like this book.

On the front cover is a picture of a small sailboat in a stormy sea. The size of those waves makes me remember when my family went on a cruise, and I got so sick. I feel sorry for the boy inside the boat because the sky looks dark, and the storm might last a long time. In the picture I can't see the boy, but the boat looks modern, so it looks like this is a realistic story that takes place in modern times.

On the title page, I see the book was published in 1989. That explains why the boy didn't take a cell phone. Everybody didn't carry them around back then. The table of contents doesn't tell me much, but after it is a diagram of the sailboat with all the parts labeled. I don't know much about boats, so I'll look back at this while I'm reading when I don't know what a term means. The next page contains only a quote from someone named Joseph Conrad: "Only the young have such moments." I don't know what that means, but I'll look at it again after I read the book to see if I understand it then.

And now, I'm ready to read.

Literature Activity: **Building Schema**

Select a popular picture book or juvenile novel, and use the prereading schema-building process to deduce as many clues as you can about the story before reading it. After you finish reading, check your list of clues to see if they were all accurate. If not, determine what led you to form a misconception. ■

CHILDREN'S   BOOKS CITED IN CHAPTER 2

Aardema, Verna. *Why Mosquitoes Buzz in People's Ears.* Illus. Leo D. Dillon & Diane Dillon. Dial, 1975.

Armstrong, William H. *Sounder.* Harper & Row, 1969.

Applegate, Katherine A. *Animorphs: The Andalite's Gift.* Scholastic, 1997.

Babbitt, Natalie. *Knee-Knock Rise.* Farrar, Straus & Giroux, 1970.

Blume, Judy. *Are You There God? It's Me, Margaret.* Bradbury, 1970.

———. *The Pain and the Great One.* Illus. Irene Trivas. Dell, 1974.

Brown, Marcia. *Once a Mouse . . . : A Fable Cut in Wood.* Scribner, 1961.

Cleary, Beverly. *Dear Mr. Henshaw.* Morrow, 1983.

Creech, Sharon. *Absolutely Normal Chaos.* Macmillan, 1990.

Fish, Helen Dean. *Animals of the Bible.* Illus. Dorothy Lathrop. Lippincott–Raven, 1937.

Forbes, Esther. *Johnny Tremain.* Houghton Mifflin, 1943.

George, Jean Craighead. *Julie of the Wolves.* HarperCollins, 1972.

Hall, Donald. *Ox-Cart Man.* Illus. Barbara Cooney. Viking, 1979.

Houston, Gloria. *The Year of the Perfect Christmas Tree.* Illus. Barbara Cooney. Dial, 1988.

Konigsburg, E. L. *From the Mixed-up Files of Mrs. Basil E. Frankweiler.* Atheneum, 1967.

Kroeber, Theodora. *Ishi, Last of His Tribe.* Houghton Mifflin, 1964.

L'Engle, Madeleine. *A Wrinkle in Time.* Farrar, Straus & Giroux, 1962.

Lewis, C. S. *The Lion, the Witch and the Wardrobe.* HarperCollins, 1950.

✓ Lionni, Leo. *Swimmy.* Knopf, 1963.

———. *Frederick.* Pantheon, 1967.

Lobel, Arnold. *Frog and Toad Together.* HarperTrophy, 1971.

———. *Frog and Toad All Year.* HarperTrophy, 1976.

Lowry, Lois. *The Giver.* Houghton Mifflin, 1993.

MacLachlan, Patricia. *Sarah Plain and Tall.* Harper & Row, 1985.

McCloskey, Robert. *Make Way for Ducklings.* Viking, 1941.

Mitchell, Margaree King. *Uncle Jed's Barbershop.* Illus. James Ransome. Simon & Schuster, 1993.

O'Dell, Scott. *Island of the Blue Dolphins.* Houghton Mifflin, 1960.

Paterson, Katherine. *Bridge to Terabithia.* HarperCollins, 1977.

Patterson, Lillie. *Martin Luther King, Jr.: Man of Peace.* Garrard, 1969.

Paulsen, Gary. *Hatchet.* Viking Penguin, 1987.

———. *The Voyage of the Frog.* Orchard, 1989.

———. *The Rifle.* Harcourt Brace, 1995.

Rowling, J. K. *Harry Potter and the Sorcerer's Stone.* Arthur A. Levine, 1998.

Scieszka, Jon. *The True Story of the 3 Little Pigs.* Illus. Lane Smith. Viking Penguin, 1989.

Scott, Sir Walter. *Ivanhoe.* New American Library, 1820/1987.

Sendak, Maurice. *Where the Wild Things Are.* Harper & Row, 1963.

Slote, Alfred. *Finding Buck McHenry.* Harper-Collins, 1991.

Speare, Elizabeth George. *The Witch of Blackbird Pond.* Houghton Mifflin, 1958.

Spinelli, Jerry. *Wringer.* HarperCollins, 1997.

Taylor, Mildred D. *Roll of Thunder, Hear My Cry.* Viking Penguin, 1976.

Van Allsburg, Chris. *The Polar Express.* Houghton Mifflin, 1985.

van Loon, Hendrik Willem. *The Story of Mankind.* Liveright, 1921.

White, E. B. *Charlotte's Web.* Illus. Garth Williams. Harper & Row, 1952.

Wilder, Laura Ingalls. *Little House on the Prairie.* Illus. Garth Williams. HarperTrophy, 1935.

Yolen, Jane. *The Devil's Arithmetic.* Viking Penguin, 1988.

KEY TERMS

 Explore the E-Glossary at **www.ablongman.com/anderson**

aesthetic stance (p. 35)

alternating point of view (p. 28)

backdrop setting (p. 29)

book talk (p. 34)

circular plot (p. 31)

conflict (p. 32)

cumulative plot (p. 30)

dynamic character (p. 26)

efferent stance (p. 35)

episodic plot (p. 31)

evocation (p. 35)

exposition (p. 31)

first-person point of view (p. 27)

flashback (p. 31)

flat character (p. 26)

foreshadowing (p. 31)

integral setting (p. 30)

limited omniscient point of view (p. 28)

linear plot (p. 30)

literary elements (p. 26)

literature circles (p. 38)

objective point of view (p. 28)

omniscient point of view (p. 28)

point of view (p. 27)

plot (p. 30)

prereading schema-building process (p. 39)

protagonist (p. 26)

reader response theory (p. 35)

round character (p. 26)

schema (p. 38)

schemata (p. 38)

setting (p. 29)

static character (p. 26)

story mapping (p. 31)

stereotype character (p. 26)

style (p. 33)

suspense (p. 32)

theme (p. 32)

tone (p. 34)

How many things start with B?

Ed Emberley's ABC
Written and illustrated by
Ed Emberley.

3

Illustration and Early Childhood Books

Have you ever had a young child turn a page too early while you were reading a picture book? When you say, "Wait, I'm not finished reading this page!" the child looks up quizzically and thinks, "Well, *I* am!" Young children believe that the illustrations, rather than the printed words, tell the story. When you read to them, they conceptualize that you are *telling* a story from the pictures. Indeed, a good picture book does tell a story through its art. After listening to a book once and looking at the pictures, most young children can retell the story.

Recall the definitions of books with illustrations presented in Chapter 1.

- *Picture books* convey their message through a series of pictures with only a small amount of text (or none at all). The illustrations are as important as— or more important than—the text in conveying the message.
- *Picture storybooks* are picture books with a plot, and the text and illustrations equally convey the story line. (Most people simply call these picture books as well.)
- *Illustrated books* are for older children. The illustrations are fewer and more limited in color, sometimes only black and white. The illustrations are extensions of the text and may add to the story, but they are not necessary to convey its meaning.

Keep in mind that *picture book* is a format. It is found in all genres and all forms of books. The illustrations in a children's book (or lack thereof) play an important part when younger children select books. Therefore, it is important that illustrations appeal to young readers and complement the text in telling a story. Because the illustrations in children's books are art, they are best discussed and evaluated by artistic standards.

The Union of Art and Text

Art and text were forever bonded when Beatrix Potter published *The Tale of Peter Rabbit* in 1901. Today, artistic excellence is increasingly apparent and appreciated in children's literature, thanks to artists such as Leo and Diane Dillon, Chris Van Allsburg, Maurice Sendak, and a multitude of others (Lukens 1999). After all, even adults, when they first pick up a book or magazine, tend to look at the pictures before reading the words (Nodelman 1996); that is why many advertisers put attractive pictures and minimal print in their ads.

"Illustrators of children's books realize the importance of conveying, through illustrations, the excitement, beauty, and meaning of the story" (Rothlein & Meinbach 1996, p. 326). In picture storybooks (hereafter referred to as picture books), the two arts of storytelling and illustration are combined; thus, both the text and the illustrations convey the story. Neither could carry the story line alone. Illustrations have both meaning and content—just like the printed words of the story. Also like words, pictures are representations of concrete things, and the meaning of these representations must be learned. This is not an automatic process with young children, especially when the drawings are not intended to convey what an object actually looks like. Therefore, parents and teachers need to encourage a young child's capacity to obtain meaning from pictures. As children learn to construct meaning from pictures, they are developing their **visual literacy**—the ability to interpret graphic stimuli. Just as people learn to read by reading, it only makes sense that people learn visual literacy by viewing.

The ability to interpret and communicate through visual symbols in art is one aspect of visual literacy. Long before children are able to read (that is, to construct meaning from print by interpreting written symbols), they are able to obtain ideas and meaning from pictures and can express these ideas orally. Parents and teachers enhance visual literacy when they focus children's attention on the illustrations as part of reading and sharing books. Even after children learn to read, illustrations aid their comprehension of the story. Among the many components of a child's visual world (including television, movies, videotapes, and computers), book illustrations are a beautiful medium through which to learn about the world.

Responding to Literature

Comparing Illustrations in Folktales

Select two or three different versions of picture books of a favorite folktale—for example, "Stone Soup" or "Hansel and Gretel." Carefully compare the illustrations in the different versions, and tell which pictures enhance the story the most. Explain the reasons for your choice.

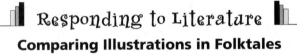

Visual Elements of Artistic Design

Good illustrations evoke a variety of emotions from both child and adult viewers. Artists use certain methods to create the effects that stimulate these emotions, and examining the elements will help children appreciate the artist's skill in creating a final effect (Stewig 1980). The elements of space, line, shape, color, texture, and composition are central to artistic design.

Space

Space refers to the areas objects take up (positive space) and the areas that surround shapes and forms (negative space). Space draws the viewer's attention to the elements the artist wishes to emphasize. A page with much negative space draws a viewer's immediate attention to the object or character depicted. However, a page with little negative space will divide the viewer's attention. Space can be used to create the illusion of distance, but it can also create emotional effects. For example, an illustration with generous use of negative space can suggest emptiness, loneliness, and isolation, whereas an illustration with only positive space can evoke feelings of claustrophobia, confusion, or chaos.

Line

Line is a horizontal, vertical, angled, or curved mark made by a tool across a surface. Lines are used to define the shape of objects and to convey the sense of movement and distance. Lines can be heavy, boldly defining forms and creating shapes, or they can be thin and delicate. They can express movement or appear static. Lines may be regular throughout a book or varied in each picture of the book. Artists use the element of line to suggest certain emotional responses. For example, curves and circles are used to suggest warmth. Sharp or zigzag lines are used to show excitement, rapid movement, and energy. Horizontal lines suggest calm and stability, and vertical lines are employed to show height and distance.

Shape

Shape refers to the two dimensions of height and width arranged geometrically. Shape is created when spaces are contained by a combination of lines. A shape can appear flat and two-dimensional, or, through the artist's shading techniques (with a buildup of small strokes), a shape may appear fully rounded and three-dimensional. Sutherland (1997) contrasts shapes as "distinct or vaguely suggested, simple or ornamented, free-flowing or rigid" (p. 116). Various types of lines that define predominant objects in an illustration can be used to depict a variety of emotions. Squarish, angular shapes are used to elicit an excited response from the viewer; rounded shapes—such as curved lines—are used to achieve a sense of warmth, coziness, and security. Large grouped shapes may suggest confinement and awkwardness, but also stability. Lighter, more delicate shapes may suggest freedom, movement, and grace. Some art forms, such as collage, consist almost entirely of shapes with little or no use of singular lines.

Color

Color refers to the variety of hues that are the different parts of the spectrum. In art, color is achieved through pigments and light. An artist can make many colors from the pigment of a single **hue** (pure color) by adding differing amounts of *white* to achieve variations of **tints,** or by adding differing amounts of *black* to achieve variations of **shades.** Illustrators may use little color—for example, black ink on white paper, as in Shel Silverstein's *The Giving Tree* (1964), or monochrome techniques with a variety of tints and shades.

Colors can be bold and brilliant or subtle and vaporous. Reds and yellows are warm colors that suggest excitement, warmth, and happiness. Greens and blues are cool colors and suggest calm, quiet, peaceful, or melancholy feelings. Lighter shades are associated with cheeriness, whereas darker shades are associated with gloominess; thus, pastel colors can induce a feeling of happiness, and darker tones can induce a somber mood. Certain colors have historically been associated with particular traits in Western culture: Purple signifies royalty, yellow signifies cowardice, blue signifies depression, and green signifies envy or illness.

Texture

Texture is the illusion of a tactile surface (e.g., rough, soft, smooth, hard, furry) created in an illustration by such methods as lines and shading. For example, a thin wash of watercolor can be used to represent a diaphanous fabric or a vapor of fog. Collage can be used effectively to obtain textural contrast. Russell (1997) comments that "an artist who wants to emphasize the realistic quality of a picture may pay greater attention to texture. . . . However, less realistic styles may make use of texture to enrich the visual experience and to stimulate the viewer's imagination" (pp. 119–120).

Composition

Composition is the combination and arrangement of the elements in an illustration. For example, varying placements of the focal point and the angle from which the scene is viewed convey different moods. A well-composed illustration shows unity and focus, and all the elements are in balance. Another important aspect of composition is **perspective,** the vantage point from which the viewer is looking at the objects or events depicted. When the vantage point is close, the viewer is brought into the scene and is mentally engaged in the action or mood. When the vantage point is far away, the viewer is more detached. Point of view is an aspect of perspective in art as well as in the literary elements, and it is an important part of the composition of an illustration. For example, a scene can be depicted from a small child's viewpoint looking up or from the panoramic viewpoint of a bird flying over the scene. The events depicted in a story are understood differently when they are seen from different points of view; for example, see *UFO Diary* by Satoshi Kitamura (1989), in which the story is illustrated from the alien's perspective.

Artistic Styles

Another way to enhance children's appreciation of book illustration is to look at the techniques artists use to compose their artwork.

Representationalism depicts objects realistically, with recognizable shapes, realistic color (if used), and proper perspectives and proportions. Because representationalism endeavors to depict the world as we see it in real life, it is the easiest of the art styles to recognize. Beatrix Potter used this technique in *The Tale of Peter Rabbit* (1902), and it continues to be the predominant style for illustrations in children's books today.

Expressionism leans toward the abstract, focusing on depicting emotions. It employs color, line, space, and the other elements in a highly individualistic and subjective manner in which the artists paint what they feel, rather than simply what they see. It includes deliberate distortion and exaggeration and is highly subjective. An example of expressionism is the *Madeline* (1967) series by Ludwig Bemelmans. Expressionism has several variations:

- *Cubism* juxtaposes various geometric shapes.
- *Fauvism* employs bold black lines and richly contrasting colors, sometimes with a stained-glass effect.
- *Art deco* employs bold sleek designs and sharp contrast.
- *Pointillism* is a technique in which carefully positioned dots of equal size and pure color build up form. The many round dots of different colors suggest, rather than depict, objects in the painting. Today, black-ink pointillist designs are also found.

Impressionism uses an interplay of color and light created with splashes, speckles, or dots of paint (as opposed to longer brush strokes) to create a dreamlike, romantic effect. The artist's concern is with the transient appearance—"the way things momentarily look in particular circumstances of light and shade" (Nodelman 1996, p. 229). The effect is a view from afar. An example is *Mr. Gumpy's Outing* by John Burningham (1970).

Surrealism distorts and plays with images, conveying a fantasy quality. It represents the artist's intellectual (as opposed to emotional) response to a subject. Artists who wish to evoke strangeness employ surrealism to "depict unrealistic situations in a highly representational way that makes the impossible seem strangely possible" (Nodelman 1996, p. 227). That is, objects can be rendered quite realistically, but they are juxtaposed unnaturally with contrasting realistic objects to create a world that is surprising, puzzling, and even shocking. Surrealistic elements often appear in books of fantasy, such as *Jumanji* by Chris Van Allsburg (1981).

Folk art is based on designs and images peculiar to a specific culture. There are innumerable folk art styles, each attempting to recreate the atmosphere or the pervasive mood of a specific culture. Folk art is characterized by imaginative use of color, repeated stylized patterns, lack of perspective, simple childlike forms, and flat patterns. An example is Blair Lent's artwork for Arlene Mosel's *Tikki Tikki Tembo* (1968).

Cartoon drawings are reduced to their essentials with simple lines and primary colors. The simplified figures and exaggerated proportions are particularly effective in achieving movement and humor. Dr. Seuss's unique cartoon style with gross exaggerations and zany creatures created a humorous effect in his many books. Other artists who have been successful with this style are Syd Hoff (e.g., *Sammy the Seal,* 1959) and William Steig (e.g., *Doctor De Soto,* 1982).

Artistic Media and Techniques

Some illustrators have such a unique style that you can recognize one of their books just by looking at the illustrations. For many artists, their own style combined with their favorite technique and medium make their work easily recognizable. For example, Tomie dePaola's characteristic folk art style in watercolor is his signature. Other artists, such as Marcia Brown, prefer versatility and use different combinations of style, technique, and media, depending on how they want to express a particular story.

The materials that artists use to make the original artwork for book illustrations are called *media*. Artists select media carefully in order to give optimal expression to their ideas. Otherwise, the images they wish to create would be limited by the wrong selection. For example, block prints are bold, but they rarely reveal texture. Collage can easily depict texture but seldon gives the perception of depth. Black ink on white paper can be used to achieve depth, but it will not convey the moods of the story the way color can. Tempera can be used to achieve myriad colors, but it will not create the impression of light the way translucent watercolor does.

Painting

Watercolor is the most popular medium for book illustrations. Watercolor combines water with either a dry form of pigment or a pigment bound with a water-soluble solution of gum arabic and glycerin. It produces a transparent look and will provide a more fluid or loose effect if more water is added, or a highly controlled effect with strong colors when mixed with less water. The color itself can define the form, or ink lines can be added to produce definition. Tomie dePaola used watercolor to create the illustrations for *Strega Nona* (1975).

Tempera consists of pigment mixed with egg yolk or a gelatinous or glutinous substance. It is less transparent than watercolor, so it can be used to produce brilliant hues. Maurice Sendak used tempera in *Where the Wild Things Are* (1963).

Gouache is powdered paint similar to tempera, but it is mixed with a white base, resulting in an opaque color. Gerald McDermott's *Arrow to the Sun* (1974) is an example of illustration using this medium.

Oil paints combine color pigment with a linseed oil base and turpentine or other thinners. These paints are usually opaque; layering can produce effects of depth and dimension. Nonny Hogrogian used oil paint to create the illustrations in *One Fine Day* (1971).

In **acrylic paints** liquid acrylic plastic (polymer) is used to bind color pigment. Acrylics can be used to produce brilliant and even shocking colors. Like oil paint, acrylic dries slowly, and it can be manipulated, changed, or covered with varnish or gel. Barbara Cooney's illustrations in Donald Hall's *Ox-Cart Man* (1979) were done with acrylic paints.

Drawing

Drawing is a linear art technique done with instruments such as pencil, pen and ink, charcoal, marker, or crayon. Pencil drawings may be in black, as in *Jumanji* by Chris

Van Allsburg (1981), or in color, as in Stephen Gammell's illustrations in *Song and Dance Man* by Karen Ackerman (1988). Pencils can be used to create strong lines, shaded areas, smudged shadows, and details.

Pen-and-ink drawings can be achieved with different shapes and kinds of pen points and with either black or many colors of ink. Pen and ink is often used to give definition in watercolor washes, but it can be used alone with no colors, as in Shel Silverstein's *Lafcadio, the Lion Who Shot Back* (1963).

Pastels are soft-colored chalks for drawing, but they can also be applied by hand in their powdered form. Pastels produce an opaque image. Nonny Hogrogian used this medium in *Always Room for One More* by Sorche Nic Leodhas (1965).

Other Techniques

Woodcut is the oldest medium for making art prints. More recently, linoleum has been substituted for hardwood because it is easier to cut. The artist first cuts away the background of the picture, applies ink or color to the surface, and presses the block against paper. Ed Emberley employed this technique to illustrate *Drummer Hoff* by Barbara Emberley (1967).

In **airbrushing,** a form of stenciling, the artist uses a compressed-air atomizer to spray paint on a surface. This technique was used by Leo and Diane Dillon in Verna Aardema's *Why Mosquitoes Buzz in People's Ears* (1975).

Collage, first made famous by the Cubist painter Pablo Picasso, is a technique of cutting or tearing paper or fabric shapes that are then assembled and glued on a surface. Ezra Jack Keats made this form popular in children's books with *The Snowy Day* (1962), and artists such as Leo Lionni (*Frederick,* 1967) and Eric Carle (*The Very Hungry Caterpillar,* 1976) carry on the tradition. Carle's signature style is created with transparent tissue papers, which he lightly streaks with paint. In **montage,** a similar technique, several distinct pictures are combined to make a composite picture. Joan Steiner introduced an innovative three-dimensional form of collage in *Look-Alikes* (1998).

Photography has been called the art of composition, but it was initially questioned as an artistic technique by critics who considered it more of a technical skill than an artistic ability. It was made popular by Tana Hoban, who used a combination of her artist's eye and photographer's skill to produce true works of art in her many children's books (Cullinan 1989). Initially Hoban worked in black and white, and she produced popular concept books such as *Push–Pull Empty–Full* (1976). Other photographer–illustrators of children's books include George Ancona and Bruce McMillan.

Computer-generated graphics constitute the newest technology-based art form to find its way to the pages of children's picture books. Digital art was pioneered by J. Otto Seibold with *Mr. Lunch Takes a Plane Ride* (1993). Lisa Desimini used computer-generated graphics for *Love Letters* (Adoff 1997) and *Doodle Dandies: Poems That Take Shape* (Lewis 1998). Veteran illustrators Don and Audrey Wood now work exclusively as digital artists.

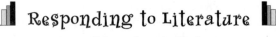

Responding to Literature

Searching for Subplots

Some books have subplots in their illustrations that are not mentioned in the text. These sub-plots can tie into the story's plot, run parallel to the plot, or have little to do with the plot. Look for this subtle technique in the picture books you read. Read *Love You Forever* by Robert N. Munsch (1989), and make up a story about the cat that is not a character in the story but that parallels the actions of the main character in each illustration.

Integrating Art and Literature

Ideas for art lessons based on book illustrations are abundant in *Art Projects Plus* (Blount & Webb). This book presents many ideas for introducing art forms, media, and techniques with children's picture books. Additionally, in *The Arts as Meaning Makers* (1999), Cornett describes methods of integrating literature and all the arts throughout the curriculum to enhance learning and motivation. Cornett discusses how the study of art

- activates the emotional intelligence and motivates children
- provides a way of communicating through visual and spatial symbols
- allows children to think through their senses
- develops aesthetic sensitivity and satisfies the basic need for beauty
- develops higher thinking, creativity, and problem-solving capabilities
- strengthens self-understanding and a child's sense of confidence about his or her own uniqueness
- creates respect and sensitivity for diversity
- develops responsibility, focus, concentration, and self-discipline
- reflects life and pertains to all curricular areas
- provides a way to understand children

Responding to Literature

Looking for Plot Clues in Illustrations

In *The Arts as Meaning Makers,* Cornett recommends that we guide children to become "picture book detectives" by drawing their attention to aspects of book illustrations that enhance the plot. For example, before reading a book, ask children to look and listen actively so they will be able to identify the following:

- story events in the art that are not in the text
- parts of illustrations that foreshadow coming events
- elements of the illustrations that help to create tension in the plot

Evaluating Illustrations

Ask yourself the following questions to judge the appropriateness of the illustrations in a book.

- Are the illustrations appealing to children?
- Do the illustrations enhance the story?
- Are the pictures a reflection of the tone of the story?
- Are all the pictures and details in harmony with the text?

ILLUSTRATED BOOKS CITED

Aardema, Verna. *Why Mosquitoes Buzz in People's Ears.* Illus. Leo D. Dillon & Diane Dillon. Dial, 1975.

Ackerman, Karen. *Song and Dance Man.* Illus. Stephen Gammell. Knopf, 1988.

Adoff, Arnold. *Love Letters.* Illus. Lisa Desimini. Blue Sky Press, 1997.

Bemelmans, Ludwig. *Madeline.* Viking, 1967.

Burningham, John. *Mr. Gumpy's Outing.* Holt, Rinehart & Winston, 1970.

Carle, Eric. *The Very Hungry Caterpillar.* Collins World, 1976.

dePaola, Tomie. *Strega Nona.* Prentice-Hall, 1975.

Emberley, Barbara. *Drummer Hoff.* Illus. Ed Emberley. Prentice-Hall, 1967.

Hall, Donald. *Ox-Cart Man.* Illus. Barbara Cooney. Viking, 1979.

Hoban, Tana. *Push–Pull Empty–Full.* Collier, 1976.

Hoff, Syd. *Sammy the Seal.* HarperCollins, 1959.

Hogrogian, Nonny. *One Fine Day.* Macmillan, 1971.

Keats, Ezra Jack. *The Snowy Day.* Viking, 1962.

Kitamura, Satoshi. *UFO Diary.* Farrar, Straus & Giroux, 1989.

Lewis, J. Patrick. *Doodle Dandies: Poems That Take Shape.* Illus. Lisa Desimini. Atheneum, 1998.

Lionni, Leo. *Frederick.* Pantheon, 1967.

McDermott, Gerald. *Arrow to the Sun.* Viking, 1974.

Mosel, Arlene. *Tikki Tikki Tembo.* Illus. Blair Lent. Holt, Rinehart & Winston, 1968.

Munsch, Robert N. *Love You Forever.* Illus. Sheila McGraw. Firefly, 1989.

Nic Leodhas, Sorche. *Always Room for One More.* Illus. Nonny Hogrogian. Holt, Rinehart & Winston, 1965.

Potter, Beatrix. *The Tale of Peter Rabbit.* Frederick Warne, 1902.

Seibold, J. Otto, & Vivian Walsh. *Mr. Lunch Takes a Plane Ride.* Viking, 1993.

Sendak, Maurice. *Where the Wild Things Are.* Harper, 1963.

Silverstein, Shel. *Lafcadio, the Lion Who Shot Back.* HarperCollins, 1963.

———. *The Giving Tree.* Harper & Row, 1964.

Steig, William. *Doctor De Soto.* Farrar, Straus & Giroux, 1982.

Steiner, Joan. *Look-Alikes.* Little, Brown, 1998.

Van Allsburg, Chris. *Jumanji.* Houghton Mifflin, 1981.

Early Childhood Books

What are your earliest memories of books? Did you have access to picture books before you entered school? Being regularly read to and having access to appropriate books before school age makes a big difference in children's achievement once they start school. Children who have listened to many readings of books and who have been encouraged to look through the books and retell the stories have a much greater likelihood of becoming good readers.

Board Books

I have stressed that it is never too early to begin reading to your own children, and I suggest you start with the books made especially for the very young. Little ones not only love to look at books—they also like to gnaw, throw, and pull at them, so these books must be sturdy. In past years, cloth and even plastic books were popular, but in recent years, these have largely been replaced with board books.

In **board books,** the content and format are designed for very young children. These durable books usually consist of twelve sturdy cardboard pages that have a glossy wipe-off finish on each side. They range in size from three inches square to twelve inches square, and all corners are rounded to prevent a poke in the eye. Each page is illustrated with a clear and simple picture, often with just a one-word caption. Though some board books tell a simple story, many are concept oriented. For example, David Bennett's book *Home* (1992) has the following captioned illustrations (each including a child): high chair, table, telephone, pillow, pot, laundry basket, books, plant, door, and curtain. The book provides a label for each of these familiar objects. Following is a list of some popular first books.

▌ RECOMMENDED BOARD BOOKS

- Bennett, David. **Home.** Dutton, 1992.
- Boynton, Sandra. **Moo, Baa, La La La.** Little Simon, 1995.
- Bunting, Jane. **My Little ABC Board Book.** DK, 1997.
- Carle, Eric. **The Very Hungry Caterpillar.** Philomel, 1994.
- Day, Alexandra. **Carl Goes Shopping.** Farrar, Straus & Giroux, 1992.
- dePaola, Tomie. **Strega Nona.** Little Simon, 1997.
- Fox, Mem. **Time for Bed.** Illus. Jane Dyer. Harcourt, 1997.
- Gomi, Taro. **Spring Is Here.** Chronicle, 1999.
- Johnson, Angela. **Joshua by the Sea.** Illus. Rhonda Mitchell. Orchard, 1994.
- Lilly, Kenneth. **My Little Animals Board Book.** DK Publications, 1998.
- Martin, Bill, Jr. **Brown Bear, Brown Bear, What Do You See?** Illus. Eric Carle. Holt, 1996.
- McBratney, Sam. **Guess How Much I Love You?** Illus. Anita Jeram. Candlewick, 1996.
- McMullan, Kate. **If You Were My Bunny.** Illus. David McPhail. Cartwheel, 1998.
- Oxenbury, Helen. **I Hear.** Candlewick, 1995.
- Pingry, Patricia A. **The Story of Easter.** Candy Cane, 1998.
- Rathman, Peggy. **Good Night, Gorilla.** Putnam, 1996.
- Wade, Lee. **The Cheerios Play Book.** Little Simon, 1998.
- Wells, Rosemary. **Max's Chocolate Chicken.** Dial, 1999.

■ Wilkes, Angela. *My First Word Board Book.* DK Publications, 1997.

■ Yaccarino, Dan. *Five Little Pumpkins.* HarperCollins, 1998.

Concept Books

Concept books are picture books that present numerous examples of a particular concept. Because children are never too young to listen to and look at books, they are also never too young to learn about the world around them. One of the most delightful ways children learn about their world is through concept books. The focus of concept books is a particular body of knowledge, so they could be considered informational books for the very young. Concept books do much to help children discover labels of familiar objects and living things. Good concept books also present beautiful images and entertaining language to attract young listeners and readers. These books help activate children's thinking, and they are a stimulus for children to construct schemata for new concepts through their own mental relationships. Some of the common concepts presented in these books include:

- letters of the alphabet (e.g., a, b, c)
- counting numbers (e.g., 1, 2, 3)
- colors (e.g., red, yellow, blue)
- shapes (e.g., circle, square, triangle)
- opposites (e.g., hot/cold, fast/slow)
- size relationships (e.g., big/small, short/tall)

Alphabet Books. **Alphabet books**, also called ABC books, are concept books that present the letters of the alphabet. These are often a young child's first introduction to the symbols that represent our language. It is desirable for alphabet books to present the letters in alphabetical order in both lower- and uppercase forms (or little and big letters as children call them). Commonly, one **two-page spread** (two facing pages in a book) is devoted to each letter. For example, the featured letter and one or more words that begin with that letter are on one page, and an illustration depicting the things named is on the facing page.

Russell (1997) identified three patterns of alphabet books. Potpourri books have no uniformity in subject matter. For example, the featured objects in *From Acorn to Zoo* (Kitamura 1992) range from armadillo, airplane, balloon, and book to yo-yo, yogurt, zoo, and zebra.

Sequential story books have a continuous story line throughout, as in *ABC Bunny* (Gag 1933). Finding a word for each letter of the alphabet to fit in the story line can be quite difficult, and the examples sometimes appear contrived. *Albert B. Cub & Zebra* (Rockwell 1977) is one such book, containing only a very loose story line. However, the illustrations are colorful and invite conversation between a child and adult.

Themed books depict objects that are linked by a theme or topic, as in *Ashanti to Zulu: African Traditions* (Musgrove 1976). These books can be helpful when you are teaching thematic units to children of all ages. The bibliography at the end of this section includes alphabet books with themes of animals, bugs, coral reef creatures, dinosaurs, and flowers—to name a few. Themed books are a colorful and interesting way to convey information. However, as with sequential story alphabet books, finding an appropriate example for each letter is challenging, and sometimes authors resort to words from other languages. For example, *Eating the Alphabet* (Ehlert 1989) contains the words *jalapeno* and *jicama* for the letter *J*. Both vegetables are native to Mexico, and their names are pronounced as if the *j* were an *h* (hah-lah-PAY-nyoh and HEE-cah-mah). This could be confusing to young children who are just beginning to match letters with the language sounds they represent.

One delightful book falls in none of the previous categories, because it does not match letters with sounds; rather, it presents the alphabet in verse with strong rhythm. *Chicka Chicka Boom Boom* (Martin & Archambault 1989) is a fabulous book to read aloud, and it could rival the traditional "Alphabet Song" in helping children remember alphabetical order.

> *A* told *B*, and *B* told *C*,
> "I'll meet you at the top
> of the coconut tree."
> "Whee!" said *D* to *E F G*,
> "I'll beat you to the top
> of the coconut tree."

Because there is a myriad of alphabet books available, teachers and parents can afford to be quite discriminating when selecting them. I mentioned that it is desirable for books to depict both forms of the alphabet—uppercase (capital) and lowercase (small) letters. At least 90 percent of the letters young children encounter in print are lowercase, so it is the most desirable form to learn first. Unfortunately, many otherwise excellent alphabet books present only the uppercase letters, for example, *A Apple Pie* (Greenaway 1993).

Annie's abc (Owen 1987) is a potpourri book that exclusively depicts lowercase letters. With hundreds of small pictures to match with words and sounds, it provides both an exercise in observation and a way for the adult to introduce the letters and their corresponding sounds. It also presents an excellent example of a clear, non-ornamental typeface that is easily recognizable to young children. Even the manuscript forms of lowercase *a* and *g* (ɑ and ɡ) are utilized instead of the printing forms found in nearly all other books.

Ed Emberley's ABC (Emberley 1978) uniquely shows how to form uppercase letters. (See the illustration at the beginning of this chapter.) Each letter is presented on a two-page spread that is divided into four frames, showing animals engaged in a variety of activities that demonstrate the sequence of strokes that form each letter. For example, the letter *B* is formed by a beetle that takes blueberries out of a basket and places them on a table in front of a bear. At the end of the book, all the letters are labeled with the numbered sequence and direction of the strokes. Other books that use graphics to present the letters include *Alphabatics* (MacDonald 1986) and *The Alphabeast Book* (Schmiderer 1971). In both books, letters are reshaped through a series of frames to form a picture of the object named. For example, in *Alphabatics* the illustrations show the lowercase letter *m* reshaping to form a mustache. These books are good for children who are strong visual learners.

In addition to presenting the sequence of letters and the unique forms of each, ABC books introduce other concepts of our alphabetic language. Nearly all children (and adults) say that "letters make sounds" (e.g., "What sound does the letter *B* make?"). In actuality, people make speech sounds, and *letters represent sounds*. A grasp of which letter (or letter cluster) represents which sounds is known as **letter–sound correspondence.** By listening to and experimenting with the **phonemes** (sounds) that letters represent, children grow in their phonemic awareness that spoken words are made up of various sounds. Children who are adept in phonemic awareness are better able to decipher the code of our written language and become independent readers.

For children to grasp letter-sound correspondence in alphabet books, it is essential that the featured words and their corresponding illustrations be within the child's realm of knowledge. For example, "*A* is for apple" is preferable to "*A* is for anvil" (Anno 1975). Even if children have never eaten an apple, most likely they have seen one. However, young children probably do not have a mental schema for *anvil*, because they have had no experience with one. Nor would they likely be able to grasp the meaning if it were explained, because the use of anvils is quite limited today.

Books such as Maurice Sendak's *Alligators All Around* (1962), which uses abstract examples (e.g., "forever fooling," "never napping," and "quite quarrelsome"), are limited in their use for nonreaders. However, they do make delightful reading experiences for older children who enjoy alliteration. Other books that older children are likely to enjoy include *The Z Was Zapped* (Van Allsburg 1987) and *The Handmade Alphabet* (Rankin 1991). In the latter, the readers are introduced to the manual alphabet of sign language. Cefali (1995) provides an annotated list of alphabet books suitable for children who have already mastered the alphabet.

To help young children make the connection between letter and sound, the featured letter should represent the first sound in the illustrative word. For example, "*P* is for puppy" is far preferable to "*P* is for lip." This rule is not simply for consistency or for the delight of alliteration. Beginning readers initially learn to segment the first phoneme of words. Once that is mastered, they learn to segment the last phoneme. Finally, they learn to segment the phonemes in between.

Because all vowels in the English language represent more than one sound, they are a particular challenge to authors of alphabet books. In *Dr. Seuss's ABC* (Seuss 1963), the author is masterful in his representation of one vowel:

O is very useful. You use it when you say:
"Oscar's only ostrich oiled an orange owl today" (p. 34)

Seuss ingeniously represented this vowel in five ways—short vowel (Oscar and ostrich), long vowel (only), *r*-controlled vowel (orange), and both diphthong vowels (oiled and owl).

Consonants are more consistent than vowels in their representation of sounds. However, there are a few that commonly represent more than one sound. Both C and G represent *hard* and *soft* sounds. *Dr. Seuss's ABC* (1963) demonstrated this with

"BIG C, little c, / What begins with C? / Camel on the ceiling / C . . . c. . . . C" (p. 10). In *From Acorn to Zoo*, Satoshi Kitamura (1992) used *girl, grass,* and *goat* to illustrate the hard sound of *G* and illustrated the soft sound with *giraffe* and *ginger.* However, most books do not contain examples of both the soft and hard sounds for these two letters.

The letter *X* represents different sounds when it appears in the beginning, middle, or end of words. (Listen for these sounds when you say *xerography, exit,* and *fox.*) Few common words begin with *X,* so *xylophone* has been the classic word to exemplify this letter, because it is within most children's realm of knowledge. However, in recent years, authors have become creative, particularly in themed books. Examples are:

- *xenotarsosaurus*—a small meat-eating dinosaur that walked on two legs (Dodson 1995)
- *Xhosa*—an African tribe (Musgrove 1976)
- *xigua*—the Chinese name for watermelon (Ehlert 1989)

Good alphabet books present more than letter forms, letter sequence, and letter–sound correspondence. Vocabulary growth can be encouraged when an adult reads the book with a child, pointing out and naming the various things in each picture. Some potpourri books—such as *From Acorn to Zoo: And Everything In Between in Alphabetical Order* (Kitamura 1992)—have numerous objects on all pages with a small label conveniently placed under each item. Others, such as *Albert B. Cub & Zebra* (Rockwell 1977), do not label the targeted objects on the page, but the reader can turn to the back of the book to find the names. In addition to the main animal depicted, each page of *Animalia* (Base 1987) contains multiple other objects that are spelled with the same beginning letter, so children can play a game of finding and naming as many as possible.

Some alphabet books, such as *Ashanti to Zulu: African Traditions* (Musgrove 1976), are obviously geared not for early childhood but for more able readers. Often these are themed books that present much content on a particular topic, such as *The Underwater Alphabet Book* (Pallotta 1991), and therefore are similar to informational books. However, these books were included in this chapter because they are alphabet books.

▌ RECOMMENDED ALPHABET BOOKS

- Ada, Alma Flor. ***Gathering the Sun: An Alphabet in Spanish and English.*** Illus. Simon Silva. Lothrop Lee & Shepard, 1977.
- Anno, Mitsumasa. ***Anno's Alphabet.*** Crowell, 1975.
- Barker, Cicely Mary. ***A Flower Fairy Alphabet.*** Frederick Warne, 1990.
- Base, Graeme. ***Animalia.*** Abrams, 1987.
- Brown, Marcia. ***All Butterflies: An ABC.*** Scribner, 1974.
- Bruchac, Joseph. ***Many Nations: An Alphabet of Native Americans.*** Illus. Robert F. Goetzl. Bridgewater, 1997.

- Chin-Lee, Cynthia. *A Is for Asia.* Orchard, 1997.
- Demi. *Demi's Find the Animal ABC.* Grosset & Dunlap, 1985.
- Das, Prodeepta. *I Is for India.* Silver Press, 1996.
- Dodson, Peter. *An Alphabet of Dinosaurs.* Scholastic, 1995.
- Ehlert, Lois. *Eating the Alphabet: Fruits & Vegetables from A to Z.* Harcourt Brace Jovanovich, 1989.
- Emberley, Ed. *Ed Emberley's ABC.* Little, Brown, 1978.
- Feelings, Muriel L. *Jambo Means Hello: Swahili Alphabet Book.* Dial, 1985.
- Feeney, Stephanie. *A Is for Aloha.* University of Hawaii Press, 1985.
- Gag, Wanda. *ABC Bunny.* Paper Star, 1933.
- Greenaway, Kate. *A Apple Pie.* Derrydale, 1873/1993.
- Hoban, Tana. *26 Letters and 99 Cents.* Mulberry, 1995.
- Kitamura, Satoshi. *From Acorn to Zoo: And Everything in Between in Alphabetical Order.* Farrar, Straus & Giroux, 1992.
- Lobel, Arnold. *On Market Street.* Greenwillow, 1980.
- MacDonald, Suse. *Alphabatics.* Bradbury, 1986.
- Martin, Bill, Jr., & John Archambault. *Chicka Chicka Boom Boom.* Simon & Schuster, 1989.
- Martin, Jordan. *Amazon Alphabet.* Kingfisher, 1996.
- Musgrove, Margaret. *Ashanti to Zulu: African Traditions.* Dial, 1976.
- Owen, Annie. *Annie's abc.* Knopf, 1987.
- Pallotta, Jerry. *The Icky Bug Alphabet Book.* Charlesbridge, 1986.
- ———. *The Underwater Alphabet Book.* Charlesbridge, 1991.
- Rankin, Laura. *The Handmade Alphabet.* Dial, 1991.
- Red Hawk, Richard D. *A, B, C's: The American Indian Way.* SCB Distributors, 1992.
- Rockwell, Anne. *Albert B. Cub & Zebra: An Alphabet Storybook.* Crowell, 1977.
- Schmiderer, Dorothy. *The Alphabeast Book: An Abecedarium.* Holt, 1971.
- Sendak, Maurice. *Alligators All Around.* HarperCollins, 1962.
- Seuss, Dr. *Dr. Seuss's ABC.* Random House, 1963.
- Van Allsburg, Chris. *The Z Was Zapped.* Clarion, 1987.
- Wells, Ruth. *A to Zen: A Book of Japanese Culture.* Simon & Schuster, 1992.
- Yolen, Jane. *All in the Woodland Early: An ABC Book.* Philomel, 1979.
- Zaslavsky, Claudia. *Count on Your Fingers: African Style.* Illus. Jerry Pinkney. Crowell, 1980.

Counting Books. Counting books, sometimes called number books, are concept books that present the counting numbers. Like alphabet books, they can be used to prepare young children for school while offering many enjoyable reading experiences. These concept books typically devote one or two pages to each of the counting numbers 1 through 10, and they include illustrations of objects for counting. Many of these books are themed, such as Pattie L. Schnetzler's delightful *Ten Little Dinosaurs* (1996), in which a pair of wacky plastic eyeballs are built into the back cover of the book. Through the holes in the pages, the eyeballs jiggle from page to page and dinosaur to dinosaur.

Other counting books may follow a story line. Eric Carle's *The Very Hungry Caterpillar* (1987) is my favorite counting storybook. A tiny (and hungry) caterpillar pops from an egg, and the readers follow as he satisfies his appetite throughout the week with one apple, two pears, three plums, four strawberries, five oranges, and ten pieces of junk food! At the end of the week, he is neither tiny nor hungry, but there is something wonderful in store for him—metamorphosis into a beautiful butterfly. In Carle's signature style, there are pages of differing sizes with die cuts to represent holes where the caterpillar has eaten through the food. (In Carle's other books—featured in Chapter 6—look for the unusual: different page sizes and shapes, die cuts in the pages, textures, microchips for sound effects, and even tiny blinking lights!)

In all counting books it is important that featured objects on each page be familiar, so children can readily identify them; and the relationship of the objects should be obvious to the viewer. To make it easier to select objects for counting, the illustrations should not be visually overloaded. It is desirable for counting books to depict all of the following concepts:

- numbers—the amount of things to be counted (e.g., *, **, ***)
- numerals—the symbolic representation of numbers (e.g., 1, 2, 3)
- number words (e.g., *one, two, three*)

A book that meets all these criteria is *Over in the Meadow,* an old nursery counting rhyme that was adapted and illustrated by Paul Galdone (1986). It opens with "Over in the meadow in the sand in the sun, lived an old mother turtle and her little turtle one." Helton (1995) provided a kindergarten activity using this book and incorporating mathematics and journal keeping: The children draw pictures of each set of animals and write the numbers both as words and symbols.

There are some excellent counting books that do not contain the number words because their targeted audience is prereaders. An example is Eric Carle's *My Very First Book of Numbers* (1974). This appealing book is spiral bound, and the sturdy pages are cut in half. The top parts of the pages contain the numerals 1 to 10, each with the appropriate number of small black squares for a child to point out and count. The challenge is to turn the bottom parts of the pages and match the numeral on the top part with the correct number of colorful objects on the bottom part by achieving one-to-one correspondence.

There is variety in the numbers depicted in counting books; they are not restricted to the first ten numbers. Tana Hoban used photographs of common objects and events to illustrate the numbers 1 through 100 in *Count and See* (1972). However, some books for younger children include only the first five or six numbers. Two examples are Eileen Christelow's *Five Little Monkeys Jumping on the Bed* (1989) and Jeffie Ross Gordon's *Six Sleepy Sheep* (1991). Once children have learned to count from 1 to 10, it is fun to share books that count backward, such as Molly Bang's *Ten, Nine, Eight* (1983).

In counting books children can identify the counting numbers and discover seriation (i.e., the order of numbers). In addition, when adults or older siblings sit with children while they view the books, they can tell children the names (labels) for all the things depicted in the illustrations and engage the children in conversation about what they see. This is a fun way for children to expand their vocabularies.

After children master the counting numbers, they can enjoy books that introduce more sophisticated math concepts. One such book is *Anno's Counting Book* (Anno 1975), which depicts the changing seasons (represented by the twelve months) with beautiful watercolor paintings that progressively show the growth of a rural village. It is the only counting book I have read that begins with zero and extends to twelve. Zero is a critical concept for understanding place value in our base-ten number system, and yet it is overlooked in other counting books. Anno also depicts one-to-one correspondence by means of a stack of cubes at the left of the pictures and the corresponding numerals at the right of the pictures. Older children can be introduced to set theory through the multiple sets of objects on each two-page spread (e.g., buildings, animals, children, adults, and trees). Each set corresponds with the featured number, and each set increases by one on the following page.

In *Sea Squares* (1991), Joy N. Hulme uses the theme of sea creatures to depict the numbers 1 to 10 and the squares of these numbers, for example, "Ten squirmy squids squirting ten inky trails / Pulling ten tentacles like ten wagging tails / When *10* squids retreat so fast, / *100* tails go swishing past." In *The Butterfly Counting Book* (1998), Jerry Pallotta describes butterflies and uses the odd numbers to count from 1 to 21 by *twos* (e.g., 1, 3, 5, 7). In a similar manner, Elinor J. Pinczes (1996) counts from 5 to 30 by *fives*. In a cumulative fashion, she describes the animals that have come to view the Northern Lights in *Arctic Fives Arrive*:

> That's five, ten, fifteen, twenty, twenty-five, thirty:
> Five musk oxen who timely arrive;
> five Arctic hares whose ears dip and dive;
> five fat walrus with tusks sharpened keen;
> five sly ermine all pop-eyed and lean;
> five polar bears on pigeon-toed paws;
> and five snowy owls with long, curvy claws.

In *One Hundred Hungry Ants* (1993), Elinor J. Pinczes tells a humorous story of 100 ants that are marching in rows to a picnic. By showing the ants in lines of varying numbers, she introduces the factors of 100 (i.e., 1 and 100, 2 and 50, 4 and 25, 5 and 20, 10 and 10). This is a clever and fun way to discover the math concepts of factoring and multiplication.

Paul Giganti's *How Many Snails?* (1988) presents yet other challenges and learning opportunities. I would not recommend this book for younger children, because it does not contain the numerals; nor does it present the quantities of things to be counted in numerical order. Rather, the readers are asked to name the total number of objects on each two-page spread, then to distinguish among the objects. For example, "I went walking to the meadow and I wondered: How many flowers were there? How many flowers were yellow? How many flowers were yellow with black centers?" On the two pages are fifteen flowers, nine of which are yellow; eight of them have black centers. This book presents opportunities to learn about sets and subsets while affording the child practice with visual acuity.

The Math Counts series from Children's Press covers the following concepts: pattern, shape, size, sorting, counting, numbers, time, length, weight, and capacity. For example, *Math Counts: Numbers* (Pluckrose 1995) contains colorful photographs to depict how numbers are an integral part of the world from telephones and money to time and addresses.

Math and social studies are joined in Jim Haskins's "Count Your Way around the World" series, which includes more than sixteen counting books with settings in various countries from Africa to Russia. Using the numbers 1 to 10, the author introduces readers to the land and people of each country. Of particular interest is *Count Your Way through Israel* (Haskins 1990), in which the numerals are presented both in the familiar Arabic form and also in Hebrew.

RECOMMENDED COUNTING BOOKS

- Anno, Mitsumasa. **Anno's Counting Book.** HarperTrophy, 1975.
- Bang, Molly. **Ten, Nine, Eight.** Greenwillow, 1983.
- Carle, Eric. **1, 2, 3 to the Zoo.** Putnam & Grosset, 1968.
- ———. **My Very First Book of Numbers.** HarperCollins, 1974.
- ———. **The Very Hungry Caterpillar.** Philomel, 1987.
- Christelow, Eileen. **Five Little Monkeys Jumping on the Bed.** Clarion, 1989.
- ———. **Five Little Monkeys Sitting in a Tree.** Houghton Mifflin, 1991.
- Galdone, Paul. **Over in the Meadow.** Simon & Schuster, 1985.
- Giganti, Paul, Jr. **Each Orange Had 8 Slices.** Greenwillow, 1993.
- ———. **How Many Snails?** Illus. Donald Crews. Greenwillow, 1988.
- Gordon, Jeffie Ross. **Six Sleepy Sheep.** Puffin, 1991.
- Haskins, Jim. **Count Your Way through Israel.** Carolrhoda, 1990.
- Hoban, Tana. **Count and See.** Macmillan, 1972.
- Hulme, Joy N. **Sea Squares.** Hyperion, 1991.
- Medearis, Angela Shelf. **Picking Peas for a Penny.** Illus. Charles Shaw. Scholastic, 1990.
- Morozumi, Atsuko. **One Gorilla.** Farrar, Straus & Giroux, 1990.
- Pallotta, Jerry. **The Butterfly Counting Book.** Scholastic, 1998.
- Pinczes, Elinor J. **One Hundred Hungry Ants.** Houghton Mifflin, 1993.
- ———. **Arctic Fives Arrive.** Houghton Mifflin, 1996.
- Pluckrose, Henry. **Math Counts: Numbers.** Children's Press, 1995.
- Schnetzler, Pattie L. **Ten Little Dinosaurs.** Accord, 1996.
- Sendak, Maurice. **One Was Johnny.** Harper & Row, 1962.

- ————. *Seven Little Monsters.* Harper & Row, 1977.
- Walsh, Ellen Stoll. *Mouse Count.* Harcourt Brace, 1991.
- Yolen, Jane. *An Invitation to the Butterfly Ball: A Counting Rhyme.* Parents' Magazine Press, 1976.

Other Concept Books.   In addition to the alphabet and counting numbers, there are numerous other concepts presented in books for the very young. One popular topic for concept books is color. Authors and illustrators have imaginative ways to introduce colors to young readers. Ann Jonas uses lovely watercolors in *Color Dance* (1989) to reveal the primary (red, yellow, and blue), secondary (orange, green, and purple), and tertiary (vermilion, marigold, chartreuse, aquamarine, violet, and magenta) colors as the children in her illustrations dance with translucent scarves. Shelly Harwayne uses a combination of painting crayons and water to illustrate *What's Cooking?* (1996), a story about the cooking sprees of the kids in Mrs. Peabody's class, who prepare meals of yellow, red, and green foods.

Some books are designed to present more than one concept. In *Planting a Rainbow* (1988), Lois Ehlert uses graphic designs with bold colors on a white background to show the primary and secondary colors through a variety of plants and flowers. Because of the author's use of labels, this book introduces children to the concepts of both colors and flowers.

Perhaps the most unusual presentation of the concept of color is employed by Annette Tison and Talus Taylor in *The Adventures of the Three Colors* (1971). A little boy learns about mixing colors when he tries to reproduce all the rainbow colors with the only three colors left in his paint box. The illustrators achieved this by colored transparent overlays superimposed on the illustrations.

CONCEPT BOOKS ON COLOR

- Ehlert, Lois. *Planting a Rainbow.* Harcourt Brace Jovanovich, 1988.
- Harwayne, Shelley. *What's Cooking?* Mondo, 1996.
- Hoban, Tana. *Colors Everywhere.* Greenwillow, 1995.
- Jonas, Ann. *Color Dance.* Greenwillow, 1989.
- Kunhardt, Edith. *Red Day Green Day.* Greenwillow, 1992.
- Tison, Annette, & Talus Taylor. *The Adventures of the Three Colors.* World, 1971.
- Walsh, Ellen. *Mouse Paint.* Harcourt Brace, 1989.

In addition to color, **shape** is a concept that children are expected to understand before starting first grade. *Shapes* by Rosalinda Kightley (1986) presents the basic shapes and lines: circle, square, rectangle, triangle, diamond, semicircle, straight line, right angle, zigzag, and wavy line. Each shape is introduced on a full page with a white background, and facing it is a graphic illustration that contains several sizes and colors of the featured shape. For example, the illustration for *triangle* is a Christmas tree with gifts. Children are challenged to find the two dozen or more triangles in the illustration. However, the picture also includes circles, squares, and rectangles, which were previously introduced, so children will have an opportunity to practice their visual acuity in distinguishing among the shapes.

In Eric Carle's *My Very First Book of Shapes* (1974), young children can be shown how to match a black shape with an object that has a similar shape. For example, the circle matches an illustration of the sun; the square matches a framed picture; a triangle is matched with a teepee. As in *My Very First Book of Numbers* (1974), Carle designed a spiral-bound book with sturdy pages cut in half, so the young viewer can flip through the bottom parts of the pages to find an object to match the black shape on the top part of the page.

In Tana Hoban's characteristic style, attractive colored photographs adorn the pages of *Dots, Spots, Speckles, and Stripes* (1987). In this book Hoban portrays the circles and straight lines that the world contains. For example, circles (dots, spots, and speckles) are found in her photographs of polka-dotted dresses, freckles, and sunflowers. Straight lines are represented by a striped dress, slats in patio furniture, and a zebra.

CONCEPT BOOKS ON SHAPE

- Allington, Richard L. **Shapes.** Steck-Vaughn, 1991.
- Carle, Eric. **My Very First Book of Shapes.** HarperCollins, 1974.
- Hoban, Tana. **Dots, Spots, Speckles, and Stripes.** Greenwillow, 1987.
- Kightley, Rosalinda. **Shapes.** Little Brown, 1986.

Eric Carle's *My Very First Book of Words* (1974) completes his trio of concept books—on numbers, shapes, and words. Like the other two, this book is spiral bound with cut pages that children can flip to find a match between top and bottom. In this case, the child can match simple objects with their labels, for example *cat, star, boy,* and *clock*. With the uncluttered arrangement of this book, children can see that a word is a string of letters that represents the name of something in the world around them. I have known children as young as three who mastered the words in this book as their first sight words and knew the meanings of the words without the help of the pictures. (When parents say to me, "Well, he's not really reading it; he has just memorized the words," I remind them that fluent readers must memorize many hundreds of words.)

Words and their relationships are additional concepts that are important for young children. Prepositions are particularly challenging, because they are not as concrete as many familiar nouns or verbs. *Rosie's Walk* (Hutchins 1968) depicts illustrations of Rosie the hen going *across, around, over, past, through,* and *under* things during her walk. Unbeknownst to Rosie, however, a fox is trying to catch her for dinner. In the clever and humorous illustrations, the fox encounters some mishap each time he tries to grab her. For example, as Rosie walks across the yard, the fox lands on the prongs of a rake, which smacks him in the head. Each two-page spread illustrating a preposition (e.g., around the pond) contains a picture clue that readers can use to predict the mishap that will befall the fox on the following page. When children are listening to this book for the first time, be sure to stop and ask them to predict what might happen next to the fox. This will encourage their search for picture clues to aid comprehension.

Inside, Outside, Upside Down by Stan and Jan Berenstain (1968) is also a good book for helping children explore the meanings of prepositions. This book shows a young bear in relation to a large box he has hidden in. In the process of the box being transported, the following prepositions and relationships are illustrated: in/out, on/off, inside/outside, upside down/right side up.

Reading books about antonyms will encourage children to think about many different concepts in our language (e.g., knowing what one word means, such as *high*, and finding a word that represents an opposite concept, such as *low*). Many enjoyable books introduce antonyms and help children gain mastery of their language; one good example is Tana Hoban's *Exactly the Opposite* (1990).

▌ CONCEPT BOOKS ON WORDS

- Bailey, Liza. ***My First Book of Opposites.*** Derrydale, 1996.
- Berenstain, Stanley, & Janice Berenstain. ***Inside, Outside, Upside Down.*** Random House, 1968.
- Carle, Eric. ***My Very First Book of Words.*** HarperCollins, 1974.
- Heller, Ruth. ***Mine, All Mine: A Book about Pronouns.*** Grosset & Dunlap, 1997.
- ———. ***Many Luscious Lollipops: A Book about Adjectives.*** Paper Star, 1998.
- ———. ***Merry Go Round: A Book about Nouns.*** Paper Star, 1998.
- ———. ***Kites Sail High: A Book about Verbs.*** Paper Star, 1998.
- Hoban, Tana. ***Exactly the Opposite.*** Greenwillow, 1990.
- Hutchins, Pat. ***Rosie's Walk.*** Macmillan, 1968.
- Kightley, Rosalinda. ***Opposites.*** Little, Brown, 1986.
- Spier, Peter. ***Fast–Slow, High–Low: A Book of Opposites.*** Doubleday, 1972.
- Tullet, Herve. ***Night/Day: A Book of Eye-Catching Opposites.*** Little, Brown, 1999.

Most children love animals and flowers and other living things, and there are wonderful concept books that present the names of these. For ideas on how to use literature on gardening topics to teach many exciting lessons, see *Cultivating a Child's Imagination Through Gardening* (Jurenka & Blass 1996).

▌ CONCEPT BOOKS ON PLANTS

- Ehlert, Lois. ***Growing Vegetable Soup.*** Harcourt Brace Jovanovich, 1987.
- ———. ***Planting a Rainbow.*** Harcourt Brace Jovanovich, 1988.
- ———. ***Eating the Alphabet: Fruits & Vegetables from A to Z.*** Harcourt Brace Javonovich, 1989.
- Kuchalla, Susan. ***All about Seeds.*** Illus. Jane McBee. Troll Associates, 1989.
- Maass, Robert. ***Garden.*** Henry Holt, 1998.

CONCEPT BOOKS ON ANIMALS

- Baker, Keith. *Who Is the Beast?* Harcourt Brace, 1990.
- Ehlert, Lois. *Feathers for Lunch.* Harcourt Brace Jovanovich, 1990.
- Fox, Mem. *Zoo-Looking.* Illus. Candace Whitman. Horwitz, 1986.
- ———. *Time for Bed.* Illus. Jane Dyer. Harcourt Brace, 1993.
- Koch, Michele. *Hoot Howl Hiss.* Morrow, 1991.
- Martin, Bill, Jr. *Polar Bear, Polar Bear, What Do You Hear?* Illus. Eric Carle. Henry Holt, 1991.

CONCEPT BOOKS ON TRANSPORTATION

- Crews, Donald. *Freight Train.* Greenwillow, 1978.
- ———. *School Bus.* Greenwillow, 1984.
- ———. *Truck.* Mulberry, 1991.
- Delafosse, Claude. *Cars and Trucks and Other Vehicles.* Illus. Sophie Kniffke. Cartwheel, 1996.
- Steedman, Scott. *Cars.* Franklin Watts, 1995.

CONCEPT BOOKS ON HOLIDAYS

- Hoagland, Victor. *Christmas Traditions for Children.* Illus. William Luberoff. Regina, 1997.
- Kolatch, Alfred J. *A Child's First Book of Jewish Holidays.* Illus. Harry Araten. Jonathan David, 1997.
- Tudor, Tasha. *A Time to Keep.* Rand McNally, 1977.
- Winchester, Faith. *Ethnic Holidays Series.* Capstone, 1996.
- Zolotow, Charlotte. *Over and Over.* Harper, 1987.

Pattern Books

Pattern books are picture books that contain repetitive words, phrases, questions, or some other structure that makes them predictable. The repeated element helps listeners remember what comes next so they can join in as you read aloud. These simple books are easily committed to memory, making them useful in initial reading instruction. My favorite pattern book is *The Wheels on the Bus* (Kovalski 1987), an adaptation of a traditional song. The first verse is:

> The wheels on the bus go round and round,
> Round and round, round and round.
> The wheels on the bus go round and round,
> All around the town.

Each subsequent verse follows the pattern:

> The wipers on the bus go swish, swish, swish.

The people on the bus hop on and off.

The horn on the bus goes toot, toot, toot.

Pattern books make great **lap reading.** When a child sits in an adult's lap, the adult can talk about and point to things in the text and illustrations. When lap reading with a familiar pattern book, encourage children to focus on the printed words and join in on parts they recognize or remember. For example, you can pause at the end of a sentence or line and allow the child to complete it. If you point *under* each word as the child says it, that will help the child learn the **concept of word:** the idea that a written word is a string of letters bounded by spaces. Once children can match spoken words to their written counterparts, they have made an important discovery called **speech-to-print match,** and most children will then begin to learn some of the words by sight.

Some of the advantages of lap reading can be obtained for groups of children when teachers use **big books**—books that are enlarged to about four times their normal size. Big books are great for teaching emergent readers the **concepts of print:** the conventions that a page is read from top to bottom, lines are read from left to right, and books are read from front to back. (Not all written languages are arranged in this manner.) For more ideas on using early childhood books to develop children's beginning reading processes, see "Developing and Assessing Emergent Literacy through Children's Literature" in *Literacy Assessment for Today's Schools* (Anderson 1995).

Pattern books are wonderful for initial reading instruction because they are predictable, the vocabulary is limited, and the illustrations reinforce the text. Though they usually contain characters, setting, and a few events, most do not have full plots. Therefore, like concept books, they can rarely be used to teach story structure. However, children who have listened to a book several times can usually recite it by looking at the illustrations. This practice is helpful later when children begin reading independently and realize they can look to illustrations for clues on unknown words. It is also important because when children have a simple pattern book memorized, an adult can help them focus on the printed words by pointing under each word as they say it. Through this process children can add these words to their sight vocabulary and become ready to tackle harder books. Box 3.1 is an example of how a very young child can become attached to a pattern book.

▌ RECOMMENDED PATTERN BOOKS

- Baer, Gene. *Thump, Thump, Rat-a-Tat-Tat.* HarperCollins, 1989.
- Cameron, Polly. *"I Can't" Said the Ant.* Coward-McCann, 1961.
- ———. *Today Is Monday.* Scholastic, 1993.
- Cole, Henry. *Jack's Garden.* Greenwillow, 1995.
- Cowley, Joy. *Mrs. Wishy-washy.* Wright, 1980.
- Emberley, Barbara. *Drummer Hoff.* Simon & Schuster, 1967.
- Fox, Mem. *Shoes from Grandpa.* Orchard, 1989.

Box 3.1

It's Never Too Early

When my niece's first child was born, I sent her a large box of books with a note that said, "It's never too early to read to your child." She and her husband frequently read to Justin. By the time he turned one, he had started to walk, could speak four words, and *loved* books! His mother wrote:

He already loves books. *Mrs. Wishy-washy* [Cowley 1980] is his favorite. He insists we read it at least 40–50 times a day. Well, maybe it's only 8 or 9 times, but it sure seems like more. I've got the whole thing committed to memory. I actually have to hide that book from him because as soon as he spots it, he'll pick it up, and give you this pitiful, neglected, don't-you-love-me-anymore look. Then he'll start whining and waving the book around till you read it to him. And *then* after you read the last page, he starts crying until you start reading it again!

- Kovalski, Maryann. **The Wheels on the Bus.** Little, Brown, 1987.
- Martin, Bill, Jr. **Brown Bear, Brown Bear, What Do You See?** Henry Holt, 1983.
- Oppenheim, Joanne. **"Not Now!" Said the Cow.** Bantam, 1989.
- Scarffe, Bronwen. **Oh No!** Mondo, 1986.
- Sweet, Melissa. **Fiddle-I-Fee.** Little, Brown, 1992.
- Westcott, Nadine Bernard. **The Lady with the Alligator Purse.** Little, Brown, 1988.
- ———. **Peanut Butter and Jelly.** Dutton, 1987.
- Wood, Audrey, & Don Wood. **The Napping House.** Harcourt Brace Jovanovich, 1984.
- Williams, Sue. **I Went Walking.** Harcourt Brace Jovanovich, 1989.
- Wilson, Etta. **Music in the Night.** Penguin, 1993.

Wordless Picture Books

In **wordless picture books,** also known as textless books, the story is revealed through a sequence of illustrations with no—or very few—words. Wordless picture book is a format, so it is found in all genres. In these books, skillful illustrators develop a full plot through their artwork, making printed words unnecessary. In the preface to his wordless book *Sing, Pierrot, Sing: A Picture Book in Mime* (1983), Tomie dePaola wrote, "The words, as in all mime, are in the eyes of the listener."

Wordless books first gained popularity in the late 1960s. In 1980 John Warren Stewig found the value of wordless picture books so significant that he devoted an entire chapter to them in his children's literature textbook. Stewig asserted it was not a new idea that pictures alone could reveal a story. He cited examples of the pictures in cave dwellings, medieval tapestries, and cathedral stained-glass windows that portrayed stories hundreds and even thousands of years ago. Stewig named several advantages of making wordless picture books accessible to children:

- They aid the development of visual literacy—the language of images.

Pierrot climbs to the moon. From *Sing, Pierrot, Sing: A Picture Book in Mime,* illustrated by Tomie dePaola.

- They can be interpreted and enjoyed by children who do not read well (or do not read at all), such as preschool children, children who are learning disabled in reading, and children with limited English proficiency.
- They can help parents and teachers assess and develop children's thinking and language abilities.
- They can serve as a stimulus for a language experience account (LEA) that can be used for early reading instruction.
- They develop imagination by stimulating an oral or written interpretation of the plot.

For an example of plot interpretation, Box 3.2 presents a 9-year-old girl's written interpretation of the wordless book *A Boy, a Dog, and a Frog* (Mayer 1967). She wrote the story independently, and I have reproduced it as written, so you can see the spellings she invented for words when she did not know the standard spelling.

Cianciolo (1973) was one of the first to extol the value of wordless picture books in enhancing visual literacy. Believing that pictures tell a universal language, she purported that viewers "must be able to bring meaning and significance to the shapes,

Box 3.2

Janelle's Interpretation of *A Boy, a Dog, and a Frog*

Once upon atime ther was a boy. Today the boy went fishing. When he got ther he saw someing! What did he see? He saw a frog! It was a big green frog. He ran to catch the frog. He tripped over a dead branch of the tree! He fell in the lake head first.

The boy is mad at the frog. The frog jumps off the lilly pad, and the boy tries to catch him. The boy misses him. The boy, and his dog go over to the place ware the frog is sitting. The boy tells his dog to do someing. What does he tell him? The boy is trying to trap the frog. So he can catch the frog. He is ready to catch the frog. He puts the net down, and. . . . He catches his dog instead. He picks up the net with his dog in it.

The frog is mad for being tricked. The boy yells at him saiding "come back here frog." The frog was not about to let the boy catch him. So he steyed. The boy goes home with out the frog. The frog fells sad. He wants some fun. The boy is mad becous he did not catch any fish today. Will the frog follow the boy? The frog is blank. He donesn't know what to do.

"Hows tracks are thes?" Aask the frog. He flows the trackes to here. They keep on going! The boy is taking a bath. The dog is in ther too! "At last I found some water." Said the frog. The frog says here I go. He jumps off of the flowr, and into the bath tube. The frog lands on the Dog's hade. The boy his dog, and the frog are friends.

The END!

positions, and movements that are depicted by the book artist as he tells his stories in pictures" (p. 226). She encouraged using wordless books to help children express a verbal translation of objects or situations in illustrations.

D'Angelo (1981) elaborated on the use of wordless picture books to develop language. She asserted that "interpreting pictures in wordless books can provide opportunities for developing the child's vocabulary and syntax by naming objects, inventing dialog, making comparisons, describing and interpreting actions, and predicting and evaluating outcomes" (p. 37). D'Angelo suggested the following classic wordless books for language development:

- building vocabulary: *Noah's Ark* (Spier 1977), *Do You Want to Be My Friend?* (Carle 1971), *Anno's Alphabet* (Anno 1975)
- producing phrases and sentences: *Frog Goes to Dinner* (Mayer 1974), *Changes, Changes* (Hutchins 1971), *The Great Cat Chase* (Mayer 1974)
- developing sequence and prediction skills: *Apples* (Hogrogian 1972), *The Silver Pony* (Ward 1973), *The Self-Made Snowman* (Krahn 1974)

 Responding to Literature

Using Illustrations to Predict Plot

Select one of Mercer Mayer's wordless picture books, such as *Oops* or *Frog, Where Are You?* Study the body language, especially the facial expressions, of the characters on each page. What do you think the characters are saying or thinking? Based on what you view on each two-page spread, predict what will happen on the next page.

When wordless books were first introduced, some individuals did not consider them literature books. After all, a book has to tell a story, and how can a book tell a story if there are no words? Groff (1974) issued an early caution not "to wrongly accredit pictures as literature. Nor to give way to wishful thoughts that wordless books will motivate children to read and appreciate literature" (p. 303).

However, young children—from prereaders to proficient readers—have been enjoying wordless picture books for more than three decades now. I recommend that you select a wordless picture book and determine if you can evaluate the artist's ability to develop all the components of a good story (setting, characterization, plot, and theme) through his or her illustrations. Then you can judge whether the book qualifies as literature.

 ## Responding to Literature

Identifying Elements of Story Structure in a Wordless Book

Select a wordless picture book from the following bibliography. Using the story map format provided in Figure 2.1, outline each of the elements of story structure that you identify from the illustrations. Do you believe this book qualifies as literature?

 RECOMMENDED WORDLESS PICTURE BOOKS

- Aliki. *Tabby: A Story in Pictures.* HarperCollins, 1995.
- Anno, Mitsumasa. *Anno's Alphabet.* Crowell, 1975.
- ———. *Anno's Journey.* Paper Star, 1997.
- Briggs, Raymond. *The Snowman.* Random House, 1978.
- Carle, Eric. *Do You Want to Be My Friend?* HarperCollins, 1971.
- Day, Alexandra. *Good Dog, Carl.* Simon & Schuster, 1985.
- ———. *Carl's Christmas.* Farrar, Straus & Giroux, 1994.
- dePaola, Tomie. *The Knight and the Dragon.* Putnam, 1980.
- ———. *The Hunter and the Animals.* Holiday House, 1981.
- ———. *Sing, Pierrot, Sing: A Picture Book in Mime.* Harcourt Brace Jovanovich, 1983.
- ———. *Pancakes for Breakfast.* Harcourt Brace, 1990.
- Hogrogian, Nonny. *Apples.* Macmillan, 1972.
- Hutchins, Pat. *Changes, Changes.* Macmillan, 1971.
- Keats, Ezra Jack. *Clementina's Cactus.* Viking, 1999.
- Krahn, Fernando. *The Self-Made Snowman.* Lippincott, 1974.

- Martin, Rafe. *Will's Mammoth.* Putnam, 1989.
- Mayer, Mercer. *A Boy, a Dog, and a Frog.* Dutton Books, 1967.
- ———. *Frog, Where Are You*? Dial, 1969.
- ———. *Frog Goes to Dinner.* Dial, 1974.
- ———. *The Great Cat Chase.* Four Winds, 1974.
- ———. *Oops.* Dial, 1977.
- Spier, Peter. *Noah's Ark.* Doubleday, 1977.
- ———. *Peter Spier's Rain.* Doubleday, 1997.
- Ward, Lynd. *The Silver Pony.* Houghton Mifflin, 1973.
- Wiesner, David. *Free Fall.* Lothrop Lee & Shepard, 1988.
- ———. *Tuesday.* Clarion, 1991.
- Wildsmith, Brian. *The Nest.* Oxford University Press, 1987.

Other Kinds of Books

Before closing this chapter on early childhood books, I must share a few more thoughts. Many good books for young children were not included because they did not fit into any of the categories discussed. For example, *Look-Alikes* (Steiner 1998) challenges young readers to find assorted everyday objects in the three-dimensional dioramas that were photographed to illustrate the book. *Look-Alikes* is not a storybook, nor does it present concepts, but it will give children many wonderful hours of perusing the beautiful and clever illustrations while sharpening their visual acuity. Numerous other good books do not neatly fall into a genre but are wonderful reading experiences for young children.

Some of the books listed in this chapter are not restricted to early childhood. I have already mentioned that some alphabet books are aimed at older children, and there are books in other categories as well. For example, the wordless book *The Silver Pony* (Ward 1973) appears to be geared for intermediate-grade children. However, I included these books in this chapter in order to discuss them within appropriate categories.

If you are overwhelmed with the volume of good books and do not know where to begin building your collection, consider investing in an anthology. *The Random House Book of Easy-to-Read Stories* (Ehrlich 1993) contains the full content and illustrations of four books by Dr. Seuss and twelve other popular picture books by such beloved authors and illustrators as Marc Brown, Tomie dePaola, P. D. Eastman, and Deborah Hautzig.

Another outstanding anthology was compiled by children's book editor Janet Schulman. She selected forty-four classic stories that she believed were the best published in the twentieth century and compiled them in *The 20th Century Children's Book Treasury* (1998). In order to include all the books in fewer than 300 pages, it was necessary to omit some illustrations and to reduce others in size. (For example, four original pages are depicted on one large anthology page.) Featured authors and illustrators include Virginia Lee Burton, Janell Cannon, Lois Ehlert, Pat Hutchins, Ezra Jack Keats, Leo Lionni, Arnold Lobel, Maurice Sendak, and Judith Viorst.

CHILDREN'S BOOKS CITED IN THIS SECTION

Ehrlich, Amy. *The Random House Book of Easy-to-Read Stories.* Illus. Diane Goode. Random House, 1993.

Schulman, Janet (Ed.). *The 20th Century Children's Book Treasury.* Knopf, 1998.

Steiner, Joan. *Look-Alikes.* Little, Brown, 1998.

Ward, Lynd. *The Silver Pony.* Houghton Mifflin, 1973.

KEY TERMS

 Explore the E-Glossary at **www.ablongman.com/anderson**

acrylic paint   (p. 50)
airbrushing   (p. 51)
alphabet book   (p. 55)
big book   (p. 67)
board book   (p. 54)
cartoon   (p. 49)
collage   (p. 51)
color   (p. 47)
composition   (p. 48)
concept book   (p. 55)
concept of word   (p. 67)
concepts of print   (p. 67)
counting book   (p. 59)
drawing   (p. 50)
expressionism   (p. 49)
folk art   (p. 49)
gouache   (p. 50)
hue   (p. 47)
impressionism   (p. 49)
lap reading   (p. 67)
letter-sound correspondence   (p. 57)

line   (p. 47)
montage   (p. 51)
oil paint   (p. 50)
pastels   (p. 51)
pattern book   (p. 66)
perspective   (p. 48)
phonemes   (p. 57)
representationalism   (p. 48)
shades   (p. 47)
shape   (p. 47)
space   (p. 46)
speech-to-print match   (p. 67)
surrealism   (p. 49)
tempera   (p. 50)
texture   (p. 48)
tints   (p. 47)
two-page spread   (p. 55)
visual literacy   (p. 46)
watercolor   (p. 50)
woodcut   (p. 51)
wordless picture book   (p. 68)

Grasshopper watches the ants work.
Aesop's Fables Collected and illustrated by Charles Santore.

Traditional Literature

Stories, songs, and rhymes with unknown authorship that were passed down orally from one generation to the next before being written down

People have always told stories; it is the oldest form of remembering. In ancient times, long before written language was developed, people told stories to preserve the history, traditions, desires, and taboos of their social groups. Each generation told their stories to the next, which in turn told the stories to the youth of the generation that followed them.

Since prehistory, all cultures have passed along such tales through the **oral tradition,** and they have always been an essential part of our humanness (Yolen 1981). Some stories were told just for entertainment. Others were used to share the history of a group of people and also to teach lessons and transmit values and beliefs. Still others were intended to explain natural phenomena—such as the changing of the seasons and the cycle of night and day—and usually involved the people's gods and other religious beliefs. Certain stories were accompanied by music and were sung instead of recited. These stories remained in a constant process of variation, depending on the memory, talent, or purpose of the storytellers.

Evaluating Traditional Literature

Because of its antiquity and its multicultural origins, **traditional literature** (also known as folk literature) is a unique genre, and a special set of evaluation criteria should be applied (Norton 1999). The following questions can guide you as you select traditional literature books:

- Does the book help children better understand the nonscientific traditions of early cultures?
- Will it help children appreciate the culture and art of a different country?
- Does it familiarize children with another dialect or language of the world?
- Can it be used to stimulate creative drama, writing, and other forms of artistic expression?
- Will it help children realize that people from another part of the world have inherent goodness, mercy, courage, and industry?
- Is it void of unwholesome ethnic and racial stereotyping?
- If adapted, does the language retain the flavor of the older form, or is it oversimplified?
- Do the illustrations complement and extend the narrative while maintaining the heritage of the tale?

History

Stories, songs, and poetry passed from one generation to the next in the oral tradition are collectively called **folklore.** Historically, folklore was not intended specifically for children but was for the enjoyment and enlightenment of the whole family. The origin of each tale has been lost in antiquity. Indeed, each tale had a multitude of contributors, for in the course of retellings, the tales were altered as storytellers modified them to suit their own times and audiences. This modification process continues today, making folklore an ever changing body of work. Rosemary Sutcliff (1981) wrote in her author's note to *The Sword and the Circle,* "No minstrel ever follows exactly the songs that have come down to him from the time before. Always he adds and leaves out and embroiders and puts something of himself into each retelling" (p. 8).

Even after written language was developed and paper was invented, stories continued to be transmitted through the oral tradition because books had to be hand copied. This slow process made books rare and valuable. Few people were literate because there was so little available for the general population to read. After the development of the printing press in the late 1400s, books became more affordable and accessible, and there was then a greater reason to learn to read and write. Many children were schooled to become literate, but not all; especially not children from poor families or those living in rural areas. So the oral tradition of storytelling continued for many more years.

Then, in 1697, a Frenchman named Charles Perrault did a remarkable thing. He recorded the tales his nursemaid had told him as a child and published eight of them in a book he titled *Stories or Tales from Past Times with Morals.* This book included classic stories such as "The Sleeping Beauty," "Little Red Riding Hood," and "Cinderella." Perrault's book was enormously popular in Europe, both in French and in English editions. Soon after, another Frenchman named Antoine Galland translated Asian and North African traditional tales into French, and in 1704 Galland published the first volume under the title *The Arabian Nights, or Tales Told by Sheherezade.* This collection included such well-known tales as "Aladdin and the Wonderful Lamp," "The Seven Voyages of Sinbad the Sailor," and "Ali Baba and the Forty Thieves." The books published by Perrault and Galland were prototypes of the traditional literature genre.

Some of the most enduring tales were collected by two German brothers, Jakob and Wilhelm Grimm. Their first volume, *Nursery and Household Tales,* was published in 1812, and a second volume followed in 1815. Favorites from this collection included "Hansel and Gretel," "Rumpelstiltskin," and "Snow White." Even in their day, the tales were criticized as gruesome, violent, and not appropriate for children. However, the collection had begun as a linguistic—rather than a literary—project in which the brothers preserved and studied the old German language. The Grimms recorded the stories told to them by peasants, whose language and way of life had changed little for many decades. Nonetheless, the stories did entertain readers of all ages. Today compilers of folktales have adapted many of the Grimms' stories for children by toning down the violence.

In 1841 Peter Asbjørnsen and Jorgen Moe published a compilation of the popular lore of Norway. Their joint collection, *Norwegian Folk Tales,* included such favorites as "The Three Billy Goats Gruff" and "East of the Sun and West of the Moon." In 1845 Asbjørnsen published an additional collection titled *Norwegian Fairytales and Folklore.*

Because the United States is a relatively young country, little true folklore in the oral tradition had time to develop. One major collection of American folklore was recorded by Joel Chandler Harris. In 1881 Harris published a volume of African American traditional stories, which he titled *Uncle Remus, His Songs and Sayings.* The escapades of Brer (short for brother) Rabbit and his nemeses, Brer Fox and Brer Bear, are hilarious. "The Tar Baby" was my favorite as a child. Unfortunately, Harris wrote the tales in a nearly undecipherable dialect that was his exaggerated attempt to reproduce the language of the elderly former slaves from whom he had heard the tales in rural Georgia. Harris presented the tales within a loose story he created of an old slave named Uncle Remus, who is telling stories to the child of his white "master." The stories themselves are delightful and entertaining. However, the context in which they were presented is replete with racist remarks, which has resulted in the book's being banned from most school libraries and from many public libraries as well. Fortunately, adapted versions of the stories are now available in picture books retold by such talented writers as Julius Lester (1987, 1990) and Van Dyke Parks (1986, 1987).

Other significant works include the collections of Scottish scholar and folklorist Andrew Lang, who published *The Blue Fairy Book,* the first of twelve volumes, in 1889. Joseph Jacobs's collection of English and Irish tales, titled *English Fairy Tales,* was published in 1898. Some well-known stories included in Jacobs's collection were "The Three Little Pigs," "Henny Penny," and "Jack and the Beanstalk."

Characteristics

What makes traditional stories different from other types of stories? How can they be so readily identified? The major difference between a traditional story and all the other stories you will be reading about in this textbook is that its *authorship is unknown.* The reason the author is not known is that each traditional tale is so ancient that it has had a multitude of contributors, all of whom helped craft the story as you read it today. This fact also explains why there are many variations of each tale. For example, there are both French and German versions of "Cinderella." In fact, several hundred Cinderella-type stories have been found in Europe, and more than a hundred have been identified in other parts of the world as well. Indeed, there is much similarity in folklore throughout the world.

When students ask me to identify the original version of a particular tale, I explain that the closest we can come to the "original" is to read the oldest recorded version—a version captured by one of the early compilers of traditional literature, such as Aesop, Asbjørnsen, Bechstein, Galland, Grimm, Jacobs, La Fontaine, Lang, Moe, or Perrault.

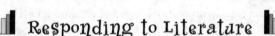

Responding to Literature

Comparing Two Variations of a Traditional Tale

Read the English tale *Duffy and the Devil* (Zemach 1973), and compare it to one of the many versions of the German tale "Rumpelstiltskin"; or read the Chinese tale *Lon Po Po* (Young 1989) and compare it to one of the several versions of "Little Red Riding Hood." What are the common elements of the two versions? What are the differences? Write your answers in the form of a Venn diagram (see Chapter 11, Figure 11.5).

The easiest way to identify traditional literature is to look in the J398 section of a library that uses the Dewey decimal system of classification. (Nearly all school libraries do.) Every book with J398 marked on the spine should be traditional literature. To identify traditional literature in a store or private collection, look for the following characteristics:

1. Unknown authorship. Words such as *retold by* or *adapted by* usually appear on the book cover or title page, or you may recognize the "author" as one of the early compilers of traditional literature. Clues may also be found in the book jacket copy, in phrases such as *an old tale.* If there is an identifiable author—meaning that the story is the product of a single person's mind—it is *not* traditional literature.

2. Conventional introductions and conclusions. The phrases *Once upon a time* and *They lived happily ever after* represent the conventional introductions and conclusions that are either explicit or implied in most tales of traditional literature. The stories are timeless, and the reader has the "secure knowledge that no matter what happens, love, kindness, and truth will prevail—and hate, wickedness, and evil will be punished" (Huck et al., p. 271).

3. Vague settings. Backdrop settings are used; as readers we are not told when the story took place, nor are we usually told where it took place. An indeterminate past time at an unspecified location is sometimes the best description of the setting of a traditional tale. The illustrations will probably reveal the most information, such as a castle, forest, peasant village, and the like.

4. Stereotyped characters. Because characters represent values and attributes, not real humans, they are stereotyped. These flat characters are either all good or all evil. Following are some of the most common types:

- *Beautiful daughter:* There are rarely any plain-looking daughters in traditional literature. Daughters who are good are beautiful, and daughters who are beautiful are good. Intelligence or any other virtue is rarely mentioned. Examples are the female protagonists in "Sleeping Beauty," "Snow White," "Rapunzel," and "Beauty and the Beast."
- *Handsome prince:* When there are beautiful daughters in distress, there are usually handsome princes to save them. They appear in all the "beautiful daughter" stories just mentioned. There are rarely any ugly princes who save the day—if you do not count the ones under evil spells, as in "The Frog Prince" and "Beauty and the Beast." Even they eventually turn into handsome princes.
- *Evil stepmother:* Quite often, the handsome prince saves the beautiful daughter from the evil stepmother, as in "Cinderella," "Snow White," and "Rapunzel." The evil stepmother is often a witch as well. (I hope my stepdaughter is not reading this.)

- *Weak father:* Of course, when there is an evil stepmother, there is usually a weak father who wimps out and does not help his daughter, as in "Snow White" and "Hansel and Gretel." But sometimes the father wimps out on his own, even without a second wife, as in "Rumpelstiltskin" and "Beauty and the Beast."
- *Simpleton:* A boy who is mentally challenged or walks to the beat of a different drummer is the simpleton. He is often abused by family members or others in the community, though he usually comes out ahead in the end. Some examples of this type character are found in "Jack and the Beanstalk," "Hans in Luck," and *Strega Nona* (dePaola 1975).

 ## Responding to Literature
Rewriting Tales

Read a tale with an evil main character, such as the Queen in "Snow White." Referring to the section in Chapter 2 on point of view, rewrite the tale from the villain's perspective.

---

5. Anthropomorphism. In traditional literature, human characteristics are frequently attributed to animals, plants, and objects. Some examples of **anthropomorphic** characters are the hungry wolf in "Little Red Riding Hood," who talks and dresses in Grandmother's clothing; the lively cookie in "The Gingerbread Man," who talks and runs away; and the magic mirror in "Snow White," which not only talks but is omniscient, possessing knowledge of things happening far away.

6. Cause-and-effect. Cause-and-effect relationships are quite apparent in traditional literature. Good characters prevail and are rewarded. Evil characters get their just punishment, which is frequently banishment or even, in the older versions of tales, a painful death. For example, the evil Queen in "Snow White" meets a dreadful end.

> The looking-glass answered, "Oh Queen, although you are of beauty rare, the young bride is a thousand times more fair." Then she railed and cursed, and was beside herself with disappointment and anger. First she thought she would not go to the wedding; but then she felt she should have no peace until she went and saw the bride. And when she saw her she knew her for Snow-white, and could not stir from the place for anger and terror. For they had ready red-hot iron shoes, in which she had to dance until she fell down dead. (Crane 1973, p. 102)

7. Happy ending for the hero. The ending is always a happy one for the good characters, who are often rewarded by great wealth or marriage to royalty. For example, in "Hansel and Gretel" the father and stepmother leave the two children in the forest because there is not enough food for them all. The children fall prey to an evil witch, but they outsmart and kill her. Then they fill their pockets with her treasures and find their way back to their father's house.

> Then they ran till they came up to it, rushed in at the door, and fell on their father's neck. The man had not had a quiet hour since he left his children in the wood; but

the wife was dead. And when Gretel opened her apron the pearls and precious stones were scattered all over the room, and Hansel took one handful after another out of his pocket. Then was all care at an end, and they lived in great joy together. (Crane 1973, p. 44)

8. Magic accepted as normal. One reason children love traditional literature is that the element of magic is a foundation in most stories. No one questions the logic when wolves talk, pigs build houses, little men spin straw into gold, cookies run away, or rags are turned into a ball gown because the magical element is anticipated in traditional tales.

9. Brief stories with simple and direct plots. It was necessary for traditional tales to be brief and simple, so storytellers could more easily remember them. As a result, these stories are appealing to children, who find them easy to comprehend. Although traditional tales were not originally targeted for children, today they are found almost exclusively in the children's sections of libraries and bookstores, because the stories are brief, simple, and direct.

10. Repetition of actions and verbal patterns. Another way storytellers remembered their tales—and made them memorable—was by reciting them in a cumulative manner, with repetition of actions and verbal patterns. An example of this type of *cumulative tale* is "The Gingerbread Man." A runaway cookie escapes from the little old woman who baked him, and he continues to run on past the little old man, some apple pickers, some reapers, a cat, a dog, and a pig before he meets his demise with a fox. Each time he escapes another character, he calls out a refrain and repeats the names of the characters he has evaded so far.

> Run, run, run as fast as you can. You can't catch me. I'm the gingerbread man. I ran away from the little old woman, and the little old man, and some apple pickers, and . . . I can run away from you too, I can.

Although not an exhaustive list, this summary has covered the more common characteristics of traditional literature. However, be aware that you may encounter some stories that, although they contain many of these characteristics, are not true traditional literature—because they were not orally passed from one generation to the next. Rather, they were written by an individual as the product of his or her creative mind. These stories are called literary tales, and they belong to the fantasy genre. There are literary fairy tales, literary myths, literary fables, literary ballads, and even literary nursery rhymes. Keep in mind that when you see the term "literary" in front of *any* category of traditional literature, it means the story was written by an individual.

The first author to successfully employ the literary style of writing was Hans Christian Andersen, starting in 1835. His original stories are often confused with the traditional ones because he emulated fairy tales so well. Indeed, you are most likely to find Andersen's stories in the traditional literature section rather than the fiction section of the library. In addition, his works are frequently included in anthologies of traditional literature. Further discussion of Hans Christian Andersen appears in Chapter 5, Modern Fantasy, where his stories more appropriately belong.

Themes of Traditional Literature

Recall from Chapter 2 that the *theme* of a story is its central idea or underlying message. Often this message is a significant truth, a value-laden statement—or, more simply, the moral of the story. Because one of the purposes of folklore was to transmit cultural values and beliefs, the theme is usually quite apparent. Several common themes or *motifs* in traditional literature follow.

- **Triumph of good over evil.** Good versus evil is surely the most prevalent theme in all literature, regardless of genre. In traditional literature the good prevails, sometimes with the help of a magical being, such as the fairy godmother in "Cinderella," but sometimes because of the characters' ingenuity, as in "Hansel and Gretel." It is unfortunate that stepmothers are nearly always portrayed as evil (Warner 1991).
- **Trickery.** The theme of trickery sometimes constitutes the reverse of the first theme. In trickery the protagonist is successful—not because he is good, but because he is a clever deceiver. For example, in "Puss-in-Boots" the cat kills other animals without mercy, deceives the king, threatens to chop the field workers into small pieces, and steals a vast estate for his master, who is the son of a poor miller. For his deeds, the cat becomes a great lord when his master marries the king's daughter. However, not all tricksters scheme for gain; some do so to preserve their lives, as in the case of Brer Rabbit in "The Tar Baby." Trickster characters are usually small, resourceful animals, such as Anansi the Spider in West African tales and Coyote and Raven in Native American tales.
- **Hero's quest.** Stories with the **hero's quest** theme contain a protagonist who is on a long journey fraught with trials and impossible tasks, in which he or she is searching for something of great importance or value. The character may be searching for riches, a specific treasure, wisdom, a loved one, or even his or her own identity. In *Jason and the Golden Fleece* (Naden 1980), the hero searches for the fleece that was shorn from Hermes's magic ram. In *The Fool of the World and the Flying Ship* (Ransome 1968), the simpleton protagonist seeks a flying ship so he can marry the princess. In *Arrow to the Sun* (McDermott 1974), the boy is seeking his father, whom he has never seen.
- **Reversal of fortune.** In the rags-to-riches theme, a story usually begins with a downtrodden underdog character who becomes blessed with luck and good fortune through a series of unpredictable events. Examples of stories with this theme are "The Elves and the Shoemaker," "Puss-in-Boots," and "Hansel and Gretel." Occasionally the reversal of fortune may be from richer to poorer, as in "Hans in Luck": Hans, being burdened by a large lump of gold to carry, successively trades with passersby until he has nothing but a stone. The greed of the wife in "The Fisherman and His Wife" causes the couple to go from poverty to great wealth and back to poverty.
- **Small outwitting the big.** The theme of the victorious little guy is especially appealing to children, who readily identify with small characters. Quick-

wittedness, rather than brawn, makes the protagonists successful in stories such as "Jack and the Beanstalk," "Hansel and Gretel," "Puss-in-Boots," and "Tom Thumb." The Brer Rabbit stories (Harris & Parks 1986, 1987) always show the rabbit pitted against larger animals, which he repeatedly outwits. This theme is also known as the "triumph of the underdog."

CHILDREN'S BOOKS CITED IN PRECEDING SECTIONS

Crane, Lucy. *Household Stories from the Collection of the Bros. Grimm.* Avenel Books, 1922.

dePaola, Tomie. *Strega Nona.* Simon & Schuster, 1975.

Harris, Joel Chandler, Van Dyke Parks, & Malcolm Jones. *Jump! The Adventures of Brer Rabbit.* Illus. Barry Moser. Harcourt Brace Jovanovich, 1986.

Harris, Joel Chandler, & Van Dyke Parks. *Jump Again! More Adventures of Brer Rabbit.* Illus. Barry Moser. Harcourt Brace Jovanovich, 1987.

Lester, Julius. *The Tales of Uncle Remus: The Adventures of Brer Rabbit.* Illus. Jerry Pinkney. Dutton, 1987.

———. *More Tales of Uncle Remus: Further Adventures of Brer Rabbit, His Friends,* *Enemies, and Others.* Illus. Jerry Pinkney. Dial, 1990.

McDermott, Gerald. *Arrow to the Sun.* Puffin, 1974.

Naden, Corinne J. *Jason and the Golden Fleece.* Illus. Robert Baxter. Troll Associates, 1980.

Ransome, Arthur. *The Fool of the World and the Flying Ship.* Illus. Uri Shulevitz. Farrar, Straus & Giroux, 1968.

Sutcliff, Rosemary. *The Sword and the Circle.* Puffin, 1981.

Young, Ed. *Lon Po Po: A Red Riding Hood Story from China.* Philomel, 1989.

Zemach, Harve. *Duffy and the Devil.* Illus. Margot Zemach. Farrar, Straus & Giroux, 1973.

The Subgenres of Traditional Literature

The bulk of traditional literature consists of *folktales,* the generic term for the various kinds of narrative literature found in the oral traditions of the world. These tales convey the legends, customs, superstitions, and beliefs of people in past times. Dividing this large genre into smaller categories or **subgenres** makes the field easier to study and ensures that nothing important is overlooked. The subgenres of folktales are (1) myths, (2) fables, (3) ballads and songs, (4) legends, (5) tall tales, and (6) fairy tales. Nursery rhymes (which are closer to poetry than to tales), along with other **traditional rhymes** and riddles, make up a final category of traditional literature.

Before you begin reading about the various categories of traditional literature, it is important to remember two things. First, to be true folk literature, a story must have *no known author.* I stress this once again because many good books appear to be traditional literature and share some of the same characteristics; these books may even have a term such as "legend," "fable," "ballad," or "myth" in the title. But if the story is the idea of one person (i.e., not passed orally from one generation to the next), then these stories are literary folktales, which are a form of fiction and are presented in Chapter 5, Modern Fantasy.

Second, for the time being, suspend your own definitions of terms such as *fairy tale, myth, fable,* and *legend.* In everyday language we often use terms to mean any highly imaginative story. However, folklorists define these as distinct forms of folktales. Even when you are certain a story is true traditional literature, you cannot always count on the title to let you know what form it is—because even writers sometimes use the terminology interchangeably. However, by the time you finish this chapter, you will understand the distinctions and will be able to recognize the various forms of traditional literature.

Myths

With one exception, all traditional literature is shelved in the J398 section of the library. The exception is mythology, which is shelved in J292. In the Dewey decimal system, the 200 section is for books about religion; and **myths** belong here because they deal with the religious beliefs of past cultures.

This is a good place to address a question I am often asked by preservice teachers: "Is it legal to use literature books about religion in public schools?" The answer is *yes.* Please see Box 4.1 for clarification on this question, provided by former president Bill

---

Box 4.1

Excerpt from President Clinton's Statement of Principles on Religious Expression in Public Schools

Teaching about Religion

Public schools may not provide religious instruction, but they may teach ABOUT religion, including the Bible or other scripture: The history of religion, comparative religion, *the Bible (or other scripture)-as-literature* [italics mine], and the role of religion in the history of the United States and other countries, all are permissible public school subjects.

Similarly, it is permissible to consider religious influences on art, music, *literature* [italics mine], and social studies. Although public schools may teach about religious holidays, including their religious aspects, and may celebrate the secular aspects of holidays, schools may not observe holidays as religious events or promote such observance by students.

Student Assignments

Students may express their beliefs about religion in the form of homework, artwork, and other written and oral assignments free of discrimination based on the religious content of their submissions. Such home and classroom work should be judged by ordinary academic standards of substance and relevance, and against other legitimate pedagogical concerns identified by the school.

Note: The president's statement does not have the force of law. However, it was promulgated to summarize court holdings on religion in the schools, and former Secretary of Education Richard Riley sent it to all 15,000 public school districts in the United States. This excerpt relates to literature, but the full statement is available in the July 13, 1995, issue of the *New York Times,* which can be accessed through the LEXIS-NEXIS Academic Universe database. These guidelines were reaffirmed with minor changes in May 1998, and again in December 1999 through a letter from former Secretary Riley that was mailed to all principals.

Clinton. I hope that after you read it, you will be encouraged to share mythology, Bible (and other scripture) stories, and stories about various religions with your pupils. Two books I highly recommend are *Celebrate! Stories of the Jewish Holidays* (Berger 1998) and *Tomie dePaola's Book of Bible Stories* (1990). More books on religion are presented in Chapter 7 under religious cultures and in Chapter 11 under informational books on religion. Also, I encourage you to look through the books about various religions in the J200 section of your library.

Mythology was perhaps the earliest form of folklore because it filled an essential need. Humans have always sought to understand the world and its inhabitants, and myths provided an explanation for otherwise unexplainable events. The plots of myths usually include heroes and supernatural beings, including gods who control natural forces such as the seasons and death. The intent of myths was to offer imaginitive interpretations of natural phenomena and other mysteries of life as acts (or influences) of deities. For example, all cultures had myths of the creation of the world and of the origins of the first man and woman. The mythology of many cultures is lengthy and complex, with episodic plots and continuing characters, in contrast to other types of folktales. However, individual stories from collections have been adapted into picture books appropriate for elementary children.

Gerald McDermott used a colorful picture book format in *Raven: A Trickster Tale from the Pacific Northwest* (1993), which tells of a time when the men and women of earth lived in cold darkness. Raven becomes the boy child of the Sky Chief's daughter in order to steal the sun and give it to the people.

Classic myths are narratives with a somewhat formal or dignified tone. Children may find it easier to enjoy and comprehend myths if you read them aloud. Also, keep in mind that like all folklore, myths were not originally intended for children. Although they may be shelved in the children's section, they are not always appropriate for children. Some involve violent acts such as murder, rape, and incest. It is a good rule to preview *everything* before you read it to children or make it available for their independent reading.

Although Greek, Roman, and Norse myths are likely the most familiar, myths from all cultures are worth exploring. They can be included in studies of ancient cultures to provide insight into the people's religion and philosophy, as well as into their ideas, modes of life, and the nature of their civilization (Evslin, Evslin, & Hoopes 1966). Myths also lend themselves as models for creative writing. See Box 4.2 for an idea on how to help children write modern creation myths.

Mythology's influence in modern culture is quite evident. Some of the English-language names of the days of the week were derived from Norse mythology. For example, Thursday comes from "Thor's day." With the exception of Earth, all the planets of our solar system were named for Greek and Roman mythological characters. In fact, references to mythology regularly crop up in our daily lives in various forms such as modern plays, novels, television programs, movies, and advertisements. The following quiz will test your knowledge of how mythology has enhanced our modern language.

Literature Activity: **Testing Your Cultural Literacy**

In our language, many terms, names, and figures of speech were derived from the names of characters in Greek and Roman mythology. Test what Hirsch (1987) calls your *cultural literacy* by naming a mythological character for each of the following. (No character is used more than once.) Answers are available at **www.ablongman.com/anderson.**

1. Early space mission
2. Company that repairs auto exhaust systems
3. Reverberation of the voice
4. Candy bar
5. Liquid metal
6. Vain self-centered person
7. Disney canine character
8. The inner self or mind
9. Name of a large planet and a small automobile
10. Name of ill-fated passenger ship
11. Planet next to Earth
12. A process to strengthen rubber ■

Box 4.2

Writing Your Own Myth

Medicine Hawk Wilburn (1998) encourages his students to make up their own modern creation myths about unexplained things around them. He provided the following example.

How Interchanges Came to Be

As Sakane (the Great Spirit in the designs of man) looked out upon the cars which criss-crossed the land she had created, it looked to her as if they were just moving too fast. "Something must be done to slow these little ants down!" she muttered to herself one day from the clouds. Thoughtfully, the Great Spirit watched the cars moving about. "They can only speed around on these little *roads,*" she decided. The idea sparked across the sky, clapping thunder, as it became clear what the Great Spirit must do. She reached down, grasping the highways like little ropes. With her mighty hands, she tied them in huge knots. As the Great Spirit continued, she began to tie them into designs, such as cloverleaves and flowers. "That should slow them down," she stated perfunctorily, observing her work. To this day, you will see these little knots periodically in the highways.

Ideas for other modern creation myths:
Why computers have viruses
How country music started
Where schools came from
How basketball was invented
Where supermarkets came from
How wars came to be
Where telephones came from
(Or invent your own)

RECOMMENDED BOOKS OF MYTHOLOGY

- Anderson, David A. *The Origin of Life on Earth: An African Creation Myth.* Illus. Kathleen Atkins Wilson. Sights Productions, 1991.

- Bernhard, Emery. *The Tree That Rains: Flood Myth of the Huichol Indians of Mexico.* Illus. Durga Bernhard. Holiday House, 1994.

- Climo, Shirley. *Stolen Thunder: A Norse Myth.* Illus. Alexander Koshkin. Clarion, 1994.

- ———. *Atalanta's Race: A Greek Myth.* Illus. Alexander Koshkin. Clarion, 1995.

- D'Aulaire, Ingri, & Edgar Parin D'Aulaire. *D'Aulaire's Book of Greek Myths.* Doubleday, 1962.

- French, Fiona. *Lord of the Animals: A Miwok Indian Creation Myth.* Millbrook, 1997.

- Jackson, Ellen. *The Precious Gift: A Navajo Creation Myth.* Illus. Woodleigh Hubbard. Simon & Schuster, 1996.

- Jaffe, Nina. *The Golden Flower: A Taino Myth from Puerto Rico.* Illus. Enrique O. Sanchez. Simon & Schuster, 1996.

- McCaughrean, Geraldine. *The Crystal Pool: Myth and Legends of the World.* Illus. Bee Willey. Simon & Schuster, 1999.

- McDermott, Gerald. *Raven: A Trickster Tale from the Pacific Northwest.* Harcourt Brace, 1993.

- ———. *The Voyage of Osiris: A Myth of Ancient Egypt.* Harcourt Brace, 1995.

- Moore, Christopher. *Ishtar and Tammuz: A Babylonian Myth of the Seasons.* Illus. Christian Balit. Larousse Kingfisher Chambers, 1996.

- Ober, Hal. *How Music Came to the World: An Ancient Mexican Myth.* Illus. Carol Ober. Houghton Mifflin, 1994.

- Osborne, Mary Pope. *Favorite Norse Myths.* Illus. Troy Howell. Scholastic, 1996.

- Strauss, Susan. *When Woman Became the Sea: A Costa Rican Creation Myth.* Illus. Cristina Acosta. Beyond Words, 1998.

- Waldherr, Kris. *Persephone and the Pomegranate: A Myth from Greece.* Dial, 1993.

- Wolfson, Margaret Olivia. *Marriage of the Rain Goddess: A South African Myth.* Illus. Clifford Alexander Parms. Marlowe, 1996.

RECOMMENDED BOOKS OF RELIGIOUS STORIES

- Berger, Gilda. *Celebrate! Stories of the Jewish Holidays.* Illus. Peter Catalanotto. Scholastic, 1998.

- dePaola, Tomie. *Tomie dePaola's Book of Bible Stories.* Putnam, 1990.

Fables

Fables, like myths, were likely one of the earliest forms of folklore—because they, too, served an essential purpose. They taught lessons about behavior, thereby transmitting cultural values from one generation to the next. Although fables appear to be simple beast stories, they are allegorical; you may need to generate discussion to help younger children understand the underlying meaning of fables. The fables encountered in traditional literature today come from a variety of cultures, but most of them share several distinct characteristics.

- They are very brief, simple narratives, usually less than one page long.
- The tone is didactic, because the purpose was to instruct the listener in a universal moral truth, often a lesson on how to behave.
- Typically, the characters are anthropomorphic animals that are unnamed. Characters are simply called by what they are, such as Fox, Crow, or Mouse. Occasionally a human ("The Boy Who Cried Wolf") or even an element of nature ("The Wind and the Sun") can be a character.
- The setting is a rural area in the distant past.
- Plots generally involve only one event, usually a conflict between animal characters portraying human faults, that provides a simple example of right from wrong.
- The intended moral is often stated at the end of the story, though some fables have only an implied moral.

Undoubtedly, the most popular fables today are those attributed to Aesop, a freed slave from Thrace who purportedly lived in Greece during the sixth century B.C. His name became attached to a collection of beast fables that had long been transmitted through oral tradition. Aesop circulated these fables orally, and they continued to be transmitted in the oral tradition for several centuries until they were written down by Greek and Roman writers around the first century A.D.

In Europe, France was the most voluminous producer of fables. A common character in these stories is a wily fox known as Reynard. Jean de la Fontaine (1661–1694) is believed to be the greatest of all French fabulists. His fables, written in verse, were extensively imitated by later writers from many countries.

Children can enjoy fables from collections such as Charles Santore's *Aesop's Fables* (1988) in which twenty-four animal tales are beautifully illustrated. This book is impressive, both in content and in size. Younger children can enjoy fables in a picture book written in an easy-to-read format with John Wallner's *City Mouse— Country Mouse* (1987), which contains three mouse tales charmingly illustrated. Fables from various cultures are also available in picture book format; for example, *Once a Mouse . . .* (Brown 1961) and *Chanticleer and the Fox* (Chaucer 1958).

Cultural Literacy. Numerous figures of speech have come from the morals of fables. From the Greek fable "The Boy Who Cried Wolf" comes the phrase "crying wolf," which refers to the fact that giving false alarms will keep people from believing you when a real problem arises. "The Fox and the Grapes" gave rise to the expression "talking sour grapes"—that is, speaking in a derogatory manner about something you were not able to obtain. Fables and all other folklore constitute an essential part in the process of learning one's culture—what Hirsch (1987) called **cultural literacy**. Houston (1999) speaks to the importance of cultural literacy.

For instance, the term, *a wolf in sheep's clothing*, conveys the image of a person who is not what she seems to be. The image is drawn from *Aesop's Fables*. If we know the story, we understand the allusion. . . . Lack of knowledge [of cultural literacy] is a handicap in communication in many situations.

The set of stories we assume our listeners/readers know becomes the shorthand of a culture. That is, a great deal of information can be conveyed in just a word or phrase taken from one of these stories. It is quite possible that students who do not know the stories are handicapped in reading the required canon of books in high school and therefore handicapped on standardized tests, the effects of which may reach on to adulthood. (p. 9)

Throughout this chapter, titles of stories that are italicized refer to specific published books. However, titles of stories encased in quotation marks are common folktales that can be found in print in several versions. When I use these general folktales as examples of concepts, I have assumed you are familiar with these tales. In other words, I have assumed you are culturally literate in terms of these stories. However, if there are titles in quotation marks you are not familiar with, I urge you to locate copies in your library and read them.

▌ RECOMMENDED BOOKS OF FABLES

- Bierhorst, John. ***Doctor Coyote: A Native American Aesop's Fable.*** Illus. Wendy Watson. Simon & Schuster, 1987.
- Brown, Marcia. ***Once a Mouse . . . : A Fable Cut in Wood.*** Scribner, 1961.
- Carle, Eric. ***Twelve Tales from Aesop.*** Philomel, 1980.
- ———. ***Eric Carle's Treasury of Classic Stories for Children.*** Orchard, 1988.
- Chaucer, Geoffrey. ***Chanticleer and the Fox.*** Illus. Barbara Cooney. Crowell, 1958.
- Climo, Shirley. ***The Little Red Ant and the Great Big Crumb: A Mexican Fable.*** Illus. Francisco X. Mora. Clarion, 1995.
- Hooks, William H. ***Feed Me! An Aesop Fable.*** Illus. Doug Cushman. Bantam, 1992.
- Santore, Charles. ***Aesop's Fables.*** Random House, 1988.
- ———. ***The Fox & the Rooster.*** Random House, 1998.
- Stevens, Janet. ***Androcles and the Lion.*** Holiday House, 1989.
- Wallner, John. ***City Mouse—Country Mouse: And Two More Mouse Tales from Aesop.*** Scholastic, 1987.
- Ward, Helen. ***The Hare and the Tortoise.*** Millbrook, 1999.

Ballads and Folk Songs

Not all folktales were told or recited; some stories, called **ballads,** were sung as narrative poems. Folk ballads are one of the newer forms of traditional literature, having developed across Europe in the late Middle Ages. Wandering minstrels earned their living by traveling from village to village and from one manor house to another, performing and entertaining the occupants with popular ballads and news from other regions. Coffin (1999) gives high praise to this form of folklore: "Aesthetically, the ballad is considered by many to be the most remarkable and beautiful art form that the folk traditions of the world have developed" (p. 2).

It was during the Middle Ages that collections of ballads arose about the legendary Robin Hood and King Arthur's Knights of the Round Table. English and Scottish ballads were first compiled by Bishop Thomas Percy in 1765. And from 1882 to 1898, Francis James Child published five volumes of English and Scottish popular ballads, which remain the definitive canon of ballads for that region.

Though the Robin Hood and King Arthur ballad collections were detailed narratives with full plots, many ballads are simple stories sung in rhymed stanzas, such as "On Top of Old Smoky." Many popular ballads and other folk songs have been retold in picture book format, usually with musical scores in the back. Because ballads are meant to be sung, they are best enjoyed with music. If you are musically challenged (like me), obtain a recording from the library, so you can help your children grow in cultural literacy by learning the folk songs of their culture. Learning American ballads and folk songs can be a fun way to learn about U.S. history.

 Literature Activity: Historical Settings of Ballads

Name the historical period and place the following ballads depict: "She'll Be Comin' Round the Mountain," "My Darling Clementine," "The Erie Canal," "Sweet Betsy from Pike," "On Top of Old Smoky," and "John Henry." ■

RECOMMENDED BOOKS OF BALLADS AND FOLK SONGS

- Brett, Jan. *The Twelve Days of Christmas.* Dodd, Mead, 1989.
- Coplon, Emily, Doris Orgel, & Ellen Schecter. *She'll Be Coming around the Mountain.* Illus. Rowan Barnes-Murphy. Bantam, 1994.
- Delacre, Lulu. *Arroz con Leche: Popular Songs and Rhymes from Latin America.* Scholastic, 1992.
- Ginsburg, Mirra. *Where Does the Sun Go at Night?* Illus. Jose Aruego. Morrow, 1987.
- Ivimey, John. W. *Three Blind Mice.* Illus. Paul Galdone. Clarion, 1987.
- Karas, G. Brian. *I Know an Old Lady.* Scholastic, 1994.
- Keats, Ezra Jack. *John Henry.* Random House, 1965.
- Kidd, Ronald. *On Top of Old Smoky: A Collection of Songs and Stories from Appalachia.* Illus. Linda Anderson: Ideals, 1992.
- Langstaff, John. *Frog Went A-Courtin'.* Illus. Feodor Rojankovsky. Harcourt Brace Jovanovich, 1955.
- Lomax, Alan, J. D. Elder, & Bess Lomax Hawes. *Brown Girl in the Ring: An Anthology of Song Games from the Eastern Caribbean.* Pantheon, 1997.
- Medearis, Angela Shelf. *The Zebra-Riding Cowboy: A Folk Song from the Old West.* Illus. Maria Christina Brusca. Henry Holt, 1997.

- Nic Leodhas, Sorche. ***Always Room for One More.*** Illus. Nonny Hogrogian. Holt, Rinehart and Winston, 1965.

- ———. ***By Loch and by Lin: Tales from Scottish Ballads.*** Illus. Vera Bock. Holt, Rinehart and Winston, 1969.

- Plotz, Helen. ***As I Walked Out One Evening: A Book of Ballads.*** Greenwillow, 1976.

- Silverman, Jerry. ***Ragtime Song and Dance: Traditional Black Music.*** Chelsea House, 1995.

- Slavin, Bill. ***The Cat Came Back: A Traditional Song.*** Illus. Kathleen Tucker. Albert Whitman, 1992.

- Spier, Peter. ***The Fox Went Out on a Chilly Night.*** Doubleday, 1961.

- ———. ***The Erie Canal.*** Doubleday, 1970.

- Westcott, Nadine Bernard. ***There's a Hole in the Bucket.*** HarperCollins, 1990.

- Wood, Douglas. ***Northwoods Cradle Song.*** Illus. Lisa Desimini. Simon & Schuster, 1996.

- Yolen, Jane. ***Tam Lin: An Old Ballad.*** Illus. Charles Mikolaycak. Voyager, 1998.

- Zalinsky, Paul O. ***The Wheels on the Bus: The Traditional Song.*** Dutton, 1990.

Legends

Legends, including epic poems, are a combination of history and myth. Typically, **legends** are based in part on real characters or historical events, such as the tales of King Arthur, Robin Hood, and Joan of Arc. However, the truth is distorted; attributes of courage, goodness, wisdom, or beauty are often highly exaggerated. The plots of legends often contain a challenge, a quest, enchantment, and battle with an evil force—with justice finally triumphing over injustice. The heroes and heroines are noble, courageous, and willing to avenge a wrong (Norton 1999).

A legend differs from a myth by portraying a human hero rather than a deity. Also, whereas myths are set in a remote time, legends are set in a specific place and time, especially when the protagonist is a historical hero. The specific setting distinguishes the legend from all other forms of folktales. Legends can overlap with ballads when the ballads are about legendary people. The difference is not in the subject but in the format: Ballads are songs, and legends are narratives (stories or tales).

Legendary heroes include a variety of characters from different times and places. According to legend, Ulysses was a Greek warrior who fought in the Trojan War and then struggled through many trials to find his way home. Beowulf was a courageous Scandinavian who slew the monster Grendel and its mother to save the thanes (feudal barons) under his protection. The English King Arthur formed the Knights of the Round Table, who searched for the Holy Grail and avenged wrongs throughout the kingdom. Robin Hood and his band of men lived in England's Sherwood Forest; they robbed well-to-do travelers and gave to the poor people in the countryside. Grania O'Malley was an Irish heroine—a great sea captain and pirate. Hua Mu Lan was a brave Chinese woman who disguised herself as a man and took the place of her elderly father when he was called to war. The Swiss hero William Tell fought for freedom and independence. Rabbi Löw of Prague created the Golem from clay to help the Jewish people of the city who were being persecuted. Children's books are available about these and other heroes.

▌RECOMMENDED BOOKS OF LEGENDS

- Brooks, Felicity, & Anna Claybourne. *King Arthur & His Knights.* EDC Publications, 1999.
- Brown, Marcia. *Backbone of the King: Story of Pakaa and His Son Ku.* University of Hawaii Press, 1984.
- Chin, Charlie. *China's Bravest Girl: The Legend of Hua Mu Lan.* Illus. Tomie Arai. Children's Book Press, 1993.
- Claybourne, Anna. *The Adventures of Ulysses.* Illus. Jeff Anderson. EDC Publications, 1998.
- Cohen, Barbara. *Robin Hood and Little John.* Illus. David Ray. Philomel, 1995.
- Fisher, Leonard Everett. *William Tell.* Farrar, Straus & Giroux, 1996.
- Geringer, Laura. *Ulysses: The Soldier King.* Scholastic, 1996.
- McCully, Emily Arnold. *The Pirate Queen.* Putnam, 1995.
- Paterson, Katherine. *Parzival: The Quest of the Grail Knight.* Lodestar, 1998.
- Singer, Isaac Bashevis. *The Golem.* Illus. Uri Shulevitz. Farrar, Straus & Giroux, 1982.
- Sutcliff, Rosemary. *Dragon Slayer: The Story of Beowulf.* Bodley Head, 1961.
- Williams, Marcia. *The Adventures of Robin Hood.* Candlewick, 1995.

Tall Tales

In the 1800s the U.S. frontier spawned the tall tale, making it the youngest form of folktales. **Tall tales** can best be described as exaggerated storytelling with gigantic, extravagant, restless, and flamboyant characters (Osborne 1991). The tales describe stupendous feats of courage and endurance by historical figures such as Davy Crockett and Johnny Appleseed, as well as the exploits of imaginary heroes such as Paul Bunyan and Pecos Bill. Other heroes of tall tales include Sally Ann Thunder Ann Whirlwind, Stormalong, Mose, Febold Feboldson, Mike Fink, and John Henry. Often the stories center on a conflict between two rogue traders or bragging brawlers, with each outdoing the other. Characters in tall tales, always larger than life, include pioneer settlers, backwoods people, farmers, cowpokes, loggers, and others.

Tall tales combine the storytelling of ordinary people and the imaginations of professional writers. Today it is difficult to disentangle the oral from the written stories, because these tales moved in and out of the oral and literary modes. Considering that the United States is a comparatively young country, there was little time for a large body of stories to develop in the oral tradition. Even the Brer Rabbit stories collected by Joel Chandler Harris go back to the West African countries from which the slaves unwillingly came. Whereas Native American tales represent the folklore of the indigenous people in the Americas, tall tales represent the folklore of the Euro-American pioneers who set out to win the continent (from the Native Americans, unfortunately).

At one time, tall tales were presented to city dwellers as true pictures of life out west, supposedly to dupe naive listeners; however, the fantastic elements of the stories are absurdly exaggerated. The behemoth lumberjack Paul Bunyan (Kellogg 1984) was so quick on his feet he could blow out a candle and leap into bed before the room became dark. He was so big, he combed his beard with the top of a pine tree. No wonder that Paul managed to dig the Great Lakes and gouge out the Grand Canyon, despite the hardships he and his crew of lumberjacks encountered—such as a blizzard that lasted for several years.

American legends overlap with tall tales when the subject is a real person, such as Davy Crockett. However, the tall tale version of a person is preposterous because of its exaggerations ("Davy killed him a bear, when he was only three"), whereas the legendary version is believable but romanticized. It is interesting to note that the African American steel driver, John Henry, has been the subject of ballads, legends, and tall tales. There is some historical evidence that John Henry was a real person who drove steel into mountainsides to help blast a passage for the railroads. Mary Pope Osborne's (1991) collection of American tall tales gives this and other interesting historical facts behind some of the tales.

▌RECOMMENDED BOOKS OF TALL TALES

- Dadey, Debbie. ***Shooting Star: Annie Oakley, the Legend Walker.*** Illus. Scott Goto. Walker, 1999.
- Dewey, Ariane. ***The Narrow Escapes of Davy Crockett.*** Mulberry, 1993.
- Johnson, Janet P. ***Keelboat Annie: An African-American Legend.*** Illus. Charles Reasoner. Troll Associates, 1998.
- Kellogg, Steven. ***Paul Bunyan.*** Morrow, 1984.
- ———. ***Pecos Bill.*** Mulberry, 1992.
- ———. ***Sally Ann Thunder Ann Whirlwind Crockett.*** Morrow, 1995.
- ———. ***Johnny Appleseed.*** Mulberry, 1996.
- ———. ***Mike Fink.*** Mulberry, 1998.
- Lester, Julius. ***John Henry.*** Illus. Jerry Pinkney. Dial, 1994.
- Osborne, Mary Pope. ***American Tall Tales.*** Illus. Michael McCurdy. Knopf, 1991.
- Rounds, Glen. ***Casey Jones: The Story of a Brave Engineer.*** Golden Gate, 1968.
- San Souci, Robert D. ***Cut from the Same Cloth: American Women of Myth, Legend and Tall Tale.*** Illus. Brian Pinkney. Philomel, 1993.
- Shepard, Aaron. ***The Legend of Slappy Hooper: An American Tall Tale.*** Illus. Toni Goffe. Atheneum, 1993.

Fairy Tales or Märchen

Fairy tales are by far the most abundant of folktales, but they are difficult to define because they are so varied. To make matters more confusing, most fairy tales do not

Shang, Tao, and Paotze escape from the wolf.
From *Lon Po Po: A Red-Riding Hood Story from China,* translated and illustrated by Ed Young.

contain fairies, which is why folklorists prefer to call this category by its German name—**Märchen.** I usually tell my students to use the rule of exclusion—meaning that if it *is* a folktale and it is *not* a myth, fable, ballad, legend, or tall tale—then it *must* be a fairy tale.

The original purpose of most fairy tales was to entertain and enchant listeners with stories of supernatural events in a wonderland setting filled with magic and strange, fantastical characters. They serve the same purpose for children today. Fairy tale characters may be anthropomorphic animals ("The Three Little Pigs"), imaginary beings with magical powers such as fairies and trolls ("Rumpelstiltskin"), humans ("Snow White"), plants (*The Tale of Three Trees,* Hunt 1989), or even inanimate objects ("The Gingerbread Man"). In American fairy tales, a boy named Jack is a common human character—as in *Jack and the Bean Tree* (Haley 1986), the Appalachian version of "Jack and the Beanstalk." In addition to fairies, unusual characters that appear in these tales are elves, brownies, gnomes, goblins, trolls, dwarves, pixies, and banshees. Fairies can be good or evil, but even good fairies are prone to play pranks on humans. Bad fairies can cause the sudden death of cattle, bewitch children, and even substitute **changelings** (ugly fairy babies) for human infants.

Fairy tales deal with a great range of subject matter, but Coffin (1999) described a typical fairy tale plot as involving "an underdog hero or heroine who is put through great trials or must perform seemingly impossible tasks, and who with magical assistance secures his or her birthright or a suitable marriage partner" (p. 5).

Because fairy tales constitute the largest subgenre of traditional literature, they can best be appreciated when they are grouped by commonalties. There are six major groups with recognizable literary patterns: beast stories, trickster tales, pourquoi tales, cumulative tales, simpleton tales, realistic tales, and wonder stories.

Beast stories. **Beast stories,** also called animal stories, have anthropomorphic animals as characters. These characters act, talk, and reason as humans do, though they may retain a few animal traits as well. Perhaps the best-known beast tale is "Goldilocks and the Three Bears." In a Native American tale, *The Story of Jumping Mouse* (Steptoe 1984), a young mouse journeys to reach the land of his dreams. Though he retains all his animal habits, he is able to talk with other animals, and he portrays the human emotions of desire, discontent, dismay, hope, sadness, courage, unselfishness, and compassion.

A common theme, especially in African lore, is a smaller animal's outwitting a larger animal or other foe. Because the trickster is most often portrayed as an animal, most of the trickster tales described in the next section are also beast stories. Many cumulative tales, such as *Three Little Pigs and the Big Bad Wolf* (Rounds 1992), are also beast stories. The activity in Figure 4.1 can be used to compare various versions of beast stories or other folktales.

Trickster tales. Usually an animal is the protagonist in a **trickster tale.** The trickster is able to outsmart others because he is cunning, shrewd, or deceptive. Often tricksters are small or weak creatures such as spiders or rabbits. They must use their wits to get the better of more powerful characters. In *Jump Again!* (Harris & Parks 1987), when Brer Rabbit is captured, he pleads over and over for just one thing: " 'Please, Brer Fox, don't fling me in that briar patch.' Of course, Brer Fox wants to hurt Brer Rabbit as bad as he could, so he caught him up and flung him into the middle of the briar patch" (p. 11). But that was exactly where Brer Rabbit wanted to go because he was "bred and born in a briar patch," and there was no place he loved better. This is an example of how a trickster uses shrewd thinking to get out of trouble.

 Responding to Literature

Interpreting Cultural Literacy

Have you ever heard someone say, "I think he is telling us not to throw him in the briar patch"? Explain what this means and give an example. What would listeners think if they were not familiar with the Brer Rabbit story? In what ways does cultural literacy through literature affect your communication (e.g., "Your nose is going to grow" and "a real Cinderella story")?

• Title	*The Three Little Pigs*	*Three Little Pigs and the Big Bad Wolf*	*The Three Little Pigs*
• **Illustrator**	Gavin Bishop	Glen Rounds	Paul Galdone
• Style of illustrations			
• Setting			
• Description of mother			
• Pig # 1 building supplies			
• Pig # 2 building supplies			
• Pig # 3 building supplies			
• Description of wolf			
• Encounters with wolf			
• Conclusion (who gets eaten)			

FIGURE 4.1 **Responding to Literature by Comparing and Contrasting Folktales.** Read two or more versions of a beast story and compare them, using a matrix. An example comparing versions of "The Three Little Pigs" is provided here. *Source:* Adapted from an activity by Pam Kuzminski.

The trickster is an exception to the stereotyped characters in traditional literature who are either all good or all bad. Tricksters are typically amoral—neither good nor bad. Sometimes they are wise and helpful, but they can also be sly and mischievous; and they are always up to something. Tricksters can be arrogant, greedy, and self-centered. However, they are also charming and likeable, and they always manage to escape severe punishment.

In Native American lore, the trickster is most often Coyote, and Susan Strauss provided several good examples in *Coyote Stories for Children* (1991). Coyote tricks both animals and people out of their possessions. He likes to poke fun at other characters by "messin' with them" and making them look foolish. According to Medicine Hawk Wilburn (1988), the tales of Coyote serve a number of valuable purposes for humankind.

> He shows us our weaknesses. He teaches us how to be wily and aware of our surroundings. He teaches us by reverse example how to behave; how to act; how to treat others. He reflects our selfish ways back to us. He brings us face to face with our dark (or lighter) side. Most of all, Coyote teaches us how to laugh at the world, and therefore laugh at ourselves.

Pourquoi Tales. *Pourquoi* (poor-QWAH) means "why" in French, and **pourquoi tales** answer questions about the way things are, particularly natural phenomena: Where does the sun go at night? Why does the elephant have a long nose? Where did the river come from? *Fire Race* (London 1993) explains how fire came to the animals. This Karuk Coyote tale also has the characteristics of a beast tale and a trickster tale because Coyote tricks the Yellow Jackets and steals their fire.

Pourquoi tales should not be confused with myths that explain natural phenomena as actions or influences of deities; rather, it is usually animals who bring things about in pourquoi tales. In addition to explaining natural phenomena, pourquoi tales explain certain animal traits or characteristics. *Rainbow Crow* (Van Laan 1989) is a beautiful story, both in text and illustrations, that explains why the courageous crow changed from a lovely bird of rainbow colors and pleasing voice to the bird it is today. These tales can also explain human customs. *Tikki Tikki Tembo* (Mosel 1968) explains why Chinese parents give their children short names.

Cumulative Tales. In **cumulative tales** the storyteller accumulates an additional event each time he or she repeats the refrain, and each event grows from the preceding one. Each time the refrain is repeated, a new item is added to the story, which expands the list of events or participants. Cumulative tales can have as few as three repetitive events, as in *The Three Billy Goats Gruff* (Asbjørnsen & Moe 1957) and *The Three Little Pigs* (Bishop 1989). Others sound like a chant, where only one new phrase or sentence is added, and the full refrain is repeated each time, such as "The House that Jack Built." The Nandi tale *Bringing the Rain to Kapiti Plain* (Aardema 1981) has a similar structure:

> This was the shot that pierced the cloud
> And loosed the rain with thunder LOUD!

A shot from the bow, so long and strong,
And strung with a string, a leather thong;
A bow for the arrow Ki-Pat put together,
With a slender stick and an eagle feather,
From the eagle who happened to drop a feather,
A feather that helped to change the weather. . . .

Some cumulative tales are called **chaining tales,** because each part of the story is linked to the next. Cullinan (1989) explained that "The initial incident reveals both the central character and problem; each subsequent scene builds onto the original one. The accumulation continues to a climax and then unravels in reverse order . . . " (p. 239). In *One Fine Day* (Hogrogian 1971), a fox drinks an old woman's milk, so she cuts off his tail. In order to get her to sew his tail back on, he must replace the milk. He goes from one character to another, but each requires the fox to give something, until he meets a kind miller who "gave him the grain to give to the hen to get the egg to pay the peddler to get the bead to give the maiden to get the jug to fetch the water to give the field to get the grass to feed the cow to get the milk to give the old woman to get his tail back."

Simpleton Tales. The protagonists of **simpleton tales** are not too smart. They are sometimes called noodle head, droll person, or numbskull. Their escapades are frequently humorous, and they often make a mess of things with their absurd mistakes—as does Big Anthony in *Strega Nona* (dePaola 1975), who makes the town overflow with pasta because he cannot figure out how to turn the magic pasta pot off.

Sometimes, however, simpletons succeed where more intelligent people do not. In *The Fool of the World and the Flying Ship* (Ransome 1968), two clever brothers and one foolish brother set out on the same quest. The two clever brothers are never heard of again, but the foolish brother finds the flying ship, takes it to the Czar, and—after meeting numerous trials—marries the princess. The ancient and magical man who first befriended him reveals the theme to this tale: "You see how God loves simple folk. Although your own mother does not love you, you have not been done out of your share of the good things. . . ."

Simpletons are usually good-hearted underdogs who are thought to be idiots by the people around them. But they usually triumph in the end, as in *Jack and the Beanstalk:* Although Jack trades his mother's cow for five magic beans (Faulkner 1986), he brings home the giant's treasure in the end.

Realistic Tales. Perhaps the smallest group of fairy tales is the **realistic tales.** In these stories, the characters, settings, and events are realistic. That is, although the plots may be far-fetched, they follow all the laws of the physical world. Because there are no elements of fantasy, realistic tales are void of talking animals, fantasy creatures, and magical objects or powers.

Uri Shulevitz gives us two such stories, both with a humble old man as the protagonist. In *The Secret Room* (1993), an old man wins the favor of the king through his clever and wise responses, and he is made the king's chief counselor. In

The Treasure (1978), an old man living in poverty follows a message in a dream and goes on a quest to a faraway city, but to no avail. When he returns home, the treasure he was seeking is found hidden under his stove. The theme is captured in one sentence: "Sometimes one must travel far to discover what is near."

In a Norse tale, *The Farmer in the Soup* (Littledale 1987), a farmer and his wife trade places for a day. She works in the fields, and he stays home, watches the baby, and cooks dinner. When the wife comes home for lunch, she cleans up the disaster he has made of the house, and the farmer never complains again. He tells his wife, "Everything you do is always right."

Wonder Stories. Enchantments and other magic abounds in **wonder stories.** These stories' characters include supernatural beings such as fairy godmothers, helpful elves, and evil trolls. Magical objects, such as mirrors, cloaks, oil lamps, and rings are common. The plots of wonder stories center on common people who need supernatural assistance in order to solve their problems. Often these stories involve adventure and romance. In *Saint George and the Dragon* (1984), Margaret Hodges retells a segment from Edmund Spenser's epic *The Faerie Queene* (1590), in which George, the Red Cross Knight, slays the dreadful dragon that has been terrorizing the countryside for years. He brings peace and joy to the land. This book is beautifully illustrated by Trina Schart Hyman.

Unusual characters in wonder stories include the princes in *Beauty and the Beast* (Brett 1989) and *The Frog Prince* (Galdone 1975), both of whom have been turned into ugly animals by evil enchantresses. A similar theme is found in *Sir Gawain and the Loathly Lady* (Hastings 1985) in which a woman who was under an evil spell had been transformed into an ugly hag. Sometimes characters are humans with amazing powers, such as the three women who were so strong they could carry cows and toss trees, in *Three Strong Women* (Stamm 1962).

In wonder tales, dreams come true—literally. In *The Mud Pony* (Cohen 1988), the boy's clay horse comes to life. Similarly, a childless old couple make a snow girl who comes to life in *The Snow Child* (Littledale 1989). Baba Yaga's dream comes true when she is adopted as a *babushka* (grandmother) by a young boy in *Babushka Baba Yaga* (Polacco 1993). Duffy gets a life of ease and marries the squire when an impish creature does her spinning for her in *Duffy and the Devil* (Zemach 1973).

Virtue and wisdom are rewarded in wonder tales. In *The Talking Eggs* (San Souci 1989), the younger sister is respectful and obeys an old woman, for which she is rewarded with magic eggs that provide her with many riches. In *The Legend of Scarface* (San Souci 1978), a young warrior wins the heart of the chief's beautiful daughter because he is generous and honest: The beautiful woman overlooks the disfiguring scar on his face that caused others to taunt him. The miller's youngest daughter in *The Enchanted Book* (Porazinska & Smith 1987), unlike her older sisters, chooses wisdom over vanity and gaiety. Later, because she can read, she is able to free her sisters and other peasant girls from the spell of an evil enchanter. In *The Fourth Question* (Wang 1991), a young man unselfishly gives up his one chance to have the Wise Man answer his pressing question. Instead, he asks three questions for three people who befriended him—and, because of this, his own problem is solved.

It is traditional to illustrate fairy tales in a setting near the time the story first appeared in print. However, some artists have taken traditional tales and illustrated them with contemporary settings. This approach may appeal to older children who think they have outgrown folktales. Anthony Browne's illustrations of the Grimms' *Hansel and Gretel* (1981) depict the brother and sister as impoverished children living in a dirty, run-down two-story brick house. The pictures are artfully drawn and amusing, from the bottle of Oil of Olay and panty hose on the dresser to the stepmother's heavy makeup and the flowered wallpaper in the witch's kitchen. In a similar manner, Gavin Bishop depicted a modern setting for a classic version of *The Three Little Pigs* (1989). In the opening picture, the mother pig is pushing a lawnmower while her three sons lounge around the swimming pool listening to their boom box. Later, the third little pig buys a truckload of bricks to build a solid home to withstand the wolf—who sports a warm-up jacket, sunglasses, and a Walkman radio.

Traditional literature is the original multicultural literature, and nowhere is this more evident than with Märchen, the largest category of traditional literature. Following are recommended books from several cultures.

▌AFRICAN MÄRCHEN

- Aardema, Verna. **Why Mosquitoes Buzz in People's Ears.** Illus. Leo D. Dillon & Diane Dillon. Dial, 1975.
- ———. **Bringing the Rain to Kapiti Plain.** Illus. Beatriz Vidal. Dial, 1981.
- ———. **Misoso: Once upon a Time Tales from Africa.** Illus. Reynold Ruffins. Knopf, 1994.
- Diop, Birago, & Rosa Guy. **Mother Crocodile.** Illus. John Steptoe. Doubleday, 1981.
- Haley, Gail E. **A Story—a Story: An African Tale.** Atheneum, 1988.
- McDermott, Gerald. **Anansi the Spider: A Tale from the Ashanti.** Henry Holt, 1998.
- Steptoe, John. **Mufaro's Beautiful Daughters.** Lothrop Lee & Shepard, 1987.

▌AMERICAN MÄRCHEN

- Abrahams, Roger D. **African American Folktales: Stories from Black Traditions in the New World.** Pantheon, 1999.
- Haley, Gail E. **Jack and the Bean Tree: A Mountain Tale.** Crown, 1986.
- ———. **Mountain Jack Tales.** Dutton, 1992.
- Hamilton, Virginia. **The People Could Fly: American Black Folktales.** Knopf, 1985.
- ———. **Her Stories: African American Folktales, Fairy Tales, and True Tales.** Illus. Leo D. Dillon & Diane Dillon. Blue Sky Press, 1995.
- Harris, Joel Chandler, Van Dyke Parks, & Malcolm Jones. **Jump! The Adventures of Brer Rabbit.** Illus. Barry Moser. Harcourt Brace Jovanovich, 1986.
- Harris, Joel Chandler, & Van Dyke Parks. **Jump Again! More Adventures of Brer Rabbit.** Illus. Barry Moser. Harcourt Brace Jovanovich, 1987.

- Hunt, Angela Elwell. *The Tale of Three Trees: A Traditional Folktale.* Illus. Tim Jonke. Lion, 1989.
- Lester, Julius. *The Tales of Uncle Remus: The Adventures of Brer Rabbit.* Illus. Jerry Pinkney. Dutton, 1987.
- ———. *More Tales of Uncle Remus: Further Adventures of Brer Rabbit, His Friends, Enemies, and Others.* Illus. Jerry Pinkney. Dial, 1990.
- San Souci, Robert D. *The Talking Eggs: A Folktale from the American South.* Illus. Jerry Pinkney. Dial, 1989.

NATIVE AMERICAN MÄRCHEN

- Bruchac, Joseph. *Flying with the Eagle, Racing the Great Bear: Stories from Native North America.* Troll Associates, 1993.
- Caldwell, E. K., & Vic Warren. *Animal Lore and Legend: Bear.* Illus. Diana Magnuson. Scholastic, 1996.
- Cohen, Caron Lee. *The Mud Pony: A Traditional Skidi Pawnee Tale.* Illus. Shonto Begay. Scholastic, 1988.
- Goble, Paul. *Paul Goble Gallery: Three Native American Stories.* Simon & Schuster, 1999.
- ———. *Adopted by the Eagles: A Plains Indian Story of Friendship and Treachery.* Simon & Schuster, 1994.
- ———. *Crow Chief: A Plains Indian Story.* Orchard, 1992.
- Hinton, Leanne. *Ishi's Tale of Lizard.* Illus. Susan L. Roth. Farrar, Straus & Giroux, 1992.
- Jones, Jennifer Berry. *Heetunka's Harvest: A Tale of the Plains Indians.* Roberts Rinehart, 1994.
- London, Jonathan. *Fire Race: A Karuk Coyote Tale.* Illus. Sylvia Long. Chronicle, 1993.
- San Souci, Robert. *The Legend of Scarface.* Illus. Daniel San Souci. Doubleday, 1978.
- Steptoe, John. *The Story of Jumping Mouse: A Native American Legend.* Morrow, 1984.
- Strauss, Susan. *Coyote Stories for Children: Tales from Native America.* Illus. Gary Lund. Beyond Words, 1991.
- Van Laan, Nancy. *Rainbow Crow: A Lenape Tale.* Illus. Beatriz Vidal. Knopf, 1989.

ASIAN MÄRCHEN

- Climo, Shirley. *The Korean Cinderella.* Illus. Ruth Heller. Harper, 1996.
- Eimon, Mina Harada. *Why Cats Chase Mice: A Story of the Twelve Zodiac Signs.* Heian International, 1993.
- Meeker, Clare Hodgson. *A Tale of Two Rice Birds: A Folktale from Thailand.* Sasquatch Books, 1994.
- Mosel, Arlene. *Tikki Tikki Tembo.* Illus. Blair Lent. Henry Holt, 1968.
- ———. *The Funny Little Woman.* Illus. Blair Lent. Dutton, 1972.

- Rinpoche, Ringu Tulku. *The Boy Who Had a Dream: A Nomadic Folk Tale from Tibet.* Findhorn Press, 1997.
- Stamm, Claus. *Three Strong Women: A Tall Tale from Japan.* Illus. Jean Tseng & Mou-sien Tseng. Viking, 1962.
- Walker, Barbara K. *The Most Beautiful Thing in the World: A Folktale from China.* Scholastic, 1993.
- Wang, Rosalind C. *The Fourth Question: A Chinese Tale.* Illus. Ju-Hong Chen. Holiday House, 1991.
- Young, Ed. *Lon Po Po: A Red Riding Hood Story from China.* Philomel, 1989.
- ———. *Night Visitors.* Philomel, 1995.

BRITISH MÄRCHEN

- Bishop, Gavin. *The Three Little Pigs.* Ashton, 1989.
- dePaola, Tomie. *Fin M'Coul: The Giant of Knockmany Hill.* Holiday House, 1992.
- Faulkner, Matt. *Jack and the Beanstalk.* Scholastic, 1986.
- Galdone, Paul. *The Gingerbread Boy.* Clarion, 1979.
- ———. *The Three Little Pigs.* Houghton Mifflin, 1984.
- Hastings, Selina. *Sir Gawain and the Loathly Lady.* Illus. Juan Wijngaard. Lothrop, Lee & Shepard, 1985.
- Hodges, Margaret. *Saint George and the Dragon: A Golden Legend.* Illus. Trina Schart Hyman. Little, Brown, 1984.
- Kellogg, Steven. *Jack and the Beanstalk.* Morrow, 1991.
- Lang, Andrew. *The Blue Fairy Book: Selected Tales from the Collection.* Junior Deluxe Editions, 1969.
- McDermott, Gerald. *Daniel O'Rourke: An Irish Tale.* Viking, 1986.
- Rounds, Glen. *Three Little Pigs and the Big Bad Wolf.* Holiday House, 1992.
- Shulevitz, Uri. *The Treasure.* Farrar, Straus & Giroux, 1978.
- Zemach, Harve. *Duffy and the Devil.* Illus. Margot Zemach. Farrar, Straus & Giroux, 1973.

FRENCH MÄRCHEN

- Brett, Jan. *Beauty and the Beast.* Clarion, 1989.
- Brown, Marcia. *Stone Soup.* Atheneum, 1989.
- Perrault, Charles. *Perrault's Complete Fairy Tales.* Dodd, 1961.
- ———. *Cinderella.* Illus. Marcia Brown. Atheneum, 1954.
- ———. *Puss in Boots: A Fairy Tale.* Illus. Hans Fischer. Chronicle Books, 1996.
- ———. *Little Red Riding Hood and Other Stories.* Illus. W. Heath Robinson. Random House, 1996.

- ———. *Sleeping Beauty.* Illus. Sheilah Beckett. Dover, 1997.
- ———. *Cinderella: A Fairy Tale.* Illus. Loek Koopmans. North-South Books, 1999.

GERMAN MÄRCHEN

- Brett, Jan. *Goldilocks and the Three Bears.* Dodd, Mead, 1992.
- Corrin, Sara, & Stephen Corrin. *The Pied Piper of Hamelin.* Illus. Errol Le Cain. Harcourt Brace Jovanovich, 1988.
- Galdone, Paul. *The Frog Prince.* McGraw-Hill, 1975.
- ———. *The Elves and the Shoemaker.* Houghton Mifflin, 1986.
- Grimm, Jacob, & Wilhelm Grimm. *Hansel and Gretel.* Illus. Arnold Lobel. Delacorte, 1971.
- ———. *Hansel and Gretel.* Illus. Anthony Browne. Knopf, 1981.
- ———. *Snow-White and the Seven Dwarfs.* Illus. Nancy Ekholm Burkert. Farrar, Straus & Giroux, 1972.
- ———. *The Complete Grimm's Fairy Tales.* Illus. Josef Scharl. Random House, 1976.
- ———. *Rapunzel.* Illus. Paul O. Zalinsky. Dutton, 1997.
- ———. *Rumpelstiltskin.* Illus. Bernadette Watts. North-South, 1993.
- Grimm, Wilhelm. *Dear Milli.* Illus. Maurice Sendak. Farrar, Straus & Giroux, 1988.
- Jarrell, Randall. *Snow-White and the Seven Dwarfs.* Illus. Nancy Ekholm Burkert. Farrar, Straus & Giroux, 1972.
- Van Der Grient, Katrien. *The Castle of Birds: A Grimm's Fairy Tale.* Anthroposophic Press, 1998.

HISPANIC MÄRCHEN

- Aardema, Verna. *Borreguita and the Coyote: A Tale from Ayutla, Mexico.* Illus. Petra Mathers. Knopf, 1991.
- Ada, Alma Flor. *Medio Pollito / Half Chicken.* Illus. Kim Howard. Bantam, 1997.
- Anaya, Rudolfo. *Farolitos of Christmas.* Illus. Edward Gonzales. Hyperion, 1995.
- ———. *Maya's Children: The Story of La Llorona.* Illus. Maria Baca. Hyperion, 1997.
- ———. *Farolitos for Abuelo.* Illus. Edward Gonzales. Hyperion, 1999.
- dePaola, Tomie. *The Legend of the Poinsettia.* Putnam & Grosset, 1994.
- Gonzalez, Lucia M. *The Bossy Gallito.* Illus. Lulu Delacre. Scholastic, 1999.
- Mike, Jan M. *Opossum and the Great Firemaker: A Mexican Legend.* Illus. Charles Reasoner. Troll Associates, 1993.
- ———. *Juan Bobo and the Horse of Seven Colors: A Puerto Rican Legend.* Illus. Charles Reasoner. Troll Associates, 1995.
- Palazzo-Craig, Janet. *When Sun Ruled the Land: A Story from Cuba.* Illus. Dave Albers. Troll Associates, 1997.
- Shute, Linda. *Rabbit Wishes.* Lothrop Lee & Shepard, 1995.

ITALIAN MÄRCHEN

- Calvino, Italo. *Italian Folktales.* Harcourt, 1980.
- dePaola, Tomie. *Strega Nona.* Simon & Schuster, 1975.
- ———. *Days of the Blackbird: A Tale of Northern Italy.* Putnam, 1997.
- Sanderson, Ruth. *Papa Gatto: An Italian Fairy Tale.* Little, Brown, 1995.

MIDDLE EASTERN MÄRCHEN

- Ahmed, Prince. *The Flying Carpet.* Illus. Marcia Brown. Scribner, 1956.
- Alderson, Brian. *The Arabian Nights, or Tales Told by Sheherezade.* Illus. Michael Foreman. Morrow, 1995.
- Schwartz, Howard. *Elijah's Violin & Other Jewish Fairy Tales.* Illus. Linda Heller. Oxford University Press, 1994.
- ———. *Next Year in Jerusalem: 3000 Years of Jewish Stories.* Illus. Neil Waldman. Viking, 1996.
- Shulevitz, Uri. *The Secret Room.* Farrar, Straus & Giroux, 1993.

RUSSIAN MÄRCHEN

- Aksakov, Sergi. *The Scarlet Flower: A Russian Folk Tale.* Illus. Boris Diodorov. Harcourt Brace Jovanovich, 1989.
- Cole, Joanna. *Bony-Legs.* Illus. Dirk Zimmer. Scholastic, 1983.
- Hoffman, Mary. *Clever Katya: A Fairy Tale from Old Russia.* Barefoot Books, 1998.
- Littledale, Freya. *The Snow Child.* Illus. Barbara Lavallee. Scholastic, 1989.
- McDermott, Beverly Brodsky. *The Crystal Apple: A Russian Tale.* Viking, 1974.
- Polacco, Patricia. *Babushka Baba Yaga.* Philomel, 1994.
- Ransome, Arthur. *The Fool of the World and the Flying Ship.* Illus. Uri Shulevitz. Collins, 1968.
- Robbins, Ruth. *Baboushka and the Three Kings.* Houghton Mifflin, 1960.

SCANDINAVIAN MÄRCHEN

- Asbjørnsen, Peter Christen. *East of the Sun and West of the Moon.* Illus. Kathleen Hague & Michael Hague. Harcourt Brace, 1989.
- ———. *The Three Billy Goats Gruff.* Illus. Stephen Carpenter. HarperCollins, 1998.
- Asbjørnsen, Peter Christen & Jorgen Moe. *The Three Billy Goats Gruff.* Illus. Marcia Brown. Harcourt Brace Jovanovich, 1957.
- ———. *Norwegian Folk Tales.* Pantheon, 1982.
- Cauley, Lorinda Bryan. *The Pancake Boy: An Old Norwegian Folk Tale.* Putnam, 1988.
- Littledale, Freya. *The Farmer in the Soup.* Illus. Molly Delaney. Scholastic, 1987.

- Phelps, Ethel J. *Tatterhood and Other Tales: Stories of Magic and Adventure.* Illus. Pamela Baldwin Ford. Feminist Press, 1989.

- Shepard, Aaron. *The Maiden of Northland: A Hero Tale of Finland.* Atheneum, 1996.

▌ADDITIONAL MÄRCHEN

- Araujo, Frank. *Nekane, the Lamina & the Bear: A Tale of the Basque Pyrenees.* Rayve Productions, 1993.

- Carle, Eric. *Eric Carle's Treasury of Classic Stories for Children.* Orchard, 1988.

- Claire, Elizabeth. *The Little Brown Jay: A Tale from India.* Mondo, 1994.

- Ehrlich, Amy. *The Random House Book of Fairy Tales.* Illus. Diane Goode. Random House, 1985.

- Hogrogian, Nonny. *One Fine Day* (Armenian). Macmillan, 1971.

- Hollis, Susan Tower. *The Ancient Egyptian Tale of Two Brothers.* University of Oklahoma Press, 1990.

- Impey, Rose. *Read Me a Fairy Tale: A Child's Book of Classic Fairy Tales.* Illus. Ian Beck. Scholastic, 1993.

- Porazinska, Janina, & Bozena Smith. *The Enchanted Book: A Tale from Krakow.* Illus. Jan Brett. Harcourt Brace Jovanovich, 1987.

- Rose, Deborah Lee. *The People Who Hugged the Trees* (India). Roberts Rinehart, 1994.

- Zemach, Margot. *It Could Always Be Worse: A Yiddish Folk Tale.* Farrar, Straus & Giroux, 1990.

Traditional Rhymes and Riddles

Nursery rhymes are traditional verses intended for very young children. Often these simple rhymes are a child's first contact with literature. Most of the rhymes are non-sensical, but they have several features that make them enjoyable. Their musical language, often created with strong rhythm, makes them appealing to children; and they contain action, humor, and entertaining incidents.

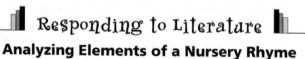
Responding to Literature

Analyzing Elements of a Nursery Rhyme

Read the following nursery rhyme aloud, and then describe how it exemplifies the elements of *musical language, rhythm, action, humor,* and *entertaining incident.*

> Hey, diddle, diddle,
> The cat and the fiddle,
> The cow jumped over the moon;
> The little dog laughed
> To see such sport,
> And the dish ran away with the spoon.

Most likely, the nursery rhymes you heard as a child were of British origin and were called **Mother Goose** rhymes. There are several explanations of how the term Mother Goose became associated with these rhymes, but I will provide the one I find most plausible. In 1729, an English translation of Perrault's fairy tales was published and became very popular in England. In addition to the enchanting tales, it contained nursery rhymes. The book was subtitled "Tales of My Mother Goose," and the **frontispiece** (the illustration preceding the title page) depicted an old woman. A caption within the illustration read "Mother Goose's Tales." Some believe the woman was a Ms. Goose, perhaps the nursemaid who first told Perrault the fairy tales. (At that time, "Mother" was added to the names of women as a sign of respect.) Interestingly, the term Mother Goose became associated with the nursery rhymes rather than with the fairy tales in the book.

Among the subjects of nursery rhymes are festivals, vocations, courtship, marriage, and death—topics that more closely match adults' interests. However, long before these rhymes were recorded, they were entertainment for adults as well as children, as is true for all folklore. Most nursery rhymes do not make sense today, but they have historical links to their originating cultures. Many developed from humorous verses that were based on real people, events, or customs. Some of the sources for the rhymes were old proverbs, street cries, games, ballads, and even tavern songs. Others were political satires, masked by allegory to lampoon political and religious leaders. The popular "Ring-a-Ring o' Roses" is said to have its origins in the history of England.

> Ring-a-ring o'roses,
> A pocket full of posies;
> A-tishoo! A-tishoo!
> We all fall down.

Chisholm's (1972) research led her to conclude that this rhyme originated during the time of the Great Plague in England in 1664. The first symptom of the plague was a rosy rash that broke out on the victim's face and body, which the rhyme refers to as "roses." The "pocket full of posies" refers to the herbs or flowers people carried in their pockets in an effort to ward off the plague. "A-tishoo! A-tishoo!" refers to the next symptom, which was violent sneezing; then death is described as "We all fall down."

All cultures have nursery rhymes and riddles—including the United States. My favorite collection of American rhymes is *A Rocket in My Pocket: The Rhymes and Chants of Young Americans* (Withers 1988). First published in 1948, this collection includes hundreds of jump rope rhymes, jingles, chants, riddles, and tongue twisters. Following are a couple of favorites I loved to recite as a child.

> A peanut sat on the railroad track.
> His heart was all a-flutter.
> Along came a train—the 9:15—
> Toot, toot, peanut butter!

> Fuzzy Wuzzy was a bear.
> Fuzzy Wuzzy had no hair.
> Fuzzy Wuzzy wasn't fuzzy,
> Was he?

Another fun collection of American traditional rhymes is *The Rooster Crows* by Maude and Miska Petersham (1945). It contains nursery rhymes, skipping rhymes, counting-out rhymes, finger games, and jingles.

Riddles are questions that initially seem incomprehensible, and they fascinate young people because of the challenge to figure them out. John Bierhorst published a collection of Native American riddles, titled *Lightning inside You: And Other Native American Riddles* (1992). It contains more than a hundred riddles from many different tribes, with subjects such as nature, animals, plants, and people. For example, here is an Eastern Cherokee riddle: What goes all around the house and never comes in? (Answer: a path.)

There are several excellent collections of nursery rhymes. I especially like *Hey Diddle Diddle & Other Mother Goose Rhymes* by Tomie dePaola (1985). This book is very appealing to young children because the illustrations are colorful and uncluttered as well as enchanting. In addition to collections, individual nursery rhymes can be subjects of picture books. Maurice Sendak used two nursery rhymes with a total of only twelve lines to write and illustrate the picture book *Hector Protector and As I Went over the Water* (1965). Understandably, many of the pages contain only Sendak's charming illustrations.

▌ RECOMMENDED BOOKS OF TRADITIONAL RHYMES AND RIDDLES

- Ainsworth, Catherine H. **Jump Rope Verses around the United States.** Clyde Press, 1976.
- Benjamin, Floella. **Skip across the Ocean: Nursery Rhymes from around the World.** Illus. Sheila Moxley. Orchard, 1995.
- Bierhorst, John. **Lightning inside You: And Other Native American Riddles.** Illus. Louise Brierley. Morrow, 1992.
- Cooney, Barbara. **Tortillas Para Mama and Other Rhymes in Spanish and English.** Henry Holt, 1987.
- dePaola, Tomie. **Hey Diddle Diddle & Other Mother Goose Rhymes.** Putnam & Grosset, 1985.
- Edens, Cooper. **The Glorious Mother Goose.** Atheneum, 1998.
- Greenaway, Kate. **Mother Goose, or, The Old Nursery Rhymes.** Grammercy, 1881/1978.
- Grover, Eulalie Osgood. **The Original Volland Edition of Mother Goose.** Illus. Frederick Richardson. Outlet, 1915.
- Jaramillo, Nelly Palocio. **Grandmother's Nursery Rhymes / Las Nanas de Abuelita.** Illus. Elivia Savadler. Henry Holt, 1994.
- Lobel, Arnold. **The Arnold Lobel Book of Mother Goose.** Knopf, 1997.
- Petersham, Maud, & Miska Petersham. **The Rooster Crows.** Simon & Schuster, 1945.
- Schwartz, Alvin. **And the Green Grass Grew All Around: Folk Poetry from Everyone.** Illus. Sue Truesdell. HarperCollins, 1999.
- Sendak, Maurice. **Hector Protector and As I Went over the Water.** HarperCollins, 1965.
- Sutherland, Zena. **Orchard Book of Nursery Rhymes.** Illus. Faith Jaques. Orchard, 1990.

- Wildsmith, Brian. **Nursery Rhymes: Mother Goose.** Oxford University Press, 1987.

- Withers, Carl. **A Rocket in My Pocket: The Rhymes and Chants of Young Americans.** Illus. Susanne Suba. Henry Holt, 1948/1988.

- Yolen, Jane. **Jane Yolen's Mother Goose Songbook.** Illus. Rosekrans Hoffman. Boyds Mills, 1992.

Violence in Traditional Literature

In recent years some critics have argued that traditional literature is too violent to share with children. Inasmuch as the genre was not specifically intended for children, this is a claim worth investigating. First, let us look back at some of the literature I have discussed in this chapter.

Snow White's wicked stepmother had to dance in red-hot iron shoes until she fell down dead. The gingerbread man was eaten alive by a fox. Puss-in-Boots killed other animals without mercy and threatened to chop the field workers into small pieces. Some myths contain events that include murder and rape. And, although I failed to mention this earlier, in older versions of "The Frog Prince" the Frog was not kissed by the beautiful princess—he was thrown against the wall! (But he turned into a prince anyway.)

Not even nursery rhymes can be excluded from this investigation. Consider the words to the familiar rhyme "Goosey, Goosey Gander."

> Goosey, goosey gander,
> Whither shall I wander?
> Upstairs and downstairs
> And in my lady's chamber.
> There I met an old man
> Who would not say his prayers,
> I took him by the left leg
> And threw him down the stairs.

I agree that a certain amount of violence in nursery rhymes and folktales has come down from the cultures of past centuries. People today are more conscious of children's exposure to violence, given the frequent news reports of violent crimes committed by children against both children and adults. However, because of most children's viewing habits, television and motion picture violence have far more influence than children's literature. By the time the average child graduates from high school, he or she will have spent more time viewing television than being in school, never mind reading or being read too.

Grover (1971) focused on the positive aspects of traditional literature when she wrote of nursery rhymes that "The healthy moral, so subtly suggested in many of the rhymes, is unconsciously absorbed by the child's receptive mind, helping him to make his own distinction between right and wrong, bravery and cowardice, generosity and selfishness" (p. 7).

I raise this issue because I have talked with parents who say that because of violence they do not share traditional literature with their children. I would point out that traditional literature is an ever changing body of works, and that most of the popular tales have been adapted for younger children. To withold the entire genre of traditional literature from children is to deprive them of cultural literacy. I advocate *selection* rather than censorship. Teachers and parents can select appropriate books from the vast body that is available, and ignore the rest.

Censorship

by Jenifer Jasinski Schneider

The following section on censorship applies to all the genres. It was written by Jenifer Jasinski Schneider, associate professor at the University of South Florida, who is a strong proponent of First Amendment rights.

What Is Censorship?

Censorship of children's literature is a major issue for parents, teachers, and librarians. Because children's literature deals with children's thoughts and imaginations as well as with real-life problems, it is under attack by some parents and political groups. According to the American Library Association (ALA) Office of Intellectual Freedom (2000c), **censorship** is

> the suppression of ideas and information that certain persons—individuals, groups or government officials—find objectionable or dangerous. . . . Censors try to use the power of the state to impose their view of what is truthful and appropriate, or offensive and objectionable, on everyone else. Censors pressure public institutions, like libraries, to suppress and remove from public access information they judge inappropriate or dangerous, so that no one else has the chance to read or view the material and make up their own minds about it. The censor wants to prejudge materials for everyone.

Censorship of children's literature can occur in various forms and for various reasons. Often the primary goal is to keep children from being exposed to knowledge the censors do not want them to have. In most cases adults do this out of genuine concern for children's welfare—to protect them from what they see as harmful.

In the journal *Reading Today* (2001), the following reasons were most frequently cited for book challenges in schools and libraries:

- Sexually explicit episodes
- Offensive language
- Topics unsuitable for targeted age group
- Occult or Satanist themes
- Homosexual themes
- Religious viewpoints
- Nudity

- Violence
- Racism
- Sex education
- Anti-family themes

For example, a commonly challenged book is *Scary Stories to Tell in the Dark* (Schwartz 1981) because it contains violence. *Daddy's Roommate* (Willhoite 1990) and *Heather Has Two Mommies* (Newman 1989) are often challenged because they contain homosexual themes. Even the much-acclaimed *Bridge to Terabithia* (Paterson 1977) has been challenged because it contains a topic (death) unsuitable for the targeted age group. However, the *most* frequently challenged books in the past few years are J. K. Rowling's Harry Potter books because their focus on witchcraft and wizardry supposedly promotes the occult (see Box 5.1).

Challenges to children's books are widespread, and the most popular books read by children are often the ones that garner the most criticism. The ALA compiles an annual list of the year's most frequently banned books and their authors. In the 1990s the ALA recorded 5,718 reported challenges to library materials. (Many more go unreported.) Of those challenges, 71 percent were made about materials in schools or school libraries; nearly 60 percent of all challenges were made by parents (ALA 2000a).

Parents and organizations have strong convictions that guide their attempts to censor particular reading material. However, ignorance is likely to do more harm than knowledge (Nodelman 1996). In addition, librarians and other educators argue that censorship violates the Constitution's Bill of Rights guarantee of freedom of expression. The ALA (2000d) developed the Library Bill of Rights to help protect this basic freedom and to provide a philosophical basis for opposing censorship. In its Bill of Rights the ALA affirms that all libraries are forums for information and ideas, and that the following basic policies should guide their services:

- Books and other library resources should be provided for the interest, information, and enlightenment of all people of the community the library serves. Materials should not be excluded because of the origin, background, or views of those contributing to their creation.
- Libraries should provide materials and information presenting all points of view on current and historical issues. Materials should not be proscribed or removed because of partisan or doctrinal disapproval.
- Libraries should challenge censorship in the fulfillment of their responsibility to provide information and enlightenment.
- Libraries should cooperate with all persons and groups concerned with resisting abridgment of free expression and free access to ideas.
- A person's right to use a library should not be denied or abridged because of [the person's] origin, age, background, or views.
- Libraries that make exhibit spaces and meeting rooms available to the public they serve should make such facilities available on an equitable basis, regardless of the beliefs or affiliations of individuals or groups requesting their use (ALA 2000d).

Selecting versus Censoring

If people find something objectionable in a book, they can keep it away from their own children, but they should not be able to prevent all children from reading the book. As an alternative to censorship, which prohibits children from reading books by removing them from library shelves and bookstores, selection helps readers locate good books among the vast body of works of differing quality. Librarians practice selection when they order books for their libraries and share books with children. Teachers practice selection when they choose books for the classroom shelves and for read-alouds and other literature-based activities. Parents practice selection when they purchase books and check out library books for their children. And, of course, children practice selection when they pick books to read on their own.

The difference between censorship and selection is the removal of choice. Censorship removes the "objectionable" materials. Therefore, an individual's ability to choose a book is eliminated. Selection is an individual process of choosing reading material for oneself and family. With selection, controversial books are still available, but it is each individual's choice whether or not to read them.

In schools and classrooms selection becomes a little more difficult, because teachers and librarians make decisions for many different children. For this reason, books should not be censored or removed, but selected by and for children. The educational organizations listed at the end of this section have created support networks and materials to help educators and parents make informed decisions in their selection of materials. For example, the ALA website (ALA 2000b) contains information about the role of libraries in serving children, how librarians select their collections, and how parents can help children and teens make the best use of the library. The National Council of Teachers of English (NCTE) also provides a website with guidelines for selecting materials in English language arts programs. NCTE suggests that the criteria for selecting materials should include a clear connection to educational objectives and should address the needs of students. By drawing upon these resources, teachers can select diverse books that reflect their students' interests and cultures while maintaining high academic standards. If parents know the reasons behind teachers' choices, they are less likely to attempt to censor them.

However, when proactive selection policies and procedures do not satisfy all parents or organizations, there are other resources available to help teachers oppose censorship restrictions and maintain the academic freedom of their classrooms. For example, the ALA's website contains detailed information on coping with challenges and conducting challenge hearings. In addition, the NCTE website has numerous resources for teachers and schools faced with censorship challenges. It provides guidelines, sample forms, and suggested procedures and approaches for dealing with challenges to literary works, for dealing with censorship of nonprint materials, for defining and defending instructional methods, and for providing rationales for challenged books.

Above all, because the selection of children's literature for the classroom must be an informed process that accounts for children's interests while meeting academic and aesthetic objectives, it is imperative that teachers preview all books to be shared with a group of children. Teachers should also develop a rationale for their use of certain books with particular children.

The following organizations are dedicated to securing the open use of literature and nonprint materials for use by children:

- American Booksellers Foundation for Free Expression: http://www.abffe.org
- American Library Association: http://www.ala.org
- Freedom to Read Foundation: http://www.ftrf.org
- National Coalition against Censorship: http://www.ncac.org
- National Council of Teachers of English: http://www.ncte.org
- PEN American Center: http://www.pen.org

For a direct link to these and other Internet sites listed in this textbook, go to http://www.ablongman.com/anderson

CHILDREN'S BOOKS CITED IN THIS SECTION

Newman, Leslea. *Heather Has Two Mommies.* Alyson Wonderland, 1989.

Paterson, Katherine. *Bridge to Terabithia.* Crowell, 1977.

Rowling, J. K. *Harry Potter and the Sorcerer's Stone.* Scholastic, 1998.

Schwartz, Alvin. *Scary Stories to Tell in the Dark.* Lippincott, 1981.

Willhoite, Michael. *Daddy's Roommate.* Alyson Wonderland, 1990.

KEY TERMS

 Explore the E-Glossary at **www.ablongman.com/anderson**

anthropomorphism (p. 79)
ballad (p. 88)
beast stories (p. 94)
censorship (p. 108)
chaining tale (p. 97)
changeling (p. 93)
cultural literacy (p. 87)
cumulative tale (p. 96)
fable (p. 86)
fairy tale (p. 92)
folklore (p. 75)
frontispiece (p. 105)
hero's quest (p. 81)
legend (p. 90)

Märchen (p. 93)
Mother Goose (p. 105)
myth (p. 83)
nursery rhymes (p. 104)
oral tradition (p. 75)
pourquoi tale (p. 96)
realistic tale (p. 97)
simpleton tale (p. 97)
subgenre (p. 82)
tall tale (p. 91)
traditional literature (p. 75)
traditional rhymes (p. 82)
trickster tale (p. 94)
wonder story (p. 98)

Harry catches the golden snitch.

Harry Potter and the Sorcerer's Stone
Written by
J. K. Rowling
and illustrated
by Mary Grandpre.

chapter

5

Modern Fantasy

Fiction: A literary work that is designed to entertain, the content of which is produced by the imagination of an identifiable author

Modern fantasy: A fiction story with highly fanciful or supernatural elements that would be impossible in real life

This is the first of four chapters on **fiction.** This chapter will explore modern fantasy; Chapter 6, animal fantasy; Chapter 8, contemporary realistic fiction; and Chapter 9, historical fiction. All fiction books, regardless of genre, are located in the *unnumbered* section of the library. Storybooks or juvenile novels are separated from picture books and have a *J* (Juvenile) on the spine. (A few libraries use *F* for Fiction.) Picture books have an *E* (Easy) on the spine. Both J and E books will have the first letters of the author's last name underneath, and both are shelved alphabetically by *authors'* last names (not illustrators').

Fantasy was the inevitable offspring of traditional literature. Today, because both genres still share so many elements, we distinguish them by referring to them as traditional fantasy stories and **modern fantasy** stories. What is it that makes fantasy so different from other forms of fiction? Fantasy contains some type of unreality or enchantment—what children call magic. The story elements break the natural physical laws of our world without explanation. When you were a child (or maybe even an adult), did you pretend your pets could talk or your toys came to life? Did you ever pretend you could fly or become invisible? Did you wish you had a fairy godmother who would take you to wonderful places, or that you lived with both parents happily ever after? Did you ever wish you could acquire great riches (like win the lottery)? In fantasy people can live out their desires, but to fully enjoy fantasy, readers must suspend their disbelief of the impossible and accept that anything is possible within the covers of a book.

Evaluating Modern Fantasy

The following questions can guide you as you select modern fantasy books:

- Is the theme worthwhile for children?
- Is the plot original?
- Are the fantasy elements of the story well developed?
- Is the setting authentic and integral to the story?
- Does the author's characterization allow readers to suspend disbelief?
- Is the story logical and consistent within its chosen format?
- Is the point of view consistent?
- Does the author use appropriate language that is believable and consistent with the story?

For high fantasy:

- Is the main character truly heroic?
- Are all the characters plausible in their own settings?
- Is the secondary world believable?
- Is the quest purposeful?

For science fiction:

- Is the technology convincing?
- Are purposeful questions about the future raised?

The Beginnings of Fiction and Modern Fantasy

In the late 1400s the development of the printing press using movable metal type made the mass publication and circulation of literature possible. Once reading materials were readily available, more people became literate. When people could read stories, listening to and telling stories became less important, and the ancient art of storytelling gradually diminished. Had it not been for the efforts of the early compilers of traditional stories, the tales might have been lost entirely.

Storytellers of the new era—such as Perrault, Galland, and Grimm—recorded old tales in print. Their published stories ultimately reached a far greater audience than was possible in the oral tradition. The new literate population clamored for more stories to read, and storytellers began to write their own tales, albeit still with the heavy influence of folktales. Eventually, the literary storytellers deviated from the folktale mold and became increasingly more individual in their subject matter and writing styles. These unique stories were the early beginnings of children's fiction and modern fantasy.

Hans Christian Andersen

The first of these modern storytellers to meet with great success was Hans Christian Andersen, born in 1805 in Odense, Denmark. He was the son of a poor cobbler who died when Hans was 11. As a child Hans never demonstrated any skill in shoemaking; his desire was to be a performer. He ran away to Copenhagen when he was 14, and he nearly starved trying to work as a singer, dancer, and actor—all with little success—before realizing his talent was for writing. Jonas Collin, director of the Royal Theater, recognized Andersen's potential and procured a royal scholarship for him, which permitted Andersen to continue his studies for many years.

Andersen probably began his career as a storyteller by telling traditional tales. Eventually his own creative genius molded the tales, and he wrote original stories. Today we call these stories **literary fairy tales** because they retained many of the characteristics of traditional fairy tales.

Starting in the 1830s, Andersen began writing and publishing his stories in a series of pamphlets. These were later collected and published in books, the first of which appeared in 1835. Before his death in 1875, Andersen published 168 tales.

Some of his best known stories include "The Little Mermaid," "The Emperor's New Clothes," "Thumbelina," "The Brave Tin Soldier," "The Nightingale," "The Little Match-Seller," "The Fir Tree," and "The Ugly Duckling." The latter story, Andersen said, was based on his own years as a gangly and homely young man.

For a complete collection of his literary fairy tales with contemporary translations, see *Hans Christian Andersen: The Complete Fairy Tales and Stories* (Andersen & Haugaard 1974). Many of his individual stories are available in picture book format as well, for example, *The Little Match Girl* (Andersen & Isadora 1987).

Andersen's writing style was unique for his day. He wrote with deliberate simplicity yet with wisdom and even humor. Consider Kai in "The Snow Queen." The young man had fallen prey to the evil enchantress, and his sled was tied to the back of hers as she sped farther and farther away from town. "The boy was frightened, and tried to say a prayer, but he could remember nothing but the multiplication table" (Andersen 1845).

Literary Fairy Tales

There has always been much confusion about whether Andersen's stories were traditional literature or fiction. Cullinan (1989) wrote that "Andersen was the first to use the classic fairy tale form to write stories of his own, which are often confused with the traditional ones because he emulates them so well" (p. 312). Indeed, you are most likely to find his stories in the traditional literature section of the library rather than the fiction section. In addition, Andersen's works are frequently included in anthologies of traditional literature. For example, *The Random House Book of Fairy Tales* (Ehrlich 1985) contains five of Andersen's stories along with traditional stories from Perrault, Grimm, and de Beaumont. *Eric Carle's Treasury of Classic Stories for Children* (1988) contains seven of Andersen's stories along with traditional stories from Grimm and Aesop.

Part of the confusion in classifying Andersen's stories arises because his first volume of original stories was titled *Andersen's Fairy Tales* (1835). Even his autobiography was titled *The Fairy Tale of My Life* (1855). Because his work was the prototype of modern fantasy short stories, I suppose no one (including himself) knew what else to call his stories. However, Andersen's well-known stories are literary fairy tales, a type of modern fantasy.

The themes of Andersen's tales have much in common with those of traditional literature. For example, trickery is the theme of "The Emperor's New Clothes." In other stories, good triumphs over evil, heroes are successful in quests, the poor become rich, and underdogs triumph. Andersen's stories also share many of the characteristics of traditional literature. His stories contain talking animals and many forms of magic, such as young men who are turned into swans and the birth of the miniature child Thumbelina. And his stories do contain stereotyped characters, such as handsome princes and evil stepmothers, but they also contain vivid original characters, such as the little mermaid who falls in love with a mortal and the fir tree that learns too late that it should have been happy with its life the way it was.

There is one characteristic of Andersen's tales that sets them far apart from traditional stories—and that has caused some critics to say his works are unsuitable for young children. Whereas traditional tales always have a happy ending for the hero, not all of Andersen's tales do. Consider the following excerpts from the endings of some of his more popular stories (accessible at http://www.math.technion.ac.il/~rl/Andersen/vt/).

The Little Mermaid (1836)
She cast one more lingering, half-fainting glance at the prince, and then threw herself from the ship into the sea, and thought her body was dissolving into foam.

The Brave Tin Soldier (1838)
Presently one of the little boys took up the tin soldier, and threw him into the stove. . . . He felt himself melting away, but he still remained firm with his gun on his shoulder. Suddenly the door of the room flew open and the draught of air caught up the little dancer, she fluttered like a sylph right into the stove by the side of the tin soldier, and was instantly in flames and was gone.

The Fir Tree (1845)
"Oh, had I but enjoyed myself while I could have done so! but now it is too late." Then a lad came and chopped the tree into small pieces, till a large bundle lay in a heap on the ground. The pieces were placed in a fire under the copper [kettle], and they quickly blazed up brightly, while the tree sighed so deeply . . . . till at last it was consumed.

The Little Match-Seller (1846)
In the dawn of morning there lay the poor little one, with pale cheeks and smiling mouth, leaning against the wall; she had been frozen to death on the last evening of the year; and the New-year's sun rose and shone upon a little corpse! The child still sat, in the stiffness of death, holding the matches in her hand, one bundle of which was burnt. "She tried to warm herself," said some.

Unlike traditional literature, Andersen's fiction stories deal with deep feelings such as love, remorse, longing, and the agony of death. Not all of his tales have such melancholy endings, but many contain serious moral meanings intended more for adults than for children.

In Denmark Andersen also had success writing adult stories, novels, plays, poetry, songs, and travel books. However, it was his literary fairy tales that gained him international fame. The popularity of Andersen's stories spread from Denmark to all of Europe and then throughout the world. He remains Denmark's most famous author, and his stories have been translated into more than eighty languages. Despite his ardent effort, Andersen was never successful as a performer; therefore, it is fitting that his stories have inspired plays, ballets, films, paintings, and works of sculpture throughout the world.

While Hans Christian Andersen was still writing fantasy short stories, Lewis Carroll published the first entertaining novel for children in England in 1865—*Alice's Adventures in Wonderland*. With these works the era of modern children's literature was launched. Though the early fiction works for children were modern fantasy, it was not long before entertaining realistic fiction became available as well; contemporary and historical fiction are discussed in Chapters 8 and 9.

Types of Fantasy

The genre of fantasy is vast, particularly for preschool and primary-grade children, so I have broken it into ten groups:

1. Animal fantasy
2. Literary fairy tale
3. Animated object fantasy
4. Human with fantasy character
5. Extraordinary person
6. Enchanted journey
7. High fantasy
8. Supernatural fantasy
9. Science fiction
10. Unlikely situation

Animal Fantasy

In animal fantasy the main—and often all—characters are anthropomorphic animals. They possess human speech and can think and express emotions like humans. Often they live like humans, wearing clothing, living in houses, cooking food, and the like. Favorite animal characters are found in *Frog and Toad Are Friends* (Lobel 1970), *The Very Lonely Firefly* (Carle 1995), and *Berlioz the Bear* (Brett 1991).

Animal fantasy is so popular with younger children that when you look through the picture book sections of bookstores and libraries, about half of the books have fantasy animal characters. Because of its popularity with children, I have devoted all of the next chapter to animal fantasy.

Literary Fairy Tale

A literary fairy tale, as discussed earlier, follows the patterns set by the oral tradition of folklore but is written by an identifiable author. Though Hans Christian Andersen was the first to write original stories in fairy tale format, many writers followed his lead, and even today some authors choose this style.

The most enchanting and absorbing literary fairy tale I have read is undoubtedly *The Moorchild* by Eloise Jarvis McGraw (1996). Set in medieval times, this novel opens with, "It was Old Bess, the Wise Woman of the village, who first suspected that the baby at her daughter's house was a changeling" (p. 3). Old Bess's granddaughter had indeed been stolen by the Moor fairies, and in her place a half-fairy, half-human baby had been left—a changeling. Saaski grows into a child who is considered a freak because of her unusual appearance and strange behaviors, not the least of which is her ability to play haunting melodies on the bagpipes without instruction. Her memory and perception of the Fairy Folk gradually return. After being driven from the village,

Saaski and her only friend, Tam the goatherd boy, embark on a quest. They attempt to find her parents' real child—for which she was exchanged—and to return the child to them.

Natalie Babbitt also writes literary fairy tales for intermediate-grade children. In *Knee-Knock Rise* (Babbitt 1970), young Egan is the hero who sets out to find the Megrimum—the source of the mysterious and unearthly wailing from the misty peak of Knee-Knock Rise. There he finds something the villagers will never believe.

Sometimes authors emulate the traditional tale so well that it is difficult to determine without research whether a story is folktale or fiction. One such story is *The Hole in the Dike* by Mary Mapes Dodge (adapted by Norma Green 1974). On his way home, Peter, a young Dutch boy, discovers a leak in the dike that keeps his city from flooding. He puts his finger in the hole to stop the leak and remains there until the next morning when help arrives.

In Katherine Paterson's *The King's Equal* (1992), a vain and cruel young king must leave his kingdom and live as a goatherd for one year before he is able to marry the woman he loves. He is befriended by a talking wolf who helps him learn humility and kindness.

As a young boy, Tomie dePaola learned the traditional story of Strega Nona from his Italian grandmother. The story of the Grandma Witch and her noodle-head helper, Big Anthony, was so popular that dePaola published several original stories. In *Big Anthony and the Magic Ring* (1979), the noodle head once more experiments with Strega Nona's magic by using her magic ring to make himself handsome. Predictably, Strega Nona must intervene to straighten things out when the ladies pursue him relentlessly. Big Anthony's incompetence can be useful, however. When Strega Amelia threatens to put Strega Nona out of business, Big Anthony goes to work for the competition and, with his usual bumbling, ends up putting the competitor out of business in *Strega Nona Meets Her Match* (1993).

Paul Goble's *The Girl Who Loved Wild Horses* (1978) is written in the style of a Native American folktale. When a Plains Indian girl is lost in the mountains during a storm, a wild stallion becomes her friend. Although she loves her people, she develops a much deeper affinity for the wild horses who graze near her village. She prefers to live among the wild horses, where she is truly free, and eventually she is transformed into a wild horse.

Teresa Bateman's original Irish tale, *The Ring of Truth* (1997), has all the charm of a traditional Irish tale with leprechauns, magic, and gold. The leprechaun king punishes Patrick O'Kelley for his fibbing and boastfulness with a magic ring that will forever make him tell the truth. However, the truth is stranger than his blarney, and no one believes the story.

Pete Seeger got the idea for his story-song *Abiyoyo* (1986) while reading to his children from a book of South African lullabies. In this story a little boy with a ukulele and his magician father come up with a plan to rid the town of the fearsome giant Abiyoyo. The boy plays a song to make the monster dance, and when Abiyoyo falls down exhausted, the father touches him with his magic wand and makes him disappear.

The Fortune-Tellers (1992) by Lloyd Alexander has a contemporary setting in Cameroon, Africa, but the story has the earmarks of a traditional tale. A young carpenter is unhappy in his trade, so he journeys to see a fortune-teller. When the fortune-teller meets with a series of terrible mishaps, the young man successfully assumes his role. He has learned from the old fortune-teller to give answers such as "You shall wed your true love, if you find her and she agrees. And you shall be happy as any in the world if you can avoid being miserable."

In addition to literary fairy tales, there are literary pourquoi stories—stories that explain natural phenomena or the way things are. The earliest enduring tales were published by Rudyard Kipling in *Just So Stories* in 1902. Influenced by the Jataka tales of India, he wrote a collection of tales that explain certain animals' features, such as "How the Leopard Got His Spots." "The Elephant Child" gives an explanation of how the elephant got its long trunk in the setting of the "great, gray-green, greasy Limpopo River."

In the title story of *Why Does It Always Rain on Sukkot?* (1990), Susan Schaalman Youdovin provides an explanation for rain during a Jewish holiday. When the chief angel gave the Jewish holidays their gifts, Sukkot feared he was left out and cried. Each year he remembers that sadness and weeps again. The book includes a story for each of the nine major Jewish holidays, explaining some of the symbolism of the artifacts used during each celebration, and provides factual descriptions of the holidays at the end.

In *We Are All in the Dumps with Jack and Guy* (1993), Maurice Sendak wove together two lesser known traditional rhymes and used the lines to illustrate a saga with the theme of current social realities. When the book came out, some critics said it was suited only for adults (and indeed it was sold to that market) because of the realities of homelessness, hunger, child abuse, and other social ills that are either in the story line or seen in newspapers appearing in illustrations. The story is of two homeless orphans living in a New York City garbage dump; they rescue a helpless waif who was abducted by rats. I think this is a good book to read to children who are unaware that not everyone has the necessities (much less the conveniences) of life.

Some stories that use fairy tale themes are spoofs on traditional tales. It is the princess who saves the prince from the dragon in *The Paper Bag Princess* (Munsch 1980). The prince is depicted as vain and haughty, whereas the princess is depicted as strong and resourceful—a real switch from the traditional stereotyped roles.

A master of fairy tale parody is Jon Scieszka, who first captured children's attention with *The True Story of the 3 Little Pigs* (1989). The traditional story is told from the point of view of the wolf, who claims that he was out to borrow a cup of sugar for his granny's birthday cake and he was framed. In the traditional story of the Frog Prince, the princess turns the frog into a prince by kissing him (or throwing him against the wall, depending on the version you read). Did they live happily ever after? In Scieszka's *The Frog Prince Continued* (1991), the prince does not like being human, and he searches for a witch to turn him back into a frog.

Responding to Literature

Interpreting Cultural Literacy

In *The Great Gilly Hopkins* (Paterson 1978), Gilly reflects on Agnes, an irritating and somewhat disgusting classmate, and says to herself, "Alas, Agnes, the world is woefully short on frog smoochers" (p. 126). Explain what Gilly means by this statement. What might be the interpretation for readers who lack the needed cultural literacy?

Perhaps Scieszka's best work is the collection of fractured fairy tales titled *The Stinky Cheese Man: And Other Fairly Stupid Tales* (1992). The Stinky Cheese Man is made by a lonely old woman from stinky cheese. When she pulls him out of the oven, he runs away, but the little old woman and the little old man do not chase him. In fact, no one wants to chase him. They all run away from his funky smell! Other great stories in this collection include "Little Red Riding Shorts," "Cinderumpelstiltskin," and "Jack's Bean Problem." The author's humor permeates the book to the very end, where in small print on the copyright page he writes, "The illustrations are rendered in oil and vinegar. Anyone caught telling these fairly stupid tales will be visited, in person, by the Stinky Cheese Man."

Mike Thaler has also published several funny parodies of fairy tales. These include *Schmoe White and the Seven Dorfs* (1997), *Cinderella Bigfoot* (1997), and *Hanzel and Pretzel* (1997). Bobbi Salinas's bilingual book, *The Three Pigs / Los Tres Cerdos* (1998), is a hilarious version of the familiar tale, featuring Nacho, Tito, and Miguel as the three pigs.

 Responding to Literature

Drama

Children love to express themselves through drama, and fairy tales and literary fairy tales lend themselves especially well to this response. **Spontaneous reenactment** requires no props, costumes, or scripts, but it does require that children be very familiar with the story, so they can spontaneously become characters and recreate story events. Following are steps to prepare your children for dramatizing a story.

- Select one of the literary fairy tales in the preceding discussion and read it several times to your children.
- Divide the children into groups of three or four (depending on the number of characters in the story), and help members of each group decide which parts to take and how the story events will be sequenced.
- Allow each group to freely reenact the story.
- After the drama, have children evaluate themselves to determine if they can improve the next time.

Groups may take turns observing each other—although this kind of reenactment does not require an audience to be an enjoyable experience. Dramatizing promotes purposeful dialogue among children and helps them expand their responses to a story. In addition to bringing literature to life, drama helps children begin to view their own world from multiple perspectives (Schneider & Brindley 1997).

Animated Object Fantasy

When you were a child, did you talk to your dolls or stuffed animals? If so, did they answer? Many young children fantasize that their dolls and toys are real. Usually children do the talking for both themselves and their toys, but imagine what would happen if the toys could really talk! Authors of animated object fantasy stories bring to life inanimate objects such as a comical doll, a toy boat, a big machine, or a loving tree.

Most common in this category are talking toys, usually dolls or stuffed animals with the ability to move about. One of the earliest toy fantasy books was *The Adventures of Pinocchio: The Story of a Puppet* (1883), written by Carlo Lorenzini under the pen name of Carlo Collodi. The book was based on a traditional story Lorenzini heard while growing up in the village of Collodi, Italy. Pinocchio is a wooden puppet who is painstakingly carved by a kindly old man named Geppetto. The puppet comes to life; that is, he can talk and walk, but he wants to be a real flesh-and-blood boy. Because Pinocchio is lazy and selfish, he experiences many unhappy adventures, though the Blue Fairy saves him time and again. He is constantly dishonest, and his nose grows each time he lies. Eventually he learns to be honest, generous, and a hard worker, and the Blue Fairy turns him into a real boy.

The Tub People (Conrad 1989), like Pinocchio, are wooden toys: a doctor, policeman, grandmother, mother, father, child, and dog. They talk to one another, and each night they float and play in the bath water. The rest of the time, they stay lined up on the edge of the bathtub. When the Tub Child accidentally goes down the drain, it is some time before one of the big people rescues him.

A toy who yearns to be real is *The Velveteen Rabbit* (1922) by Margery Williams. A stuffed rabbit is given to a little boy as a Christmas gift, and he eventually becomes the little boy's constant companion. The stuffed rabbit can understand what humans say, and he can talk with the other nursery toys, but he is painfully aware that he is made only of cloth (which is becoming shabby), and he is not able to jump like real rabbits. The boy contracts scarlet fever, and when he recovers, the toy rabbit is put in a bag with contaminated sheets, bedclothes, and other things that must be burned. At this point readers fear that the rabbit may meet the same fate as Andersen's little fir tree—but nursery magic intervenes for a happy ending.

Leo Lionni presents a beautiful tale of two mice, a real one named Alexander and a toy one named Willy, in *Alexander and the Wind-Up Mouse* (1969). When Alexander makes friends with Willy, he is sad because Willy is loved and played with by the child. Alexander has experienced only screams and broom swats from humans. He asks the lizard wizard in the garden to change him into a toy mouse, so he can play and be loved like Willy. But before the moon becomes full and the spell can take effect, Alexander finds the toy mouse in a box of trash; Willy had been discarded when the child got new toys for her birthday. Alexander rushes back to the lizard wizard to ask if the magic can be used to make Willy into a real mouse instead.

A. A. Milne's classic book *Winnie-the-Pooh* (1926) began as bedtime stories for Milne's son, Christopher Robin. Christopher and the stuffed animals in his bedroom were the story characters: Winnie-the-Pooh (a naive but loving stuffed bear), Piglet, Kanga, Roo, Eeyore, Tigger, Rabbit, and Owl. The book and its sequel, *The House at Pooh Corner* (1928), contain episodic chapters that center on the antics of the stuffed animals. They live in the Hundred Acre Wood and act much like real animals. For example, Rabbit lives in a hole in the ground (though it does have furniture), and Winnie loves to eat honey. Today both books are available under one cover (Milne 1996).

Raggedy Ann, one of the most famous American toy fantasy characters, was created by cartoonist Johnny Gruelle in 1918 with *Raggedy Ann Stories*. The adventures of Raggedy Ann start when she first arrives in young Marcella's nursery. She takes the other dolls on a series of adventures that include saving the family dog from the dogcatcher. Because of her popularity Raggedy Ann was quickly merchandized in the form of a real cloth doll. Two years later Gruelle added the character of her twin brother, Raggedy Andy, to his new books. Both doll characters became known by their red-and-white-striped legs, red yarn hair, and shoe button eyes. Unfortunately, the original book contains some racial stereotypes that are unacceptable today.

Don Freeman's lovable *Corduroy* (1968) tells the story of a little stuffed bear in a large store. Corduroy has lost a button on his overalls. He goes through the store searching for his lost button, so he will look good enough for someone to buy. His heart's desire is met when Lisa buys him with the money from her piggy bank, brings him home, and sews on his lost button. In the sequel, *A Pocket for Corduroy* (1978), the toy bear again tries to add something to his wardrobe. This time he searches in a laundromat for a pocket for his overalls. He gets lost, but Lisa finds him and sews on a pocket.

 ## Responding to Literature

Writing Fantasy

When you were a child, did you have a favorite doll, stuffed animal, or other toy? Read a toy fantasy, and then write a story about your favorite toy's coming to life. Recreate the setting of your childhood in your story.

As a child, did you own a copy of *Scuffy the Tugboat* (Crampton 1946)? (My mother bought me one in the grocery store for a quarter.) Literally millions of copies of this book have been sold (*Publishers Weekly* 1995a). Scuffy, a little boy's toy boat, is bored floating in the bathtub. When taken outside, he floats away downstream to a large river that takes him into the sea. There he longs for the safety of his home and the little bathtub.

Animated dolls, stuffed animals, and toys have always been favorite subjects of fantasy stories. However, Virginia Lee Burton was a master at bringing larger inanimate objects to life, and her picture books are classics that remain in print. Main characters in her most memorable stories include a lovable steam shovel named Mary Anne in *Mike Mulligan and His Steam Shovel* (1939) and a naughty train engine in *Choo Choo: The Story of a Little Engine Who Ran Away* (1937).

Gertrude Crampton also wrote a best-selling book about a train engine. *Tootle* (1945) is a little engine who is in locomotive school. Like Burton's Choo Choo, he is willful, and he would much rather play in the meadow than stay on the tracks.

Shel Silverstein gives life to a lovely apple tree in *The Giving Tree* (1964). The tree loves the little boy, and he plays on and around her until he grows older. Then worldly things and money become the objects of his love. To meet his desires, the boy/man takes and takes from the selfless tree until there is nothing left of her but an old stump. When he is an old man, he returns to the tree, no more contented than when he left. Never does the boy/man say "thank you" in this story. Though this book has been enormously popular, I agree with Jane Yolen (Alter 1995) that it more rightly should be titled "The Taking Boy."

Silverstein animates imaginary objects in *The Missing Piece* (1976) and in the companion book *The Missing Piece Meets the Big O* (1981). With simple but appealing ink line drawings of circles, triangles, and Pac-Man-like characters, Silverstein depicts characters trying to find the right fit for a relationship to roll along through life. As in his other prose books, there is a story for children on one level and a message for adults on another. By providing some help, you can generate thought-provoking discussion among children about Silverstein's stories.

With similar characters but with a very different theme, Leo Lionni tells the story of *Little Blue and Little Yellow* (1959), blobs of color that are best friends. They live with their papas and mamas (who are bigger blobs). They have many friends to play games with, and they go to blob school together. One day, when Little Blue and Little Yellow hug too hard, they turn green, and neither set of parents recognizes them.

Responding to Literature

Puppets

Young children should be encouraged to retell favorite storybooks in their own words. A good way to do this is through simple puppets, such as the ones children make with small paper lunch bags they decorate with construction paper and crayon drawings. With the book *Little Blue and Little Yellow,* help your children retell the story with puppets. Divide the class into groups of four to play the parts of Little Blue, Little Yellow, the mothers, and the fathers. Two children can play the parts of both sets of parents by drawing the Blue parent on one side of the bag and the Yellow parent on the other. Similarly, the puppets for Little Blue and Little Yellow should be colored green on the back, so the children can turn the bag puppets around to show how they turned green when they hug too hard. It is important to remember that the children should retell the story in their own words while they act it out with the puppets.

Human with Fantasy Character

Some fantasy books have an ordinary human and a fantasy creature as main characters. The fantasy creature can be a monster, a strange beast, or even an element of nature.

In Mercer Mayer's *There's a Nightmare in My Closet* (1968), a young boy overcomes his fear of the monster in his closet by waiting for him one night and shooting him with a popgun. The boy ends up bringing the monster into bed with him to stop him from crying. (Be cautious if you plan to share this book with very young children to help them overcome their fears. A teacher told me that after she read it to her three-year-old son, he believed that not only was there a monster under his bed, but now there was one in his closet, too.)

When a boy tells a lie about eating a jar of cookies in *A Big Fat Enormous Lie* (Sharmat 1978), his lie comes alive in the form of a monster—who grows and grows until the boy tells the truth. Parents could use this book to talk with their children about the importance of telling the truth.

Another young boy finds himself facing a monster in *The Teacher from the Black Lagoon* (Thaler 1989). The title is a spoof on the old movie *The Creature from the Black Lagoon*. The teacher in this book does not come from a lagoon; rather, she shows up the first day of school as Mrs. Green, the boy's new teacher. She's a real monster (literally) with a long green snout and tail. Undoubtedly, this is *the* funniest picture book I have read. However, it may not be appropriate for very young children, as Mrs. Green is prone to munching children for discipline! This book is a great icebreaker on the first day of school. (It makes children wonder what *your* discipline program will be.)

Tomie dePaola's *Little Grunt and the Big Egg* (1990) has a prehistoric boy and a baby dinosaur as main characters. When Little Grunt finds the hatchling, he is allowed to keep it as a pet. The little dinosaur, George, becomes part of the Grunt family until he outgrows the cave and becomes a bit clumsy. He is sent away, but when a volcano threatens the Grunt clan, George returns to carry them to safety.

In *Flossie & the Fox* (McKissack 1986), a young girl carries a basket of fresh eggs to Miz Viola's, and she encounters a sly old fox along the way. Because Flossie has never seen a fox, she insists upon proof that he is what he says. Flossie skips all the way through the woods while the fox tries to convince her that he *is* a fox and she should be afraid of him. McKissack beautifully captures the language of the pre–Civil War South in her dialogue: "Flossie stopped. Then she turned and say 'I aine never seen a fox before. So, why should I be scared of you and I don't even-now know you a real fox for a fact?' "

Sometimes the fantasy creature is an element of nature, as in *My Life with the Wave* (Paz & Cowan 1997). On a boy's first trip to the seashore, a wave breaks away from the sea and joins him. The boy takes the wave home for a liquid pet, and she floods the house. At first the wave is playful and full of joy, but eventually her mood changes. With the onset of winter storms, she becomes unruly, and when she freezes into an icy statue, the boy and his father return her to the sea. Long after you finish reading, the intriguing illustrations can keep you engrossed in searching for the many hidden figures and images. Careful observers will find a very small mouse in each illustration. Sometimes the mouse has a bodily form, as when it is paddling a little canoe or riding a tiny surfboard in the background; at other times it appears as an image in the sand or a hole in the cloud. Other characters and images to search for include a cat, a dog, a whale, and a sea horse, all of which can be found in most of the illustrations.

The wind is a popular element for fantasy characters. In *Mirandy and Brother Wind* (McKissack 1988), Mirandy wants to catch Brother Wind so he will be her partner in the junior cakewalk, but he skillfully eludes her. In *Old Hannibal and the Hurricane* (Amos 1991), Matt and Sophie help Old Hannibal launch the *Sally Sue* as he describes his encounter with Bellowing Bertha, a hurricane of tremendous fame. Arnold Lobel tells of an afternoon when happy people are walking and talking in the countryside until the fierce rushing wind blows to earth and turns everything upside down, inside out, and topsy-turvy in *The Turnaround Wind* (1988). Starting on page 10, each illustration represents two scenes. The first shows a character setting out for a walk (when the book is held right side up). The second shows the chaotic aftermath of the Turnaround Wind, appearing only when the book is held upside down. Searching the illustrations for details can help children sharpen their visual acuity.

James and the Giant Peach by Roald Dahl (1961) has some of the most memorable characters in children's literature. With the help of magic green crystals, James escapes his hideous, cruel aunts by sailing away inside an enormous peach. He is accompanied by friendly giant insects: Old-Green-Grasshopper, Miss Spider, Ladybug, Centipede, Earthworm, Silkworm, and Glow-worm. When they are threatened by sharks, 502 seagulls carry them through the air with threads spun by Miss Spider and Silkworm. They land in New York City, where they are warmly received.

Extraordinary Person

Not all fantasy books contain fantasy creatures. Sometimes the characters are humans who are preposterous or extraordinary in some way, such as possessing strange powers or unusual size.

Miniature Humans. The idea of miniature beings has always fascinated children, and there are many good books with miniature human characters. Folklore contains stories of diminutive people, such as "Tom Thumb." However, *Thumbelina* by Hans Christian Andersen (Andersen & Haugaard 1997) was one of the earliest fiction stories about a tiny person. A childless woman goes to a fairy and asks for a child. The fairy gives her a seed, and when the woman plants and cultivates it, it grows into a plant with a beautiful flower. When the flower opens, out pops a very tiny maiden about half the size of the woman's thumb. When Thumbelina is kidnapped by a horrible toad, she embarks on misadventures that culminate in her finding a group of flower people her own size.

Mary Norton's *The Borrowers* (1952) and its sequels have captivated children for several decades. Pod, Homily, and Arrietty Clock are a family of tiny people no more than two inches tall. They live beneath the floorboards of a quiet country house in England, and they outfit their living quarters as well as meeting their other needs by "borrowing" things from the big people. The Borrowers are quite resourceful in the way they recycle trinkets and bits of household objects into clothing, tools, and furnishings. One day the boy of the house spots Arrietty, and the Clock family's adventures begin.

The characters in John Peterson's series about *The Littles* (1967) are a group of tiny people only a few inches tall who live in the Biggs house. The Littles look like humans in every way except for their size and their mouselike tails. These factors become a problem when the house's new residents bring a cat.

In one famous setting, it is the regular-size human who is the novelty. Margaret Hodges's *Gulliver in Lilliput* (1995) is an adaptation of Jonathan Swift's classic story of the Englishman, Lemuel Gulliver, who is shipwrecked in Lilliput, a land of people only six inches high.

In *George Shrinks* (Joyce 1985), George's parents leave the house early, and while he is still asleep, he dreams he is very small. When he wakes up, he finds it is true! Despite his size, George comically tries to take care of his "little" brother and complete all the tasks his parents have assigned him for the day. When he unwraps a package in the mail and finds a toy airplane, he flies it over the house and into his bedroom window. The family cat swipes the airplane wing, causing it to crash land on George's bed. When it appears the cat is going to eat him, George pops back to his regular size—just before his parents arrive home. In case you were thinking it was all a dream, the author shows the damaged toy airplane in the last three illustrations after George has returned to full size.

William Steig presents a similar theme in *The Toy Brother* (1996). When Magnus Bede, the famous alchemist, and his wife go on a journey, their older son, Yorick, sneaks into his father's lab. In the course of attempting to find a potion to change donkey dung into solid gold, Yorick accidentally makes himself shrink to about two inches. The younger brother, Charles, whom Yorick has always mistreated, enjoys his new power; however, Charles tries to make a potion to reverse the process.

Younger siblings are often frustrated with their inability to do things their older siblings do. In *I'll Fix Anthony* (1969) Judith Viorst depicts a younger brother who believes that he will grow bigger, stronger, and smarter but his big brother, Anthony, will remain the same. This book and *The Toy Brother* could be used with younger siblings to help them deal with the frustrations of being smaller.

Flying People. In fantasy stories people sometimes possess extraordinary powers, such as the ability to fly. These stories are exciting for young children, who often fantasize about flying. In *Abuela* (Dorros 1991) a young girl is feeding a flock of birds in the park with her grandmother. She imagines that the birds pick her up and she can fly. Her grandmother joins her, and they fly over and around New York City.

A similar theme and setting is found in *Tar Beach* (Ringgold 1991), which takes place in New York in 1939. An 8-year-old girl can fly when she thinks about "somewhere to go that you can't get to any other way." From the tar rooftop of her Harlem apartment building, she flies over the buildings of New York City. She especially likes flying over the George Washington Bridge, which she claims as her own.

Bertie, who is overweight because he eats only chocolate bars, seeks a magic potion that will make him lighter in *Pie Magic* (Forward 1995). Unfortunately, the potion does not make him smaller; it just makes him weightless, and he floats around like a cloud. The magical English nanny in *Mary Poppins* (Travers 1934) defies gravity in various ways. The wind lifts her parrot-headed umbrella and carries her to the Banks household. She levitates to have tea, slides up the banister, and flies around the world in two minutes, along with many other magical feats.

Talking with Animals. What would our pets tell us if they could talk? The ability to talk with animals is a coveted power. A human character who fluently speaks with all animals is the good country doctor in Hugh Lofting's *The Story of Doctor Dolittle* (1920) and *The Voyages of Doctor Dolittle* (1922). In the first book the doctor sails to Africa to treat an epidemic among the monkeys. In the sequel Dolittle and friends journey to Spidermonkey Island in the tropical seas to search for a missing colleague. Karen Hesse also creates a memorable character in 14-year-old Mila in *The Music of Dolphins* (1996). A feral child is discovered on an unpopulated island, where she has spent the last ten years living with the dolphins who saved her after a wreck at sea. Mila is able to speak with her dolphin family, and she greatly prefers her life among the dolphins to what she experiences living among humans.

Extraordinary Abilities. Fantasy characters possess many other extraordinary abilities. The outrageous and incorrigible 9-year-old in *Pippi Longstocking* (Lindgren 1950) has superhuman strength. For example, she carries her horse outside every morning, and she carries away two annoying police officers (one in each hand). Pippi often uses her strength and eccentric attitude to make fun of adults. The little girl in *Matilda* (Dahl 1988) uses telekinesis and her genius intellect to annoy and scare off people who are unkind to the schoolchildren.

Another unforgettable character from Roald Dahl is the eccentric Willy Wonka in *Charlie and the Chocolate Factory* (1964). Charlie and other children meet Willie Wonka, creator of the famous and magical chocolate factory that produces the world's greatest candy delights. However, great perils await undeserving children who enter the factory. In *Sideways Stories from Wayside School*, Louis Sachar (1978) devotes one short chapter to each of the thirty children in the classroom on the top floor of Wayside School. Each is a funny and bizarre tale of unusual children with an unusual teacher in a very unusual school—which was accidentally built sideways, resulting in a building with thirty floors of one classroom each.

Natalie Babbitt's *Tuck Everlasting* (1975) leaves readers pondering if they would want to live forever. The Tuck family unknowingly drank water from a spring that prevents them from ever growing older. Every ten years, the family of four meets at the secret spring in a secluded wood. In the 1880s they are observed by 10-year-old Winnie Foster when she is exploring the woods near her house. She learns about their terrible secret, so they prevent her from returning to her home, fearing the ill that would come to the world if anyone else drank from the magic spring.

Picture books with extraordinary humans include Dr. Seuss's *Daisy-Head Mayzie* (1994), in which young Mayzie McGrew has a flower growing from the top of her head. Chris Van Allsburg's *The Sweetest Fig* (1993) is a story of a man whose dreams literally come true. Unfortunately for him, his mistreated dog acquires the same power. Dav Pilkey created a hilarious character in *The Adventures of Captain Underpants: An Epic Novel* (1997). Two boys hypnotize their principal into thinking he is a superhero—Captain Underpants. When he is put under a spell, he tears off all his clothes except his briefs, yanks off his toupee, ties a red curtain around his neck, and jumps out the school window singing "Tra-la-laaaa!"—his battle cry as he goes out to fight evil forces such as the nefarious Dr. Diaper or the voracious Talking Toilets. (From my experience, do not show this book to a principal; she will want to throw *it* out the school window!)

Enchanted Journey

Many of the classic fantasy stories are **enchanted journeys.** The story begins in the real world, but the main character is soon transported to another world, which is often an enchanted realm. The characters enter the fantasy world by some type of magic. At the end of the story, the protagonist usually returns to the real world, but it is not always by the same manner in which she or he left.

Journey to Fantasyland. *Alice's Adventures in Wonderland* by Lewis Carroll (1865) is perhaps the earliest example of an enchanted journey to a fantasyland. Alice is sitting on the riverbank with her sister when a big white rabbit runs past, talking to himself. When he pops down a large rabbit hole, Alice follows him and floats down a long passageway to Wonderland. She experiences many bizarre situations, such as changing sizes and swimming in her own tears, and she meets equally bizarre characters, including the Cheshire Cat, the Mad Hatter, the Mock Turtle, the Queen of Hearts, and the deck of cards that comes to life. Alice returns to the real world when her older sister awakens her.

L. Frank Baum's *The Wonderful Wizard of Oz* (1900) was the first modern fantasy novel for children that was written by an American. It begins in Kansas when Dorothy's house is lifted into the air by a cyclone (tornado). When it lands, Dorothy and her dog, Toto, find themselves in the Land of Oz. She desperately wants to return home to her family. The little munchkins advise her to find the great wizard in the wonderful Emerald City of Oz. Along her way, she meets the brainless Scarecrow, the Tin Woodsman, and the Cowardly Lion. Though the wizard turns out to be a humbug, the good witch Glenda tells Dorothy she can return home by clicking the heels of her silver slippers and saying, "Take me home to Aunt Em!" Dorothy finds herself back home in front of the farmhouse Uncle Henry had rebuilt after the storm. Baum wrote thirteen more books about adventures in the Land of Oz.

The beloved story of Peter Pan, the boy who would not grow up, was written first as a play and later as a book by the Scottish novelist and dramatist Sir James Matthew Barrie. Wendy, John, and Michael Darling are children living in London when Peter Pan persuades them to return with him to Neverland, a place where chil-

Wendy sews on Peter's shadow. From *Peter Pan,* written by J. M. Barrie and illustrated by Diane Goode.

dren never grow up. With a little fairy dust, the children fly off to Neverland with Peter and his fairy Tinker Bell, so Wendy can tell stories to the six Lost Boys. During their stay the children encounter the evil pirate Captain Hook, a hungry crocodile, and the Indian Princess Tiger Lily. The Lost Boys beg Wendy to stay and be their mother, but she and her brothers fly back to London and take the boys along instead. Mr. and Mrs. Darling are so happy to have their children back that they adopt the Lost Boys. Peter Pan, however, refuses the offer, saying, "I don't want to go to school and learn solemn things. I don't want to be a man. I want always to be a boy and have fun" (Barrie & Goode 1983, p. 64). (Have you ever known anyone like that?)

Barrie's original *Peter Pan and Wendy* (1906) deals with two serious themes, the retention of childhood innocence and the feminine instinct for motherhood. If you read the book as a child, I encourage you to read it again and look for the messages Barrie included for adults. Be certain to read the original unabridged edition, such as the one published by Viking Press in 1991. For younger children, Diane Goode beautifully illustrated an abridged and adapted version in 1983.

Norton Juster's *The Phantom Tollbooth* (1961) is likely the most brilliant and hilarious work of satire, irony, and double entendre the world of children's literature has known. The protagonist is Milo, a boy who is utterly bored with life. When a box containing a magic tollbooth appears in his room, he puts it together and drives his small electric automobile through. He enters a land full of strange characters and settings, masterpieces of puns and wordplay. In the Kingdom of Wisdom, one can visit the area of the Doldrums, the city of Dictionopolis, the Forest of Sight, the Foothills of Confusion, the Mountains of Ignorance, the Castle in the Air (where the twin princesses Rhyme and Reason are imprisoned), and the Sea of Knowledge, where the Island of Conclusions is located. (One gets there by jumping.)

Milo meets Tock the watchdog (who has a watch for a body) and Humbug the lovable bug, who accompany him in his travels. When Milo visits the King, he learns of the accomplishments of the King's cabinet members.

> "The duke here can make mountains out of molehills. The minister splits hairs. The count makes hay while the sun shines. The earl leaves no stone unturned. And the undersecretary," he finished ominously, "hangs by a thread. Can't you do anything at all?" (p. 85)

Another example of Juster's linguistic ingenuity is his description of the menacing demon Threadbare Excuse, who was

> a small, pathetic figure whose clothes were worn and tattered and who mumbled the same things again and again, in a low but piercing voice: "Well, I've been sick—but the page was torn out—I missed the bus—but no one *else* did it—well, I've been sick. . . . " (p. 239)

Milo eventually says goodbye to his friends and returns home the same way he came. The next day, the tollbooth is gone—off to awaken another lazy mind.

There are also excellent picture books of enchanted journeys. In *Where the Wild Things Are* (Sendak 1963), Max is reprimanded for his wild behavior and sent to his room. There a forest grows up with an ocean tumbling by, and Max sails to the land of the Wild Things. When he gets lonely, he sails back the way he came to his bedroom. In case you are thinking his enchanted journey was a dream, Maurice Sendak shows the passage of time by the moon first seen through the bedroom window. When Max leaves, it is a quarter moon; when he returns, it is a full moon.

A Sendak book that can be explained as a dream is *In the Night Kitchen* (1970). When Mickey is awakened by noise in the night, he falls off his bed and into the comic baker's kitchen (sans clothing). The frontal nudity in the illustrations gained Sendak criticism. (I even saw a copy in a public library where someone had colored dark breeches on the boy!) However, Mickey's fanciful journey delights young children as he travels from the batter to an airplane he makes out of dough to the giant milk bottle where he obtains the cup of milk the bakers need to finish the batter. Mickey slides down the milk bottle and lands in his bed, thus ending his journey to the Night Kitchen.

Completing Sendak's trilogy of enchanted journey books is *Outside Over There* (1981). A young girl discovers that goblins have stolen her baby sister when the icy changeling they left in her place begins to melt. She crawls outside her bedroom window backward, falling "outside over there," and is therefore unable to follow the faceless goblins. After hearing a mystical message from her father, who is away at sea, she tumbles "right side round" and lands in the goblin's cave. She destroys the goblins by playing her wonder horn, recovers her baby sister, and follows the stream home to her waiting mother.

In *Hey Al* (Yorinks 1986), Al the janitor and his faithful dog Eddie are totally miserable in their dingy Manhattan West Side apartment until a large mysterious bird takes them on a journey to a paradise island in the sky. However, they return home when their comfortable paradise existence threatens to turn them into birds as well.

In *The Polar Express* by Chris Van Allsburg (1985), a boy is awakened by the sound of a train in his front yard on Christmas Eve. He runs outside and catches the Polar Express, a train carrying children to the North Pole. After a trip with fabulous sights, the children meet Santa, who selects the boy to receive the first gift of Christmas. The boy asks for a silver bell from Santa's sleigh, and he is then returned home on the Polar Express; however, he loses his bell on the way. In the morning, the boy finds the silver bell in a small box behind the Christmas tree, but only those who truly believe in Santa can hear its beautiful sound.

Responding to Literature

Story Boxes

A concrete way to respond to literature is with a **story box** (Tompkins & McGee 1993), also called a jackdaw (after the bird that collect trinkets). To make a story box, gather or make things that represent the events, images, characters, or topics of a story or poem and place them in a shoebox. For example, a story box for *The Polar Express* could contain a bedroom slipper, a toy train, a jingle bell, and some Christmas wrapping. Write the title of the book and the names of the author or poet and illustrator on paper taped to the lid of the box. You may also choose to decorate the title paper with a motif from the story. When your children look at the contents, they can make predictions as to what the book is about. If they have already read the book, they should be able to recall the story by looking at the various objects.

In another Van Allsburg book, *Jumanji* (1981), Judy and Peter experience a reverse enchanted journey. Playing a mystical board game they find in the park results in their house's being transformed into an exotic jungle that includes a roaring lion, destructive monkeys, and an erupting volcano. Each turn of play plunges them from one perilous predicament into another, but only by finishing the game can they restore their house to normal.

Sometimes an enchanted journey is experienced through a story the narrator is recalling. In *Cloudy with a Chance of Meatballs* (Barrett 1978), Grandpa tells his grandchildren about a faraway town called Chewandswallow. The residents did not have to buy and prepare food because the sky supplied all the food they wanted, three times a day. For example, it rained soup and juice, snowed mashed potatoes, and stormed hamburgers. One day the food and portions started getting larger. When they became gigantic, the people glued together giant pieces of stale bread with peanut butter and sailed on these rafts to a new land.

An enchanted journey can even be taken with a vivid imagination. Edward likes to read all kinds of books in *Edward and the Pirates* (McPhail 1997), but his favorite is adventure stories. One night Edward is reading an old book about lost pirate treasure when he suddenly finds his bed surrounded by fierce pirates who want to use his book to find their treasure. Threats and a battle ensue, and Edward's parents come to his aid (in the guise of story heroes). In the end the pirates find they cannot use the book because they do not know how to read, so Edward reads it to them.

Journey to the Historical Past. An enchanted journey can take the protagonist from the modern world to a real time in the historical past. Such a book is Jane Yolen's *The Devil's Arithmetic* (1988). Hannah resents the traditions of her Jewish heritage. During a long Seder ceremony in her grandfather's apartment, she is asked to perform the ritual of opening the door for Elijah. When she does, she has opened a door in time that places her in the middle of a small Jewish village in Nazi-occupied Poland. Because the time-travel door closes behind her, she must follow the inevitable course of history, which takes her to a concentration camp. How Hannah reenters her own time makes for a gripping and unforgettable story.

A similar journey takes place in *The Orphan of Ellis Island* by Elvira Woodruff (1997). Dominic Cantori is an orphan who takes a trip with his fifth-grade class to Ellis Island, and he accidentally gets left behind. Trying to call for help, he picks up a display telephone that connects him to an old Italian immigrant who talks to him about his life in Italy. The voice lulls Dominic to sleep, and when he awakes, he is in the old man's beautiful Italian village in the year 1908. There he suffers the hunger and abuse that the other village orphans experience, and he emigrates with them when they sail for America in the crowded, filthy, stinking steerage compartment of a ship. During the difficult voyage Dominic finds proof that one of the orphans traveling with him is his great-grandfather! He falls asleep while waiting in a long line at Ellis Island, and he awakes back in his own time. However, an artifact in a museum display case lets him know it was not a dream.

In *The Castle in the Attic,* Elizabeth Winthrop (1985) spins a tale of 10-year-old William, who receives an old, realistic-looking miniature castle from his beloved housekeeper, Mrs. Phillips. He accidentally brings to life the miniature knight, Sir Simon. Together with a magic token, they manage to shrink the housekeeper, who must then stay in the castle with Sir Simon. When William allows himself to be shrunk, he finds he is in a real castle in the Middle Ages. However, he must battle a fiery dragon and an evil wizard before he can find the means to return Mrs. Phillips and himself to their own world.

In Jon Scieszka's typical style, he has created a zany series of books called the Time Warp Trio. Three wacky boys—Joe, Sam, and Fred—travel both back and forward in time by means of Joe's magical blue book. The mixture of adventure, comedy, and hocus-pocus makes for fast reading. In the first book, *Knights of the Kitchen Table* (1991), the boys end up in King Arthur's court with a fire-breathing dragon, a belligerent knight, and a vile-smelling giant. They must locate the magical blue book before they can be transported back to their own time. Scieszka does much research for each book in the series, so in addition to being hilarious, the books include historical details, interesting facts, and even some basic math and physics.

 Responding to Literature

Dialogue Response Journals

One way to combine children's responses to literature with writing is to keep a **dialogue response journal** with each of your children. In these journals you and the children conduct a written conversation about what they are reading. You read and respond to each entry. (This works particularly well when both you and the child are reading the same book.) One entry a week is generally appropriate for younger children, but older children may write several times a week or even daily. It is important for the child to select the topic of each entry, or else it becomes an essay exam. To achieve maximum expression of ideas, do not correct grammar and spelling. **Invented spelling,** in which children spell words the way they sound, needs to be encouraged. (See Box 3.2 for examples.) Children can write their true ideas rather than limiting themselves to words they can spell correctly. Response journals can also be kept between two children.

High Fantasy

Colorful adventure, enchantment, and heroism are the hallmarks of **high fantasy** (Colbath 1971). The protagonist in high fantasy engages in a monumental struggle against a powerful evil force in the ageless struggle of good and evil. Like enchanted journeys, they may begin in the real world, or the **primary world**, but the major setting in high fantasy is a self-contained fictional world that is inhabited by imaginary creatures and has its own time frame. These settings are called **secondary worlds.** The setting typically has an aura of medieval times because writers have often drawn from mythology and legends for their characters and settings. In high fantasy books the author develops the secondary world in detail, describing the history, dress, housing, lifestyles, language, and occupations of the inhabitants. Creators of high fantasy, such as those I'll feature here, frequently write a series of books in order to develop their secondary worlds and its inhabitants in depth (Goforth 1998).

J. R. R. Tolkien and the Lord of the Rings. J. R. R. Tolkien is the writer of high fantasy against whom all other writers in the field are measured (Donelson & Nilsen 1997). The secondary world he created in his stories, Middle-earth, has been used as a touchstone for all who write high fantasy. Tolkien was a professor at Oxford University in England, specializing in Anglo-Saxon and medieval literature. His scholarship is evident in the cycle of fantasy books that were launched with *The Hobbit*

(1937), which grew out of bedtime stories Tolkien told his children. This book was the gateway to his celebrated Lord of the Rings trilogy. The trilogy is a sophisticated, complex epic and quite lengthy, making it more suitable for adolescents.

Even *The Hobbit* is a challenging read for most elementary children. However, I recommend it for advanced readers who are bored with other books. The story is an adventurous quest set in Middle-earth, which is inhabited by mythical creatures such as hobbits, dwarves, elves, trolls, goblins, the wizard Gandalf, the dragon Smaug, and the disgusting creature Gollum. The protagonist, Bilbo Baggins, is a typical hobbit about three feet tall. Like other hobbits in the Shire, he is plump and has very large and hairy feet that do not require shoes. Bilbo embarks on a quest to help the dwarves, and he confronts the great dragon Smaug—the terror of the countryside. He returns home with a priceless magic ring that makes the wearer invisible.

C. S. Lewis and the Chronicles of Narnia. C. S. Lewis wrote his Narnia series specifically for children, though adult readers likely understand more of the Christian symbolism that he wove into the books. The land of Narnia gets its magic from the majestic lion, Aslan, who is the Lord of the Wood and the son of the great Emperor-Beyond-the-Sea. Unlike the typical heroes of high fantasy, the protagonists of these chronicles are children from earth. They magically make the crossing between our world and the secondary world of Narnia by Aslan's bidding.

The first book to be published was *The Lion, the Witch and the Wardrobe* (Lewis 1950). Four siblings enter Narnia through a magical wardrobe. Lucy, Edmund, Susan, and Peter find themselves in a mystical land that is under an evil spell: It is always winter, but never Christmas. The children battle the White Witch to rescue the talking beasts of Narnia; meanwhile, the majestic Aslan is drawing near, causing the spell to weaken. Father Christmas arrives, followed by the melting of snow and ice. However, Edmund has crossed over to the side of the White Witch. By the law of the Deep Magic, the White Witch has the right to kill him, but Aslan forgives Edmund and takes on his cruel punishment. The children are despondent when Aslan dies—but the next morning, by the working of the Deeper Magic Before the Dawn of Time, he is resurrected, and the White Witch is defeated.

When Lewis wrote *The Lion*, he probably did not intend to write a series of books. So as he continued to write others one by one, the stories were not in chronological order. Therefore, if you plan to read them all, Lewis recommended that you read them in the order of Narnian chronology, rather than the order in which they were published. The proper sequence follows.

1. *The Magician's Nephew* (1955)
2. *The Lion, the Witch and the Wardrobe* (1950)
3. *The Horse and His Boy* (1954)
4. *Prince Caspian* (1951)
5. *The Voyage of the "Dawn Treader"* (1952)
6. *The Silver Chair* (1953)
7. *The Last Battle* (1956)

Notice that *The Magician's Nephew* is the **prequel** (book that takes place at a time before the action of the preexisting work) to *The Lion, the Witch and the Wardrobe*. It tells how Narnia came to be and how the evil witch entered the land. It explains why the wardrobe was a passageway from earth to Narnia and why the professor was not surprised by the children's story. It even explains the presence of the lamppost in the middle of the wood.

To fully enjoy the series, I recommend that you acquire *A Book of Narnians: The Lion, the Witch and the Others*, compiled by James Riordan (1994) and magnificently illustrated by Pauline Baynes, whose drawings adorn each book in the Chronicles as well. *A Book of Narnians* devotes one or two full-color pages to each of the Narnian creatures—Aslan, the White Witch, Doctor Cornelius, Eustace the Dragon, Puddleglum, the Centaurs, and others. In addition to the illustrations, a brief narrative sets each character in the context of the Narnian stories. At the end of the book, there is a short description of each character arranged alphabetically, a summary of each book, a map of Narnia and the surrounding countries, and a time line of Narnian history.

I find it interesting that Charles Dodgson (Lewis Carroll), J. R. R. Tolkien, and C. S. Lewis were all professors at Oxford University in England. Dodgson was a professor of mathematics in the mid-1800s; Tolkien and Lewis were contemporaries in the mid-1900s, and both were scholars of English literature.

Lloyd Alexander and the Prydain Chronicles. The books of Lloyd Alexander are also outstanding high fantasy for children. In his five books about the secondary world of Prydain, Alexander developed engaging and memorable characters and situations that are heavily drawn from the ancient Welsh legends known as the *Mabinogion*. The books in the Prydain Chronicles include *The Book of Three* (1964), *The Black Cauldron* (1965), *The Castle of Llyr* (1966), *The Taran Wanderer* (1967), and *The High King* (1968).

The Book of Three introduces the series and the character Taran, a boy of unknown parentage who is a ward of the wise sorcerer Dalben. Taran works as an assistant pig-keeper, but he longs to be a hero. He joins Prince Gwydion in the struggle to save Prydain from the forces of evil marshaled by the Arawn Death-Lord and his deathless warriors, the Cauldron-Born. Taran dreams of winning the love of the fearless Princess Eilonwy, who possesses magical powers. In the final book, *The High King*, Taran achieves ultimate victory over the army of the dead after a mighty clash, and the Death-Lord is vanquished. But it is his own struggle and sacrifice that save Taran from destruction, not magic.

Susan Cooper and The Dark Is Rising. Susan Cooper borrowed concepts from Celtic, Welsh, and Arthurian legends when she wrote the series known as The Dark Is Rising. The protagonist, Will Stanton, learns on his eleventh birthday that he is the last of the Old Ones destined to battle the evil forces of the Dark. He recognizes that he is endowed with strange powers, including a release from the hold of ordinary time. He is able to travel back to earlier centuries on earth and to mystical lands. Will is entrusted with the quest to unite the six magical Signs of Light that will enable the Old Ones to triumph over the Dark. Books in the series include *Over Sea, under Stone* (1966), *The Dark Is Rising* (1973), *The Grey King* (1975), *Greenwitch* (1976), and *Silver on the Tree* (1977).

 ## Responding to Literature

Art

After reading the first book in a high fantasy series, draw a picture of what you think the secondary world looks like. For ideas reread some of the early chapters in which the author describes the fantasy world.

Storybox
Supernatural Fantasy

Supernatural fantasy explores the possibilities offered by the supernatural—for example, by beings that exist outside the natural world (such as ghosts) or by powers that go beyond natural forces (such as telepathy).

Supernatural Powers. The wild success of J. K. Rowling's series of books on Harry Potter, the boy wizard, clearly demonstrates children's (and adults') fascination with supernatural powers. Each Harry Potter book has soared to the top of the *New York Times* best-seller list and stayed there—the first book in the series stayed for more than two years! However, great controversy surrounds this series, and you can read about it in Box 5.1.

In *Harry Potter and the Sorcerer's Stone* (Rowling 1998), when Harry turns 11, he is informed by a lovable giant that his parents were not killed in a car wreck, as he had been told by his wretched muggle aunt and uncle. Harry's mother was a witch and his father a wizard. Both were murdered by a sorcerer of such evil magnitude that his name cannot be spoken; however, as an infant, Harry survived the attack. Harry is called to Hogwarts School of Witchcraft and Wizardry to receive his formal training. Nearly all of the wizard masters and wizards-in-training are in awe of Harry, because he is the only person ever to survive an attack by the unspeakable Lord Voldemort, master of the Dark Arts. However, there are enemies at the school who want Harry to fail. The series is a humorous look at witchcraft and wizardry, and it pokes fun at the English boarding school system as well. The following excerpt is from a scene in Charms class, where the students are learning how to make objects fly.

"Now, don't forget that nice wrist movement we've been practicing!" squeaked Professor Flitwick, perched on top of his pile of books as usual. "Swish and flick, remember, swish and flick. And saying the magic words properly is very important, too—never forget Wizard Baruffio, who said 's' instead of 'f' and found himself on the floor with a buffalo on his chest."

Box 5.1

Censorship and *Harry Potter*

by Jenifer Jasinski Schneider

Although children (and adults) all over the world have fallen in love with the Harry Potter stories, the books have been the target of one of the most visible and widely reported censorship/anticensorship campaigns in children's literature. And despite varying opinions on the literary merits of the Potter series, these books have forced many children, parents, educators, and communities to examine and take a stand on issues of censorship.

The story lines of Harry Potter books deal with good versus evil, wizardry and witchcraft, magic, and adventure. Consequently, although they are lauded by elementary children, they are simultaneously the target of strong opposition from some people. For example, one critic wrote:

> Hidden in the . . . pages of the Harry Potter books is a very dangerous main theme. Harry . . . a nerdy, family-less, abused, unhappy, 11 year old kid discovers he is actually a powerful wizard and leaves his adoptive home to attend a school of witchcraft and wizardry. Here he finds new life, success, friendship and that he has great powers (wizardry) within him that can

be used to gain victory and respect in his life. To suggest to any child (especially underprivileged ones like Harry) that there is a way to escape the unhappy, real-life world they live in and retreat into a mystical fantasy world to find happiness is totally irresponsible and deceitful. To then suggest that the world of the occult (witchcraft) can be the power that can make it all happen is in fact evil and ultimately a lie. (Family Friendly Libraries 2000)

In response to ideas such as these, the "Muggles for Harry Potter" campaign emerged. Several groups of "muggles" (i.e., regular nonmagical humans) banded together to fight censorship of the Potter series. Specifically, their purpose is to "support kids, parents and teachers who are fighting school officials and others who want to ban classroom 'read alouds' of Potter books and other controversial works, remove the books from library shelves and otherwise restrict their use" (American Booksellers Foundation for Free Expression 2000). You may visit the campaign's website at http://www.mugglesforharrypotter.org.

It was very difficult. Harry and Seamus swished and flicked, but the feather they were supposed to be sending skyward just lay on the desktop. Seamus got so impatient that he prodded it with his wand and set fire to it—Harry had to put it out with his hat. (p. 171)

J. K. Rowling plans to publish one book for each of Harry's seven years at Hogwarts. Already in print are *Harry Potter and the Sorcerer's Stone* (1998), *Harry Potter and the Chamber of Secrets* (1999), *Harry Potter and the Prisoner of Azkaban* (1999), and *Harry Potter and the Goblet of Fire* (2000). Even two of Harry's Hogwarts textbooks are available: *Fantastic Beasts and Where to Find Them* by Newt Scamander (2001) and *Quidditch through the Ages* by Kennilworthy Whisp (2001). Both textbook authors are pseudonyms for J. K. Rowling, of course. Fans of Harry Potter should be able to identify the unique names and terms in the wizardspeak activity on page 138. (A few answers are found in this text.)

Literature Activity: **Wizardspeak**

How good is your Harry Potter "wizardspeak"? Match the following words to their definitions. Answers are available at **www.ablongman.com/anderson.**

1. Bertie Botts		A.	Harry's mean nonwizard relatives
2. Dursleys		B.	Harry's best friend
3. Hagrid		C.	Giant-size gamekeeper of school grounds
4. Hedwig		D.	The evil wizard who killed Harry's parents
5. Hogsmeade		E.	The School of Witchcraft and Wizardry
6. Hogwarts		F.	An all-wizard village near school
7. Lord Voldemort		G.	Station track where students board the express train to school
8. Muggles		H.	Harry's pet owl and courier
9. Nearly Headless Nick		I.	The school's mischievous poltergeist
10. Peeves		J.	The resident ghost of Harry's dorm
11. Platform 9¾		K.	Nonmagical people
12. Quidditch		L.	A wizard sport with four balls, played on flying brooms
13. Ron Weasley		M.	The brand name for every-flavor candy beans ■

Another light look at wizardry is *Pet-rified!* (1997) by Dean Marney. When someone moves into the spooky house next door to Becky, strange things begin to happen to her neighborhood. The plants on her block suddenly start growing into a tropical rain forest, and the pets are *pet*rified into things that look like plastic lawn ornaments. The wizard version of Doctor Jekyll and Mr. Hyde is responsible, and he has worse things in store for the neighborhood.

A variety of magic tales are contained in *Bruce Coville's Book of Magic: Tales to Cast a Spell on You* (1996). Children can read short stories by eleven authors, including Bruce Coville's "Wizard's Boy" and Jane Yolen's "Phoenix Farm."

Some supernatural powers are passed down from parents to children for generations. Such is the case with *In the Eye of the Tornado* (Levithan 1998). After the death of their parents, Adam and Stieg Atwood fulfill their destiny to use the supernatural power that has been in their family for countless generations. The Atwoods are able to foretell meteorological disasters, and their destiny is to try to save people from these disasters. The government knows that "he who controls the weather, controls the world," and Agent Taggert pursues them—as he pursued their parents, which led to their deaths in the eye of a tornado.

Communication with Spirits. Communicating with spirits or ghosts is a common motif of supernatural fantasy. Rarely do you find picture books in this category, but White Deer of Autumn's *Ceremony—in the Circle of Life* (1983) is one. Nine-year-old Little Turtle is a Native American boy who has grown up completely in the mainstream of a large city. In his loneliness and deep sorrow, he is visited by Star Spirit, and the walls in his room become the Earth and Sky. Star Spirit tells him, "I am from a long time past, yet I live today. I have traveled from the Seven Dancing Stars to teach you what many of Earth's people have forgotten" (p. 6). Star Spirit teaches Little Turtle about the Circle of Life, the animals that live in the wild, and the Pipe Ceremony. After offering prayers to the four directions, Star Spirit returns him to his home in the city.

Behind the Attic Wall (1983) by Sylvia Cassedy is a serious and compelling story about spirits. When 12-year-old Maggie—orphaned, rejected, and expelled from boarding school—goes to live with her two great-aunts in their gloomy ancestral home, she hears mysterious voices. She searches for the source and in a closet discovers a hidden panel that leads to stairs to the attic. There, shockingly, she finds china dolls inhabited by the spirits of Maggie's ancestors, who built the great house. Maggie frequently visits the dolls, Timothy John, Miss Cristabel, and their dog Juniper, who are forever locked in the time when they tragically died in a fire. She grows to love them, and they are her family. The ending is bittersweet and can move readers to tears.

In some supernatural fantasy books, spirits are in the form of angels. In *Answer My Prayer* (Hite 1995), Ebol became an angel when he gave up his life to save another passenger on a sinking ship. He is assigned to help Lydia Swain, who lives with her parents in the imaginary land of Korasan, in a cottage in the jeffwood tree forest. Against a medieval setting, the story tells of Lydia's love for the wood carver Aldersan and of Ebol and Lydia's adventures in trying to save the treasured jeffwood forest.

There also is an angel in Douglas Kaine McKelvey's *The Angel Knew Papa and the Dog* (1996). When a sudden flood rushes across the land, sweeping her father away, a girl must battle the rising flood waters alone with her mule. When it appears the flood will overtake them, the girl encounters an angel who gives her the courage she needs to survive.

E. L. Konigsburg masterfully blends a story of angelic beings, medieval history, and humor in *A Proud Taste for Scarlet and Miniver* (1973). For centuries Eleanor of Aquitaine has been patiently waiting for her husband, King Henry II, to meet her in Heaven. Before beings can come Up, they must be judged; but they can have the help of someone to argue their cases. Abbot Sugar asks Eleanor,

> "Who is pleading Henry's case?"
> "Lawyers," Eleanor answered. "I always knew that if we ever got enough lawyers into Heaven, they would plead for him. . . . Henry was due Up long before this, but it has taken almost eight hundred years to get enough lawyers Up to make a case."
> "Yes," Abbot Sugar agreed, "in Heaven lawyers are as hard to find as bank presidents." (p. 8)

Communication with Ghosts. Many elementary children are fascinated with the prospect of ghosts. The plots of ghost stories most often involve a child's encounter with another child from the past. In *The Doll in the Garden* (Hahn 1989), 10-year-old Ashley finds a beautiful antique doll buried in the forbidden garden. She discovers that it belonged to a girl who lived next door who had died of tuberculosis at the turn of the century. Ashley can hear the girl crying in the garden at night, and she is determined to find out why.

Pam Conrad's *Stonewords* (1990) presents a tale of two girls living in the same house; however, one lives there in the present, and the other lived there more than a hundred years ago. The two girls move in and out of each other's worlds by a back staircase. Eleven-year-old Zoe is determined to discover the nature of her friend's death, so she can alter the tragic event.

On a camping trip with her older sister, 13-year-old Caitlin in *A Taste of Smoke* (Bauer 1993) encounters an oddly dressed boy who is eager to befriend her. Gradually she discovers that he is an orphan who was left behind in a great fire that swept the area a century ago. He literally haunts her, appearing whenever she thinks of him. Desperate to free herself from this ghost, Caitlin must help him find what he is seeking.

In the first book of R. L. Stine's expansive Goosebumps series, *Welcome to Dead House* (1992), Amanda and Josh's parents inherit an old house in Dark Falls from Uncle Charlie. However, neither parent can remember having an uncle named Charlie. When they move there, they soon realize the house is haunted. In truth, the whole town is inhabited by "the living dead," who need new victims to stay alive. Stine has written countless other horror books in the Goosebumps series. There are also spin-off series with countless books. In some, Stine has employed other writers, though only his name appears on the cover.

Science Fiction

When magic is replaced by advanced technological wonders, a fantasy story is called **science fiction.** Incredible and inconceivable characters and events are given rational scientific-sounding explanations, which a good science fiction writer makes quite plausible. The time setting in science fiction stories does not have to be the future. It can be the present day with some type of secret advanced technology, or, if you read books that were published some time ago, the setting can even be in the past.

Science fiction is based on scientific extrapolation in which speculative scientific developments and discoveries are the reality. Stories extend current scientific developments by starting with what is known today and taking that knowledge one step farther. For example, today surgeons can transplant hearts. In the future, what will happen when they transplant brains? Some science fiction writers have been prophetic in their literary inventions. What sounded bizarre at the time it was published is now reality. For example, Jules Verne wrote about traveling to the moon in 1865 in *From the Earth to the Moon.*

Because of the technical nature of this genre, very few true science fiction books are written on the elementary level. Some books for younger children do involve space travel or extraterrestrials, but they touch very little on technology, if at all; an example is *The Little Prince* (Saint Exupéry 1943).

Science fiction plots often center on how science and technology impact human life, portraying technology's potential for both good and evil. Readers are drawn to examine the social consequences of technology, and some writers depict a very bleak picture of future societies. One such book is the acclaimed *The Giver* by Lois Lowry (1993), in which a future society of "sameness" has learned how to control everything—memory, emotion, occupation, marriage, weather, propagation, and who is allowed to live or die.

Some of my adult students told me they found *The Giver* unsuitable for children because of one particularly disturbing scene. When Jonas turns 12, he is appointed as the next Receiver of Memory and is apprenticed to the current Receiver, who then becomes the Giver (of memory). This person alone holds the memories of the true pain and pleasures of life—because generations ago, the people had all memories (beyond their own generation) removed from the people's consciousness and transferred to the Receiver. This included memories of such horrors as war and famine. Along with the memories, they gave up strong emotions such as love, fear, and pain.

Jonas's father, a Nurturer (caregiver of infants), explains that to avoid confusion, only one identical twin is allowed to live in the community. The newborn twin with the smallest birth weight must be "released." Jonas finally learns the meaning of *release* when the Giver shows him a videotape in which his father is weighing newborn twins. Jonas looks on in horror, and the Giver observes with deep sorrow, as his father dispassionately gives the smaller twin a lethal injection in a scalp vein, saying cheerfully, "I know, I know. It hurts, little guy. But I have to use a vein, and the veins in your arms are still too teeny-weeny. . . . All done. That wasn't so bad was it?" (p. 149). Then he disposes of the lifeless body in a trash chute.

The Giver is a worthy book with a profound message. Preventing people from developing memories that allow understanding of both love and pain means preventing them from developing compassion—the virtue that is missing in these futuristic people who use euthanasia to mold their society by culling out the unwanted. I fear that to shield children from learning about such horrors is to make the same mistake as is made in Lowry's futuristic society, and that it too could result in a lack of compassion.

Science fiction can be categorized into six broad topics:

Life in the Future. As in *The Giver, The Crystal Drop* (Hughes 1993) takes place in the future. The setting is Canada in 2011, after the destruction of the ozone layer has devastated the land. Megan and her little brother set off to find their uncle after their mother dies.

Space Travel. Alfred Slote has written science fiction specifically for elementary children, and one of his best loved stories is *My Trip to Alpha I* (1978). In easy-to-understand language, the reader learns how VOYA-CODE travel was developed and how it will enable Jack to get to the planet Alpha I to help his aunt. *This Place Has No Atmosphere* (1986) is Paula Danziger's story of what happens when a teenage girl's parents move the family to a small moon colony in 2057.

Life in Other Worlds. In *A Wrinkle in Time* by Madeleine L'Engle (1962), Meg's father has learned to travel instantaneously through outer space by means of a tesseract, which is explained only as a mathematical procedure. In the same manner, Meg and her brother, seeking their lost father, travel to several destinations in space inhabited by strange creatures.

Marvelous Inventions or Discoveries. *My Robot Buddy* by Alfred Slote (1975) is the story of a boy who receives a robot for his tenth birthday. After a brush with a robotnapper, Jack and his robot buddy live like brothers. In *The Duplicate* (Sleator 1999), David finds a machine that creates replicas of living organisms. He duplicates himself and then suffers horrible consequences when the duplicate turns against him. Younger children will enjoy *Cosmo and the Robot* (Pinkney 2000). After Cosmo's beloved robot, Rex, becomes damaged and is taken off to the asteroid dump, his parents try to console him with a Super Solar System Utility Belt with ten supersonic attachments.

Time Travel. In science fiction characters can travel both to the future and to the past; however, travel is accomplished by scientific technology rather than by magic. In *Singularity* (Sleator 1985) twin brothers discover an old shed built over a rock, which is the inside of a singularity to another universe. Anything or anyone shut inside the shed is caught in a time warp that makes time run exceedingly faster than it does on earth. Richard Peck's *Lost in Cyberspace* (1995) is a story of Aaron, a sixth grader who microprocesses himself into cyberspace through cellular reorganization. (He explains it as faxing himself through cyberspace.) He and his friend Josh must deal with unexpected visitors from the past. In the sequel, *The Great Interactive Dream Machine* (1996), Aaron tinkers with the programming of his computer/time machine and accidentally gives it the ability to grant wishes. Unfortunately, the wishes granted are not always those of Aaron and Josh, so they are transported through time and space to some unwanted places.

Extraterrestrials on Earth. The most popular category of science fiction for elementary children is aliens on Earth. *The Forgotten Door* (Key 1965) is an intriguing story of Jon, a boy from another planet who has accidentally fallen through a door that is a passage to Earth. He has the power to read the minds of others, but he lost his own memory in the fall. *UFO Diary* (Kitamura 1989) is a picture book narrated by an alien who takes a wrong turn in his dome-shaped rocket ship. He makes an unscheduled stop on Earth, where he visits with a young boy. In *I Was a Sixth Grade Alien* (Coville 1999), two boys tell their stories in alternating chapters on what it is like to be/have an alien from the planet Hevi-Hevi in elementary school.

The Year of the Child: Alien Exchange Students (Anders & Throop 1999) introduces Meena Biop, a visitor from beyond the stars. *When the Tripods Came* (1988) is John Christopher's first book in a trilogy about the struggle against the Tripods that descend from outer space and begin brainwashing everyone with their hypnotic caps. *Animorphs: The Invasion* (1996) is the first in a voluminous series of science fiction books by K. A. Applegate. Jake, Rachel, Cassie, Tobias, and Marco are five kids who stumble upon a crashed space ship. The mortally wounded alien warns them of the mind-controlling Yeerks who are already on Earth. Before the noble alien prince dies, he transmits to the children the power to morph (change shape), so they can better fight the Yeerks. Thereafter, the children are able to morph into the forms of any animals they touch.

 Responding to Literature

Comparing Older Books to Present Reality

Read an older science fiction book such as *Danny Dunn and the Homework Machine* (Williams 1958) or *Miss Pickerell Goes to Mars* (MacGregor 1951). Compare the book's version of futuristic technology to what has actually been achieved today. How accurate was the author in predicting the future?

Unlikely Situation

In some fantasy books there is no magic, and none of the characters is a talking animal, live toy, monster, ghost, or other unearthly creature. A book may have all human characters and a realistic setting; however, the characters may engage in some totally unrealistic situation that makes the book fantasy rather than realistic fiction.

The Miss Nelson books by Harry Allard fall in this category. In *Miss Nelson Is Missing* (1977), a teacher with an unruly class disappears, and the vile Miss Viola Swamp becomes their substitute teacher. In *Miss Nelson Is Back* (1982), the children fear they will get Viola Swamp again when Miss Nelson has an operation, so a couple of kids dress up in a Miss Nelson costume and fool the principal. However, The Swamp appears when she finds out what they have done. The Swamp returns once more in *Miss Nelson Has a Field Day* (1985), when the Horace B. Smedley School has the worst football team in the state. As their new coach, The Swamp whips them into shape while Miss Nelson looks on. Within the last couple of pages of each book, Allard reveals who the real Viola Swamp is.

In Dr. Seuss's first book, *And to Think That I Saw It on Mulberry Street* (1937), Marco's father tells him to observe carefully what he encounters on the way home from school. The boy sees only a horse and wagon on the street, but his imagination builds as he progressively envisions what *could* be on Mulberry Street: an elephant, giraffes, a wagon full of musicians, a magician, and more.

A hardworking but simple maid goes to work for the Rogers family in *Amelia Bedelia* (Parish 1963). She is great at baking, but she takes her household chores quite literally. When told to dust the furniture, she puts dusting powder on everything. When told to put the lights out, she hangs all the light bulbs on the clothesline for some fresh air. When told to dress the chicken, she sews some green pants and socks to put on it. Peggy Parish has written a number of popular books about the zany Amelia Bedelia.

Petite Madeline and eleven other little girls live "in an old house in Paris that was covered with vines," where they are cared for and tutored by the loving Miss Clavel. In the first book, *Madeline* (Bemelmans 1939), the smallest girl is rushed to the hospital to have her appendix removed. In the sequel, *Madeline's Rescue* (1953), Madeline's daring attempt to walk atop the wall of a bridge lands her in the Seine River, where a brave dog rescues her.

Robert Munsch's *Thomas' Snowsuit* (1985) is sure to make you laugh if you have ever had to get a small child into (or out of) heavy winter clothing. You can appreciate the frustrations Thomas's mother, teacher, and principal face when they somehow end up in one another's clothes.

In *Weslandia* (Fleischman 1999), Wesley is not an ordinary boy. He dislikes pizza and soda, finds professional football stupid, and refuses to shave off his hair. One summer he accidentally grows an unusual fruit-bearing plant whose juice tastes like various delicious flavors. He uses the fruit rind to make a cup for the juice he squeezes, barbecues the root tubers, weaves the bark into a hat, and uses a flower stalk as a sundial. Wesley creates a new language based on an eighty-letter alphabet and a counting system based on the number eight. His classmates, who previously tormented him, become very curious about his new world.

 ## Literature Activity: Fantasy Movies

Many of the books described in this chapter have been made into movies. Looking through the bibliography that follows, make a list of all the titles you recognize. Try to name at least one actor in each movie. To whom were the movies targeted, child audiences or general family audiences? ■

FANTASY BOOKS

Alexander, Lloyd. *The Book of Three.* Henry Holt, 1964.

———. *The Black Cauldron.* Henry Holt, 1965.

———. *The Castle of Llyr.* Henry Holt, 1966.

———. *The Taran Wanderer.* Henry Holt, 1967.

———. *The High King.* Henry Holt, 1968.

———. *The Fortune-Tellers.* Illus. Trina Schart Hyman. Dutton, 1992.

Allard, Harry. *Miss Nelson Is Missing.* Illus. James Marshall. Houghton Mifflin, 1977.

———. *Miss Nelson Is Back.* Illus. James Marshall. Houghton Mifflin, 1982.

———. *Miss Nelson Has a Field Day.* Illus. James Marshall. Houghton Mifflin, 1985.

Amos, Berthe. *Old Hannibal and the Hurricane.* Hyperion, 1991.

Anders, Isabel, & Sarah A. Throop. *The Year of the Child: Alien Exchange Students.* Guardian, 1999.

Andersen, Hans Christian. *Andersen's Fairy Tales.* Syndicate Trading Company, 1835.

———. *The Little Mermaid.* 1836. http://www.math.technion.ac.il/~rl/Andersen/vt/

———. *The Brave Tin Soldier.* 1838. http://www.math.technion.ac.il/~rl/Andersen/vt/

———. *The Fir Tree.* 1845. http://www.math.technion.ac.il/~rl/Andersen/vt/

———. *The Snow Queen.* 1845. http://www.math.technion.ac.il/~rl/Andersen/vt/

———. *The Little Match-Seller.* 1846. http://www.math.technion.ac.il/~rl/Andersen/vt/

———. *The Little Match Girl.* Illus. Rachel Isadora. Putnam, 1987.

———. *The Complete Hans Christian Andersen Fairy Tales.* Grammercy, 1993.

———. *Thumbelina.* Illus. Arlene Graston. Doubleday, 1997.

Applegate, K. A. *Animorphs: The Invasion.* Scholastic, 1996.

Babbitt, Natalie. *Knee-Knock Rise.* Farrar, Straus & Giroux, 1970.

———. *Tuck Everlasting.* Farrar, Straus & Giroux, 1975.

Barrett, Judi. *Cloudy with a Chance of Meatballs.* Illus. Ron Barrett. Macmillan, 1978.

Barrie, J. M. *Peter Pan and Wendy.* Illus. Scott Gustafson. Viking, 1906/1991.

Barrie, J. M. & Diane Goode. *Peter Pan.* Random House, 1983.

Bateman, Teresa. *The Ring of Truth.* Illus. Omar Rayyan. Holiday House, 1997.

Bauer, Marion Dane. *A Taste of Smoke.* Houghton Mifflin, 1993.

Baum, L. Frank. *The Wonderful Wizard of Oz.* Morrow, 1900/1987.

Bemelmans, Ludwig. *Madeline.* Viking, 1939.

———. *Madeline's Rescue.* Viking, 1953.

Brett, Jan. *Berlioz the Bear.* Putnam, 1991.

Burton, Virginia Lee. *Choo Choo: The Story of a Little Engine Who Ran Away.* Houghton Mifflin, 1937.

———. *Mike Mulligan and His Steam Shovel.* Houghton Mifflin, 1939.

Carle, Eric. *The Very Lonely Firefly.* Philomel, 1995.

Carroll, Lewis. *Alice's Adventures in Wonderland.* Random House, 1865/1988.

Cassedy, Sylvia. *Behind the Attic Wall.* Crowell, 1983.

Christopher, John. *When the Tripods Came.* Dutton, 1988.

Collodi, Carlo. *The Adventures of Pinocchio: The Story of a Puppet.* Illus. Mary Haverfield. Random House, 1883/1992.

Conrad, Pam. *The Tub People.* Illus. Richard Egielski. HarperCollins, 1989.

———. *Stonewords.* HarperCollins, 1990.

Cooper, Susan. *Over Sea, under Stone.* Harcourt, Brace & World, 1966.

———. *The Dark Is Rising.* Atheneum, 1973.

———. *The Grey King.* Atheneum, 1975.

———. *Greenwitch.* Atheneum, 1976.

———. *Silver on the Tree.* Atheneum, 1977.

Coville, Bruce. *Bruce Coville's Book of Magic: Tales to Cast a Spell on You.* Scholastic, 1996.

———. *I Was a Sixth Grade Alien.* Minstrel, 1999.

Crampton, Gertrude. *Tootle.* Illus. Tibor Gergely. Golden Books, 1945.

———. *Scuffy the Tugboat.* Illus. Tibor Gergely. Golden Books, 1946.

Dahl, Roald. *James and the Giant Peach.* Illus. Lane Smith. Knopf, 1961.

———. *Charlie and the Chocolate Factory.* Knopf, 1964.

———. *Matilda.* Puffin, 1988.

Danziger, Paula. *This Place Has No Atmosphere.* Delacorte, 1986.

dePaola, Tomie. *Big Anthony and the Magic Ring.* Harcourt Brace, 1979.

———. *Little Grunt and the Big Egg.* Holiday House, 1990.

———. *Strega Nona Meets Her Match.* Putnam, 1993.

Dodge, Mary Mapes, & Norma Green. *The Hole in the Dike.* Illus. Eric Carle. Scholastic, 1974.

Dorros, Arthur. *Abuela.* Illus. Elisa Kleven. Dutton, 1991.

Fleischman, Paul. *Weslandia.* Illus. Kevin Hawkes. Candlewick, 1999.

Forward, Toby. *Pie Magic.* Illus. Laura Cornell. Tambourine Books, 1995.

Freeman, Don. *Corduroy.* Viking, 1968.

———. *A Pocket for Corduroy.* Viking, 1978.

Goble, Paul. *The Girl Who Loved Wild Horses.* Bradbury, 1978.

Gruelle, Johnny. *Raggedy Ann Stories.* Simon & Schuster, 1918.

Hahn, Mary Downing. *The Doll in the Garden.* Houghton Mifflin, 1989.

Hesse, Karen. *The Music of Dolphins.* Scholastic, 1996.

Hite, Sid. *Answer My Prayer.* Henry Holt, 1995.

Hodges, Margaret, and Jonathan Swift. *Gulliver in Lilliput.* Illus. Kimberly Bulcken Root. Holiday House, 1995.

Hughes, Monica. *The Crystal Drop.* Simon & Schuster, 1993.

Joyce, William. *George Shrinks.* HarperCollins, 1985.

Juster, Norton. *The Phantom Tollbooth.* Illus. Jules Feiffer. Random House, 1961.

Key, Alexander. *The Forgotten Door.* Westminster, 1965.

Kipling, Rudyard. *Just So Stories.* Illus. Barry Moser. Morrow, 1902/1996.

Kitamura, Satoshi. *UFO Diary.* Farrar, Straus & Giroux, 1989.

Konigsburg, E. L. *A Proud Taste for Scarlet and Miniver.* Atheneum, 1973.

L'Engle, Madeleine. *A Wrinkle in Time.* Farrar, Straus & Giroux, 1962.

Levithan, David. *In the Eye of the Tornado.* Scholastic, 1998.

Lewis, C. S. *The Lion, the Witch and the Wardrobe.* Macmillan, 1950.

———. *Prince Caspian.* Macmillan, 1951.

———. *The Voyage of the "Dawn Treader."* Macmillan, 1952.

———. *The Silver Chair.* Macmillan, 1953.

———. *The Horse and His Boy.* Macmillan, 1954.

———. *The Magician's Nephew.* Macmillan, 1955.

———. *The Last Battle.* Macmillan, 1956.

Lindgren, Astrid. *Pippi Longstocking.* Illus. Nancy Seligsohn. Viking, 1950.

Lionni, Leo. *Little Blue and Little Yellow.* Astor Honor, 1959.

———. *Alexander and the Wind-Up Mouse.* Knopf, 1969.

Lobel, Arnold. *Frog and Toad Are Friends.* Harper & Row, 1970.

———. *The Turnaround Wind.* Harper and Row, 1988.

Lofting, Hugh. *The Story of Doctor Dolittle.* Illus. Michael Hague. Morrow, 1920.

———. *The Voyages of Doctor Dolittle.* Bantam, 1922.

Lowry, Lois. *The Giver.* Houghton Mifflin, 1993.

MacGregor, Ellen. *Miss Pickerell Goes to Mars.* Whittlesey House, 1951.

Marney, Dean. *Pet-rified!* Scholastic, 1997.

Mayer, Mercer. *There's a Nightmare in My Closet.* Dial, 1968.

McGraw, Eloise Jarvis. *The Moorchild.* Simon & Schuster, 1996.

McKelvey, Douglas Kaine. *The Angel Knew Papa and the Dog.* Philomel, 1996.

McKissack, Patricia. *Flossie & the Fox.* Illus. Rachel Isadora. Dial, 1986.

———. *Mirandy and Brother Wind.* Illus. Jerry Pinkney. Random House, 1988.

McPhail, David. *Edward and the Pirates.* Little, Brown, 1997.

Milne, A. A. *Winnie-the-Pooh.* Dutton, 1926.

———. *The House at Pooh Corner.* Dutton, 1928.

———. *The Complete Tales of Winnie-the-Pooh.* Illus. Ernest H. Shepard. Penguin, 1996.

Munsch, Robert. *The Paper Bag Princess.* Illus. Michael Martchenko. Annick Press, 1980.

———. *Thomas' Snowsuit.* Illus. Michael Martchenko. Annick Press, 1985.

Norton, Mary. *The Borrowers.* Illus. Beth Krush & Joe Krush. Harcourt Brace, 1952.

Parish, Peggy. *Amelia Bedelia.* Illus. Fritz Siebel. HarperCollins, 1963.

Paterson, Katherine. *The King's Equal.* Illus. Vladimir Vagin. HarperCollins, 1992.

Paz, Octavio, & Catherine Cowan. *My Life with the Wave.* Illus. Mark Buehner. Morrow, 1997.

Peck, Richard. *Lost in Cyberspace.* Dial, 1995.

———. *The Great Interactive Dream Machine.* Dial, 1996.

Peterson, John. *The Littles.* Illus. Roberta Carter Clark. Scholastic, 1967.

Pilkey, Dav. *The Adventures of Captain Underpants: An Epic Novel.* Blue Sky Press, 1997.

Pinkney, Brian. *Cosmo and the Robot.* Greenwillow, 2000.

Ringgold, Faith. *Tar Beach.* Crown, 1991.

Riordan, James (Ed.). *A Book of Narnians: The Lion, the Witch and the Others.* Illus. Pauline Baynes. HarperCollins, 1994.

Rowling, J. K. *Harry Potter and the Sorcerer's Stone.* Scholastic, 1998.

———. *Harry Potter and the Chamber of Secrets.* Scholastic, 1999.

———. *Harry Potter and the Prisoner of Azkaban.* Scholastic, 1999.

———. *Harry Potter and the Goblet of Fire.* Scholastic, 2000.

Sachar, Louis. *Sideways Stories from Wayside School.* Avon, 1978.

Saint Exupéry, Antoine de. *The Little Prince.* Harcourt, Brace & World, 1943.

Salinas, Bobbi. *The Three Pigs / Los Tres Cerdos.* Piñata Books, 1998.

Scamander, Newt. *Fantastic Beasts and Where to Find Them.* Scholastic, 2001.

Scieszka, Jon. *The True Story of the 3 Little Pigs.* Illus. Lane Smith. Viking Penguin, 1989.

———. *The Frog Prince Continued.* Illus. Lane Smith. Viking Penguin, 1991.

———. *Knights of the Kitchen Table.* Illus. Lane Smith. Viking Penguin, 1991.

———. *The Stinky Cheese Man.* Illus. Lane Smith. Viking Penguin, 1992.

Seeger, Pete. *Abiyoyo.* Illus. Michael Hays. Macmillan, 1986.

Sendak, Maurice. *Where the Wild Things Are.* Harper & Row, 1963.

———. *In the Night Kitchen.* Harper & Row, 1970.

———. *Outside Over There.* Harper & Row, 1981.

———. *We Are All in the Dumps with Jack and Guy.* HarperCollins, 1993.

Seuss, Dr. *And to Think That I Saw It on Mulberry Street.* Random House, 1937.

———. *Daisy-Head Mayzie.* Random House, 1994.

Sharmat, Marjorie Weinman. *A Big Fat Enormous Lie.* Illus. David McPhail. Dutton, 1978.

Silverstein, Shel. *The Giving Tree.* HarperCollins, 1964.

———. *The Missing Piece.* HarperCollins, 1976.

———. *The Missing Piece Meets the Big O.* Harper & Row, 1981.

Sleator, William. *Singularity.* Puffin, 1985.

———. *The Duplicate.* Puffin, 1999.

Slote, Alfred. *My Robot Buddy.* Lippincott, 1975.

———. *My Trip to Alpha I.* HarperCollins, 1978.

Steig, William. *The Toy Brother*. HarperCollins, 1996.

Stine, R. L. *Welcome to Dead House*. Scholastic, 1992.

Thaler, Mike. *The Teacher from the Black Lagoon*. Illus. Jared Lee. Scholastic, 1989.

———. *Cinderella Bigfoot*. Illus. Jared Lee. Cartwheel, 1997.

———. *Hanzel and Pretzel*. Illus. Jared Lee. Cartwheel, 1997.

———. *Schmoe White and the Seven Dorfs*. Illus. Jared Lee. Cartwheel, 1997.

Tolkien, J. R. R. *The Hobbit*. Houghton Mifflin, 1937.

Travers, P. L. *Mary Poppins*. Buccaneer, 1934.

Van Allsburg, Chris. *Jumanji*. Houghton Mifflin, 1981.

———. *The Polar Express*. Houghton Mifflin, 1985.

———. *The Sweetest Fig*. Houghton Mifflin, 1993.

Viorst, Judith. *I'll Fix Anthony*. Illus. Arnold Lobel. Harper & Row, 1969.

White Deer of Autumn. *Ceremony—in the Circle of Life*. Illus. Daniel San Souci. Carnival, 1983.

Whisp, Kennilworthy. *Quidditch through the Ages*. Scholastic, 2001.

Williams, Jay, & Raymond Abrashkin. *Danny Dunn and the Homework Machine*. McGraw-Hill, 1958.

Williams, Margery. *The Velveteen Rabbit*. Illus. Michael Green. Running Press, 1922.

Winthrop, Elizabeth. *The Castle in the Attic*. Holiday House, 1985.

Woodruff, Elvira. *The Orphan of Ellis Island*. Scholastic, 1997.

Yolen, Jane. *The Devil's Arithmetic*. Viking Penguin, 1988.

Yorinks, Arthur. *Hey Al*. Illus. Richard Egielski. Farrar, Straus & Giroux, 1986.

Youdovin, Susan Schaalman. *Why Does It Always Rain on Sukkot?* Illus. Miriam Nerlove. Albert Whitman, 1990.

Verne, Jules. *From the Earth to the Moon*. Bantam, 1865/1993.

KEY TERMS

 Explore the E-Glossary at **www.ablongman.com/anderson**

dialogue response journal (p. 133)
enchanted journey (p. 128)
fiction (p. 113)
high fantasy (p. 133)
invented spelling (p. 133)
literary fairy tale (p. 114)
modern fantasy (p. 113)

prequel (p. 135)
primary world (p. 133)
science fiction (p. 140)
secondary world (p. 133)
spontaneous reenactment (p. 120)
story box (p. 131)

Toad takes fresh-baked cookies to Frog.

Frog and Toad Together
Written and illustrated by Arnold Lobel.

6

Animal Fantasy

Library locations: J (Juvenile) for junior novels; E (Easy) for picture books

Fantasy stories in which main characters are anthropomorphic animals
that talk, experience emotions, and have the ability to reason as humans

Talking animals have always been popular story characters. The earliest were the fables and talking beast folktales of traditional lore. Animal characters are particularly adapted to expressing ideas about human foibles (Stewig, 1980), and most likely it was this quality that led ancient storytellers to employ animal characters in their tales. Whitney (1976) explained that even in contemporary fantasy, animal tales can be "filled with important truths that might make the child reader uncomfortable if presented in realistic terms involving human characters" (p. 133).

In modern **animal fantasy,** the main—and often all—characters are **anthropomorphic animals** (i.e., animals with human characteristics). They possess human language, thoughts, and emotions. An effective author of animal fantasy makes the incredible sound credible while maintaining story logic and is therefore able to create believable characters and plots. Very young children do not make a clear distinction between fact and fantasy, so they have little trouble imagining animals with human traits, or what Russell (1997) called the metaphorical use of animals in human roles. He postulated that animal characters are actually literary symbolism, in which the animals signify human counterparts. The animals are the vehicles for experiencing human emotions, values, and relationships. To demonstrate the extent to which readers accept animal characters as substitutes for humans, consider *Arthur's New Puppy* (Brown 1993), in which an animal (a young aardvark) has a pet animal!

Animal fantasy stories usually do not contain magic (outside of animals that talk and think like humans). Rather, the most common plots take place in a contemporary setting and focus on everyday issues that mimic human nature, which is in concert with Russell's (1997) theory. However Nodelman (1996) believes that animal characters represent the "animal-like" condition of children. He cited the example of *The Tale of Peter Rabbit* (Potter 1902), in which Peter is torn between the opposing forces of his mother's wishes and his natural desire to eat in the garden. Nodelman (1996) pointed out that whether or not animal characters wear clothing is of significance, marking them as either more human or more animal. When the characters are more animal-like, they typically are more focused on their concerns of finding food.

A look through the picture book sections of bookstores and libraries will reveal how popular animal fantasy is among children's books. I recently reviewed the catalogues of six imprints published by Scholastic Inc. (Scholastic Press, Arthur A. Levin Books, the Blue Sky Press, Scholastic Reference, Cartwheel Books, and Orchard Books). Animal fantasy titles accounted for 37 percent of the 129 new titles introduced—by far the largest genre when compared to the other genres presented in this textbook: concept books, traditional literature, modern fantasy, contemporary realistic fiction, historical fiction, biography, informational books, and poetry. The most prevalent characters in these new animal fantasy stories were dogs, fowl (such as chickens and ducks), cats, and rabbits.

The popularity of animal fantasy is not a new trend. Peterson (1971) identified fantasy stories about animals as the most prevalent choice of the 745 second graders in his study. Additionally, Lawson (1972) concluded that animal stories were by far the most favorite type of reading materials for the 695 fifth graders in her study. In their respective guides to aspiring authors of childrens books, both Phyllis A. Whitney (1976) and Jane Yolen (1973) spoke to the popularity of animal stories, and Yolen postulated that animal tales in general are probably the single greatest category in children's books.

In this chapter, I first trace some of the milestones in the history of animal fantasy and then I analyze the characteristics of this genre by dividing it into four main types, citing notable authors and some of their most memorable works. (Stories involving real animals are presented in Chapters 8 and 9, which discuss realistic fiction.)

Evaluating Animal Fantasy

The following questions can guide you as you select animal fantasy books:

- How believable are the anthropomorphic animals?
- Does the protagonist possess an appropriate mix of both animal and human characteristics?
- Does the book tell a good story that children will enjoy?
- Is the plot credible?

Milestones in Animal Fantasy

1877: *Black Beauty: The Autobiography of a Horse* by Anna Sewell

The first significant animal fantasy story was published in England in the nineteenth century and is still in print (Sewell 1877/1998). *Black Beauty* was not written as a children's book; rather, Sewell wrote it as a protest against the cruel treatment of animals. Its theme is a plea for the humane treatment of horses. The novel is told from the first-person point of view of the thoroughbred Black Beauty, a beautiful horse that is traded to a series of owners, some of whom severely abuse him. When the book was published, people of all ages read and loved it, and it stirred a movement to pass laws against animal cruelty. Today's readers may find the book overly sentimental and overdrawn, but adapted versions are available that target contemporary child readers.

1894: *The Jungle Book* by Rudyard Kipling

The Jungle Book is a collection of seven stories interspersed with seven poems, with settings in the jungles of India. The most popular tale is "Mowgli's Brothers," which features Mowgli, the fearless man-cub who was raised by a family of wolves. His companions include Akela his wolf father, Baloo the wise brown bear, and Bagheera the sleek black panther, all of whom help him learn the law of the jungle. While Mowgli grows in the language and ways of the jungle animals, the cunning and sinister tiger Shere Khan looms in the darkness, waiting for the right moment to pounce.

Also popular in Rudyard Kipling's collection is "Rikki-Tikki-Tavi," the story of a heroic mongoose that belongs to a small boy. True to his nature, the mongoose stalks and kills the wicked cobra Nag that lives in the garden at the boy's house. He must then face the female cobra Nagaina; she intends to avenge her mate and protect her unborn babies.

1902: *The Tale of Peter Rabbit* by Beatrix Potter

The Tale of Peter Rabbit was the prototype of children's picture storybooks. It was written and illustrated by Beatrix Potter, the daughter of a wealthy London lawyer. Beatrix's parents raised her in seclusion, allowing her no contact with any children except her younger brother. She was cared for by servants and governesses, who sneaked small field animals to her room to be her playmates. These animals became the characters in the beloved stories she wrote and illustrated.

In 1901 Potter privately printed the first edition of *Peter Rabbit* after six publishers had turned her down. Frederick Warne & Company published the second edition in color the following year, and Warne continues to publish this and Potter's twenty-two other books. *Peter Rabbit* is a cautionary tale warning children about the serious consequences of not minding their parents. Peter nearly loses his life for nibbling in Mr. McGregor's garden, but he escapes, leaving his jacket and shoes behind. His compliant sisters, Flopsy, Mopsy, and Cottontail, are rewarded with blackberries and milk. The sequel is *The Tale of Benjamin Bunny* (1904), in which Peter and his cousin Benjamin sneak back to Mr. McGregor's garden to retrieve Peter's clothes, which are being used as a scarecrow.

Potter's books have been in the public domain for some time, so they are no longer protected by copyright laws. When you look for her books to read or purchase, make sure Beatrix Potter is listed as both author and illustrator. There are many imitation books on the market in which publishers employ other illustrators for Potter's stories.

1903: *The Call of the Wild* by Jack London

In 1887 and 1889 Jack London participated in the Alaskan gold rush. When he returned to his home in San Francisco, he wrote about his experiences. *The Call of the Wild* is a survival story of a contented pet dog named Buck that is stolen from his California home to work as a rugged sled dog during the Alaskan gold rush. He receives much brutal treatment in the Klondike, and he struggles savagely to survive. When rescued by a miner in the wilderness, he loves the man unconditionally. However, Buck becomes inescapably drawn by the wild cries of a wolf pack nearby. When his beloved master is killed, the dog's long suppressed instincts overtake him. He reverts to the primitive state of his wolf ancestors and is accepted into the pack. Animal lovers will find this adventure book both exciting and heart-wrenching.

1908: *The Wind in the Willows* by Kenneth Grahame

The first major animal fantasy novel specifically for children was *The Wind in the Willows,* which became the touchstone for all animal fantasy novels that followed. Kenneth Grahame's bedtime stories—and later his letters—to his son Alastair became the episodes in the book. Grahame had spent much of his childhood living in his grandmother's house on the banks of the Thames River in Berkshire, England, and he used the riverbank as the setting of this book. The good-natured and adventurous Water Rat; the cautious and reflective Mole; the gruff but kindly Badger; and the rich, boisterous, and arrogant Mr. Toad of Toad Hall are all dear and loyal friends. Mr. Toad's cocky personality and his irrepressible passion for motorcars launch him on wild adventures. Though his friends try to reform him and even manage to take back his ancestral manor house from the evil weasels, the pompous Mr. Toad remains utterly recalcitrant. Themes of warm friendship, sympathetic understanding, and forgiveness are charming features of this book.

The Wind in the Willows was written nearly a century ago in England, and because of its different customs and vocabulary, it is difficult reading for most children. Even my adult students (mostly in their 20s) often find it slow paced, overly sentimental, and difficult to understand. Undoubtedly, the most appealing character is Mr. Toad, and the loose plot of the book concerns mostly his antics. I suggest you read this book aloud to your children starting with Chapters 6, 8, 10, 11, and 12, which describe Mr. Toad's adventures. If this part of the book is enjoyable, you may then want to read the rest of the chapters, which are episodic tales of the other characters.

1928: *Millions of Cats* by Wanda Gag

The first significant animal fantasy picture book by an American author was *Millions of Cats.* If you are a person who wants to adopt every feral cat you see, you will easily identify with Wanda Gag's book. A very old man sets out to find a pet cat for his lonely wife. However, he sees so many cats that he cannot make up his mind, so he brings them all home—"Hundreds of cats, thousands of cats, millions and billions and trillions of cats." The story is revealed as a modern-day fable of vanity versus humility when all the cats save one homely little kitten get in a fight, because each thinks he is the prettiest. After they destroy one another, the homely little kitten is selected to be the well-loved pet.

1929: *Bambi: A Life in the Woods* by Felix Salten

While living in Austria in 1929, Siegmund Salzman—using the pen name Felix Salten—published *Bambi: A Life in the Woods* (translated by Whittaker Chambers). This is the endearing tale of the life of a deer, which opens with the birth of the fawn Bambi in the middle of a forest thicket. As the story unfolds, Bambi learns both the pleasures and the dangers of forest life, such as the bitter winters and the terrors of fire. However, man—the hunter—is the greatest danger. Bambi loses his mother and a childhood friend to hunters, and later he is seriously wounded by gunfire. It is the revered old stag, the Prince of Deer, who rescues him and keeps him alive. This book stirs deep emotions in readers who believe wild animals should not be killed for sport.

1939: *Rudolph the Red-Nosed Reindeer* by Robert L. May

American culture was forever impacted by the publication of *Rudolph*. The famous story of Santa's unusual reindeer was born in 1939 when Montgomery Ward & Company asked one of their young copywriters, Robert L. May, to write a book to be used as a Christmas giveaway for the store's customers. May's book, *Rudolph the Red-Nosed Reindeer,* was enormously popular, and Montgomery Ward distributed more than 6 million copies. In 1947 John Marks, a friend of May's, wrote a song about Rudolph. Gene Autry's recording of the song sold millions of copies and quickly rose to the number one spot on the Hit Parade. Although the song about Rudolph became part of the tradition of Christmas, most people do not know *Rudolph* was first a book. This is unfortunate, because May's use of couplets to tell the story is charming.

> "Ha, ha! Look at Rudolph! His nose is a sight!"
> 'It's red as a beet!" "Twice as big!" "Twice as bright!"
> While Rudolph just wept. What else could he do?
> He knew that the things they were saying were true!
> Where most reindeer's noses are brownish and tiny,
> Poor Rudolph's was red, very large, and quite shiny.

Young children would surely enjoy this book, especially if the history (printed on the book cover) is shared.

1941: *Make Way for Ducklings* by Robert McCloskey

Robert McCloskey's time-honored classic, *Make Way for Ducklings,* is set in Boston. The reader will see the Charles River, Louisburg Square, Beacon Hill, and the Public Garden from a mallard duck's point of view. The excitement comes when Mrs. Duck starts to lead her eight little hatchlings from an island in the Charles River to the pond in the Public Garden, which requires the help of Michael the police officer.

1942: *The Poky Little Puppy* by Janette Lowrey

The Poky Little Puppy is the all-time best-selling children's picture book. According to *Publishers Weekly* (1995a), 14 million copies of Janette Lowrey's book were sold during the first fifty-three years of its publication. This cumulative tale is about five puppies who mischievously dig under the fence to explore the outside world. When they smell dinner and dessert, all but the poky puppy run home and are scolded by their mother. The four puppies are sent to bed with no dessert, but the poky puppy returns home after everyone is asleep and eats *all* the dessert. This routine continues for three days. (Somehow the mother never catches on.) But on the third night the brothers and sisters get up and fill the hole with dirt, shutting the poky puppy outside the fence while they eat dessert.

1952: *Charlotte's Web* by E. B. White

Undoubtedly, *Charlotte's Web* by E. B. White is the most-loved animal fantasy story of the twentieth century. As the only novel written specifically for children by an American in this list of classics, it has become part of our heritage. It is the all-time best-selling juvenile novel, with nearly 10 million copies sold in the first forty-three years of its publication. It opens on a farm in Maine, where a girl named Fern lovingly takes care of Wilbur, a runt pig. When Wilbur grows too big, he is sold to Fern's Uncle Zuckerman, whose farm is down the road. Wilbur becomes lonely and dejected in his new location, but Charlotte, the large gray spider who lives in the barn rafters, lovingly befriends him. When he learns from the sheep that he is destined for the dinner table, Wilbur is hysterical. However, the intelligent Charlotte, who can read and write, saves his life by weaving words in her web about how terrific Wilbur is. Though Wilbur becomes famous, he remains a humble little pig. The value of true friendship and the cycle of life and death are major themes of this classic.

1957: *The Cat in the Hat* by Dr. Seuss

Dr. Seuss's *The Cat in the Hat* was the prototype of easy-to-read picture storybooks written on a beginning reader's level. In this wildly popular book, two children are bored sitting at home on a rainy afternoon. A cat wearing an odd red-and-white top hat appears, and with hilarious antics he teaches the children some tricks and games, making quite a mess. Everything is amazingly put back in order before the parents return.

Types of Animal Fantasy

In my definition of animal fantasy, I include main characters that are imaginary animals, such as mythological creatures (*The Dragon and the Unicorn,* Cherry 1995), monsters (*Shrek!* Steig 1990), imaginative beings (*How the Grinch Stole Christmas!* Seuss 1957), and recognizable animals with some outstanding feature (*Catwings,* Le Guin 1988). From a content analysis of more than 100 popular animal fantasy books in print, I identified four major types. Following is a description of the types in the order of the most prevalent (Type I) to the least prevalent (Type IV).

Type I: Anthropomorphic Animals in an All-Animal World

In Type I animal fantasy, the anthropomorphic animals take the place of humans and exist in a totally animal world. This world may be inhabited by a single species, such as the mice in *Owen* (Henkes 1993), or it may be a world inhabited by various species, as in *Franklin in the Dark* (Bourgeois 1986). In this type the animal characters behave almost entirely as humans, talking in human speech, living in houses, eating human food, wearing clothing, and using various modes of transportation. However, some animal characters may retain a few natural traits, such as their favorite foods. Plots primarily involve the same problems encountered by the stories' child readers, whose lives these characters reflect. Quite often, only the illustrations reveal to readers that the characters are animals.

Arnold Lobel. Arnold Lobel is a master of Type I animal fantasy. Themes of unconditional friendship with sympathetic understanding are prominent in his Frog and Toad series. In the first of the four books, *Frog and Toad Are Friends* (1970), the animals are illustrated in appropriate sizes compared to the other flora and fauna (e.g., Toad sits under a mushroom and is smaller than a sparrow). However, Frog and Toad live in little houses, wear human clothing, walk upright, eat human food, and are able to read and write. Essentially, they do everything that humans do. Because they live in an all-animal world, they are able to communicate with the other woodland creatures—which, interestingly, live in natural habitats and do not wear clothing.

Lobel's stories are easy-to-read books, and each consists of five episodic chapters. My favorite episode is "The Story." One day when Frog is visiting, Toad notices that he does not look well. Toad tucks Frog in his own bed to rest and fixes him a cup of hot tea. Frog asks Toad to tell him a story while he is resting, but Toad cannot think of any, even when he walks up and down the porch for a long time, stands on his head, pours water over his head, and bangs his head against the wall. After that, Frog says he is feeling better and does not need a story.

> "Then you get out of bed and let me get into it," said Toad, "because now I feel terrible."
> Frog said, "Would you like me to tell you a story, Toad?"
> "Yes," said Toad, "if you know one." (Lobel 1970, p. 25)

Frog then tells a story about a sick frog who has a toad friend who cannot think of a story, even after walking up and down, standing on his head, pouring water over his head, and banging his head against the wall. When Frog finishes the story, Toad is asleep.

Responding to Literature
Readers Theater

Readers theater is an activity in which children take speaking parts in a brief story and then read it as if it were a radio play. To help your children prepare for readers theater, let them select parts (one part for each character with dialogue, plus the narrator). Have the group practice together until they are ready to read the story like a play. Children should not try to memorize parts, and props are optional. The story can be read from the book, or a script can be written with speaking parts identified for each character and the narrator. The following script is from the beginning of "The Swim" from *Frog and Toad Are Friends* (Lobel 1970, pp. 40–45).

> **Narrator:** Toad and Frog went down to the river.
> **Frog:** What a day for a swim.
> **Toad:** Yes. I will go behind these rocks and put on my bathing suit.

Frog: I don't wear a bathing suit.

Toad: Well, I do. After I put on my bathing suit, you must not look at me until I get into the water.

Frog: Why not?

Toad: Because I look funny in my bathing suit. That is why.

Narrator: Frog closed his eyes when Toad came out from behind the rocks. Toad was wearing his bathing suit.

Toad: Don't peek.

Narrator: Frog and Toad jumped into the water. They swam all afternoon. Frog swam fast and made big splashes. Toad swam slowly and made smaller splashes. A turtle came along the riverbank.

Toad: Frog, tell that turtle to go away. I do not want him to see me in my bathing suit when I come out of the river.

Narrator: Frog swam over to the turtle.

Frog: Turtle, you will have to go away. . . .

Lobel wrote several other Type I easy-to-read books, including *Mouse Tales* (1972), but his book of literary fables gained him the most acclaim. *Fables* (1980) comprises twenty brief stories containing important lessons with a variety of animal characters. Each two-page spread consists of a beautiful full-page illustration facing a one-page story with the moral stated at the end. Because each of these brief stories contains all the elements of story structure, they lend themselves to a variety of activities. They serve as excellent models for children to write their own literary fables, and they are fabulous for story mapping activities (see Figure 2.1). Also, because each story has a narrator and two to three characters with dialogue, they lend themselves well to readers theater.

William Steig. Another excellent Type I animal fantasy author and illustrator is William Steig, whose stories are unique because he uses magical objects in the plot. In *Sylvester and the Magic Pebble* (1969), little Sylvester (a young donkey) finds a magic red pebble and accidentally turns himself into a rock while trying to hide from a lion. Steig amusingly differentiates between adult and child animals by having only the adults wear clothing. Steig chose an array of species for the characters, but he received criticism when he depicted the police officers as pigs. It is interesting that not all the animals in the story live like humans; some retain natural characteristics—the ducks float on the pond, the lion wants to eat the little donkey, the dogs go sniffing for Sylvester's scent, and the lone wolf howls atop the rock.

 Responding to Literature

Literature Webs

An interesting way to connect children with stories and encourage their involvement is **webbing:** creating a visual display of information to represent organized relationships. Webbing can be used to foster and record responses to literature. It promotes discussion while helping chil-

Mr. and Mrs. Duncan find Sylvester. From *Sylvester and the Magic Pebble,* written and illustrated by William Steig.

dren construct shared meanings that will extend their understandings and appreciation. Because webs are versatile, they can be used to depict many types of information. The web in Figure 6.1 represents the beginning of a character study on the protagonist in *Sylvester and the Magic Pebble.* Bromley's *Webbing with Literature* (1996) has a treasure trove of ideas on webbing activities. Select another of William Steig's picture books and make a character web of one of the memorable characters.

William Steig also employs magic in *The Amazing Bone* (1984), in which a girl pig finds a talking bone that helps her outwit a band of highway robbers; and in *Zeke Pippin* (1994), in which a boy pig finds a magic harmonica that makes everyone fall asleep when he plays it. (Wouldn't parents find that handy?) In *Doctor De Soto* (1982) Steig depicts a variety of species, all of which live in a city and dress and act like humans. This story of a diminutive mouse dentist has only one character that retains natural animal instincts: The large fox plans on eating Doctor De Soto after he fixes his bad tooth.

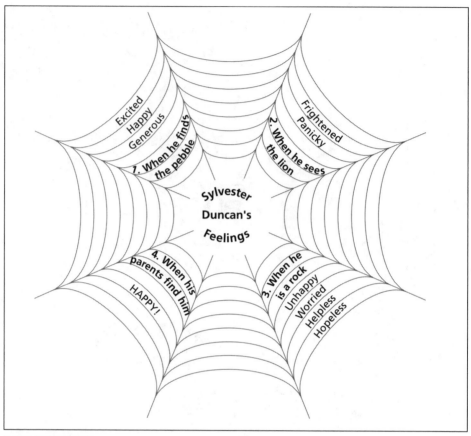

FIGURE 6.1 Web on Sylvester's Feelings

Steig also wrote Type I stories for intermediate-grade children. Juvenile novels about animals living in an all-animal world are rare, but Steig has written two that are quite popular. *Dominic* (1972) is the story of a dog that sallies forth to see the world. Through an episodic plot, Steig develops Dominic as a three-dimensional character by revealing his many fine qualities. He is clever, kindhearted, patient, generous, and courageous. Steig spoofs Victorian novels with *Abel's Island* (1976), a love story between two newlywed mice, lovely Amanda and the dapper Abel. In a ferocious hurricane Abel is marooned on an island and must learn to survive in nature, where one of his greatest adversaries is the owl. After living the Crusoe life for a year, Abel finds his way home—a much changed mouse.

William Steig frequently uses sophisticated language, even in his picture books. He uses involved syntactic arrangements, and words and concepts that are not common in children's listening vocabulary. Though child listeners usually extract meaning from the context of the passage and the illustrations, Steig's colorful language can be used to introduce new vocabulary and concepts.

Responding to Literature

Analyzing Unknown Phrases in Context

Read one of William Steig's picture books, and select five words or phrases that you believe are not in your children's listening vocabulary. Describe how you would use context and the illustrations to help children comprehend them. For example, read aloud the entire paragraph in which the phrase appears; then pinpoint the phrase and ask children, "Is there anything in the story and illustration that would help you know what this means?" Ask them to paraphrase the sentence in their own words. Following is an example list of phrases from *Zeke Pippin* (Steig 1994).

"using his father's schnapps as a disinfectant."
"and started regaling them with the prelude to *La Traviata.*"
"reviling himself for his lack of faith"
"bring them surcease for their sorrow"
"the Samaritans began researching his baggage."

Jane Yolen. Jane Yolen is an author with remarkable talent and versatility. In addition to her numerous juvenile novels and picture books, she has written Type I animal stories. *The Acorn Quest* (1981) is a parody of the Arthurian legends. When the happy kingdom of Woodland is threatened with hunger, King Earthor (an owl) chooses four of his faithful knights to go in quest of the Golden Acorn: Sir Belliful (a groundhog), Sir Tarryhere (a turtle), Sir Gimmemore (a rabbit), Sir Runsalot (a mouse), and the Wizard Squirrelin (a squirrel, of course). The names will make you laugh if you read them aloud. In an equally funny parody, Yolen's *Commander Toad in Space* (1980) pokes fun at the movie *Star Wars.* Commander Toad flies the mighty green spaceship *Star Warts* with a crew of four, including young Jake Skyjumper. In this first book of their adventures, the space crew lands on a watery planet and encounters a horrid sea monster—Deep Wader.

Marc Brown. The plots in Marc Brown's expansive series about Arthur, a young aardvark, center on holidays and issues that young children face, such as the arrival of a new baby, having chicken pox, going to camp, and sleeping over. My favorite is *Arthur's Eyes* (1979), one of the early books, in which Arthur gets eyeglasses and at first the other children laugh at him. Arthur is one of the very few picture book characters with glasses, and in this story Arthur could serve as a positive role model for children who wear glasses. New ventures for Marc Brown include a spin-off series on Arthur's little sister, D. W., and storybooks about the Arthur characters.

Other Type I Authors. Young children feel comfortable with familiar story characters, and they enjoy reading many books about them. Several Type I animal fantasy characters are memorialized in book series. Else Holmelund Minarik's stories of the adorable cub first introduced in *Little Bear* (1957) have entertained several generations of children with themes of familial relations and friendship. Russell Hoban's

Frances, the little badger (sans tail), first appeared in *Bedtime for Frances* (1960), a story about Frances's trouble sleeping because of frightening sounds and objects. In *Franklin in the Dark* (1986), Paulette Bourgeois presented Franklin, the little turtle who drags his shell behind him because he is afraid of crawling into a small dark place. I must also recognize the large and enormously popular series about the Bear family by Stan and Jan Berenstain. One of their best books came early in the series, *The Berenstain Bears and the Spooky Old Tree* (1978).

From the stories I have shared with you, you can see that a panorama of human emotions can be presented in animal guise. These fantasy stories can give children a new perspective on their own lives by allowing them to see the humor in ordinary mishaps that befall the animal characters. Because it is impossible to tell you about all the great Type I animal fantasy books, I close this section with a few more titles that are too good to miss.

- *Happy Birthday Moon* by Frank Asch (1982)
- *Berlioz the Bear* by Jan Brett (1991)
- *Goodnight Moon* by Margaret Wise Brown (1947)
- *Julius, the Baby of the World* by Kevin Henkes (1990)
- *Chrysanthemum* by Kevin Henkes (1991)
- *Toot & Puddle* by Holly Hobbie (1997)
- *Leo the Late Bloomer* by Robert Kraus (1971)
- *Guess How Much I Love You?* by Sam McBratney (1994)
- *Swine Lake* by James Marshall (1999)
- *Albert's Toothache* by Barbara Williams (1974)

Type II: Anthropomorphic Animals Coexisting with Humans

In Type II animal fantasy, animals coexist with human—sometimes in a human-dominated world, as in *Charlotte's Web* (White 1952), where they may or may not be able to speak, and other times in an animal-dominated world where humans only occasionally appear, as in *The Wind in the Willows* (Grahame 1908). In addition, some characters, such as Lafcadio (Silverstein 1963), move from the animal world to the human world and back to the animal world.

Pets. Stories about pet animals are typically set in a human-dominated world where animal and human characters have equal importance. Henry's best friend and constant companion is his dog Mudge in Cynthia Rylant's easy-to-read series on Henry and Mudge. Though Mudge does not speak, the narrator lets the reader know how he is feeling, and the dog typically reflects the boy's mood. For example, in *Henry and Mudge and the Happy Cat* (1990), we learn through text and illustrations that Mudge loves the stray cat, does not mind sharing crackers, and is sad and depressed when the cat goes home. The reader also learns the feelings of the cat, who loves Mudge and likes sleeping in the towel closet. The cat also desires to teach Mudge good manners.

Everyone who owns a dog knows dogs do not like baths, and Gene Zion tells a funny story about baths from the dog's point of view in *Harry the Dirty Dog* (1956). The police officer's pet dog in *Officer Buckle and Gloria* (Rathman 1995) peps up the officer's boring safety speeches by acting out the consequences on stage. *Clifford the Big Red Dog* (Bridwell 1963) is *really* big—taller than his owner's house! In the first book of the series, readers learn that Clifford must be bathed in a swimming pool and combed with a rake, and he generally wreaks havoc on the neighborhood. Sometimes pets have unusual abilities. The dog in *Martha Speaks* (Meddaugh 1992) learns how to talk after eating alphabet soup, and her jabber becomes quite annoying.

The rabbit in *Bunnicula* (Howe & Howe 1979) appears to have very strange abilities. In a story that mixes animal fantasy with the supernatural, Chester the household cat has trouble convincing Harold the dog that the rabbit is really a vampire. Bunnicula is a vegetarian vampire who—from his locked cage—mysteriously gets vegetables from the refrigerator and sucks them dry and colorless. In an equally funny sequel, *Howliday Inn* (Howe 1982), the family goes on vacation. Bunnicula is left with a neighbor, but Chester and Harold are boarded for a week at Chateau Bow-Wow. Cautious Chester is certain a werewolf is responsible for the eerie howling and the mysterious disappearance of other boarders. In the next book, *The Celery Stalks at Midnight* (Howe 1983), Chester and Harold follow a trail of white vegetables after Bunnicula disappears from his cage. Thinking the pale vegetables will become "veggie vampires" after Bunnicula sucks their juices, they follow with a box of toothpicks for spearing the veggies through their hearts before they can harm others.

In *Julius* (Johnson 1993) a huge Alaskan pig becomes a little girl's pet. Unfortunately, he acts like a pig around the house. The feline counterpart of Clifford (the big red dog) is Wuggie Norple in *The Wuggie Norple Story* (Pinkwater 1980). This cat arrives at normal size, but he grows daily until he is larger than an elephant. In *It's So Nice to Have a Wolf Around the House* (Allard 1977), Cuthbert the wolf (disguised as a German shepherd) is not actually a pet, but rather the caretaker of an old man and his pets.

Farm Animals. Farm animals in animal fantasy stories are often pigs. Wilbur in *Charlotte's Web* (White 1952) lives on a farm and communicates with the other animals: the comical geese, the wise old sheep, and the disgusting rat Templeton.

Like Wilbur, Daggie Dogfoot in *Pigs Might Fly* (King-Smith 1980) is a runt pig who is unwanted by the farmer. However, Daggie learns to swim and is quite helpful when the farm is flooded. King-Smith's story of another remarkable pig, *Babe: The Gallant Pig* (1988), introduces readers to an unusual pig who was raised by a sheepdog. Using his gracious manners and polite communication, Babe is able to command a herd of sheep, and he becomes a champion sheepherder. The author's many years of farming experience helped him write these humorous fantasies with very realistic settings and situations. Robert Munsch's *Pigs* (1989) is purely humorous. When a farm girl lets a herd of pigs loose, they wreak havoc on her house and the school, not to mention what they do on the principal's shoe. After commandeering a school bus, the pigs drive themselves home.

Responding to Literature

Analyzing Characters' Traits

Select a favorite animal character, such as Wilbur, the pig in *Charlotte's Web* (White 1952). Using informational books, research the characteristics of the species. Which of the characteristics of the animal did the author retain in the story?

Minnie and Moo Go to the Moon (Cazet 1998) is a hilarious story about two daring cows who watch the farmer and figure out how to drive his tractor. They even remember to say the magic words when it does not start: "YOU CHEESY PIECE OF JUNK! YOU BROKEN-DOWN, NO-GOOD, RUSTY BUCKET OF BOLTS!" (p. 18).

Mice. Fantasy stories with mice characters are numerous. This is interesting, because mice are decidedly less popular with humans than dogs, cats, birds, and horses. However, the diminutive and vulnerable qualities of mice are attractive to children, who view themselves similarly. Though juvenile novels are rare in animal fantasy, several good ones are available with mice characters.

Mrs. Frisby and the Rats of NIMH (O'Brien 1974) is a most unusual story in that it combines animal fantasy with science fiction. A group of field rats at the labs of the National Institute of Mental Health (NIMH) have been subjected to experiments that made them highly intelligent. After teaching themselves to read, they found a way to escape. Because of her late husband's bravery, the rats agree to move Mrs. Frisby and her mouse family away from the vegetable garden to safer ground where farmer Fitzgibbon will not plow. However, she must first sprinkle sleeping powder in the food of Mr. Fitzgibbon's house cat.

Redwall (1986) by Brian Jacques is the first in a series of epic adventures with mice characters. Matthias is an ambitious young mouse who must overcome his clumsy ways and prepare to defeat the savage bilge rat, Cluny the Scourge, and his villainous hordes. Matthias determines to find the legendary sword of Martin the Warrior, which he is convinced will help save the ancient realm of Redwall Abbey, the idyllic world of mice.

In *Poppy* (Avi 1995) a grumpy porcupine helps Poppy the deer mouse go to battle with Ocax the evil owl after he consumes her fiancé. Poppy then finds a safer home and helps the other mice move. A short book about field mice for younger children is *Windmill Hill* (Bryant 1992). The lives of Newly and his uncle, Old Raggedy, change forever when people move into the house on top of the hill.

Beverly Cleary's series on Ralph the Mouse started with *The Mouse and the Motorcycle* (1965). Ralph is a young, impetuous, and adventuresome mouse who lives inside the walls on the second floor of the Mountain View Inn. He becomes enchanted with a young boy's toy motorcycle, which he can ride once he learns how to make the right noise. When the boy, Keith, becomes very ill, Ralph faces danger to find an aspirin tablet to ease his fever. Keith gives him the motorcycle in return. Equally loved are the two books that followed—*Runaway Ralph* (1970) and *Ralph S. Mouse* (1982).

In Dick King-Smith's stories, the mice characters live in buildings. In the imaginative *Three Terrible Trins* (1994), three young mice living in an old farmhouse learn to play a ball game with the farmer's glass eye. In *The School Mouse* (1995), young Flora watches from a hole in the wall of the old schoolhouse, and she learns to read by observing the kindergarten teacher's instruction.

The Cricket in Times Square (Selden 1957) has a fast-talking Broadway mouse named Tucker as a central character. He and his sidekick, streetwise Harry the Cat, meet up with a Connecticut country cricket, Chester, who accidentally got transported to the Forty-Second Street subway station in New York via a picnic basket. Chester is taken in by Mario, the son of the kindly Bellinis who run the subway-station newsstand where the three animal friends hang out. Chester's melodious chirping brings attention, and much-needed business, to the Bellinis' newsstand.

Wild Animals. Robert Lawson's *Rabbit Hill* (1944) is both funny and heartwarming. Little Georgie rabbit, his parents, his aged Uncle Analdas, and the other animals on the hill are excited but a little nervous when they learn that New Folks are coming to live in the big house on the hill. They wonder how they will be treated by the new people: Will the folks plant a garden, or will they bring dangerous guns, traps, dogs, and boys? Little Georgie is quite adventurous, outrunning dogs and jumping Deadman's Brook, but when he is struck by the new folks' automobile, he disappears and the worst is feared.

Jan Brett's *Armadillo Rodeo* (1995) is a wild tale about a young armadillo that wanders away from his mother and siblings. Thinking a young cowgirl's shiny boot is a bright red armadillo, the nearsighted critter tracks her to a rodeo, where he becomes an unwanted participant. In another story by Brett, *Fritz and the Beautiful Horses* (1981), a scraggly wild pony rescues three children when they are stranded because of a cracked bridge over a steep river gully. As a reward, he is asked to come live in the great walled city with the beautiful horses.

Equally charming is Tomie dePaola's saga of *Bill and Pete* (1978). Bill (a young crocodile) and Pete (his bird friend who picks Bill's teeth clean) have a crazy adventure escaping from The Bad Guy who captures crocodiles and takes them to Cairo to become suitcases. The rear nude picture of The Bad Guy hightailing it out of town gets a lot of laughs.

H. A. Rey created an enduring character in 1941 with his first book about the little monkey, *Curious George*. "The man with the big yellow hat" captures George in Africa and takes him home on a ship to America. Though George does not talk, he is able to understand speech. He can also do everything humans can (though he bungles it), such as using the telephone and accidentally calling the fire department. Other adventures include falling overboard, breaking out of jail, and flying over the city with balloons. In the books that follow, George's curiosity continues to get him in trouble. The fast adventure and slapstick humor of this series have made George a favorite for successive generations.

Paleowolf, like Curious George, is able to understand human speech but is not able to speak himself. In *The First Dog* (Brett 1988), when a young wolf and a cave boy in Paleolithic times each face hunger and danger on their journey, they decide to join forces and help each other.

Another character who gets in trouble despite his best intentions is Paddington in *A Bear Called Paddington* (Bond 1958). The Brown family finds a bear wandering about the Paddington train station in London, where he has arrived from darkest Peru. They take him home to be part of their family, and things are never quite the same. Though Paddington desires to help out, he bungles everything—and makes it worse by trying to hide his mistakes.

In his inimitable style, Shel Silverstein created another charming children's book with a profound message for readers of all ages to ponder in *Lafcadio, The Lion Who Shot Back* (1963). While all the other lions in the jungle are fleeing from the hunters, Lafcadio finds one and eats him, keeping the fascinating gun. After a great deal of practice, Lafcadio becomes the greatest shooter in the jungle and is offered a job as a sharpshooter in a circus. As he becomes famous and very rich, he also becomes more like a man. At one time he could sign six autographs at once, using all four paws, his tail, and his teeth.

> But after a while of course he would sign only one at a time with his right front paw because that was more like a man and less like a lion and Lafcadio was becoming more and more like a man all the time. For instance, he stood on his back paws and he learned to sit at the table with his left hand in his lap and his elbows off the table. . . . And he kept his tail curled up and seldom let it hang down except when he forgot himself or he had a little too much buttermilk to drink.

Lafcadio learns to play golf, paint pictures, work out with weights, and many other things that rich and important people do. Eventually he becomes bored and desires something new and exciting, so the circus owner takes him on a hunting trip to Africa. There he is confronted by an old lion who reminds Lafcadio that he is a lion and should be eating the hunters. The hunters tell him he is a man, and he should be shooting the lions. Lafcadio, who is now neither lion nor man, drops his gun and walks away from both.

Type III: Talking Animals in Natural Habitats

The animals in Type III animal fantasy stories do not wear clothing or live in houses, and humans are not present. These animals live in natural-type habitats and display many of their animal traits. However, they are able to talk to animals of all species, and they portray human emotions and thoughts.

Eric Carle. Eric Carle is a master of creating unforgettable insect characters. His illustrations are collages made from transparent tissue papers, which he lightly streaks with paint. His style is so distinctive that you can easily recognize one of his books just by looking at the cover. I have come to expect the unexpected from Carle's books. In *The Very Hungry Caterpillar* (1969), readers will see holes in the varied-size pages where the caterpillar has eaten through. *The Grouchy Ladybug* (1977) contains progressively wider pages as the ladybug tries to pick fights with progressively larger animals. The final animal, the whale, is eight pages long and has a movable paper tail that children can flip back and forth, showing how it slaps the lady-bug back to land. *The Very Busy Spider* (1984) provides enjoyable tactile experiences as children trace parts of the illustrations embossed on each page: the spider, her web, and the unwary fly that will be the spider's supper.

The Very Quiet Cricket (1990) was Eric Carle's first book to use an embedded microchip. A little cricket tries to answer the various animals that greet him, but he is unable to chirp when he rubs his wings. Finally, when he meets a she-cricket and the last page is turned, a chirping sound is heard! Equally enchanting is *The Very Lonely Firefly* (1995), in which a newly hatched firefly is seeking others of his kind. He is attracted to a variety of lights, such as a light bulb and a candle, but at the end he finally finds other fireflies. When the reader turns the last page, eight little fireflies blink on and off via tiny light bulbs powered by a built-in replaceable battery. In Carle's most recent book, *The Very Clumsy Click Beetle* (1999), a small beetle falls on his back but is unable to click and snap back to his feet like the other beetles. Readers will hear an unusual clicking sound that emanates from a fiber-optic mi-crochip with a light sensor powered by a built-in replaceable battery.

Leo Lionni. *Inch by Inch* (1960) is Leo Lionni's story of a clever inchworm that stays alive by showing the birds how useful he can be in measuring things like bird legs and tail feathers. However, when the nightingale commands him to measure her song (or she will eat him), he inches his way out of sight as she sings. Equally charming is Lionni's book *Frederick* (1967), the story of a mouse that gathers sun rays, colors, and words while the other mice gather food to store for the winter. Frederick's stores are as important as the food when winter comes. In *An Extraordinary Egg* (1994), Jessica the frog finds an egg and brings it home to her two friends, who tell her it is a chicken egg. A few days later, when a baby alligator pops out, the three frogs call him Chicken, although he swims better than they. In *Swimmy* (1963), Lionni uses beautiful seascapes as backdrops for the clever story of how one little fish devises a plan to camouflage himself and his new school of friends.

Janell Cannon. Janell Cannon's first book, *Stellaluna* (1993), was a smash hit. Stellaluna, an adorable baby bat, is parted from her mother during an owl attack. Fortuitously, she ends up in a bird nest. Mama bird accepts Stellaluna but insists that she act like her three baby birds. Stellaluna tries to be like the birds, but the birds want to be like her, and they all hang upside down from the nest. After several ad-ventures, Stellaluna is reunited with her mother.

In *Verdi* (Cannon 1997) a baby green tree python is the protagonist. Verdi loves his bright yellow skin with bold black stripes, and he never wants to turn green like the boring older snakes. In his fast-moving lifestyle, Verdi zips around the rain for-est, taking risks. Eventually he injures himself when he discovers he cannot fly from the top of a tree. Using a tree limb as a body splint, Verdi's family helps him recover, and he settles into a more appropriate lifestyle, though not without fun.

Jane Simmons. Jane Simmons writes and beautifully illustrates Type III books for younger children. In *Come Along, Daisy!* (1997), Simmons presents a cautionary tale about a duckling that is so busy exploring the world that she loses sight of her mother. When Daisy sees threatening predators, she hides in the reeds until her mother finds her. The centerfold illustration perfectly captures the expression of a little lost child. In the sequel, *Daisy and the Egg* (1999), the little duck's mother loses heart that the green egg will hatch, but Daisy lovingly keeps it warm one more day and night—and is rewarded by a baby brother.

Type IV: Realistic Animals with Human Thinking Ability

Type IV animal fantasy is set in the real world, so all the animal characters live in appropriate habitats, such as meadows, barnyards, jungles, and stables. They have all the natural habits common to their species, which may include an instinctive fear of humans. Their knowledge of human ways is limited to what they can observe and comprehend. Usually they are able to communicate, but only with animals of the same species—never with people. In Type IV the ability to communicate human-type thoughts (and sometimes with human-type speech) is the only element of fantasy. In other words, the setting and characters are very realistic, but the narrator has access to the minds of the animals and lets the readers know what the animals think, feel, and say. The author tells the story through the animal's point of view and, in so doing, assigns some human emotions to the animal characters.

Type IV is a very small subcategory, because it requires that the author engage in painstaking research and keen observation so as to accurately represent the cultures and habitats of animals, especially animals that live in the wild. The classic example is *Black Beauty* (Sewell 1877), told as the first-person narrative of a horse that reveals his emotions and thoughts to the reader in human language. An equally loved classic is Jack London's *The Call of the Wild* (1903), told from the point of view of Buck, a dog that was stolen and sold as an Alaskan sled dog. The readability level of these two classics is beyond the reach of most elementary children, but children may enjoy listening to the books.

Dogs. Plots in Type IV animal fantasy often show animals in conflict of some kind, usually with nature, as in *The Incredible Journey* (Burnford 1961). Three loyal pets, a young Labrador retriever, a wise old bull terrier, and an adventurous Siamese cat, run away and trek through the Canadian wilderness in search of the family they love. Knowing only that the way home lies to the west, they travel steadfastly. Though they face starvation, exposure, and wild forest animals, they finally make their way home after traveling more than 250 miles. Meindert DeJong's *Hurry Home, Candy* (1953) is the story of a small dog that experiences a sad but heroic search for a home and someone to love him. Also by DeJong, *Along Came a Dog* (1958) tells of a stray dog that earns a home for himself by protecting a little red hen and her chicks from a preying hawk.

Wolves. Wolves are the main characters in *Julie's Wolf Pack* (1997) by Jean Craighead George, the third book in a trilogy about an Alaskan Inuit girl and the wolf pack she loves. The first two books are realistic fiction told through the girl's point of view, and they are discussed in Chapter 8 (Contemporary Realistic Fiction). *Julie's Wolf Pack*, however, is told from the point of view of the Avalik River wolf pack, headed by the young new alpha wolf, Kapu. The wolves display all the customary patterns of behavior of the wolf pack's complex culture—so when an outbreak of rabies threatens the wolves of the tundra, their instinct is to flee the humans who seek to save them through inoculation.

Elizabeth Hall's *Child of the Wolves* (1996) is the saga of Granite, a young Siberian husky that escapes from his kennel and is lost in the frozen Alaskan forest. He is taken in by Snowdrift, a great white wolf who is grieving the loss of her pups, which were stolen by human breeders. Because Snowdrift is the alpha male's mate, she is able to keep the puppy in the wolf pack; but he is constantly harassed by the other members because he does not know how to hunt and his short legs prevent fast running. Granite slowly adapts to the pack's way of life, and he is finally accepted when he saves Snowdrift, who has been blinded by a hunter's bullet, from falling off a cliff.

Horses. Notable among Type IV horse books is *The Blind Colt* by Glen Rounds (1941), based on a true story of a colt born blind. The little blue-gray colt roams the Montana badlands with a band of mustangs. His devoted mother cares for him, teaching him about the numerous dangers he is destined to face on the range, including the gray wolves. Miraculously, he survives the winter and is claimed and trained as a saddle horse by a young boy.

A comparison of the various types of animal fantasy is provided in Figure 6.2.

ANIMAL FANTASY BOOKS

Allard, Harry. *It's So Nice to Have a Wolf around the House*. Illus. James Marshall. Bantam Doubleday Dell, 1977.

Asch, Frank. *Happy Birthday Moon*. Prentice-Hall, 1982.

Avi. *Poppy*. Orchard, 1995.

Berenstain, Stan, & Jan Berenstain. *The Berenstain Bears and the Spooky Old Tree*. Random House, 1978.

Bond, Michael. *A Bear Called Paddington*. Illus. Peggy Fortnum. Dell, 1958.

Bourgeois, Paulette. *Franklin in the Dark*. Illus. Brenda Clark. Kids Can Press, 1986.

Brett, Jan. *Fritz and the Beautiful Horses*. Houghton Mifflin, 1981.

———. *The First Dog*. Harcourt Brace, 1988.

———. *Berlioz the Bear*. Putnam, 1991.

———. *Armadillo Rodeo*. Putnam, 1995.

Bridwell, Norman. *Clifford the Big Red Dog*. Scholastic, 1963.

Brown, Marc. *Arthur's Eyes*. Little, Brown, 1979.

———. *Arthur's New Puppy*. Little, Brown, 1993.

Brown, Margaret Wise. *Goodnight Moon*. Illus. Clement Hurd. Harper & Row, 1947.

Bryant, Hope Slaughter. *Windmill Hill*. Illus. Pamela Cote. Newfield, 1992.

Burnford, Sheila. *The Incredible Journey*. Illus. Carl Burger. Little, Brown, 1961.

Cannon, Janell. *Stellaluna*. Harcourt Brace, 1993.

———. *Trupp: A Fuzzhead Tale*. Harcourt Brace, 1995.

———. *Verdi*. Harcourt Brace, 1997.

Carle, Eric. *The Very Hungry Caterpillar*. Philomel, 1969.

———. *The Grouchy Ladybug*. Crowell, 1977.

———. *The Very Busy Spider*. Putnam, 1984.

———. *The Very Quiet Cricket*. Philomel, 1990.

———. *The Very Lonely Firefly*. Philomel, 1995.

———. *The Very Clumsy Click Beetle*. Philomel, 1999.

Cazet, Denys. *Minnie and Moo Go to the Moon*. DK, 1998.

Cherry, Lynn. *The Dragon and the Unicorn*. Gulliver, 1995.

Fantasy Type	Real-world setting	All-animal world	Wear clothing/live in houses	Coexist with humans	Communicate with humans	Possess human-type language and thoughts
Type I Animals replace humans		Yes	Yes			Yes
Type II Animals coexist with humans			Varies	Yes	Varies	Yes
Type III Animals in natural habitats without humans		Yes				Yes
Type IV Animal viewpoint in a realistic world	Yes			Yes		Yes

FIGURE 6.2   **Comparison of Animal Fantasy Types**

Cleary, Beverly. *The Mouse and the Motorcycle.* Morrow, 1965.

———. *Runaway Ralph.* Morrow, 1970.

———. *Ralph S. Mouse.* Morrow, 1982.

DeJong, Meindert. *Hurry Home, Candy.* Illus. Maurice Sendak. Harper, 1953.

———. *Along Came a Dog.* HarperCollins, 1958.

dePaola, Tomie. *Bill and Pete.* Putnam & Grosset, 1978.

Gag, Wanda. *Millions of Cats.* Coward-McCann, 1928.

George, Jean Craighead. *Julie's Wolf Pack.* Illus. Wendell Minor. HarperCollins, 1997.

Grahame, Kenneth. *The Wind in the Willows.* Atheneum, 1908/1983.

Hall, Elizabeth. *Child of the Wolves.* Houghton Mifflin, 1996.

Henkes, Kevin. *Julius, the Baby of the World.* Greenwillow, 1990.

———. *Chrysanthemum.* Greenwillow, 1991.

———. *Owen.* Greenwillow, 1993.

Hoban, Russell. *Bedtime for Frances.* Illus. Garth Williams. Harper, 1960.

Hobbie, Holly. *Toot & Puddle.* Little, Brown, 1997.

Howe, Deborah, & James Howe. *Bunnicula: A Rabbit-Tale of Mystery.* Illus. Alan Daniel. Simon & Schuster, 1979.

Howe, James. *Howliday Inn.* Illus. Lynn Munsinger. Atheneum, 1982.

——. *The Celery Stalks at Midnight*. Illus. Leslie Morrill. Atheneum, 1983.

Jacques, Brian. *Redwall*. Illus. Gary Chalk. Philomel, 1986.

Johnson, Angela. *Julius*. Illus. Dav Pilkey. Orchard, 1993.

King-Smith, Dick. *Pigs Might Fly*. Viking Penguin, 1980.

——. *Babe: The Gallant Pig*. Crown, 1988.

——. *Three Terrible Trins*. Illus. Mark Teague. Crown, 1994.

——. *The School Mouse*. Hyperion, 1995.

Kipling, Rudyard. *The Jungle Book*. Illus. Kurt Wiese. Everyman's Library, 1894/1994.

Kraus, Robert. *Leo the Late Bloomer*. Illus. Jose Aruego. HarperCollins, 1971.

Lawson, Robert. *Rabbit Hill*. Viking, 1944.

Le Guin, Ursula K. *Catwings*. Illus. S. D. Schindler. Orchard, 1988.

Lionni, Leo. *Inch by Inch*. Astor Honor, 1960.

——. *Swimmy*. Knopf, 1963.

——. *Frederick*. Knopf, 1967.

——. *An Extraordinary Egg*. Knopf, 1994.

Lobel, Arnold. *Frog and Toad Are Friends*. Harper & Row, 1970.

——. *Mouse Tales*. Harper & Row, 1972.

——. *Fables*. Harper & Row, 1980.

London, Jack. *The Call of the Wild*. Simon & Schuster, 1903/1995.

Lowrey, Janette Sebring. *The Poky Little Puppy*. Illus. Gustaf Tenggren. Golden Books, 1942.

McCloskey, Robert. *Make Way for Ducklings*. Viking, 1941.

McBratney, Sam. *Guess How Much I Love You?* Illus. Anita Jeram. Candlewick, 1994.

May, Robert L. *Rudolph the Red-Nosed Reindeer*. Illus. Michael Emberley. Modern Curriculum Press, 1939.

Marshall, James. *Swine Lake*. Illus. Maurice Sendak. HarperCollins, 1999.

Meddaugh, Susan. *Martha Speaks*. Houghton Mifflin, 1992.

Minarik, Else Holmelund. *Little Bear*. Illus. Maurice Sendak. Harper & Row, 1957.

Munsch, Robert. *Pigs*. Illus. Michael Martchenko. Annick Press, 1989.

O'Brien, Robert. *Mrs. Frisby and the Rats of NIMH*. Atheneum, 1974.

Pinkwater, Daniel M. *The Wuggie Norple Story*. Illus. Tomie dePaola. Macmillan, 1980.

Potter, Beatrix. *The Tale of Peter Rabbit*. Frederick Warne, 1902/1987.

——. *The Tale of Benjamin Bunny*. Frederick Warne, 1904.

Rathman, Peggy. *Officer Buckle and Gloria*. Putnam, 1995.

Rey, H. A. *Curious George*. Houghton Mifflin, 1941.

Rounds, Glen. *The Blind Colt*. Holiday House, 1941.

Rylant, Cynthia. *Henry and Mudge and the Happy Cat*. Illus. Suçie Stevenson. Simon & Schuster, 1990.

Salten, Felix. *Bambi: A Life in the Woods*. Illus. Barbara Cooney. Pocket Books, 1926.

Selden, George. *The Cricket in Times Square*. Illus. Garth Williams. Farrar, Straus & Giroux, 1957.

Seuss, Dr. *The Cat in the Hat*. Random House, 1957.

——. *How the Grinch Stole Christmas!* Random House, 1957.

Sewell, Anna. *Black Beauty*. Grammercy, 1877/1998.

Silverstein, Shel. *Lafcadio, the Lion Who Shot Back*. HarperCollins, 1963.

Simmons, Jane. *Come Along, Daisy!* Little, Brown, 1997.

——. *Daisy and the Egg*. Little, Brown, 1999.

Steig, William. *Sylvester and the Magic Pebble*. Simon & Schuster, 1969.

——. *Dominic*. Farrar, Straus & Giroux, 1972.

——. *Abel's Island*. Farrar, Straus & Giroux, 1976.

——. *Doctor De Soto*. Farrar, Straus & Giroux, 1982.

——. *The Amazing Bone*. Farrar, Straus & Giroux, 1984.

——. *Shrek!* Farrar, Straus & Giroux, 1990.

——. *Zeke Pippin*. HarperCollins, 1994.

White, E. B. *Charlotte's Web*. Illus. Garth Williams. HarperCollins, 1952.

Williams, Barbara. *Albert's Toothache*. Illus. Kay Chorao. Dutton, 1974.

Yolen, Jane. *Commander Toad in Space*. Illus. Bruce Degen. Coward-McCann, 1980.

——. *The Acorn Quest*. Illus. Susanna Natti. Crowell, 1981.

Zion, Gene. *Harry the Dirty Dog*. Illus. Margaret Bloy Graham. Harper & Row, 1956.

KEY TERMS

Explore the E-Glossary at **www.ablongman.com/anderson**

animal fantasy (p. 149)

anthropomorphic animals (p. 149)

readers theater (p. 155)

webbing (p. 156)

c h a p t e r

7

Multicultural
Literature

Library locations: Appears in all genres. Various locations.

Cross-cultural literature that includes books by and about peoples of *all* cultures

I remember reading in my elementary school history book about how the United States was made up of people from many nations. The text explained that through intermarriage and assimilation, the different races had been homogenized into what we call Americans. This formulation was called the "melting pot theory." My textbook even had a cartoon showing people of different races jumping into a huge cooking pot with Uncle Sam stirring them around with a big stick. According to this theory, American people abandoned all their distinguishing cultural characteristics in favor of the dominant white culture.

The melting pot theory permeated the U.S. educational system for many decades. However, there were some serious flaws in this theory. First, not all races melted equally. It is true that people of European descent melted quite nicely; even many Native Americans melted as they were assimilated through intermarriage to European Americans. However, some racial groups, such as people from Africa and Asia, did not homogenize so quickly, and because of this, they were easy targets for discrimination and other forms of racism. A second major flaw to the melting pot theory was that not all people wanted to melt. Some people desired to keep their heritage intact—to preserve the language, religion, customs, and traditions of their parents.

A more accurate description of the U.S. populace is the "salad bowl theory." When you toss a salad, all the different vegetables are mixed together. However, they do not melt into some huge veggie fondue; rather, each different vegetable in the bowl retains its own shape, texture, color, and flavor. Each component of the salad makes a contribution, and together they make one great dish.

Having a variety of vegetables makes a salad more appealing and nutritious. In a like manner, including books about a variety of cultures makes a literature program more interesting and complete. A greater variety also makes it more likely that all children will have access to literature that represents their various backgrounds. Children need to see themselves reflected in stories with positive role models; this tends to increase their self-esteem and pride in their heritage. Also, greater variety in the literature program exposes all readers to the various minority cultures in our country. Vicarious experiences—and ensuing emotional involvement with minority characters in well-written books—have the potential to correct misconceptions about people who are different from the reader. This may help children avoid developing prejudiced attitudes.

One general definition of **culture** is the totality of socially transmitted behavior patterns, arts, beliefs, institutions, and all other products of human work and thought. More specifically, the word *culture* can designate these patterns, traits, and products as the expression of a particular community or population. Cultures can be determined by national origin, ethnic origin, primary language, religion, geographic region, and other factors.

In past decades, children's textbooks and literature focused on white, middle-class Americans, but over the years, books have moved toward greater cultural diversity. Keep in mind, however, that European American is also a culture—currently the majority culture in the United States.

Good multicultural books increase readers' appreciation of persons of various cultures and help them overcome stereotypical views. **Stereotyping** is assigning a fixed image or some fixed characteristics to *all* the members of a particular cultural group. This gross overgeneralizing rests on an assumption that something identifiable is shared by *all* members of a group. Groups can be stereotyped based on gender, ethnicity, religion, culture, socioeconomic status, dialect, and other factors. Stereotyping in literature can occur when the author does not develop characters into well-rounded people who have both positive and negative attributes (Houston 1999).

It is easy to detect and understand how harmful stereotyping can be when the traits are negative, but stereotyping can also be damaging when it relates to positive qualities. Racism in stories can often be subtle, masquerading as a virtue. For example, Native Americans are often stereotyped as being close to nature, but is this a covert way of saying they are less civilized? Other positive stereotypes have to do with intelligence, athletic ability, and artistic talent. Imagine how children in the cultural group feel when they themselves do not exhibit their group's purported universal traits. To determine if a multicultural book contains "positive stereotyping," ask yourself questions such as, Are all African American characters portrayed as athletic? Are all Jewish characters portrayed as wealthy? Are all Asian American characters portrayed as highly intelligent? Are all Hispanic American characters portrayed as gregarious? Are all Native American characters portrayed as animal lovers?

Evaluating Multicultural Literature

In evaluating **multicultural literature,** first and foremost ask yourself if it is quality literature supported by a worthy theme. If it is, the following questions will further guide you.

- Is there any cultural stereotyping suggesting that all members of a specific cultural group share the same socioeconomic status, personality traits, facial features, and the like?
- Are the characters multidimensional individuals with lives rooted in their culture? *well rounded*
- Is the language authentic to the background and social environment in which the story takes place?
- Is the portrayal of the culture authentic, reflecting its values and beliefs?
- Are all factual details accurate?
- Are all cultural details authentic and naturally integrated within the story using a modern perspective?
- Are there any cultural omissions or distortions that may create misconceptions?

- Are the central issues of the culture realistically portrayed and explored in depth?
- Does the book help children value their own heritage or understand people with other backgrounds?

Categories of Multicultural Books

Bishop (1992) identified three categories of multicultural books, which she classified according to the degree of the cultural understandings they afford readers. Books representative of each of these categories are important in a balanced literature program.

Culturally Neutral Books

Culturally neutral books contain some characters from minority groups or have multicultural faces portrayed within illustrations. These books' topics contain no real cultural content; nonetheless, their inclusive nature reveals that the authors, illustrators, and publishers value diversity in children's books. These books serve to increase readers' exposure and awareness of diversity. Also, minority children can identify with these books when they belong to the same cultural group as the characters.

Examples of culturally neutral books include *The Egypt Game* (Snyder 1967), in which four children living in a neighborhood play together. Two of the children, a girl and her younger brother, are African American. Were it not for the illustrations and the author's mention of these children's ethnicity early in the book, the reader would not know that the ethnicities of the four children are not the same.

To say a book is culturally neutral does not imply it cannot be useful in helping children understand and accept diversity. For example, *What a Wonderful World* (Weiss & Thiele 1994), a book inspired by a Louis Armstrong song, depicts children of all major U.S. ethnic groups in the illustrations, though no cultural information is given in the text. However, the theme of the book is that the world is wonderful because of its diversity, and no particulars are necessary to understand the value of that message.

Michael Hays took culturally neutral books to a new high when he illustrated *Abiyoyo* (Seeger 1986). The story is set in a small village during past times, much like a folktale. The main characters, a magician and his son, are of African descent. However, all the other characters in the book are from various nations and world religions. For example, the first page shows the main characters with a blond-headed man, a Hindu woman, and an Oriental woman talking around a kitchen table. The illustrations showing all the townspeople together are intriguing for children to look at and try to determine which nationality or religious culture each character represents.

Culturally Generic Books

Culturally generic books focus on characters representing a specific cultural group, but there is little culturally specific information involved. The characters in these books are depicted as ordinary people existing within the larger American culture, and the book's themes and plots are generically American. One such book is *Short-cut* by Donald Crews (1992). The cover of this book depicts seven African American siblings, four boys and three girls, standing on a railroad track. In the story the children take a shortcut home by following the tracks. When they hear a freight train approaching, they jump off the tracks onto the steep slopes full of briers. If you did not know that the author was African American and that he wrote about his childhood experiences, only the color of the characters' skin would indicate their ethnicity. Nothing in the children's environment, clothing, or actions reveals they are African Americans. Only on the last page is there a word in the African American vernacular: The book's narrator mentions Bigmama, a common name for grandmother in the African American culture.

Another culturally generic book is *The Lost Lake* by Allen Say (1989), who is Japanese American. The book's characters are young Luke and his father. The illustrations indicate that the father and son are Asian Americans. However, what the narrator relates about the characters is common to many people within the larger American culture: The parents are divorced; the boy becomes bored in the summer; the father and son enjoy a hiking and camping trip; and they eat foods such as salami, dried apricots, beef stroganoff, and coffee on their trip.

Again, it would be a mistake to shrug off culturally generic books with the reaction that "There was nothing to be learned about this culture." On the contrary, these books help readers see past cultural stereotypes and to learn that people of all cultures have many things in common. "Readers see themselves and others as sharing universal experiences" (Temple, Martinez, Yokota, & Naylor 1998). And indeed, we are all more alike than different.

Culturally Specific Books

Culturally specific books incorporate details that help define the characters as members of a particular cultural group. In these books ethnicity is more than a superficial mask. There is a mix of distinguishing characteristics of the minority cultural group—together with elements that are characteristic of the larger cultural group to which all Americans belong. Specifics of the minority culture include such things as family relationships, religion, language, names, values, attitudes, and interactions with others both inside and outside the cultural group. Illustrations in culturally specific books also portray many cultural details.

In *Felita* by Nicholasa Mohr (1979), the author weaves some of her childhood experiences growing up Puerto Rican in New York City's *El Barrio*. The reader learns something about family relationships, language, cuisine, and customs among New York Puerto Ricans (called *Nuyoricans* by Puerto Ricans on the island). The reader also shares the hurt and humiliation young Felita experiences when her family moves to a "better neighborhood," where she receives cruel treatment from the neighborhood children.

Likewise, readers of *To Walk the Sky Path* (Naylor 1973) will learn about a Mikasuki Seminole family living in a *chickee* on a mangrove island in the Florida

Felita hugs her *abuelita.*
From *Felita,* written by
Nicholasa Mohr and
illustrated by Ray Cruz.

Everglades. Billie is the only member of his extended family to go to school and learn
how to read, and he sometimes feels he is caught between two worlds. Throughout
the book he contrasts the Seminole culture with the mainstream culture of his school
and the friends he has made there.

Common Themes

The themes of culturally specific books are usually different from those of other
books in realistic fiction. One recurring theme is the mingling of two cultures when
a family immigrates to the United States—or when, like the young Seminole boy in
To Walk the Sky Path, a character enters another culture. Obviously, the differences
between the two cultures are pointed out, but frequently this is done in a positive
manner, and the similarities among peoples are stressed.

Culturally specific books also contain quite serious themes, such as the persistence of racial oppression in the United States in both historical and modern times. Among other themes are the oppression that drove people to leave their homelands and emigrate to the United States, the prejudice the newcomers faced in this country, and the challenge of learning to appreciate one's cultural heritage while adjusting to American life. Other themes do not involve a major hardship, as in stories about characters who are awakening to the meaning and importance of their heritage.

The folktales from all over the world presented in Chapter 4 demonstrate that traditional literature was the original multicultural literature. Books introduced in this chapter represent a variety of genres, because multicultural literature comes in all genres. I encourage you to move beyond traditional literature in your readings. I believe that realistic fiction most authentically portrays culture, affording children the greatest opportunities to learn about diversity.

Misrepresentation of Culture

I caution readers to scrutinize older books, especially historical fiction and biography, to determine if they contain "white bias," a subtle form of racism that implies that the mainstream way of life is inherently superior. An example of a biased theme is that minority people achieve success only after giving up the distinctive values and lifestyles of their culture to adopt those of the mainstream society.

However, older books are not the only ones guilty of misrepresentation. I cite two examples with Native American characters. One recently published book that has been subjected to in-depth scrutiny is *My Heart Is on the Ground: The Diary of Nannie Little Rose, a Sioux Girl* (Rinaldi 1999). The narrative is set in 1880 at the Carlisle Indian School in Pennsylvania. This juvenile historical fiction book, written in the form of a diary, is part of Scholastic's Dear America series. It was the subject of a severe critique by a group of women, both Native American and non-Native (Atleo et al. 1999), who found the book to be an outrageous depiction of a tragic period in Native American history—the attempt to strip Indian children of their culture.

Survivors have told of the forced removal of Indian children from their homes during that period and of the mistreatment and humiliation they received at the boarding schools. The children were not allowed to speak their languages, wear their own clothing, or practice their tribal customs and religion. In contrast to the documented abuse and desperate situations that occurred at the Carlisle Indian Industrial School, however, *My Heart Is on the Ground* presents a picture of children who—though sad to leave their families and afraid of going to a new place—are eager to learn the language and the customs of the white people at the boarding school. Except for a couple of "troublemakers," once the children experience the good life in the boarding school, they do not want to leave. Even the troublemakers come around at the end.

Responding to Literature

Comparing Cultural Viewpoints

After reviewing the description of life in an Indian boarding school in *My Heart Is on the Ground* (Rinaldi 1999), compare the book to one of the fictional but authentic Native American books listed below. What are the major differences between the descriptions of life in the schools, and what might account for those differences?

> *Cheyenne Again* by Eve Bunting (1995)
> *Daughter of Suqua* by Diane Hamm Johnson (1997)
> *My Name Is Seepeetza* by Shirley Sterling (1997)

Another book that has received much criticism because of its historical and cultural inauthenticity is *Brother Eagle, Sister Sky: A Message from Chief Seattle* (Jeffers 1991). The book states that the text is a speech by the Suquamish Chief Seattle (Seathl), given at the signing of a peace treaty in the 1850s. However, a film writer named Ted Perry has declared that the book was based on a script he wrote for an environmental television commercial in 1971. Perry asserts that although he did base the *intent* of his text on a report by Dr. Henry Smith, who was present during Chief Seattle's speech, Smith's account was written some thirty years after the occasion and may not have accurately represented the chief's words.

Even Jeffers's illustrations in this book, though very attractive, depict cultural aspects of the Plains Indians—not of the Suquamish people of the Northwest, as the book leads the reader to believe. However, the most disturbing aspect of Jeffers's illustrations is that the Native Americans are depicted as ghostlike images. Debbie Reese (Nambe Pueblo) pointed out, "They are not in a physical form, as is the case with the white family illustrated at the end of the book. I think that is a powerful subliminal message to children that Native people are gone, that only their ghosts are left" (personal communication, November 17, 1999).

One of the most controversial topics in multicultural literature today is whether an author outside a specific culture's social group can write authentically about that group. The questions raised include: Do books by authors outside a particular culture provide a distorted view because of the authors' own cultural biases? If an author does adequate research into another culture and is able to write with sensitivity, can the author authentically write about that culture? Do authors who share the culture of their characters describe them more authentically and convincingly?

It is difficult to determine the authenticity of a book that deals with a culture outside one's own. Usually, if the authors and illustrators are of the same cultural group as their characters, this supports their credentials. However, that information is not always provided—and, hard as it may be to believe, some authors misrepresent their culture. One author whose name was changed to sound Indian has been denounced by Native Americans on several fronts as an imposter.

Readers often know when something does not sound accurate in a book, and they are able to recognize obvious stereotypes. Checking a book's copyright date may be helpful because older books were not scrutinized for stereotyping, whereas many publishers make some effort to do so today. However, most cases of cultural inauthenticity are revealed only when we read literary critiques and talk to other people who are knowledgeable in multicultural literature.

The authors and illustrators I have listed in each of this chapter's cultural sections are members of the designated cultural group. My aim is not to devalue the work of those who write authentic books about characters of another culture; rather, it is to highlight the achievements of sometimes overlooked minority authors and illustrators. Additionally, books written and illustrated by minorities—as well as books about minorities written by people outside the cultural group—are included in each of the genre chapters.

CHILDREN'S BOOKS CITED IN PRECEDING SECTIONS

Bunting, Eve. *Cheyenne Again.* Clarion, 1995.

Crews, Donald. *Shortcut.* Greenwillow, 1992.

Jeffers, Susan. *Brother Eagle, Sister Sky.* Dial, 1991.

Johnson, Diane Hamm. *Daughter of Suqua.* Albert Whitman, 1997.

Mohr, Nicholasa. *Felita.* Dial, 1979.

Naylor, Phyllis Reynolds. *To Walk the Sky Path.* Yearling, 1973.

Rinaldi, Ann. *My Heart Is on the Ground: The Diary of Nannie Little Rose, a Sioux Girl.* Scholastic, 1999.

Say, Allen. *The Lost Lake.* Houghton Mifflin, 1989.

Seeger, Pete. *Abiyoyo.* Illus. Michael Hays. Macmillan, 1986.

Snyder, Zilpha Keatley. *The Egypt Game.* Atheneum, 1967.

Sterling, Shirley. *My Name Is Seepeetza.* Douglas & McIntyre, 1997.

Weiss, George David, & Bob Thiele. *What a Wonderful World.* Illus. Ashley Bryan. Sundance, 1994.

The following section was written by Sabrina A. Brinson, assistant professor at the University of Memphis. She developed a strong interest in African American children's literature while in graduate school, and it is one of her primary areas of research.

African American Literature

by Sabrina A. Brinson

African Americans are the descendants of various indigenous people of the African continent who are American citizens. They have always had a pervasive and important influence on American life. However, as an African American child, I read only a few children's books with positive African American characters. In graduate school I looked for what I had missed as a child, and I searched school and public libraries for children's books in print with African American characters that were published before the civil rights movement. The only books I found published before 1962 were in a large university library, and these were books like *Little Black Sambo* (Bannerman

1945) and *The Pickaninny Twins* (Perkins 1931). My analysis of these books was a sad commentary. The African American characters in these books were typically depicted as a "no 'count natural thief, a flunky happily steppin' and fetchin', a pitied simpleton, a gargantuan bully, and (ever popular) a poor, helpless, inept underdog scared senseless, a shakin' and a quakin' in his shoes" (Brinson 1997, pp. 8–9). In addition, many of these characters rattled off unintelligible dialect. Accentuating the text were characters illustrated in charcoal black with out-of-control hair and absurdly overexaggerated features that seemed to leap off the pages!

Although he was not African American, Ezra Jack Keats broke ground when he published *The Snowy Day* in 1962. It is an account of a young African American boy's day of play in the snow in an urban neighborhood. Many other suitable books have followed, from individuals within and outside the cultural group. In my analysis of post–civil rights books, I found a vast difference. The derogatory, stereotyped image of African American characters, for the most part, has been eradicated in children's books. It has been supplanted with portrayals of African Americans with suitable vernacular. Illustrations of characters adorning the text are kaleidoscopic images, representative of the true variations of skin color, hair, and features. The protagonists represent cognizant, autonomous, versatile, productive characters—who incidentally are African American (Brinson 1997).

Today, African American authors and illustrators have made literary contributions in which a variety of voices are tapped. To highlight the contributions of African American authors and illustrators, the *Coretta Scott King Award* (discussed in Chapter 2) is given annually to an African American author and illustrator for their outstanding inspirational and educational books published in the previous year.

One of my favorite King Award–winning authors is Eloise Greenfield, who has written an impressive number of inspiring books, such as *Grandmama's Joy* (1980), that feature amiable intergenerational relationships and multifaceted characters. Greenfield was awarded the Coretta Scott King Award in 1978 for *Africa Dream* (1977), in which a little girl imagines a trip to Africa filled with a bounty of cherished events and loving experiences with her ancestors. The book's inclusion of some of Africa's natural resources, animals, and architecture provides opportunities for readers to learn about the continent. More importantly, Greenfield's heartwarming story encourages children to appreciate their ancestries and to dream in color with their eyes open. Greenfield received the Coretta Scott King Honorable Mention in 1978 for *Mary McCleod Bethune* (1977) and again in 1990 for *Nathaniel Talking* (1989). She described her work by saying,

> I attempt to depict African American people and their lives with accuracy, depth, and balance, always keeping in mind the need to counteract the stereotypes that are so prevalent in the general body of literature and other media. I write with the hope that my work will inspire in readers a love of language, a love of themselves, and a commitment to human values. (Pollock 1992, p. 85)

A favorite award-winning illustrator is Jerry Pinkney, an ingenious artist whose expressive illustrations illuminate a variety of books, among them *The Green Lion of Zion Street* (Fields 1988). Pinkney received the Coretta Scott King Award in 1986 for his illustrations in *The Patchwork Quilt* (Flournoy 1985) and in 1989 for his illustrations in *Mirandy and Brother Wind* (McKissack 1988), which was also named a Caldecott Honor book. In addition, he received the Coretta Scott King Honorable Mention in 1981 for his illustrations in *Count on Your Fingers: African Style* (Zaslavsky 1980) and in 1990 for his illustrations in *The Talking Eggs: A Folktale from the American South* (San Souci 1989).

My favorite Pinkney book is *Mirandy and Brother Wind,* in which he animates a young girl's determination to dance with the wind during the community's junior cakewalk. The illustrations are powerful because they capture the essence of expressive individualism, movement, harmony, verve, and affect, which are some of the interrelated dimensions of the African American culture (Boykin 1983). Because of Pinkney's exceptional artistry, Brother Wind blows to life with a commanding presence and self-important persona, and Mirandy and her partner nearly dance off the pages during the junior cakewalk!

Today there are many good books with African American characters. Nevertheless, there is still much to be done to provide literature that portrays the rich experiences representative of our multicultural society. To illustrate, African Americans have produced the largest and most rapidly growing body of multicultural children's literature, yet only 2 percent of the children's books published each year are written or illustrated by an African American. Considering that approximately 13 percent of the U.S. population is African American, 2 percent is a paltry figure.

Fortunate children are exposed to alluring stories that are treasured and remembered, even through adulthood. Children often pattern themselves after the main characters or central themes. Culturally specific issues and illustrations can help encourage positive self-attributes and high ethnic identity in African American children, and can help children of all backgrounds see African Americans in a positive light. When African American characters are portrayed in a variety of settings and involved in a variety of activities, it accentuates the uniqueness of each one of us while strengthening the common bonds that join us together. Therefore, as society moves toward greater celebration of our diverse population, it is beneficial to promote African American authors' and illustrators' contributions in literature for children.

CHILDREN'S BOOKS CITED IN THIS SECTION

Bannerman, Helen. *Little Black Sambo*. Harrison, 1945.

Fields, Julia. *The Green Lion of Zion Street*. Illus. Jerry Pinkney. Simon & Schuster, 1988.

Flournoy, Valerie. *The Patchwork Quilt*. Illus. Jerry Pinkney. Dial, 1985.

Greenfield, Eloise. *Africa Dream*. Illus. Carol Byard. Day, 1977.

———. *Mary McCleod Bethune*. Illus. Jerry Pinkney. Crowell, 1977.

———. *Grandmama's Joy*. Illus. Carol Byard. Philomel, 1980.

———. *Nathaniel Talking*. Illus. Jan Spivey Gilchrist. Black Butterfly, 1989.

Keats, Ezra Jack. *The Snowy Day*. Puffin, 1962.

McKissack, Patricia. *Mirandy and Brother Wind*. Illus. Jerry Pinkney. Knopf, 1988.

Perkins, Lucy Fitch. *The Pickaninny Twins*. Houghton Mifflin, 1931.

San Souci, Robert D. *The Talking Eggs: A Folktale from the American South*. Illus. Jerry Pinkney. Dial, 1989.

Zaslavsky, Claudia. *Count on Your Fingers: African Style*. Illus. Jerry Pinkney. Crowell, 1980.

▌ RECOMMENDED BOOKS BY AFRICAN AMERICAN AUTHORS AND ILLUSTRATORS

- Boyd, Candy D. *Circle of Gold.* Scholastic, 1984. This endearing novel reveals how the loss of a little girl's father has left the close-knit, happy family dazed and divided. Mother's Day is approaching, and Mattie desperately wants to give her mother the perfect gift in hope of reuniting their family.

- Cosby, Bill. *The Meanest Thing to Say.* Illus. Varnette P. Honeywood. Scholastic, 1997. The serious social issue of bullying is addressed in this picture book. The story promotes peace education and features children as problem solvers.

- Crews, Donald. *Bigmama's.* Greenwillow, 1991. This picture book details rich traditions and festivities enjoyed by three generations of a family during summer visits to the grandmother's house in the country.

- Curtis, Christopher Paul. *The Watsons Go to Birmingham—1963.* Delacorte, 1995. This novel is a captivating account of exciting events, revelations, and harrowing encounters in an engrossing story about a Michigan family's visit to the South. (If you read this book aloud, get ready for some raucous laughter.)

- ———. *Bud, Not Buddy.* Delacorte, 1999. Ten-year-old Bud flees from a horrendous foster home with the unyielding determination to find the man he believes is his father, the famous bandleader Herman E. Calloway.

- Flournoy, Valerie. *The Patchwork Quilt.* Illus. Jerry Pinkney. Dial, 1985. Three generations of love and keepsakes are laced into each patch of a quilt made by a little girl, her mother, and her grandmother.

- Ford, Juwanda G. *A Kente Cloth for Kenya.* Illus. Sylvia Walker. Scholastic, 1996. A little girl learns from her grandmother about the history of the kente cloth and displays her knowledge about her ethnic heritage during a special school activity.

- Greenfield, Eloise. *Grandpa's Face.* Illus. Floyd Cooper. Philomel, 1988. A little girl becomes upset when she sees her grandfather, an actor, portraying an angry role. Potentially negative feelings are released in a soothing, amiable manner that youngsters can relate to.

- Hoffman, Mary. *Amazing Grace.* Illus. Caroline Binch. Scholastic, 1991. Adversity in reference to ethnicity and gender are rejected with style and grace by a little girl who accomplishes her goal of being Peter Pan in the school play.

- Hopkinson, Deborah. *Sweet Clara and the Freedom Quilt.* Illus. James Ransome. Knopf, 1993. The essence of bravery and ingenuity are demonstrated by a little girl who weaves a map that helps guide slaves to the Underground Railroad and subsequent freedom.

- Howard, Elizabeth Fitzgerald. *Aunt Flossie's Hats (and Crab Cakes Later).* Illus. James Ransome. Clarion, 1991. Brilliant illustrations accentuate this picture book about two sisters and the magical Sunday visits shared with their Great-Great-Aunt Flossie.

- King, Martin Luther, Jr. *I Have a Dream.* Illus. Ashley Bryan et al. Scholastic, 1997. Dr. Martin Luther King Jr. soulfully expresses his dreams for a world where all people live in peace in his famous speech, which is beautifully illustrated in this picture book.

- Mathis, Sharon Bell. *Sidewalk Story.* Viking Penguin, 1971. The neighbors are sympathetic but passive when Lilly Etta's best friend, Tanya, and her family are evicted from their apartment. Lilly Etta is determined to find a way to make the men move the furniture back and let Tanya's family stay.

- Mitchell, Margaree King. ***Uncle Jed's Barbershop.*** Illus. James Ransome. Simon & Schuster, 1993. A young woman looks back over the years and marvels at her uncle's persistence in striving to achieve his dream—of opening his own barbershop—despite severe setbacks.

- Ringgold, Faith. ***If a Bus Could Talk: The Story of Rosa Parks.*** Simon & Schuster, 1999. A talking bus tells the story of Rosa Parks, thoroughly explaining the significance of her historic act of courage—remaining seated on a bus in Montgomery, Alabama.

- Small, Irene. ***Irene and the Big Fine Nickel.*** Illus. Tyrone Geter. Little, Brown, 1991. Reflections on African Americans' heritage and the Harlem Renaissance are heralded in this book that depicts the sheer happiness experienced by a little girl and her best friends when they make a wonderful discovery.

- Taylor, Mildred D. ***Roll of Thunder, Hear My Cry.*** Puffin, 1976. This powerful novel portrays a close family in Mississippi in the 1930s. The Logans hold fast to their principles and make a personal sacrifice to save the life of a young boy.

- ———. ***Let the Circle Be Unbroken.*** Dial, 1981. In this compelling sequel to *Roll of Thunder,* the Logan family rally together during a whirlwind of turmoil as an innocent friend stands trial for murder, a cousin tries to pass for white, and a neighbor is driven from her *annotated* home when she stands up for her right to vote.

- Thomassie, Tynia. ***Mimi's Tutu.*** Illus. Jan Spivey Gilchrist. Scholastic, 1996. Vibrant illustrations in this picture book spotlight a little girl who celebrates her individuality, self-confidence, and ethnic heritage when she dances with her friends.

- Yarbrough, Camille. ***Cornrows.*** Illus. Carol Byard. Coward-McCann, 1979. This book highlights African traditions and symbols, such as the cornrows hairstyle, as they are passed on to a little girl and her brother by their mother and great-grandmother.

Asian American Literature

Although the **Asian American** population (which includes descendants of peoples from Cambodia, China, Japan, Korea, Laos, Thailand, and Vietnam) throughout the United States is significant, there are relatively few quality children's books written by and about them.

A prime example of a negative portrayal of an Asian culture is the widely circulated folktale, *The Five Chinese Brothers* by Claire Huchet Bishop, which was first published in 1938 and is still in print. In the illustrations by Kurt Weise, not only are the brothers identical, but all the characters—mother, townspeople, judge, and executioners—are identically caricatured. They are all illustrated with yellow skin and slanted slits for eyes, wearing queue hairstyles and "coolie" clothing. Schwartz (1977) deemed this book a relic of historical racism, which can harm the self-image of children of Chinese descent as well as harm non-Chinese children's potential for bias-free thought and behavior. Children could form the misconceptions that all Chinese people look alike and have yellow skin and slanted eyes. To make matters worse, the book fosters old images of oppression. "The queue was a humiliating symbol of subjugation forced upon Chinese peasants by the Manchu ruling class" (p. 4), and the coolie clothes are associated with the subjugation of underpaid Chinese laborers in the United States.

In a watershed study commissioned by the Council for Interracial Books for Children (1976), eleven Asian American book reviewers located, read, and analyzed all children's books on Asian American themes that were published by establishment or commercial publishing houses and were in current use in schools and libraries. The major conclusion was that with no more than a couple of exceptions, the sixty-six books reviewed were racist, sexist, and elitist. The researchers determined that the image of Asian Americans presented in these books was grossly misleading, presenting them as "foreigners who all look alike and choose to live together in quaint communities in the midst of large cities and cling to 'outworn,' alien customs" (p. 3). From this study, the Council's criteria for analyzing books on Asian Americans were developed.

These criteria were primarily directed to authors, artists, art directors, and book editors who create and publish books with Asian American characters and themes. In the report, the ensuing discussion of each criterion largely consisted of stereotypes and negative themes to avoid. In order to benefit educators who are selecting (rather than creating) quality literature, I have extrapolated from this discussion some significant positive themes and character traits that can be used as evaluative criteria.

According to the Council for Interracial Books for Children (2000), a culturally authentic children's book about Asian Americans should achieve the following six criteria.

- **Reflect the realities and way of life of an Asian American people.** The characters should be depicted as people from a distinct Asian culture whose experiences in the United States have generated new and unique Asian American cultures. The settings, behavior, speech, clothing, and the like should be depicted accurately for the historical period and cultural context of the story. Traditional festivals should be put into perspective within typical daily activities.
- **Transcend stereotypes.** Problems should be confronted and handled by the Asian American protagonist, rather than by a benefactor from the mainstream culture. Characters should display a full range of human emotions, so the reader senses their spirit, individuality, humor, strength, and drive. Characters' occupations should be varied, and their speech should be authentic.
- **Rectify historical distortions and omissions.** Where appropriate, books should indicate that in the past, dire conditions in China encouraged emigration, and Chinese were actively recruited by agents of U.S. business interests. The historical achievements of Asian Americans—such as the Chinese who constructed the transcontinental railroad—should be valued. The internment of more than 110,000 Japanese Americans in concentration camps during World War II should be placed in the historical context of racism, rather than being dismissed as war hysteria.
- **Avoid the model- and super-minority syndromes.** Characters in the story should be respected on their own terms, rather than needing to demonstrate outstanding abilities, skills, or talents in order to gain approval and esteem.

- **Reflect an awareness of the changing status of women.** Asian American females should be presented as individual persons, not as "China dolls." Young readers should encounter positive female role models (outside the ancient Confucian model that specified a higher status for men than for women).
- **Contain art and photos that accurately reflect racial diversity.** Illustrations should reveal the differences in facial structures between individuals and among groups—for example, among Chinese Americans, Filipino Americans, Japanese Americans, Korean Americans, and other Asian Americans. In particular, illustrations should reveal the variations in Asian American eyes and skin tones. Clothing should be appropriate to the activity and occasion. When traditional clothing is called for, it should be appropriate to the culture depicted.

Currently, the body of literature about Asian cultures includes some well-written and illustrated folktales that can be helpful in establishing cultural context, interest, and meaning for children (Gerson 2000; Li 2000). There are also books of interesting memoirs and personal accounts of Asian Americans, which often fall within the historical fiction genre. There are fewer books of contemporary fiction about Asian American characters and cultures. However, even among these more recently published books, cultural authenticity is often lacking.

In an interview by Baghban (2000), renowned author Laurence Yep speaks to the problems that can occur when stories are created by someone whose ethnic background differs from the characters in the book:

> There are so many terrible books written about Chinese Americans by white writers who simply made up whatever they wanted. There is a smaller group of books where an author was conscientious enough to do interviews. Unfortunately, even those authors distorted the data to fit their cultural prejudices and stereotypes. (p. 44)

Properly selected books can help foster cultural awareness and self-concepts in Asian American children as well as help them with issues of acculturation (Chi 1993). Additionally, they can assist all children in appreciating Asian American cultures and rejecting the mass media's stereotypical representations.

To promote the publication of authentic literature, the annual Asian Pacific American Award for Children's and Young Adult Literature was recently established to encourage and honor outstanding books by authors and illustrators of Asian and Pacific Islander descent. This award is cosponsored by the Asian Pacific American Librarians Association and the Chinese American Librarians Association. The first award was given to Janet S. Wong for *The Trip Back Home* (2000). This and other authentic stories by Asian American authors and illustrators are annotated in the following list.

 ## Responding to Literature

Looking for Stereotypes

Read the folktale *The Five Chinese Brothers* by Claire Hutchet Bishop, illustrated by Kurt Wiese (Putnam 1938). Make a list of Asian stereotypes that are depicted in the illustrations and text. Compare this book to a newer tale from an Asian culture, such as *Three Monks, No Water* (Chan

1997), and describe the major differences. For criteria see http://nisus.sfusd.k12.ca.us/org/tact/analyze.html

■ RECOMMENDED BOOKS BY ASIAN AMERICAN AUTHORS AND ILLUSTRATORS

- Chan, Harvey (Chinese American). *Three Monks, No Water.* Annick Press, 1997. In a literary folktale, Chan gives an explanation for an old Chinese saying, "Three monks, no water," which refers to a child's trying to avoid chores. Illustrations contain many authentic details of the Chinese culture.

- Chang, Margaret, & Raymond Chang (Chinese American). *In the Eye of War.* Simon & Schuster, 1990. During the final days of the Japanese occupation of China, Shao-shao observes traditional Chinese customs while the chaos of war engulfs him and his family.

- Choi, Sook Nyul (Korean American). *Year of Impossible Goodbyes.* Houghton Mifflin, 1991. In an autobiographical account, 10-year-old Sookan and her family flee south to avoid an oppressive life under the Communist rule. After separation from her mother, Sookan must attempt a harrowing escape across Korea's thirty-eighth parallel with her 7-year-old brother.

- Choi, Yangsook (Korean American). *New Cat.* Frances Foster Books, 1999. New Cat lives in Mr. Kim's tofu factory, and when she chases a mouse in the production room, she discovers that a fire has broken out.

- Chin-Lee, Cynthia (Chinese American). *A Is for Asia.* Illus. Yumi Heo. Orchard, 1997. This alphabet book combines informative text with stylish illustrations to introduce the events, food, animals, crafts, and traditions of many Asian countries.

- Heo, Yumi (Korean American). *One Afternoon.* Orchard, 1994. Surrounded by the sights and sounds of an ordinary day in New York City, Minho and his mother spend a busy afternoon doing errands in the neighborhood.

- Ho, Minfong (Thai American). *Hush! A Thai Lullaby.* Illus. Holly Meade. Orchard, 1997. This bedtime story in rhyme is one mother's efforts to keep all the animals—from the mosquito to the elephant—quiet when their noise threatens to awaken her baby.

- Lee, Huy Voun (Cambodian American). *At the Beach.* Henry Holt, 1994. Xiao Ming and his mother go to the beach, where she teaches him how to make Mandarin Chinese words by drawing pictures in the sand. The book's endpapers include a pronunciation guide for the ten Chinese characters.

- Lee, Millie (Chinese American). *Nim and the War Effort.* Illus. Yangsook Choi. Farrar, Straus & Giroux, 1997. During World War II Nim, a Chinese American student, proves to her classmates that she can be true to both her country and her heritage when she collects the most papers for a war-effort paper drive.

- Lord, Bette Bao (Chinese American). *In the Year of the Boar and Jackie Robinson.* Harper & Row, 1984. Following World War II 10-year-old Shirley Temple Wong and her family emigrate from China to Brooklyn, where she enrolls at Public School 8 but remains friendless—until she earns the respect of the toughest girl in the class.

- Louie, Ai-Ling (Chinese American). *Yeh Shen: A Cinderella Story from China.* Illus. Ed Young. Putnam, 1982. A story based on an ancient Chinese manuscript tells of a young girl who overcomes the wickedness of her stepsister and stepmother to become the bride of a prince.

- Mochizuki, Ken (Japanese American). *Baseball Saved Us.* Illus. Dom Lee. Lee & Low, 1993. Despondent over the harsh conditions of a World War II internment camp, a young Japanese American boy and his father galvanize an effort to build a camp baseball diamond and form a league to give the internees something to look forward to.

- Namioka, Lensey (Chinese American). *Yang the Youngest and His Terrible Ear.* Little, Brown, 1992. The Yang family, recently arrived in Seattle from China, are all musically talented except for the youngest, Yingtao, who wishes he could play baseball with his friend Matthew instead of worrying about ruining the family's important recital.

- Nhuong, Huynh Quang (Vietnamese American). *Water Buffalo Days: Growing Up in Vietnam.* Illus. Jean Tseng & Mou-sien Tseng. HarperCollins, 1997. Nhuong is a young boy growing up in the hills of central Vietnam; his companion is Tank, the family's noble water buffalo. Together, Nhuong and Tank face the dangers of life in the Vietnamese jungle that is their home.

- Say, Allen (Japanese American). *Grandfather's Journey.* Houghton Mifflin, 1993. In a biographical account, the author tell of his grandfather's travels throughout North America as a young man. Because the grandfather is unable to forget his homeland, he returns to Japan, where the author is born.

- Uchida, Yoshido (Japanese American). *The Best Bad Thing.* Simon & Schuster, 1983. Rinko is dismayed when her parents ask her to spend the last month of her summer vacation helping the recently widowed Mrs. Hata. Though bad things do happen while she is there, Rinko discovers that things are not always as bad as they seem.

- Wong, Janet S. (Chinese–Korean American). *Good Luck Gold and Other Poems.* Simon & Schuster, 1994. Poems written from the point of view of a young Asian American girl are loving and poignant recollections of family members and of times when Korean and Chinese cultures clashed in the United States.

- ———. (Chinese–Korean American). *The Trip Back Home.* Illus. Bo Jia. Harcourt, 2000. The author recalls a childhood trip with her mother to rural Korea, where they visit her grandparents and aunt in a very traditional household. The daily rhythms of the farming family's way of life are poignantly retold.

- Yee, Paul (Chinese American). *Breakaway.* Groundwood Books, 1993. In 1932 Kwok-ken Wong, 18, the only Chinese Canadian boy at his Vancouver school, finds himself alienated by the racism that confronts him until he joins the Chinese community's soccer team.

- Yep, Laurence (Chinese American). *Dragonwings.* Harper, 1989. In the early twentieth century, a young boy and his father emigrate from China to San Francisco, where they achieve their dream of building a flying machine.

- Young, Ed (Chinese American). *Voices of the Heart.* Scholastic, 1997. Young illustrates and discusses twenty-six Chinese characters that describe a feeling or emotion and contain the symbol of the heart. He interprets the visual elements within each character and uncovers layers of meaning.

■ Xiong, Blia (Laotian American). ***Nine-in-One, Grr! Grr!: A Folktale from the Hmong People of Laos.*** Illus. Nancy Hom, 1989. When the great god Shao promises Tiger nine cubs each year, Bird comes up with a clever trick to prevent the land from being overrun by tigers.

Hispanic American Literature

The term *Hispanic* commonly refers to all native Spanish-speaking people. *Latino* and *Chicano* are also names that describe many of these people. Hispanic Americans include descendents from parts of the Caribbean, Central and South America, Cuba, Mexico, Puerto Rico, and Spain. As you can see, the cultures of Hispanic Americans are diverse, drawing from traditions of many nations. Hispanic Americans are the fastest growing minority group in the United States. There are more than 33 million Hispanic Americans today, and the U.S. Census Bureau projects that by 2025 the Hispanic/Latino population will be the country's largest single group, perhaps comprising nearly half the U.S. population. Not surprisingly, the Hispanic group expanding fastest is school-age children.

It is surprising, however, to learn that there are so few books about Hispanic Americans. Additionally, books that are published about this culture tend to go out of print faster than other books, and they are not always replaced by new ones. Since 1994 the Cooperative Children's Book Center (2001) has tracked the number of books published by or about the major minority groups. These data show there has been a steady decline in the number of books about Latinos since 1996. In 2000 only 42 out of the approximately 5,250 children's books published were about Latinos, and most likely fewer than half of those 42 were written by Latinos (see http://www.education.wisc.edu/ccbc/pcstats.htm for data on the number of books published by or about minorities).

Clearly, there is a crucial need for books with positive portrayals of Hispanic Americans. Publishing companies and bookstores should take heed that Hispanic/Latino families *do* buy books, use public libraries, read to their children, and want their children to learn to read. Also, they *do* want their children to see their own culture reflected in the books they read at school and find at the library.

It is important to review critically any older books written by non-Hispanics that are still in circulation (often because they won an award). Avoid books with stereotypic Hispanic characters who are impoverished, uneducated farm workers. Also, stereotyped illustrations commonly depict a barefooted Hispanic character wearing a wide-brimmed hat and a serape and snoozing under a cactus or riding a burro.

Even today, non-Hispanic authors have been criticized for overusing topics such as the Festival of the Dead, the ancient Aztecs and Mayas (especially human sacrifices), and formulaic descriptions of the different Latin American countries. In addition, Hispanics are frequently depicted as a singular group with no acknowledgment of the vast differences in race, class, and culture among them. However few their number, contemporary Hispanic authors and illustrators provide a realistic and positive portrayal that can help Hispanic readers feel admired and respected, while helping non-Hispanics learn to appreciate their cultures. A sample of their works is listed in the bibliography that follows this section.

Two awards promote Hispanic/Latino children's books. The *Americas Award*, begun in 1993, is sponsored by the National Consortium of Latin American Studies Programs. It is given annually in recognition of a children's or young adult book published in the United States that authentically and engagingly presents the experiences of Latinos in Latin America, the Caribbean, or the United States. The text of the book may be bilingual or English only, and the author may be of any ethnicity. By including all the Americas, the award reaches beyond both geographic borders and international boundaries to focus on cultural heritages within the whole hemisphere. In addition to naming award-winning and honor books, the committee issues each year a list of recommended books that are selected for their quality of story, cultural authenticity and sensitivity, and potential for classroom use.

Initiated in 1996, the *Pura Belpré Award* is given biennially to the author and illustrator who best portray, affirm, and celebrate the Latino cultural experience in an outstanding work of literature for children and youth. Unlike the Americas Award, the Pura Belpré Award honors only authors and illustrators of Hispanic heritage. The award is cosponsored by the Association for Library Service to Children and the National Association to Promote Library Services to the Spanish Speaking. It was named after the New York Public Library's first Latina librarian. As a children's librarian, storyteller, and author, Pura Belpré enriched the lives of Puerto Rican children in the United States through her pioneering work of preserving and disseminating Puerto Rican folklore.

RECOMMENDED BOOKS BY HISPANIC AMERICAN AUTHORS AND ILLUSTRATORS

- Ada, Alma Flor. *Under the Royal Palms: A Childhood in Cuba.* Atheneum, 1999. The author recounts short stories of growing up in the town of Camagüey, Cuba. Her remembrances—some sad and some humorous—demonstrate the importance of family, friends, neighbors, and teachers in her childhood.

- Ancona, George. *The Piñata Maker / El Piñatero.* Harcourt Brace, 1994. A photo essay in both English and Spanish records the life of 70-year-old Tío Rico, the beloved piñata maker of a southern Mexican village. Included are instructions on making piñatas at home.

- Anzaldúa, Gloria. *Friends from the Other Side / Amigos del Otro Lado.* Illus. Consuelo Mendez. Children's Book Press, 1995. Having crossed the Rio Grande into Texas with his mother in search of a new life, Joaquin receives help and friendship from Prietita, a brave young Mexican American girl.

- Blanco, Alberto. *Angel's Kite / La Estrella de Angel.* Illus. Rodolfo Morales. Children's Book Press, 1994. When the church bell disappears, Angel the kite maker designs a special kite with a beautiful replica of his small Mexican town, and the church bell mysteriously returns.

- Cisneros, Sandra. *Hairs / Pelitos.* Illus. Terry Ybanez. Dragonfly, 1997. This warm and humorous description of the many types of hair in one girl's family illuminates diversity within a loving family.

- Delacre, Lulu. ***Arroz con Leche: Popular Songs and Rhymes from Latin America.*** Scholastic, 1992. This collection of beloved Latin American songs, games, and rhymes has text in both Spanish and English and is complemented by watercolor illustrations of Latin American land- and cityscapes.

- Dorros, Arthur. ***La Isla.*** Illus. Elisa Kleven. Dutton, 1995. When Rosalba and her grandmother travel to the Caribbean island where *Abuela* grew up, Rosalba meets *Abuela's* son Fernando and his family, and together they sample the sights of the island.

- Garza, Carmen Lomas. ***In My Family / En Mi Familia.*** Children's Book Press, 1996. The author recounts loving memories of growing up in the traditional Mexican American community of Kingsville, Texas, describing religious practices, traditional forms of healing, holiday celebrations, and ordinary chores and pastimes.

- ———. ***Magic Windows: Cut-Paper Art and Stories / Ventañas Magicas: Papel Picado y Relatos.*** Children's Book Press, 1999. Garza tells stories of herself, her family, her community, and her Aztec ancestors through the intricate and beautiful folk art of *papel picado* (cut paper).

- Garcia, Maria. ***The Adventures of Connie and Diego / Las Adventuras de Connie y Diego.*** Illus. Malaquias Montoya. Children's Book Press, 1994. Tired of being laughed at because they are different, a pair of twins with multicolored skin run away to ask the animals where they really belong.

- Gonzalez, Lucia M. ***Señor Cat's Romance and Other Favorite Stories from Latin America.*** Illus. Lulu Delacre. Scholastic, 1997. This collection includes the stories of silly Juan Bobo, who challenges a three-legged pot to race him home; Martina, who conducts a zany search for the right husband; and four other popular characters from Latin America.

- Jaffe, Nina. ***The Golden Flower: A Taino Myth from Puerto Rico.*** Illus. Enrique O. Sanchez. Simon & Schuster, 1996. This origin myth of Puerto Rico tells how the Taino homeland was transformed when a large shining pumpkin broke open and released the sea that now surrounds their island.

- Jimenez, Francisco. ***The Circuit: Stories from the Life of a Migrant Child.*** University of New Mexico Press, 1997. In twelve autobiographical short stories, Jimenez portrays the tenacity and courage of a family through descriptions of their daily life and poor living conditions.

- Martinez, Floyd. ***Spirits of the High Mesa.*** Piñata Books, 1997. Flavio is torn between his love and respect for the old ways of his grandfather, El Grande, the town patriarch, and the coming of technological progress to his small New Mexican village.

- Mohr, Nicholasa. ***All for the Better: A Story of El Barrio.*** Illus. Rudy Guitars. Raintree, 1992. During the Great Depression, 11-year-old Evelyn is sent from Puerto Rico to the mainland to live with her aunt and uncle in New York. Once there, she figures out a way to get food for many neighbors who are too proud to accept charity.

- Mora, Pat. ***Pablo's Tree.*** Illus. Cecile Lang. Simon & Schuster, 1994. Each year on his birthday, a young Mexican American boy looks forward to seeing how his grandfather has decorated the tree he planted on the day the boy was adopted.

- Nodar, Carmen Santiago. ***Abuelita's Paradise.*** Illus. Diane Paterson. Albert Whitman, 1992. Although her grandmother has died, Marita sits in *Abuelita's* rocking chair and remembers the stories *Abuelita* told of her life in Puerto Rico.

- Soto, Gary. **Chato's Kitchen.** Illus. Susan Guevara. Putnam, 1995. Chato, the low-riding cat with six stripes, discovers that *ratoncitos* (mice) have moved next door in his East Los Angeles barrio, so he invites them for dinner—literally.

- ———. **Snapshots from the Wedding.** Illus. Stephanie Garcia. Putnam, 1997. This account of a Mexican American wedding is seen through the eyes of Maya, the flower girl. The illustrations are photographs of innovative three-dimensional scenes, which Garcia created using clay figures and other assorted objects.

- Stevens, Jan Romero. **Carlos and the Squash Plant.** Illus. Jeanne Arnold. Rising Moon, 1993. After ignoring his mother's warning about what will happen if he does not bathe after working on his family's farm in New Mexico, Carlos wakes up one morning and finds a squash growing out of his ear.

Native American Literature

Native Americans are the members (or the descendants) of the 500 or more tribes of the indigenous people of North America. Since 1997 there has been a decline in the number of books published by or about Native Americans. The Cooperative Children's Book Center (2001) reported that in 2000, only thirty-nine such books were published. This was the fewest of all the groups reported, which included African American (243 books), Asian American (54 books), and Hispanic American (42 books). All the books about minorities combined amount to less than 7 percent of the approximately 5,250 books published in 2000.

In the past, informational, biography, and historical fiction books by non-Natives have been most damaging to the image of Native peoples. Many of these books contained demeaning vocabulary and artificial dialogue. Frequently Native American characters were stereotyped as either cruel savages (as in *The Matchlock Gun* by Walter D. Edmonds, 1941) or docile, childlike people who were totally dependent on the mission or reservation for their existence. It comes as no surprise that non-Native people were exclusively depicted as the authority figures in those stories.

Even in current children's literature, old stereotypes live on. Too often authors and illustrators rely on old images of buckskin and feathers and fail to portray modern Indians realistically. In contrast, books that are void of stereotypes will help readers understand the realities of how Native Americans live today. Authors should convey that although many Native people maintain their tribal traditions, they also make use of modern technologies. Additionally, good books reveal the great diversity among the 500 or more American Indian tribes, each with its own history, religion, language, and government.

Authentic books about Native Americans can also help readers understand the realities of how these peoples lived in the past. Authentic books do not portray Native Americans as savages, as was done in history books and literature for many decades. They depict Native Americans defending their homeland from invaders—just as all Americans would today if the United States were invaded by foreigners. In such books, instead of being portrayed as savages or as annoying barriers to frontier settlement by white people, American Indians are portrayed within their civilized and complex cultures. Positive literature about Native Americans challenges the myths, distortions, stereotypes, and racist ideas that many people still hold.

I was dismayed to review recently published literature textbooks that almost exclusively present books *about* Native Americans instead of books *by* them. If any explanation is offered, it is that there are too few Native American authors and illustrators. However, you can see from the list that follows that there are many fine Native American authors and illustrators of children's books, though—with the exception of one or two—they have received little recognition.

Currently there is no special award given to Native American authors and illustrators. However, the *Carter G. Woodson Book Award* is given to outstanding books dealing with social studies that treat topics related to ethnic minorities with sensitivity and accuracy. Several books by or about Native Americans have won this award, for example *Battlefields and Burial Grounds: The Indian Struggle to Protect Ancestral Graves in the United States* by Roger C. Echo-Hawk and Walter R. Echo-Hawk (Lerner, 1994), and *The Life and Death of Crazy Horse* by Russell Freedman and illustrated by Amos Bad Heart Bull (Holiday House, 1996).

The books in the following bibliography were selected because they represent a variety of tribes and genres. The list is by no means comprehensive, however. There are many more children's books by Native American authors and illustrators in print. Additionally, many fine works by Natives have gone out of print but are still available in libraries. Along with a representative work of each person on the list, I have included the individual's tribe to show the great variety of First Nation cultures involved in the field of children's publications.

▌ RECOMMENDED BOOKS BY NATIVE AMERICAN AUTHORS AND ILLUSTRATORS

- Armstrong, Jeannette (Okanagan). **Neekna and Chemai.** Illus. Barbara Marchand. Theytus Books, 1994. This is a story of two girls growing up in the Okanagan culture before the coming of the Europeans.

- Ata, Te (Chickasaw), & Lynn Moroney (Chickasaw). **Baby Rattlesnake.** Illus. Mira Reisberg. Children's Book Press, 1989. Willful Baby Rattlesnake throws tantrums to get his rattle before he is mature, and when he gets it but misuses it, he learns a hard lesson.

- Begay, Shonto (Navajo). **Navajo: Visions and Voices across the Mesa.** Scholastic, 1995. Twenty of Begay's paintings, culled from his body of work, are combined with his original poetry to represent an intimate look at Navajo life today.

- Brown, Vee (Navajo). **Animal Lore and Legend: Owl.** Cartwheel, 1995. This book describes eighteen species of owls native to North America and explains their role in Native American lore.

- Bruchac, Joseph (Abenaki). **The Arrow over the Door.** Illus. James Watling. Dial, 1998. In alternating narratives, two 14-year-old boys—one Quaker and the other Abenaki—tell the story of what led to their memorable meeting in 1777 just prior to the Battle of Saratoga.

- Dorris, Michael (Modoc). *Morning Girl.* Hyperion, 1992. Morning Girl and her younger brother Star Boy alternately narrate the story of their lives on an island in pre-Columbian America. At the end of the book, Morning Girl witnesses the arrival of the first Europeans.

- Erdrich, Louise (Chippewa). *The Birchbark House.* Hyperion, 1999. Adopted as an infant when she was the sole survivor of a smallpox epidemic in her village, Omakayas—an Ojibwa girl—tells of her life on an island in Lake Superior in 1847.

- Green, Richard G. (Mohawk). *Sing Like a Hermit Thrush.* Ricara Features, 1995. Driven to solve a mysterious dream, Darrin begins an adventure that leads to discoveries about himself, and he begins to experience the ability to predict coming events.

- Lacapa, Katherine (Mohawk). *Less than Half, More than Whole.* Illus. Michael Lacapa (Apache/Hopi/Tewa). Northland, 1999. A boy of mixed heritage struggles to understand why his friend called him "less than half Indian."

- Monture, Joel (Mohawk). *Cloudwalker: Contemporary Native American Stories.* Illus. Carson Waterman (Seneca). Fulcrum, 1996. In six stories, children from various tribes come to appreciate their heritage through relationships with their elders.

- Nez, Redwing T. (Navajo). *Forbidden Talent.* Northland, 1995. In an autobiographical story, Nez tells about his childhood through the character Ashkii, who lives on the reservation with his grandparents. He finds his way of painting is in conflict with what Grandfather calls the Navajo Way.

- Ross, Gayle (Cherokee). *How Turtle's Back Was Cracked: A Traditional Cherokee Tale.* Illus. Murv Jacob. Modern Curriculum Press, 1995. When the Wolves decide to punish Turtle for bragging, they throw him in the river and his beautiful smooth, shiny shell cracks on a rock.

- Savageau, Cheryl (Abenaki). *Muskrat Will Be Swimming.* Illus. Robert Hynes. Rising Moon, 1996. With gentle guidance from her grandfather, a Native American girl learns to find strength, rather than fear, in her identity as a Native person living in a non-Native society.

- Shenandoah, Joanne (Oneida), & Douglas M. George (Mohawk). *Skywoman: Legends of the Iroquois.* Illus. John Fadden & David Fadden. Clear Light, 1998. Iroquois traditional stories—including the Iroquois concept of creation and a pourquoi story on why the maple tree loses its leaves—are illustrated in both color paintings and black-and-white etchings.

- Smith, Cynthia Leitich (Muscogee). *Jingle Dancer.* Illus. Cornelius Van Wright & Ying-Hwa Hu. Morrow, 2000. Jenna is a contemporary Creek–Ojibwe girl who brings together her jingle dress and dance regalia with the assistance of the women who inspire her—a great-aunt, a cousin, a neighbor, and her grandmother.

- Sneve, Virginia Driving Hawk (Lakota). *High Elk's Treasure.* Illus. Oren Lyons. Holiday House, 1995. While trying to locate a valuable filly lost during a storm, 13-year-old Joe High Elk discovers an object of great historical importance.

- Stroud, Virginia A. (Cherokee/Creek). *A Walk to the Great Mystery.* Dial, 1995. Grandma Ann, a medicine woman, promises to help Dustin and Rosie find the Great Mystery. She opens their eyes and hearts to the life around and within them.

- Swamp, Chief Jake (Akwesasne Mohawk). *Giving Thanks: A Native American Good Morning Message.* Illus. Erwin Printup Jr. (Cayuga-Tuscarora). Lee & Low, 1995. This book is an adaptation of a traditional Iroquois ceremony of thanksgiving for Mother Earth and her natural gifts.

- White Deer of Autumn (Wampanoag). ***The Great Change.*** Illus. Carol Grigg. Beyond Words, 1992. A wise grandmother explains their people's understanding of death, called the Great Change, to her questioning granddaughter as they work together on the land.
- Whitethorne, Baje (Navajo). ***Sunpainters: Eclipse of the Navajo Sun.*** Rising Moon, 1994. During a solar eclipse, a Navajo boy learns from his grandfather about the children of Mother Earth called the Little Painters, who restore color to the earth whenever the sun dies.

Responding to Literature

Focus Units

A **focus unit** is a series of literary experiences that integrate the language arts. It is organized around a central focus such as an author, theme, genre, topic, or literary element. Authors make great subjects for focus units. The basic procedures follow.

- With your children, select the author to study.
- Collect multiple titles and copies of books by the author from school and public libraries and personal collections.
- Arrange an attractive bulletin board and display with the books, the author's picture, and any information received from the publisher or Internet. (Many authors have their own Internet sites where you can download pictures and interesting information.)
- Encourage children to browse through the display and to add books and information they have located.
- Ask the children to collaborate to select the book you will read to the class, and allow literature circles to form around the other available books.
- Keep a dialogue response journal with each child, and ask the children to make regular entries about the book you are reading aloud as well as about the book their literature circle is reading. Respond to the journal entries on a regular basis. (Journals can also be kept between pairs of children.)
- Engage the children in meaningful projects that extend the literary experiences, such as grand conversations, webbing, story mapping, and dramatizing.

Literature of Religious Cultures

Some cultural groups, such as religious groups, cross racial lines. Numerous children's books help young readers learn about people who practice various religions.

CHRISTIANITY

- Devon, Paddie. ***The Grumpy Shepherd.*** Abingdon Press, 1995. This imaginative tale tells of a habitually grouchy shepherd, Joram, and of his reaction to a message from the angels that the Christ child is born. Though written with a humorous tone, the story carries a reverential message.

- Giff, Patricia Reilly. ***Mother Teresa: Sister to the Poor.*** Illus. Ted Lewin. Viking, 1987. This biography emphasizes the early years of the nun who became world renowned for her work with destitute and dying people in India.

- Savory, Louis. ***The Children's Book of Saints.*** Regina, 1986. The lives of fifty-two saints are vividly recounted, each accompanied by a full-color portrait. The saints' efforts on behalf of poor, needy, uneducated, abused, and otherwise forgotten people are emphasized.

- Watson, Carol. ***Christian.*** Children's Book Press, 1997. This book surveys the history, beliefs, traditions, and methods of worship of Christians.

- Wellman, Sam. ***C. S. Lewis: Author of Mere Christianity.*** Chelsea House, 1998. This is the story of Lewis's remarkable conversion to Christianity—and of his fascinating life as a scholar, a writer, and the author of the fantasy series called the Chronicles of Narnia.

ISLAM

- Husain, Shahrukh. ***What Do We Know about Islam?*** Illus. Celia Hart. Peter Bedrick Books, 1996. This book provides a brief discussion of the beliefs, worship practices, lifestyles, sacred books, sacred places, holidays, art, and music of Islam.

- Kessler, Cristina. ***One Night: A Story from the Desert.*** Illus. Ian Schoenherr. Putnam, 1995. A Tuareg boy from the Niger portion of the Sahara takes the family's flock of goats to graze. When a goat gives birth, he must stay in the desert overnight. When the boy arrives back at the tents carrying the newborn kid, his father promises him a blue turban as a mark of his manhood. Gratitude to Allah is an important theme in the story.

- Matthews, Mary. ***Magrid Fasts for Ramadan.*** Illus. E. B. Lewis. Clarion, 1996. In this story set in modern Egypt, 8-year-old Magrid wants to fast during the month of Ramadan like the rest of his family, so he secretly throws away his lunch each day to keep his promise to Allah.

- Oppenheim, Shulamith Levey. ***The Hundredth Name.*** Illus. Michael Hays. Boyds Mills, 1997. To help his dejected camel Qadlim, young Salah prays to Allah for assistance. This lyrical story evokes village life along the Nile and captures a youngster's faith.

- Wormser, Richard. ***American Islam: Growing Up Muslim in America.*** Walker, 1994. Through extensive interviews with young American Muslims together with interesting discussions of the teachings of the Koran and the history of Islam, the author debunks current myths and controversies about Muslims in America.

JUDAISM

Several awards are dedicated to encouraging quality children's novels about Jewish experiences. These include the *Sydney Taylor Award,* the *National Jewish Book Award,* and the *Charles and Bertie G. Schwartz Award.* All these awards recognize distinguished children's books that authentically and sensitively express Jewish thought and experiences.

- Cohen, Barbara. ***Yussel's Prayer: A Yom Kippur Story.*** Illus. Michael J. Deraney. Lothrop Lee & Shepard, 1981. In this folktale, Yussel, an orphaned young cowherd, is not allowed to go to synagogue on Yom Kippur, but his simple and sincere prayer is instrumental in ending the day's fast.

- ———. *Molly's Pilgrim.* Illus. Daniel M. Duffy. Morrow, 1983. Based on an account from the author's family, this is the story of Molly, whose family has emigrated from Russia to escape religious persecution. Her third-grade classmates laugh at her, but when Molly's mother makes a Russian pilgrim doll for the school's Thanksgiving celebration, they begin to see her in a new light.

- Drucker, Malka. *Grandma's Latkes.* Illus. Eve Chwast. Harcourt Brace, 1992. As Grandma and Molly prepare latkes for the family's traditional Hanukkah meal, Grandma explains the custom of eating latkes and discusses the historical background of the holiday traditions.

- Polacco, Patricia. *Mrs. Katz and Tush.* Yearling, 1994. A young African American boy and an elderly Jewish woman develop a friendship through their mutual concern for an abandoned cat. Together they explore the common themes of suffering and triumph in each of their cultures, and they celebrate their friendship by spending Passover together.

- ———. *The Keeping Quilt.* Simon & Schuster, 1998. When the author's great-great-grandmother came to America from Russia, she made a quilt out of the family's old clothes. This book tells how the quilt is lovingly passed on to each new generation and used for a variety of purposes.

- Singer, Isaac Bashevis. *The Golem.* Illus. Uri Shulevitz. Sunburst, 1996. A clay giant miraculously brought to life by a rabbi saves a Jewish banker who has been falsely accused. This traditional tale is set in Prague during the rule of Emperor Rudolf II.

- Levine, Gail Carson. *Dave at Night.* HarperCollins, 1999. Gideon and Dave are two Jewish boys growing up in New York in the 1920s. When their father dies, Dave finds himself separated from his older brother and thrust into the Hebrew Home for Boys. At night he sneaks out and explores Harlem during its renaissance.

OTHER RELIGIOUS TRADITIONS

- Ammon, Richard. *An Amish Christmas.* Illus. Pamela Patrick. Atheneum, 1996. A young Amish boy describes the joys experienced in his community during the Christmas season, such as going to an evening skating party, playing with friends, and visiting with relatives.

- Krishnaswami, Uma. *The Broken Tusk: Stories of the Hindu God Ganesha.* Illus. Maniam Selven. Linnet, 1996. This collection of seventeen Hindu folktales features stories about the god Ganesha, who has the head of an elephant.

- Landaw, Jonathan. *Prince Siddhartha: The Story of Buddha.* Illus. Janet Brooke. Wisdom, 1996. This is the story of Prince Siddhartha and how he became Buddha, the Awakened One. Illustrations depict each major life event in Siddhartha's development

- Polacco, Patricia. *Just Plain Fancy.* Bantam, 1990. Two Amish sisters find a fancy egg that hatches into an unusual chick. When it turns out to be a peacock, they fear it will bring shame on their family because it is not plain.

- Yolen, Jane. *Raising Yoder's Barn.* Illus. Bernie Fuchs. Little, Brown, 1998. After the barn and windmill burn on an Amish family's farm, the neighbors quickly respond to raise a new barn, proving a strong community allegiance.

International Literature

"The nature of the modern world demands that we all become more aware of and sensitive to the diverse cultures found not only in our own nation, but in the world at large" (Russell 1997, p. 38). What better way to accomplish this than through literature? **International literature** consists primarily of books originally written and published for children living in other lands. However, it also includes books published in the United States that were written by immigrants about their homelands. Also, some authors write about other countries where they have lived for a period of time or have visited and researched the culture.

International literature promotes social awareness, and it allows readers to consider very different points of view. Gaining an understanding and appreciation of the history and cultures of other countries helps readers attain a global perspective. Quality international literature is "culturally authentic and rich in cultural details and celebrates both diversity and the common bonds of humanity" (Siu-Runyan 1999, p. 498).

It is not surprising that the international books most widely available in the United States are those that were first published in other English-speaking countries such as the United Kingdom, Canada, and Australia. However, even books written in English undergo some revision to make them appropriate for U.S. readers. To Americanize a book a publisher may change things such as spelling, punctuation, titles, character names, vocabulary, settings, and cultural allusions. The word *barbie* is a good example. In the United States, Barbie is a doll; in Australia, a barbie is a cookout (short for barbecue). In some cases the changes may be minor; in other instances, authors complain that the intent of the book has been altered, particularly when works are translated from another language.

English author J. K. Rowling has discussed the changes that were made to her Harry Potter books before they were marketed in the United States. Changes were made only when both the author and her U.S. editor thought that what was written would create an erroneous picture in an American child's mind. For example, concerning boys' clothing, the word *jumper* was changed to *sweater*. In the title of her first book, the word *philosopher* was changed to *sorcerer* (i.e., *Harry Potter and the Sorcerer's Stone*). The original title, with the term *philosopher's stone*, would have had little meaning to American readers, and it names a very important object in the plot (O'Malley 1999).

Another example of a title change is Dick King-Smith's *Daggie Dogfoot* (1980). The special little pig in this book has front feet that look more like a dog's than a pig's, and thus he is named Daggie Dogfoot, *dag* being a word for a runt piglet in England. However, U.S. children might think the book was about a dog rather than a pig, so the title of the U.S. edition is *Pigs Might Fly*, an oft repeated phrase in the book.

Several awards honor outstanding international publications. In 1953 the International Board on Books for Young People was established, and in 1956 they initiated the international Hans Christian Andersen Award (discussed in Chapter 2). Also, the *Mildred L. Batchelder Award*, first declared in 1968, is given to a U.S.

publisher by the American Library Association Children's Services Division in recognition of the most noteworthy translated children's book (picture books and folktales excluded) of the year.

Following is a selection of noteworthy international books.

AFRICA

- Buettner, Dan. **Africatrek: A Journey by Bicycle Through Africa** (Tunisia/South Africa). Lerner, 1997.
- Gordon, Sheila. **The Middle of Somewhere: A Story of South Africa.** Orchard, 1990.
- Mbure, Sam, Valerie Cuthbert, & Kariuki Gakuo. **Beneath the Rainbow: A Collection of Children's Stories and Poems from Kenya.** Jacaranda Designs, 1995.
- Naidoo, Beverley. **Journey to Jo'burg: A South African Story.** HarperCollins, 1986.
- ———. **No Turning Back: A Novel of South Africa.** HarperCollins, 1999.
- Sacks, Margaret. **Beyond Safe Boundaries** (South Africa). Puffin, 1990.
- ———. **Themba** (South Africa). Illus. Wil Clay. Puffin, 1994.

Children picnic with their parents during the school's sportsday. From *The Bicycle Man,* by Allen Say.

ASIA

- Anno, Mitsumasa. *All in a Day* (Japan). Illus. Eric Carle et al. Putnam, 1990.
- Dolphin, Laurie. *Our Journey from Tibet.* Illus. Nancy Jo Johnson. Dutton, 1998.
- Godden, Rumer. *Premlata and the Festival of Lights* (India). HarperCollins, 1998.
- Lewin, Ted. *The Storytellers* (Morocco). Lothrop, 1998.
- Lewis, Elizabeth Foreman. *Young Fu of the Upper Yangtze* (China). Illus. Ed Young. Yearling, 1999.
- London, Jonathan. *Ali, Child of the Desert* (Morocco). Illus. Ted Lewin. Lothrop Lee & Shepard, 1997.
- Paterson, Katherine. *The Sign of the Chrysanthemum* (Japan). HarperCollins, 1973.
- Say, Allen. *The Bicycle Man* (Japan). Houghton Mifflin, 1982.
- Schlein, Miriam. *The Year of the Panda* (China). Illus. Kam Mak. Crowell, 1990.
- Staples, Suzanne Fisher. *Shabanu: Daughter of the Wind* (Pakistan). Knopf, 1989.
- Takaaki, Nomura. *Grandpa's Town* (Japan). Kane/Miller, 1991.
- Tsuchiya, Yukio. *Faithful Elephants: A True Story of Animals, People, and War* (Japan). Illus. Ted Lewin. Houghton Mifflin, 1988.
- Yumoto, Kazumi. *The Friends* (Japan). Farrar, Straus & Giroux, 1996.

AUSTRALIA

- Fox, Mem. *Wilfrid Gordon McDonald Partridge.* Illus. Julia Vivas. Kane/Miller, 1984.
- Kidd, Diana. *Onion Tears.* Orchard, 1991.

CENTRAL AND SOUTH AMERICA

- Cameron, Ann. *The Most Beautiful Place in the World* (Guatemala). Illus. Thomas B. Allen. Random House, 1988.
- Castaneda, Omar S. *Abuelita's Weave* (Guatemala). Lee & Low, 1993.
- Machado, Ana Maria. *Niña Bonita.* Illus. Rosana Farina. Aims, 1996.
- Smith, Roland. *Jaguar* (Brazil). Hyperion, 1998.
- Temple, Frances. *Grab Hands and Run* (El Salvador). Orchard, 1993.

EUROPE

- Buchholz, Quentin. *The Collector of Moments* (Germany). Farrar, Straus & Giroux, 1999.
- Bjørk, Christina. *Vendela in Venice* (Italy). Illus. Inga Karin Ericksson. R & S, 1999.
- Creech, Sharon. *Bloomability* (Switzerland). HarperCollins, 1999.
- Guettier, Benedicte. *The Father Who Had 10 Children* (Belgium). Illus. Skip Skwarek. Dial, 1999.

- Holub, Josef. *The Robber and Me* (Germany). Henry Holt, 1997.
- Innocenti, Roberto. *Rose Blanche* (France). Creative Education, 1996.
- Llorente, Pilar Molina. *The Apprentice* (Spain). Illus. Juan Ramon Alonso. Sunburst, 1994.
- Mochizuki, Ken. *Passage to Freedom: The Sugihara Story* (Lithuania). Illus. Dom Lee. Lee & Low, 1997.
- Pfister, Marcus. *The Rainbow Fish* (Switzerland). North-South Books, 1992.
- Schur, Maxine Rose. *Sacred Shadows* (Germany). Dial, 1997.
- Wild, Margaret. *Let the Celebrations Begin!* (Poland). Illus. Julie Vivas. Orchard, 1991.

MIDDLE EAST

- Dalokay, Vedat. *Sister Shako and Kolo the Goat: Memories of My Childhood in Turkey.* Lothrop Lee & Shepard, 1994.
- Heide, Florence Parry, & Judith Heide Gilliland. *The Day of Ahmed's Secret* (Egypt). Illus. Ted Lewin. Lothrop Lee & Shepard, 1990.
- ———. *Sami and the Time of Troubles* (Lebanon). Illus. Ted Lewin. Houghton Mifflin, 1992.
- Lewin, Betsy. *What's the Matter, Habibi?* (Pan-Arab). Clarion, 1997.
- McGraw, Eloise Jarvis. *The Golden Goblet* (Egypt). Puffin, 1961.
- Nye, Naomi Shihab. *Sitti's Secrets* (Palestine). Illus. Nancy Carpenter. Simon & Schuster, 1994.
- Orlev, Uri. *The Man from the Other Side* (Israel). Houghton Mifflin, 1991.
- ———. *The Lady with the Hat* (Israel). Houghton Mifflin, 1995.
- Schami, Rafik. *A Handful of Stars* (Syria). Dutton, 1990.

NORTH AMERICA AND CARIBBEAN

- Bunting, Eve. *How Many Days to America? A Thanksgiving Story* (Caribbean). Illus. Beth Peck. Clarion, 1988.
- Ekoomiak, Normee. *Arctic Memories* (Canadian Inuikitut). Henry Holt, 1990.
- Korman, Gordon. *Losing Joe's Place* (Canada). Scholastic, 1990.
- Pomerantz, Charlotte. *The Chalk Doll* (Jamaica). Illus. Frane Lessac. HarperCollins, 1989.
- Temple, Frances. *A Taste of Salt: A Story of Modern Haiti.* Orchard, 1992.

SCANDINAVIA

- Bjørk, Christina. *Linnea in Monet's Garden* (Sweden). Farrar, Straus & Giroux, 1987.
- Dexter, Catherine. *Safe Return* (Sweden). Candlewick, 1998.
- Lowry, Lois. *Number the Stars* (Sweden). Houghton Mifflin, 1989.
- Mathas, Carol. *Lisa's War* (Denmark). Scribner, 1987.
- Reuter, Bjarne. *The Boys from St. Petri* (Denmark). Puffin, 1996.

UNITED KINGDOM

- Banks, Lynne Reid. *Maura's Angel* (Ireland). Avon, 1999.
- Cooper, Susan. *The Boggart and the Monster* (Scotland). Aladdin, 1998.
- Cushman, Karen. *The Midwife's Apprentice* (England). Clarion, 1995.
- Rowling, J. K. *Harry Potter and the Sorcerer's Stone* (England). Scholastic, 1998.

Resources

Good resources for selecting multicultural literature and using it in the classroom include the following books. See the References for the full listings.

- *Building Bridges with Multicultural Picture Books* (Beaty 1997)
- *Crossroads: Literature and Language in Culturally and Linguistically Diverse Classrooms* (Cox & Boyd-Batstone 1997)
- *Latina and Latino Voices in Literature for Children and Teenagers* (Day 1997)
- *Multicultural Voices in Contemporary Literature: A Resource for Teachers* (Day 1999)
- *The New Press Guide to Multicultural Resources for Young Readers* (Muse 1997)
- *Multicultural Children's Literature: Through the Eyes of Many Children* (Norton 2001)
- *Transcultural Children's Literature* (Pratt & Beaty 1999)
- *Children's Books from Other Countries* (Tomlinson 1998) (with a companion volume in press, edited by Susan Stan, that expands the focus to include American books about other countries as well as international books)

The Council for Interracial Books for Children, 1841 Broadway, New York, NY 10023, is another helpful resource. The council's purpose is to heighten public awareness of diversity issues related to children's books, and you may write to them for brochures and other information.

KEY TERMS

 Explore the E-Glossary at **www.ablongman.com/anderson**

African Americans (p. 179)
Asian Americans (p. 183)
culturally generic book (p. 174)
culturally neutral book (p. 174)
culturally specific book (p. 175)
culture (p. 172)
focus unit (p. 194)

Hispanic Americans (p. 188)
international literature (p. 197)
multicultural literature (p. 173)
Native Americans (p. 191)
stereotyping (p. 173)
super-minority syndrome (p. 184)

c h a p t e r

8

Contemporary Realistic Fiction

Recall from Chapter 5 that fiction is divided into two major categories—fantasy and realistic fiction. This chapter and the next are devoted to realistic fiction. The division between the contemporary and historical eras is arbitrary, and not all literature specialists agree on where the separation should be made. However, because of the dramatic changes in the United States since the civil rights movement of the 1960s, I have set that era as the dividing point. In this textbook, books with settings prior to the passage of the Civil Rights Act of 1964 are considered historical fiction, and books with settings after are considered contemporary.

Evaluating Contemporary Fiction

The following questions can guide you as you select contemporary realistic fiction.

- Is the topic suitable for the age intended?
- Does the book tell a good story that children will enjoy?
- Is the plot credible?
- Are the characters convincing?
- Does the author avoid stereotyping?
- Does the theme emerge naturally from the story, rather than being stated too obviously? *evolves, not to predictable*
- Is the theme worth imparting to children?
- Does the author avoid didacticism? *teaching and preaching*

Characteristics of Contemporary Realistic Fiction

The characteristics of **contemporary realistic fiction** are quite different from fantasy. First, the setting is in modern or contemporary times—which I have defined for the purpose of this textbook as any year from 1964 to present day—in a real (or realistic) location. This means that stories take place at real locations in the world, typically the United States. The state is nearly always identified, but the cities may be either real or fictional.

Second, the characters are realistic people. There are no anthropomorphic animals or people with superhuman abilities. Sometimes characters are even based on a real person or a composite of people the author has known, although the names are typically fictional. Expect characters to be described more forthrightly in realistic fiction than with other genres. The stories are frequently narrated in first person by the main character, making them even more believable.

Because there is no magic or fantasy of any kind in this genre, the plots of contemporary realistic fiction books reflect real-life situations. In some books the tone is light and humorous; in others it is serious and reflects real-life milieus. Plots may deal with subjects such as aging, disability, illness, death, divorce, abandonment, and poverty. Unlike fairy tales, realistic fiction does not always have a happy ending, and often the major problem of the story is not solved, leaving many unanswered questions. However, the protagonist usually finds a way to cope with the problem by the end of the story. Readers who do not care for such equivocal endings can find many good contemporary fiction books with happy endings, often geared for younger children.

Around fourth grade, many children's reading preferences change from fairy tales and fantasy to stories about boys and girls their own age with plots that reflect situations similar to their own lives. Because many intermediate-grade children prefer contemporary fiction, there is an extensive roster of books from which to choose.

Themes

The themes of contemporary books tend to be abstract concepts that reflect complexities of modern life. Themes often center on people and situations that are in a child's immediate world, such as family, friendship, and school; they also include exciting situations such as adventure and mystery. Some of the more prevalent categories of contemporary themes are the following, each of which will be explored in more detail a little later in this chapter.

* *Family themes* involve plots that focus on family issues. These include stories about loving families, such as *Ramona and Her Father* (Cleary 1975), as well as stories about dysfunctional families, such as *Hannah in Between* (Rodowsky 1994).

* *Friendship themes* focus on the lives and adventures of two or more friends, such as *Bridge to Terabithia* (Paterson 1977).

* *Humorous themes* are found in lighthearted books intended to make children laugh at ridiculous situations, such as *How to Eat Fried Worms* (Rockwell 1973).

* *Adventure themes* characterize stories with fast-moving plots and exciting settings, such as *The Haymeadow* (Paulsen 1992). One category of adventure stories consists of *survival stories,* in which a character is pitted against nature, such as *Julie of the Wolves* (George 1972). The settings of survival stories are often exotic places such as oceans, the wilderness, or deserted islands. Another category is *mystery stories:* adventure stories that involve solving a puzzle or crime. These stories often contain unusual characters and clever twists of plot that surprise the readers, as in *Coffin on a Case* (Bunting 1992).

* *Social reality themes* are found in books that involve important issues facing the world today, such as racism, crime, war, poverty, and abuse. One example is *Work-*

ing Cotton (Williams 1992), a story of migrant workers and child labor. Sometimes the plots involve characters who learn to cope with their problems or characters who have hope of overcoming their hardship through perseverance—as in *Fly Away Home* (Bunting 1991), the story of a homeless father and his young son who live at an airport.

- *Personal issue themes* focus on an individual character's response to a specific personal problem or situation. Two examples are living with a disability, as in *Tangerine* (Bloor 1997), and the loss of a loved one, as in *Nana Upstairs & Nana Downstairs* (dePaola 1973).

- *Animal themes* focus on a child's relationship with a pet or other beloved animal, as in *I'll Always Love You* (Wilhelm 1985).

When I introduce these topics to my adult students, they often express horror that books for children expose them to the dire situations of modern life. I respond by asking my students if any of their children or young relatives watch television, go to movies, look at the front page of newspapers, or know another child who is experiencing a serious problem. I believe the average child witnesses more violence and is exposed to more harsh realities (both fictional and real) in a few months of watching television than in a lifetime of reading children's books. Even in the case of the few children whose television viewing is curtailed, the realities of the world cannot be hidden.

Driscoll (1999) believes that "we are becoming a nation of mourners and victims. Few communities have not experienced senseless crimes, and media coverage of tragedies perpetuates widespread grief [in all communities]" (p. 17). Most adults underestimate the capacity of children to face serious issues presented in realistic stories. Children need to know about issues that they or their peers may face. To deprive youngsters of knowledge—because we believe their ignorance will keep them safe from the problems of the world—is folly! It has the opposite effect. When children eventually face one of life's painful realities, such as the death of a beloved grandparent, they will be caught off guard. If they do not have the opportunity to think about such situations beforehand and prepare themselves, they may have great trouble coping. Attempting to protect children from painful subjects can ultimately cause them more harm, especially when children are left feeling they are alone in their painful experiences and thoughts.

If adults withhold realistic books, children will find and read them on their own but without an adult to guide them in their selections and responses. There is good reason why middle school and secondary students read more contemporary fiction than any other genre. It reflects their lives and the real world around them. Children soon learn that reading contemporary books can be both entertaining and enlightening.

It can also be therapeutic. **Bibliotherapy** is the process of mending one's life by reading books. The following section was written by Dan Ouzts, professor of education at The Citadel, who has studied and written about bibliotherapy for many years.

Bibliotherapy

by Dan Ouzts

Bibliotherapy means therapy through books. It is an effective technique that helps children cope with their problems and thus promotes mental health. It can be thought of as storybook guidance. It is a means for children to identify with a character in a story who has similar problems, which may result in improved attitudes toward books and reading. If children who are experiencing difficulties can read about others who have solved similar problems, they may see alternatives for themselves. In a study by Carter and Harris (1982), a set of books selected from the Children's Choices lists—developed by the International Reading Association and the Children's Book Council—was introduced to students. By analyzing the students' reasons for favoring certain titles, the researchers identified the attributes that made a book popular. Characterization was most frequently mentioned. Many students asserted that a character in a book was "just like me." This suggests that self-identification in books is of paramount importance for children who are experiencing attitudinal barriers to learning. Presenting possible solutions to problems through bibliotherapy can minimize and possibly help prevent difficult situations.

The word *bibliotherapy* first appeared in 1930 in an article by G. O. Ireland (Ouzts 1991). It is also known as *therapeutic reading*. In the United States, Will and Karl Menninger were among the first to foster an interest in this type of aid to healing (O'Bruba & Camplese 1983). The process of bibliotherapy used in education today is largely credited to Caroline Shrodes, whose 1949 dissertation on the subject is now a classic (Grindler, Stratton, & McKenna, 1997). Today, bibliotherapy has emerged as an important discipline in the field of reading (Ouzts 1991).

The Purpose of Bibliotherapy

Bibliotherapy can serve as an adjunct to teaching, and there are several compelling reasons for using literature to teach children both how to read and how to break attitudinal or emotional barriers to learning. Bibliotherapy offers benefits beyond the conventional methods and materials that have long been used in teaching reading. The right books can offer possible solutions to problems that create children's inner turmoil. Also, reading about a personal situation has the potential to sharpen perception and deepen understanding. Intervention through a book can make the difference between an emotionally well-adjusted child and one who may later suffer mental anguish.

We must be concerned with the emotional aspect of learning as well as the academic. Teachers and parents can sensitize children to themselves and to others through books. Bibliotherapy is particularly helpful because it has the potential to address the needs of the whole child (Grindler et al. 1997). In addition to parents, teachers occupy a strategic position in the development of children's emotions. Books allow teachers to intervene with children who are experiencing stress and crises in their lives. Caring, competent, and knowledgeable educators fully appreciate how authentic interactions with literature can contribute to overall cognitive and affective growth (Jalongo 1983).

Guidelines for Using Bibliotherapy

Jalongo (1983) recommends initiating bibliotherapy by administering an interest inventory (such as the one found in Chapter 13, Figure 13.1) in order to select several appealing books. *The Bookfinder* (Dreyer 1989), a guide to children's literature about the needs and problems of youths ages 2 and up, is an excellent resource. It lists books by subject or problem area, author, and title, and it provides appropriate age ranges for each book.

An additional resource is *The Right Book, the Right Time* (Grindler et al. 1997). It assists classroom teachers, media specialists, and parents in matching children who are facing important issues in their lives with fiction books that feature characters in similar circumstances. Jalongo (1983) identified three criteria for selecting books for bibliotherapy: potential for controversy, accuracy or credibility, and literary value.

Books need to be carefully selected. Sanacore (1982) noted that many censorship issues in public education are related to language arts materials, and he identified several controversial subjects: politics, religion, ethnic groups, strong language, drugs, alcohol, and sex. You may want to review districtwide adoption lists to determine which books are acceptable for your grade level.

I recommend the Children's Choices and the Teachers' Choices lists (discussed in Chapter 2) that are published yearly in *The Reading Teacher.* Many of the books selected for these lists present issues and topics that could be appropriate for your children; examples include self-concept, perseverance, relationships, social values, friendship, facing adversity, family values, death, illness or disease, and war (Ouzts 1998). Books should be selected because they cover possible solutions to difficulties that children may be facing, but they also must have high literary merit.

In the bibliotherapeutic process, timing and approach are of great importance. Materials should be readily available, but the choice needs to be left to the individual child. In addition, adequate time and encouragement will support the child's enjoyment of the book selected. Providing time for discussion and listening is an essential component of any bibliotherapy program; however, in class discussions of books, no single child should be targeted for responding to questions. I suggest giving students excerpts from a book to respond to in dialogue response journals between the child and teacher.

Although there are no formal processes or guidelines for bibliotherapy, I recommend the following procedures to use before, during, and after presenting books.

- *Before* children listen to or read a book, the teacher should set specific purposes for the activity.
- *During* the guided reading of the book, the teacher should set expectations, guide the discussion, and relate the text to children's experiences. (It is critical

to guide adequate discussion at this point, and to note unusual behaviors exhibited by any of the children.)
- *After* reading the book, evaluate its impact on the children and document any changes in their attitudes or behaviors.

Current Trends

The themes of children's novels today have moved away from fairy–tale type stories. Books now tend to focus more on real-life situations. Contemporary literature—particularly literature aimed at intermediate-grade children—reflects many difficult social issues, such as abuse, alcoholism, bullying, AIDS, homelessness, gang warfare, single parenthood, and even the threat of nuclear war. An examination of the content of recent Caldecott and Newbery Award–winning books also reveals issues such as divorce, death, lying, and prejudice.

Socioemotional Therapy

In bibliotherapy books are usually chosen to assist a child in dealing with his or her current situation. However, books can also be used on a broader scale in **socioemotional therapy**—the development of children's social and emotional capacities related to self and others. If children view themselves as failures, they develop irrational ideas about their self-worth and abilities. In addition to dwelling on important tasks they have been unable to perform, they often talk themselves into a corner of ugliness, ineptitude, and unpopularity on many dimensions. Anxiety sets in, and the affected individuals become their own worst enemies.

If we are to teach children well, we need to know them as individuals. It is important that teachers note any changes in behavior and watch for specific types of stress, so they can offer the right book to the right child at the right time. Children will not develop self-confidence and self-respect if they are burdened with stress. If children have unhappy home situations, academic success will be difficult or even impossible. A child's risk of failure should be the primary criterion for supplying a special book.

Remember that a poor book sets a child back, and a mediocre book leaves a child at a standstill—but a good book will assist in the development of a child's emotions. It is through this emotional development of children that bibliotherapy can break attitudinal barriers to learning.

Families

Few contemporary realistic books have only one theme. For example, a book may have a social issue theme, such as the tragedy of homelessness; however, it must also have a personal issue theme, such as the protagonist's need for a place to live. In this and the following sections I have grouped books around central themes—but as you read the books, look for other themes the author employs.

Traditional Families

First and foremost to young children are their families and homes. For younger children, happy and humorous books about families abound. Among the most enduring and warmhearted books about traditional families are Beverly Cleary's books about Ramona Quimby, her big sister Beezus, and their family. Two of the most popular of the books are *Ramona and Her Father* (1975) and *Ramona Quimby, Age 8* (1981). In the series readers follow Ramona as she grows from a pesky baby sister to a third grader whose antics include accidentally cracking a raw egg atop her head in school. In 1999, after a fifteen-year break from writing the series, Cleary published *Ramona's World,* in which the exuberant Ramona is 9 years old.

Equally popular is Judy Blume's series about Peter Hatcher, who is constantly tormented by his 2-year-old brother, Fudge. Fudge gets away with everything, including swallowing Peter's pet turtle in *Tales of a Fourth Grade Nothing* (1972). Things worsen in the sequel, *Superfudge* (1980), when Peter's parents announce there is going to be a new baby in the family, and all Peter can think of is a carbon copy of Fudge! Though Peter seems to have overcome his sibling rivalry by the time Fudge is 5, in *Fudge-a-Mania* (1990) the new menace in his life is his next-door neighbor and sworn enemy, Sheila Tubman the Cootie Queen. Chaos strikes when Peter's and Sheila's parents decide to rent adjacent cottages for the summer.

Judith Viorst's stories stem from her experiences in raising boys. Her funniest account is *Alexander and the Terrible, Horrible, No Good, Very Bad Day* (1972), in which the younger son gives a first-person account of his bad day. It includes waking up with gum in his hair, having his best friend find another best friend, not finding dessert in his lunchbox, and accidentally calling Australia on his father's office phone. In *Alexander, Who's Not (Do you hear me? I mean it!) Going to Move* (1995), he has another bad day when he must help pack for the move to a new home—where he is sure he will never have any friends.

Some books focus on a child's special experience with one parent. In *Tell Me a Story, Mama* (Johnson 1989), a young girl is getting ready for bed, and she and her mother talk about Mama's childhood memories, recounting stories of two generations of an African American family. In *A Perfect Father's Day* (1991), Eve Bunting gives a delightful account of 4-year-old Susie, who treats her father to a series of special activities for Father's Day (activities that happen to be all her own favorites). In *One Afternoon* (Heo 1994), a boy spends a day with his mother experiencing all the sights and sounds of the big city. A boy and his father take a special trip together to find the father's childhood camping spot in *The Lost Lake* (Say 1989).

Stories about grandparents abound. Tomie dePaola gives a loving account of his Irish grandfather in *Tom* (1993). When Grandpa Tom, the butcher, gives Tommy a pair of chicken feet to play with, he takes them to school and scares the other kids. In *Song and Dance Man* (Ackerman 1988), two boys and a girl delight in their grandfather's performance of his old vaudeville act. Malka Drucker's *Grandma's Latkes* (1992) is the story of a young girl who helps her grandmother make latkes (potato pancakes) for the Hanukkah dinner. *The Wednesday Surprise* (Bunting 1989) is a touching story of 7-year-old Anna, who reads with her grandmother every

Wednesday after school. At the end of the story, the reader learns that instead of the grandmother's helping the young girl practice reading, the girl is teaching her grandmother how to read. *Emma* by Wendy Kesselman (1980) is a charming account of a grandmother who, after turning 72, begins to paint pictures of all the things she loves.

Nontraditional Families

Stories of children living in nontraditional families (i.e., families in which one or both parents are absent) frequently contain themes of serious personal issues.

In many such stories, children are living with one parent. When they live with their fathers, it is frequently because their mothers have died. Eleven-year-old George, his younger brother James, and their widowed father live on Michigan's Dove Island in *The In-Between Days* by Eve Bunting (1994). When George's father begins to spend time with Caroline, who lives on the mainland, George becomes jealous. He becomes angry when 5-year-old James (who does not remember their mother) also becomes fond of Caroline. George plots a prank to show Caroline how much he dislikes her in hopes she will not return.

In *A Chair for My Mother* (Williams 1982), a young girl, her mother, and her grandmother have had all their furniture and belongings destroyed in an apartment fire, so family members and neighbors have donated furniture and household goods for them to start over. However, there is nothing comfortable for the mother to sit on when she comes home from waiting tables all day, so they save all their coins in a big jar to buy a soft armchair.

In Beverly Cleary's *Dear Mr. Henshaw* (1983), Leigh's parents are divorced, and his father undertakes a wayfaring life in his tractor-trailer with the family dog. Ten-year-old Leigh is left behind, hurt and confused. In letters to his favorite author, Leigh reveals his problems in coping with his parents' divorce, being the new boy in school, and finding his own place in the world.

Children who live in blended families with a parent and a stepparent face several serious personal issues, such as adjusting to the divorce or death of a parent, resentment in sharing their mother or father with the new spouse, dislike for the stepparent, and the presence of unwanted new siblings. *Two Under Par* by Kevin Henkes (1987) chronicles 10-year-old Wedge's personal struggle after his mother remarries. They are living over Wedge's stepfather's miniature golf course with the stepfather's drippy son Andrew. To make things worse, there is a new baby on the way. In *The Hideout* by Eve Bunting (1991), 12-year-old Andy runs away from home because he feels unloved by his mother and new stepfather. He hides out in the tower suite of a luxurious San Francisco hotel while trying to contact his father in London.

In some nontraditional families, children live with aunts and uncles or grandparents because parents are deceased or absent. Among the most poignant of these stories is *Missing May* by Cynthia Rylant (1992). Summer was 6 when her mother died and her Great Aunt May and Uncle Ob lovingly took her in. Six years later, when Aunt May dies, Summer grieves—and is frightened, because Uncle Ob does not want to go on with life. When Cletus, a strange neighbor boy, says he knows someone who can help Ob contact May's spirit, Summer goes along, looking for some sign from Aunt May to ease their sorrow.

Carolyn Coman's *Tell Me Everything* (1993) is an intense novel about 12-year-old Roz, who has lived with her Uncle Mike since her mother died from an accident in the mountains. Roz feels compelled to talk to the teenage boy who last saw her mother alive, as the mother had helped search for the boy when he was lost. Through flashbacks, Roz relives her life with her mother and the terrible event that resulted in her own birth. At the story's end, Roz and her uncle are able to confide—she about the anguish of losing her mother and he about his painful experiences in Vietnam.

Dysfunctional Families

The protagonist in a dysfunctional family setting is certain to be dealing with one or more deep personal issues. Twelve-year-old Hannah comes to the gradual realization that her mother is an alcoholic in *Hannah in Between* (Rodowsky 1994). Not knowing how to cope, she first tries to hide the problem; but when her mother is involved in a serious automobile accident, the family must come to grips with it.

It's Not the End of the World (Blume 1982) is the story of Karen Newman's family, which is torn apart by the parents' constant fighting. When her father moves out and her mother talks about divorce, Karen tries to think of a way to get them back together. However, when her parents come together briefly, the fighting resumes, and Karen begins to realize that a peaceful single-parent home is not the end of the world.

In *Always My Dad* (1995), Sharon Dennis Wyeth paints a tender picture of a young girl's love for the father she infrequently sees. Because the father, who was once an Air Force pilot, is now a laborer who changes jobs and addresses frequently, readers are led to think he may have an alcohol or drug dependency problem. When the girl and her three younger brothers unexpectedly spend part of their summer with their dad at his parents' farm, they renew their love for him. When he leaves for a new job as a truck driver, he hugs his daughter and tells her, "I love you. Just remember, wherever I am, I'm always your dad."

In *Somewhere in the Darkness* by Walter Dean Myers (1992), Jimmy's father was in prison, so when Jimmy's mother died, he lived with Mama Jean, his mother's best friend. When Crab, his father, suddenly appears to take Jimmy with him to Chicago, the boy is understandably reluctant; and rightly so, because Crab has not been paroled as he tells Mama Jean. Though dying of a kidney disease, he has escaped from the prison hospital to find Jimmy—and to prove he is innocent of the crime for which he was convicted.

Abandoned Children

Deep personal turmoil is felt by children whose mothers have abandoned them. When Jeff Green in *A Solitary Blue* (Voigt 1983) was in second grade, his mother vanished, leaving only a goodbye note. Left with his emotionless father, The Professor, Jeff learns that not caring and not feeling is the safest way to live. Five years later his mother, Melody, invites him to spend the summer at her grandmother's house, and he begins to open up and love her again. At first he does not recognize her insincere and selfish nature; he overlooks her neglect, which borders on abuse. During a second summer visit in which he sees Melody very little, he realizes he can be alone without being lonely. Upon his return he learns that his father is not without emotion after all, and a true relationship is kindled.

Journey's father deserted the family some time ago, and Journey is 11 when his mother leaves him and his older sister with their grandparents in *Journey* (MacLachlan 1991). The boy is sad and angry and spends the summer looking for clues that will explain why she abandoned them. He sifts through the box of family photos his mother ripped into pieces before she left, looking for answers. Grandfather stays busy taking new photos of the family and their farm to recreate the family's history. Along the way, Journey gains insight that it was his grandfather, not his long departed father or his absent mother, who has always cared for him like a parent.

Walk Two Moons by Sharon Creech (1994) is a poignant story of 13-year-old Salamanca's search for her mother, who did not return from a solo vacation. During a trip from Ohio to Idaho with her grandparents in search of her mother, the story of her mother's disappearance is revealed through flashbacks. To pass the time during the long car trip, Sal tells the story of her friend Phoebe, whose mother also disappeared for a while. However, Sal's mother can never return, and the author slowly and tenderly unfolds the story of why the mother did not return to the family she loved.

In *Baby* by Patricia MacLachlan (1993), 12-year-old Larkin finds a baby in a basket in her family's driveway. An anonymous note pleads for the family to take her in, and they do so—trying hard not to love her because the note says the mother will come back for her one day. In the year they care for little Sophie, the family begins to heal from the loss of their own infant, who had died a few months before.

One of the most poignant stories of abandoned children is Katherine Paterson's acclaimed *The Great Gilly Hopkins* (1978). Box 8.1 spotlights this book and how it has drawn the attention of censors over the years.

An excellent annotated bibliography of current books with family themes is "Extended Families" by Barbara N. Kupetz, published in the November 1999 issue of *Book Links: Connecting Books, Libraries, and Classrooms.*

Friendship

Books with friendship themes are frequently lighthearted and humorous. A good example is *Annie Bananie Moves to Barry Avenue* (Komaiko 1996). Libby Johnson is bored senseless during the summer. However, things take a turn for the good when Annie Bananie and her big dog, Boris, move to Barry Avenue.

A recurring problem in friendship-themed books is the moment when best friends must part. In Patricia Reilly Giff's *Adios, Anna* (1995), Sarah must say goodbye to her best friend, Anna Ortiz, for the summer. Anna is having a great time at camp while Sarah is stuck with two kindergarten babies to watch. Best friends also part in *Ira Says Goodbye* (Waber 1988). When Ira first learns that his best friend, Reggie,

Box 8.1

Censorship and *Gilly Hopkins*

Because contemporary realistic stories deal with real-life problems, they are open to attack by parents and political groups who attempt to censor books. To *censor* means to examine books or other published materials with the purpose of removing what the examiner finds objectionable (see Chapter 4).

The inherent problem with censorship is that what is objectionable to one person may not be objectionable to another. Is it right for another parent to tell you what *your* children can read? I am convinced that for every book published, there is at least one person who will find something objectionable in it, but that person should not be able to deprive *all* children from reading the book.

Katherine Paterson, the most recent U.S. winner of the Hans Christian Andersen international award, is the daughter of Christian missionaries, and she is married to a Christian minister. Therefore, I was stunned when I first learned that some of her books had been banned from schools because of bad language and un-Christian overtones! Paterson's much acclaimed *The Great Gilly Hopkins* (1978) has been the target of such attacks.

The story opens as a social worker brings 11-year-old Gilly to live in yet another foster home. Gilly is appalled by the frumpy foster mother, Maime Trotter, whom she describes as a semiliterate religious fanatic. Equally appalling is the freaky learning-disabled William Ernest, another young foster child in Trotter's care. Then Gilly learns that the blind African American man who lives next door, Mr. Randolph, is also considered part of the family. Gilly believes she can be happy only with her real mother, so she instantly rejects the affection and compassion offered by her foster family. However, she is slowly drawn into their circle of love. When a stranger, who turns out to be her grandmother, comes to claim her, she has a brief meeting with her mother, but it is a sad reunion.

Below is an excerpt from the last page, in which Gilly telephones Maime Trotter.

"If life is so bad, how come you're so happy?" [said Gilly.]

"Did I say bad? I said it was tough. Nothing to make you happy like doing good on a tough job, now is there?"

"Trotter, stop preaching at me. I want to come home."

"You're home baby. Your grandma is home."

"I want to be with you and William Ernest and Mr. Randolph."

"And leave her all alone? Could you do that?"

"Dammit, Trotter. Don't try to make a stinking Christian out of me."

"I wouldn't try to make nothing out of you." There was a quiet at the other end of the line. "Me and William Ernest and Mr. Randolph kinda like you the way you are."

"Go to hell, Trotter," Gilly said softly.

A sigh. "Well, I don't know about that. I had planned on settling permanently somewheres else."

"Trotter"—She couldn't push the word hard enough to keep the squeak out—"I love you."

"I know, baby. I love you, too."

Gilly is a child hardened by rejection, and she speaks realistically in the manner a tough sixth grader would. (Indeed, elementary children hear such language on their playgrounds.) Her speech and actions project the hard shell her life has become. Because the author is so successful in portraying Gilly's tough persona, the moment when Trotter's love breaks through becomes all the more poignant. Adult readers should consider the context in which objectionable language is used, especially when it is the same language children are allowed to hear on television and movies.

is moving, he sadly thinks of all the fun things they have done. Then, when Reggie tells him how excited he is about moving to a city where there are lots of fun things to do, Ira gets mad and thinks about all the things Reggie does that bug him.

Amber Brown Is Not a Crayon by Paula Danziger (1994) is the story of Amber and Justin, her best friend since preschool. When Amber finds out in third grade that Justin's family is moving to Alabama, she is devastated. They fall into a silly quarrel, but with some counseling they realize that the true cause of their spat is their dejection about the coming separation.

In Nikki Grimes's *Growin'* (1977), Pumpkin's father dies, and she and her mother move to a new neighborhood. She thinks nobody will ever understand her until she meets Jim Jim, the class bully who turns out to be a one-of-a-kind friend.

One of the most moving books about friendship between a girl and a boy is *Bridge to Terabithia* by Katherine Paterson (1977). Though this title is most often remembered because of Leslie's death, it is Leslie's friendship with Jess that the author says is the focus of the book. Leslie moves to a rural Virginia farmhouse adjacent to Jess's at the beginning of their fifth-grade year. Her unique and unconventional manner opens up worlds of imagination and learning that change Jess forever. He is out of town when she falls and strikes her head, and he is disbelieving and numb when he learns of her death. As is characteristic of Paterson's novels, the reader becomes so involved with the characters that it is impossible to remain unmoved by this account, even when forewarned of the death.

 Responding to Literature

Grand Conversations

Children who love stories love to talk about them. A way to encourage talk is through a **grand conversation,** a collaborative discussion that is much like natural conversation, in which the teacher is a facilitator or participant (not the inquisitor). Grand conversations can occur in a large group, such as the whole class, or in a small group, such as a literature circle. Initially it may be difficult for you to keep from falling into the old role of inquisitor—the role in which you ask a question about a book, call on a child to respond, and then mentally evaluate the child's answer before probing for more information, redirecting the question to another child, or initiating a new question. Figure 8.1 contrasts the roles of the teacher and students in traditional discussions and grand conversations. Select a book that you are reading aloud to your children or one they are all reading independently. Conduct a grand conversation, and try to assume the role of facilitator. It usually takes a few times to overcome the traditional inquisitor's role.

Humor

Some contemporary realistic books are written primarily for comic relief. Books targeted for primary-grade children often contain slapstick humor, but intermediate-grade children find light sarcasm appealing. Surely children will read more if they can self-select books they are interested in and enjoy. Because of the universal appeal of

☺ Grand Conversations ☺	☹ Traditional Discussions/Inquisitions ☹
Students are encouraged to guide the discussion and to take turns talking when they have something to contribute.	Teacher controls content of discussion and the students' verbal exchanges.
Students' discussion resembles natural conversation with shifting topics.	Students respond to inquisition.
Students describe the feelings the text evokes in an exchange that reveals their response to the passage.	Teacher controls what counts as an acceptable interpretation of the passage.
Students collaborate by building on previous comments.	Teacher controls the content and direction of discussion.
Teacher is facilitator and asks open-ended questions.	Teacher asks questions, selects who is to answer, and evaluates each answer according to his/her interpretation of the passage.
Teacher's questions are genuine quests for information or clarification.	Teacher asks questions to assess students' comprehension of a passage.

FIGURE 8.1   **Comparison of Grand Conversations with Traditional Discussions**

humorous literature, Klesius, Laframboise, and Gaier (1998) make a special case for using it with **reluctant readers**—children who tend not to choose reading as a pastime. These researchers believe that by offering a good laugh, humorous literature gives nonachievers an authentic reason to read. This can result in better comprehension and the likelihood that reluctant readers will become less reluctant.

Judy Blume's *Freckle Juice* (1971) is sure to make readers of all ages laugh. Andrew wants to have freckles like his friend Nicky, because he thinks that then his mother will never notice if his neck is dirty. So he buys Sharon's secret freckle recipe for fifty cents. But when he tries the strange combination of ingredients, he turns green—not freckled.

Thomas Rockwell's *How to Eat Fried Worms* (1973) is equally hilarious. Because of a revolting bet, Billy has to eat fifteen worms in fifteen days. The worms are supplied by his opponent, and he is allowed a choice of condiments to help get them down. The gastronomic ordeal takes a new twist each day, making the outcome of this delightfully repulsive story unpredictable.

Gary Paulsen is best known for his adventure stories, but he displays a uniquely comic vein in *The Schernoff Discoveries* (1997). The hysterically funny antics of two

14-year-old social nerds, who are "easily the most unpopular boys in the entire demographic area encompassing Washington Junior High School" (p. 1), are told in the first-person account of the main character. His best (read *only*) friend, Harold Schernoff, is a science whiz with a theory for every problem. However, nothing goes according to Harold's plans, especially his scheme on how to act on a first date. The narrator (unnamed) is willing to help Harold test his theories, though they invariably have disastrous results. At the end of the book, readers learn that the narrator is Gary Paulsen—whose aim is to show how a good sense of humor and a faithful friend can help make an outcast succeed. The book is inspiring to readers who fear that adolescent uncoolness might be a permanent state of being.

Books with themes of sibling rivalry are usually humorous—for example, Eloise Greenfield's *She Come Bringing Me That Little Baby Girl* (1974). A little boy's disappointment and jealousy over a new baby sister are gradually dispelled as he becomes aware of the importance of his role as a big brother. In *The Pain and the Great One* (Blume 1974), a story is told from two very different points of view. A 6-year-old boy (The Pain) and his 8-year-old sister (The Great One) each see the other as the troublemaker, but yet the best loved in the family.

Outrageously funny events occur in Barbara Robinson's *The Best Christmas Pageant Ever* (1972) when the Herdmans ("the worst kids in the history of the world") invade church one Sunday and decide to take over the annual Christmas pageant.

Humorous stories that feature a class or group of children at school are always fun, especially when the readers are in the same grade as the characters. Some examples are *Second-Grade Pig Pals* (Larson 1994), *How to Be Cool in the Third Grade* (Duffey 1993), *Fourth Grade Rats* (Spinelli 1991), *Nothing's Fair in Fifth Grade* (DeClements 1981), and *Sixth Grade Secrets* (Sachar 1992). Another great book with sixth-grade characters is E. L. Konigsburg's much acclaimed *The View from Saturday* (1996). For an excellent review of books with school settings, see the article by Radencich and Harrison (1997).

Adventure

Adventure stories typically have fast-moving plots that take place in unusual settings. The quest theme is prevalent: Protagonists in adventure tales often embark on arduous journeys in search of a deeper understanding of themselves. **Survival stories** are adventure stories in which the protagonist is pitted against the elements of nature. In regular adventure stories the main characters may contend with severe weather in remote locations, but they embark on their adventures by choice, and they can return to a safe haven if they desire. In contrast, the protagonists in survival stories are not in their hostile settings by choice, and they must struggle to survive until they find their way to a safer environment or are rescued. Because of the exciting plots, even reluctant readers used to a steady diet of television can often be induced to read adventure stories with absorbing, breathtaking action. Both Gary Paulsen and Jean Craighead George are well known for their lively adventure stories.

Gary Paulsen draws from many exciting episodes of his own life for background in the survival stories he writes. His adventures include hunting and trapping in winter as a young person and twice running the Iditarod Trail sled dog race across more than 1,100 miles of grueling Alaskan terrain. Paulsen's experiences with the latter is clearly seen in *Dogsong* (1985), the story of a 14-year-old Eskimo boy, Russel Susskit, who is troubled by the impact of modernity on his life. His longing for the old ways and the songs that celebrated them takes him to the elder, Oogruk, who is the only one in the village who owns a team of dogs. Russel lives and learns with Oogruk and then embarks on an arduous trek by dogsled across the frozen Alaska wilderness. His 1,400-mile journey across ice, tundra, and mountains brings him self-discovery and his own song, as well as an unexpected encounter with another sojourner.

Fourteen-year-old John Barron is the protagonist in *The Haymeadow* (Paulsen 1992). He is asked to spend the summer taking care of the family sheep herd in the ranch's hay meadow, and he is left there alone (except for two horses, four dogs, and 6,000 sheep). John desperately wants to please his father, but a river flood, coyote attacks, and an injured dog make it seem less likely that he will. His resourcefulness, ingenuity, and talent help him survive the summer and to succeed in the rite of passage like his father and grandfather before him.

The Voyage of the Frog (Paulsen 1989) is the story of 14-year-old David Alspeth's ordeal at sea. In the sailboat his uncle left him, David sets out to fulfill his uncle's last wish by scattering his ashes at sea. However, he is caught in a savage storm; when it passes he is lost and becalmed on a windless sea. There is no radio and only a little water and seven cans of food on board the twenty-two-foot boat. As David drifts southward, he experiences a near collision with an oil tanker as well as frightening encounters with sharks and killer whales. How he survives until he is rescued by a whale research ship off the coast of Baja California is a thrilling tale.

Surely Paulsen's best loved survival story is *Hatchet* (1987), the first book in an unusual trilogy. Thirteen-year-old Brian Robeson is stranded in the Canadian wilderness after the single-engine airplane he was on crashes into a lake. Brian is the sole survivor, escaping with nothing but the clothes he is wearing and a hatchet buckled to his belt, which was a parting gift from his mother. Each of his fifty-four days living in the treacherous wilderness is filled with Brian's perseverance in finding food, shelter, and protection from the elements. When part of the wrecked plane finally floats to the surface of the lake, Brian is able to remove a survival pack that includes an emergency transmitter. He unwittingly turns on the transmitter—and it is heard by a fur buyer flying a bush plane with floats, which allow the pilot to land on the lake and rescue Brian.

The sequel, *The River* (Paulsen 1991), takes place two years after Brian's rescue. Government officials ask him to go back into the wilderness so the military can learn the survival techniques that kept Brian alive. Derek Holtzer, a government psychologist, accompanies him to observe and take notes. During a freak storm, however, Derek is hit by lightning and falls into a coma. With their radio transmitter dead, Brian fears that Derek will die of dehydration unless he can get him to a doctor. He builds a raft and begins a hazardous hundred-mile trip down the river to transport Derek to a trading post, hoping his only map is accurate.

Thousands of readers (as many as 200 a day) wrote Gary Paulsen, wanting to know what would have happened to Brian Robeson had he not been rescued from the Canadian wilderness at the end of the summer in the first book. Paulson wrote an alternate sequel to *Hatchet* to satisfy their curiosity. The reader is asked to imagine that although Brian did retrieve the survival pack, he did not trigger a radio signal and was not rescued. In the alternative sequel, *Brian's Winter* (1996), Brian has the survival kit from the crashed plane with its supply of freeze-dried food, two butane lighters, a rifle, a fishing line, and a sleeping bag. Like the ancient indigenous people, he has to learn to make arrowheads and snowshoes, and he learns the sounds, tracks, and weather of Canada's wild North Slopes. Brian's extraordinary resourcefulness keeps him alive, even after he weathers a ceaseless blizzard and is knocked unconscious by a 700-pound moose. At last, wearing skins for clothes and carrying his handmade weapons, he encounters a Cree trapping family, with whom he stays until he can finally be flown out.

Jean Craighead George, the daughter of an entomologist, had early exposure to natural habitats in the Florida Everglades. Today she is a respected naturalist who travels extensively to observe and report on the behavior of animals in the wild. In her children's books she blends her profound respect for nature with her deep understanding of the reciprocal relationship between humans and their natural surroundings. She has spent much time in Alaska, where her grandson Luke lives, and has traveled by dogsled far out on the Arctic Sea to climb blue pressure ridges and view the natural settings of the animals in her books.

The protagonist in *Julie of the Wolves* (George 1972) is a 15-year-old Inuit girl named Miyax, whose English name is Julie. She escapes from a dreadful arranged marriage by fleeing across the tundra. She naively thinks she can reach her pen pal in San Francisco, but instead she becomes lost in the Alaskan wilderness without food or a compass. Near starvation, she closely observes an Arctic wolf pack and mimics their behavior until they accept her into the group and provide food. With their help and by drawing upon her early training by her father, Julie struggles day by day to survive. She comes to love the wolves as her brothers and is devastated when the leader, Amaroq, is shot from an airplane. After many months of life in the wilderness, she is found by a hunter and taken to her father.

Julie (George 1994) is the sequel to *Julie of the Wolves*. After many years of separation, Julie tries to adjust to living with her father, Kapugen, and her new white stepmother. When Julie finds her father's pilot helmet and goggles, she recognizes him as the man who killed the beloved leader of her wolf pack. Kapugen is determined to kill any wolves that appear near the Kangik village's musk oxen herd, even if they are members of Julie's beloved pack. When she hears the calls of her pack nearby, she prepares for a long solitary journey. She finds the pack (now led by Kapu, son of the slain Amaroq), renews their friendship, and regains their confidence. By carrying Kapu's pup in her backpack, she gets the wolves to follow her across the tundra to an area where they can find wild game.

The Talking Earth (1983) is possibly George's best portrayal of the reciprocal relationship between humans and nature. The protagonist, 13-year-old Billie Wind, is a Florida Seminole living on the Big Cypress Reservation. When she scoffs at the old legends and beliefs of her people, such as the animal gods who talk, the tribal council decides to punish her by requiring her to spend two days alone in the *pa-hay-okee,* the Everglades. Billie takes her punishment as a challenge, and she willingly prolongs her sojourn in the Everglades for twelve weeks. After surviving a raging forest fire and threats from dangerous animals, she discovers that she must listen to the animals and the land in order to survive.

Mystery

Mystery stories are a special category of adventure tales. They usually involve solving some type of puzzle, which may or may not be a crime. Though Joan Lowery Nixon has written several good murder mysteries for children (such as *A Candidate for Murder,* 1991), murder is not typically involved in children's mystery books. However, they do contain unusual characters and clever twists of plot that will surprise readers—unless they have been able to interpret the clues that are interwoven in the story.

Sutherland (1997) described the unique positive effects that reading mysteries can have on young readers. The element of mystery evokes excitement and suspense, so it can rouse the interest of reluctant readers. Because children often speed up their usual reading rate under the stimulus of suspense, mysteries encourage rapid silent reading, a critical skill for fluent readers. In addition, a carefully structured mystery story can help develop logical reasoning.

Responding to Literature

Looking for Mystery Clues

To get the most enjoyment from reading mysteries and to help develop logical reasoning skills, try to solve the mystery in the story before it is revealed to you. Use the following steps:

1. Identify the mystery or puzzle of the book as soon as possible, and write it in a complete sentence in the form of a question (e.g., "Who stole Thomas's money?").
2. List each clue in the plot as it is disclosed by the author.
3. Cross through any clues that turn out to be irrelevant.
4. Using the relevant clues, form one or more possible answers to your question before it is revealed by the author at the end of the story.

Practice this method with one of the short mysteries provided in *Encyclopedia Brown and the Case of the Slippery Salamander* by Donald J. Sobol (1999). Each chapter is a separate mystery, and the solutions are revealed at the end of the book, allowing you to try your skill at solving them yourself.

Since 1962 the *Edgar Allen Poe Award* has been given yearly by the Mystery Writers of America for the best juvenile novel in the field of mystery, suspense, crime, or intrigue. Authors who have won this award in recent years—some of whom are not normally associated with mystery writing—include Robbie Branscum, Eve Bunting, Betsy Byars, Dorothy R. Miller, Phyllis Reynolds Naylor, Joan Lowery Nixon, Willo Davis Roberts, and Susan Shreve. In this section I will touch on books by some of these authors as well as on some of the classics of mystery.

Younger children delight in the series of crime-solving stories that started with *Encyclopedia Brown: Boy Detective* (1963) by Donald J. Sobol. Leroy Brown's father is the chief of police in Idaville. Leroy's computerlike brain has won him the nickname Encyclopedia, and he helps his father solve the tough cases. Most books in the series consist of ten or so chapters, each with a different crime. The readers are invited to interpret the clues and solve the cases along with Encyclopedia. In the event readers need help, the answers are in the back of the book.

When Melanie and April stumble upon a deserted storage yard with a shed behind the A-Z Antiques and Curio Shop, they decide it is the perfect spot to transform into the Land of Egypt in *The Egypt Game* (Snyder 1967). They spend every available moment playing the Egypt game, and eventually other children join. Everyone thinks it is just a game—until strange things begin happening to the players, and a young girl is found murdered in the neighborhood. The children are involved in the events that lead to the capture of the murderer.

E. L. Konigsburg's acclaimed books of intrigue include *From the Mixed-up Files of Mrs. Basil E. Frankweiler* (1967). Claudia decides to run away to teach her parents to appreciate her. She invites her brother Jamie, and they take up residence in the Metropolitan Museum of Art. Claudia finds a statue so beautiful that she will not go home until she discovers its maker, but that question has baffled even the experts. They go to the home of the statue's former owner, Mrs. Frankweiler, to find the answer.

The House of Dies Drear by Virginia Hamilton (1970) is an absorbing mystery about 13-year-old Thomas and his family, who move into a huge old house with secret tunnels, a cantankerous caretaker, and legends of buried treasure. Thomas senses something strange about the Civil War–era house, which used to be a critical stop on the Underground Railroad. Exploring the hidden passageways in and under the house, he pieces together clues in an increasingly dangerous quest for the truth.

In *The Westing Game* (Raskin 1978), sixteen heirs of the eccentric multimillionaire Samuel Westing are assembled in the old Westing house for the reading of his very strange will. To their surprise, the will turns out to be a contest, challenging the group to find out who among them is Westing's murderer. The heirs are paired off and given clues to a puzzle they must solve in order to inherit the money.

There are many fearful night noises on the Mississippi backwoods farm where Ellen lives in *Night Cry* by Phyllis Reynolds Naylor (1984). She is often alone because her father travels a lot and her brother was recently killed in a riding accident. When a local boy is kidnapped and she is awakened before dawn by a cry, Ellen finds the courage to search through the dark alone, believing the scream is from the boy.

In Susan Shreve's *Lucy Forever and Miss Rosetree, Shrinks* (1987), sixth graders Lucy and Rosie love to invent psychiatric case histories, such as the woman whose husband comes home in a bear costume and says he is going to eat her. However, no case they have ever imagined has prepared them for the day a little mute girl with a scar across her throat walks through the door of Shrinks, Incorporated.

Megan's Island by Willo Davis Roberts (1988) is the story of 11-year-old Megan Collier's search for her identity. The book opens when, a week before school is out, her mother insists on taking Megan and her younger brother to their grandfather's isolated lake cottage in the middle of the night. Megan is astonished by her mother's actions—and is further disturbed by evidence that they have been followed and are being spied upon by three mysterious strangers.

Alfred Slote skillfully blends suspense and baseball in *Finding Buck McHenry* (1991). Jason is moved to his Little League's not-yet-formed expansion team of rejected players. He finds a sponsor, and school custodian Mack Henry agrees to be their coach. Soon Jason wonders if the baseball-wise Mr. Henry could really be Buck McHenry, a famous pitcher from the old Negro League. Mr. Henry says his identity is a secret, but Jason is determined to find the truth.

One of Betsy Byars's funniest books in the Blossom series is *Wanted . . . Mud Blossom* (1991). The school hamster that Junior brought home for the weekend is missing; the evidence points to Mud, Pap Blossom's dog, who is hiding under the porch. Meanwhile, old Mad Mary (the Vulture Lady who is Junior's best friend) also has disappeared. Her bag and cane are found by the side of the road, and Junior knows she would never leave them behind voluntarily. The book is full of delightfully comic twists.

Eve Bunting's *Coffin on a Case* (1992) features 12-year-old Henry Coffin, the son of a private investigator. When his father is called out of town, Henry helps Lily—a gorgeous high school girl—search for her kidnapped mother. His powers of observation, intuition, and logic help save not only Lily's mother but a valuable art object as well.

Willo Davis Roberts spins a humorous tale in *The Absolutely True Story . . . How I Visited Yellowstone Park with the Terrible Rupes* (1994). Twelve-year-old twins Lewis and Alison Dodge realize that their dream vacation to Yellowstone with the Rupe family is a nightmare. They are disgusted when they find out their hosts are more annoying than fun. They must baby-sit for two rambunctious preschoolers, cope with Mr. Rupe's terrible driving in the motor home, and track two suspicious-looking men trailing them. The humorous story turns suspenseful when the Rupes' children are kidnapped.

In *The Clearing* by Dorothy Reynolds Miller (1996), Amanda is excited about spending the summer with her cousin, who lives in a remote clearing in rural Pennsylvania. When Amanda learns that a mysterious man called Spook Wade lives nearby and that everyone believes he killed little Bucky Mead ten years before, she wants to find the truth. She and her cousin Nelson set out to discover the long hidden secrets of the clearing.

In *Search for the Shadowman* (1996), four-time Edgar Allen Poe Award winner Joan Lowery Nixon combines contemporary and historical fiction in an exciting mystery. Twelve-year-old Andy Thomas delves into his family tree and uncovers a secret kept hidden for generations. Though his own family discourages him and he receives mysterious threats, he is determined to clear the name of the family's black sheep, Coley Joe Bonner.

In *Holes* (1998), a darkly humorous tale of crime and punishment, Louis Sachar tells the story of young Stanley Yelnats, who has been sent to a boys' juvenile detention center at Camp Green Lake, Texas. Though Stanley is innocent of the crime, the camp seems a better alternative than jail. At the waterless camp, Stanley and the other boys must suffer the punishment of digging a hole a day in the hot sun—five feet deep and five feet across—in the hard earth of the dried-up lakebed. Stanley discovers that the wicked warden is really using the boys to dig for loot buried by the Wild West outlaw Kissin' Kate Barlow. The author masterfully weaves a narrative puzzle that tangles and untangles with increasing suspense.

Social Reality

I have emphasized more than once that attempting to keep children ignorant of social realities will not keep them safe from the problems of the world. The realities of the world cannot be hidden from children, and most of them are quite capable of facing serious issues. Indeed, children need to know as much as possible about the global society in which they live. Attempting to protect them from painful subjects could, among other things, prevent them from understanding the plight of less fortunate people.

War

Stories that deal with war and its aftermath are less prevalent in contemporary fiction than in historical fiction. However, four great books deal with the aftermath of the Vietnam conflict. *The Wall* by Eve Bunting (1990) is a heartrending story of a little boy and his father who travel a great distance to visit the Vietnam Veterans Memorial in Washington, D.C. They find the name of the boy's grandfather, who was killed in the conflict, and make a pencil rubbing of his name. The man says he is the same age his father was when he was killed, and the boy silently wishes that his grandfather could be with them instead of having his name on the wall.

Mick Strum is an artist who is commissioned to design a Vietnam War memorial to honor the casualties of Bolton, Kansas, in Gary Paulsen's *The Monument* (1991). However, the town is appalled by Mick's drawings, because they reveal too much about the community. As Mick anticipates, people react most negatively to what he considers his strongest work. Then he skillfully leads the townspeople to accept a dignified monument to please everyone: eighteen trees, one for each of Bolton's military dead, going back to the Civil War.

In *Journey Home* by Laurence McKay (1998), a 10-year-old Vietnamese American girl tells of the journey with her mother to Vietnam to search for her mother's birth family. Mai's mother was left as a baby at an orphanage in Saigon during the Vietnam conflict and was subsequently adopted by a loving American family. Mai's mother locates the man who saw her parents die in the bombing of their village. The old man recounts how he took her from the rubble and carried her through the devastated village to the orphanage.

Katherine Paterson's *Park's Quest* (1988) is the story of an 11-year-old boy's search for information about his father, who was killed in Vietnam a decade earlier.

Park's mother refuses to speak about his father, but when Park finds he has a grandfather and uncle in rural Virginia, he goes to spend the summer on their farm. Among Park's startling discoveries are that his parents were divorced before his father died and that he has a Vietnamese half sister.

Homelessness

Eve Bunting's *Fly Away Home* (1991) is the story of a man and his young son, Andrew, who live at the airport because the father's job does not pay enough for a deposit on an apartment. They must avoid detection, so father and son keep to themselves, change terminals every night, sleep sitting up, wash in the rest rooms—and, above all, try not to be noticed. Andrew feels hope when he sees a bird trapped in the terminal find its freedom.

The plight of poverty and homelessness is spotlighted when 11-year-old Clay struggles to survive on the street after his father and then his mother abandon him in *Monkey Island* (Fox 1991). He is compelled to stay near the welfare hotel where he and his mother were living. To avoid being taken away by social workers, Clay escapes to the street, where two homeless men, Buddy and Calvin, take him under their wing.

Bye, Bye, Bali Kai (Luger 1996) is the story of a middle-class family's descent into homelessness. Suzie's father loses his job and cannot find another, and her mother's new job does not cover the bills. After eviction from the Bali Kai Apartments and a week in a cheap motel, Suzie and her parents sleep in their car behind a dingy abandoned building. Suzie must spend her afternoons in the public library, alone except for Dawn, the school outcast who latches onto her.

Poverty and Child Labor

Working Cotton by Sherley Anne Williams (1992) is a somber look at a long workday in the life of a migrant family in which everyone except the smallest child must labor in the fields harvesting cotton. The story is told through the eyes of Shelan, a young girl who works in the fields with her family in central California.

Lupita Mañana by Patricia Beatty (1981) is the tale of 13-year-old Lupita, whose father died in an accident near their small Mexican village. Her mother tells Lupita and her older brother Salvador that they must cross the border into the United States to earn enough money to support her and their younger siblings. The children enter California illegally and work at menial jobs, constantly on the watch for *la migra,* the immigration officers who will deport them if found.

In a similar story, Fran Leeper Buss presents the plight of 15-year-old Maria in *Journey of the Sparrows* (1991). Fleeing El Salvador and eager for a new life in the United States, Maria, her pregnant older sister, her little brother, and a stranger endure a terrifying journey nailed inside a crate in the back of a truck that crosses the border and drives on to Chicago. There they find work cleaning, sewing, and washing dishes—always careful to remain invisible so the authorities will not arrest and deport them.

Gangs and Crime

Smoky Night by Eve Bunting (1994) is a child's view of the Los Angeles riots, complete with burning buildings and feuding neighbors. The mother explains to her child that rioting happens when people get angry; they only want to smash and destroy because they do not care anymore about right and wrong.

Walter Dean Myers's *Scorpions* (1988) is a look at gang life. Twelve-year-old Jamal Hicks is having a tough time at school, with Dwayne always pushing him to fight. Jamal worries about his mother, who is working hard to save enough money for an appeal for his jailed older brother, Randy. Randy was the leader of the Harlem Scorpions, and he wants Jamal to take his place until he gets out, but the gang members, especially Angel and Indian, do not like the idea. The only one who approves is Mack, and he gives a gun to Jamal, who reluctantly takes on the leadership of the gang. Jamal finds that when he carries the gun, his enemies treat him with respect. Then a tragedy occurs. Though Jamal survives the experience, he sacrifices his innocence and his best friend.

In Alice Mead's *Junebug* (1995), Reeve McLain Jr., known as Junebug, is approaching his tenth birthday—the age at which boys in the projects are forced into gangs or ensnared by drug dealers. He dreams that someday he and his younger sister and mother will move from the awful housing project, where drugs, gangs, and guns are part of everyday life. Before the gangs and drug dealers come after him, he launches his collection of fifty glass bottles, each carrying a message about his desire to be a sailor and his wish for his family to escape their project home.

Racism

Jerry Spinelli's *Maniac Magee* (1990) is the story of a remarkable homeless orphan named Jeffrey "Maniac" Magee, who confronts racism in the small town of Two Mills, Pennsylvania. This 12-year-old seeks a home where there is no racism, and he attempts to soothe tensions between rival factions on the tough side of town. The story is presented as an urban legend, extolling Magee's ability to do the unthinkable, such as crossing the boundary between the white West End and the black East End, confronting prejudice and racism head on.

Nicholasa Mohr's *Felita* (1979) is a story of the heartache a young Puerto Rican girl in New York experiences when her parents move from *El Barrio* to what they believe is a better neighborhood and school district for their children. Instead of the better future that her father promised, the children are faced with racism and hatred. The kids in the new neighborhood taunt Felita, and her family finally moves back to their old block. In an interesting contrast, Felita also faces prejudice and ridicule from children who are native to Puerto Rico when she goes with her uncle to visit the island in *Going Home* (1986). Among other things, the children laugh at her Spanish and call her a *Nuyorican*.

In Laurence Yep's *Thief of Hearts* (1995), Stacy has always felt comfortable in her suburban middle school. Things begin to go downhill when her family assigns her to escort Hong Ch'un, the new girl from China. When Stacy defends Hong Ch'un against false charges of petty thievery, her friends accuse her of blind loyalty to another culture. When she is called a half-breed, she is shocked and finds herself caught between her Chinese and American heritages. Stacy's mother and great-grandmother take her back to San Francisco's Chinatown, where Stacy learns about their immigrant past and the struggles they faced.

In Judy Blume's *Iggie's House* (1982), an African American family with three children moves into an all-white neighborhood on Grove Street. Eleven-year-old Winnie is the only one who welcomes them, and they soon find a hate sign posted in their front yard: "Go back where you belong. We don't want your kind around here." Winnie learns the difference between being a good neighbor and being a good friend. The author provides a perceptive interpretation of the black family's reaction.

Personal Issues

Except for books that are strictly humorous, most contemporary realistic books contain one or more personal issues. Frequently the character's personal issue is the major theme of the story. Below is a list of popular contemporary realistic books with personal issue themes that are relevant to elementary school children.

▌ ADOPTION

- *Absolutely Normal Chaos* (Creech 1990). In 13-year-old Mary Lou's summer journal, she writes about the unexpected visit of Cousin Carl Ray from West Virginia. During his long-term stay Carl Ray hopes to overcome the anger he felt when he learned his father was not his birth parent, and to search for his biological father, who lives nearby.

- *Tell Me Again about the Night I Was Born* (Curtis 1994). A small child asks her adoptive parents to tell her again about the night of her birth, demonstrating that it is a cherished tale she knows by heart.

- *Tell Me a Real Adoption Story* (Lifton 1994). A child asks his mother to tell him a story before bed. The mother relates the account of the child's adoption, after which he asks several questions before falling asleep, satisfied to know the real history of his beginnings.

- *Mother Help Me Live* (McDaniel 1992). Because she has leukemia, 15-year-old Sarah Mac-Greggor needs a bone marrow transplant. She is stunned and then angry when her parents tell her they cannot be donors because she is adopted. She searches for and finds her birth mother but is disappointed by the woman's response.

- *Come Sing, Jimmy Jo* (Paterson 1985). When his family starts a successful country music group and he becomes the featured singer, 11-year-old James has to deal with big changes. He is not prepared when a stranger approaches and says he is his real father.

- *The Chosen Baby* (Wasson 1977). Because they want to share their home with children, a couple adopts a boy and later a girl.

▌ DEATH

- *Nana Upstairs & Nana Downstairs* (dePaola 1973). Every Sunday 4-year-old Tommy and his parents visit his grandparents and his 94-year-old great-grandmother, who is always in bed upstairs. Tommy is greatly saddened when his upstairs Nana dies, but his mother comforts him by explaining that she will come back in his memory.

- **My Brother Joey Died** (Houston 1982). A child goes through the difficult process of adjusting to the sudden illness and death of her older brother from Reye's syndrome.

- **Abuelita's Paradise** (Nodar 1992). Marita is sad because her grandmother has died, but it helps to sit in *Abuelita's* rocking chair and remember the stories *Abuelita* told of her life in Puerto Rico.

- **Mick Harte Was Here** (Park 1993). Phoebe copes with the painful loss of her 12-year-old brother, who died in a bicycle accident because he was not wearing a helmet. She reminisces about the many happy and funny things they did together.

- **Flip-Flop Girl** (Paterson 1994). Vinnie Matthews is devastated when her father dies, and her little brother is so traumatized that he stops speaking. When they must move in with their grandmother, Vinnie is unhappy in her new school until she is befriended by Lupe, a girl so poor she wears flip-flops instead of shoes to school.

- **The Tenth Good Thing about Barney** (Viorst 1971). When their pet cat Barney dies, everyone in the family is sad. They have a funeral and think of good things to remember about Barney.

DETERMINATION

- **Sticks** (Bauer 1996). There's only one thing in the world Mickey Vernon really wants—to win the 10- to 13-year-olds' nine-ball championship; but to win he has to beat Buck Pender, who is three years older. An old friend of Mickey's father turns up and offers to coach him, but his mother does not trust the man.

- **Oliver Button Is a Sissy** (dePaola 1979). Oliver Button would rather dance and draw pictures than play football like the other boys. His classmates' taunts do not stop him from doing what he likes best, and his practice and persistence pay off when he performs in a talent show.

- **Amazing Grace** (Hoffman 1991). A classmate tells Grace she cannot play Peter Pan in the school play because she is black and a girl, but Grace discovers that she can do anything she sets her mind to.

- **Sidewalk Story** (Mathis 1971). The neighbors are sympathetic but passive when Lilly Etta's best friend, Tanya, and her family are evicted from their apartment. Lilly Etta is determined to find a way to make the men move their furniture back and let them stay.

- **Forbidden Talent** (Nez 1995). Ashkii lives on a Navajo reservation with his grandparents and is determined to be a painter, although his way of painting is in conflict with what his grandfather calls the Navajo Way.

- **William's Doll** (Zolotow 1972). More than anything, William wants a doll, but his brother and the boy next door make fun of him. His father buys him a basketball and an electric train set, but only his grandmother understands he wants a doll to practice being a father.

DILEMMA

- **Are You There God? It's Me, Margaret.** (Blume 1970). When Margaret's family moves to Farbrook, she learns that everybody belongs to either the Y or the Jewish Community Center, but she does not have a religion because one of her parents was raised Christian and the

Ashkii's art wins first prize. From *Forbidden Talent,* written and illustrated by Redwing T. Nez.

other Jewish. Margaret has many conversations with God in hopes of getting some help in choosing a religion and in coping with the problems of puberty.

- *Tangles* (Broome 1993). Sophie does not have enough money to buy a kitten she wants at the fair. When her elderly neighbor drops her wallet, Sophie takes the money she needs but is plagued by guilt.

- *Yang the Youngest and His Terrible Ear* (Namioka 1992). Newly immigrated from China, Yingtao struggles between his desire to please his musically talented parents and his desire to play baseball with his new friend Matthew.

- *To Walk the Sky Path* (Naylor 1973). Billie Tommie, a 10-year-old Seminole Indian, is the first in his family to attend school and learn how to read. He is torn between the ways of his traditional grandfather and the desire to learn more about the white man's ways.

- *Shiloh* (Naylor 1991). When Marty Preston finds a young beagle that is obviously being abused by its owner, his parents insist he return it. When the dog comes back, Marty finds a way to hide him, but lying to his family is extremely difficult.

- *Wringer* (Spinelli 1997). Palmer LaRue dreads the day he turns 10, when he will be expected to take his place beside the other boys in town and become a "wringer" at the annual Pigeon Day shooting contest. Wringers wring the necks of wounded pigeons, but Palmer is repulsed by the slaughter.

- *Ira Sleeps Over* (Waber 1972). When Ira gets ready for his first sleepover, he is torn between taking his teddy bear, Tah Tah, or leaving it home. He has never slept without it before, but his big sister says Reggie will laugh at him.

- ***Shadow of a Bull*** (Wojciechowska 1964). Eleven-year-old Manolo Olivar's father was killed in a bullfight, and everyone expects Manolo to become a famous matador as well. He does not want to disappoint his father's fans, but he is tortured by his fear of fighting the bulls and his aversion to killing the noble beasts.

▌ DISABILITY

- ***Tangerine*** (Bloor 1997). Paul Fisher is legally blind, and he has lived most of his life in the shadow of his football star brother, whom he fears. When his family moves to Tangerine County, Florida, Paul gains friends and confidence by playing goalie on the soccer field, and he finally is able to confront his parents to learn the truth about the accident that damaged his sight.
- ***The Summer of the Swans*** (Byars 1970). A 14-year-old girl gains new insight into herself and her family when her mentally handicapped brother gets lost one summer day.
- ***Yellow Bird and Me*** (Hansen 1991). Doris reluctantly starts helping Yellow Bird, the class clown, with his studies. She finds out that his learning disability makes it difficult for him to learn to read, and in caring for and helping Bird with his reading and his part in the school play, she develops a new friend.
- ***I Have a Sister, My Sister Is Deaf*** (Peterson 1977). A young girl describes how her deaf sister experiences everyday things.

▌ ILLNESS

- ***Now One Foot, Now the Other*** (dePaola 1981). When his grandfather suffers a stroke, which results in partial paralysis, Bobby teaches him to walk, just as his grandfather once taught him.
- ***Alex, the Kid with AIDS*** (Girard 1991). Alex, a fourth grader with AIDS, makes a new friend and learns that even though he is sick, he will not be permitted to misbehave in school.
- ***You Shouldn't Have to Say Good-bye*** (Hermes 1982). Hearing the unbearable news that her mother is dying of cancer, 13-year-old Sarah Morrow throws herself into her gymnastics and tries not to think about it until she and her father can come to terms with their impending loss.
- ***Mama One, Mama Two*** (MacLachlan 1982). A young girl's mother falls into a deep depression, and the child goes to live with a foster family until her mother is well enough to care for her.
- ***The Hundred Penny Box*** (Mathis 1975). Michael loves his frail Great-Great-Aunt Dew. Fearing she will die, he intercedes when his mother says she is going to toss out Aunt Dew's old things—among them her old box containing one hundred pennies, one for each year of her life.

 Responding to Literature

Reacting to Controversial Situations

Encourage your children to respond to the controversial situations in a book. In *Creative Teaching Strategies*, Wynn (1996) described a response activity called "Save the Last Word for Me." While children are reading a book in their literature circle, ask each student to write notes about at least two controversial statements or situations in the story. These should be written on sep-arate index cards, with a personal reaction written on the back of each card. One child in the group is appointed to collect the cards and guide a discussion about each situation. At the end of the discussion, the group leader turns over the card and reads "the last word." For example, in writing about *On My Honor* (Bauer 1986), one child noted the following situation: "Joel feels responsible for Tony's death. Is he responsible?" On the back of the card, the child wrote, "We all make mistakes. It will probably take Joel a long time to realize that even though he is not re-sponsible, he should keep his word and maintain his honor."

Animals

Animal stories most often deal with warm relationships between young people and their animal companions, and stories involving dogs and horses are the most popu-lar. There is much for children to gain by reading these stories. In stories about pets, children can enjoy the "vicarious experience of giving love to and receiving devotion and loyalty from animals" (Huck, Hepler, Hickman, & Kiefer 1997, p. 496). Stories can also help children learn to breed and raise young animals and can teach lessons about the proper training of pets. Perhaps most important, reading about the nurture and care required for a pet helps children recognize others' needs.

In stories involving wild animals, children can learn about the animals' natural habitats and the impact of predators, weather, and seasons. They can vicariously ex-perience the maturity cycles of animals as they grow and develop, mate, raise young, and die.

Popular animal story plots include children who desire pets but must first con-vince their parents, or who gain self-confidence and mature along with a beloved pet. Plots can also involve sad but real issues such as the death of a pet or the sorrow a child experiences when a wild baby animal matures and must be returned to its nat-ural habitat. Other serious themes involve humans' cruel treatment of animals and the illegal hunting of wild animals. More often, though, stories for elementary chil-dren center on the positive effects of loyalty and devotion between pets and children.

Unlike the animal fantasy stories discussed in Chapter 6, real animal stories should portray animals objectively; that is, the author should refrain from interpret-ing behavior or motives for the animals, and the characteristics of animals depicted should be true to their species and breed qualities. Also, there should be a balance among the animals' natural world, human beings, and the special bond of friendship with children. Following is a selection of recommended animal stories.

❙ ANIMAL STORIES

- *The Cry of the Crows* (George 1988). While caring for a baby crow, Mandy begins to look at her family and herself in a different light.
- *Sable* (Hesse 1994). Tate Marshall is delighted when a stray dog turns up in his yard one day, but Sable—named for her dark, silky fur—causes trouble with the neighbors and has to go.

- **Wilderness Cat** (Kinsey-Warnock 1992). When Serena's family moves fifty miles to a wilderness area in Canada, they must leave their cat, Moses, behind, but he shows up on the doorstep of their new home.

- **Gift Horse** (Levine 1996). Matt's dream of owning a horse comes true when his great-uncle sends him one, but being responsible for the horse's care and maintenance in a suburban community is filled with obstacles.

- **Puppies, Dogs, and Blue Northers: Reflections on Being Raised by a Pack of Sled Dogs** (Paulsen 1996). This is a tender account of the sled dog Cookie, who was the lead dog when Paulsen ran the Iditarod sled race in Alaska. The story begins with her last litter and continues to her death of old age.

- **My Life in Dog Years** (Paulsen 1998). In eight chapters, one for each of the significant dogs in his life, Paulsen recounts how his canine friends kept him from harm and made his life richer.

- **I'll Always Love You** (Wilhelm 1985). A child's sadness at the death of his beloved dachshund, Elfie, is tempered by his remembrance of saying to it every night, "I'll always love you."

CONTEMPORARY REALISTIC FICTION BOOKS

Ackerman, Karen. *Song and Dance Man.* Illus. Stephen Gammell. Knopf, 1988.

Bauer, Joan. *Sticks.* Delacorte, 1996.

Bauer, Marion Dane. *On My Honor.* Houghton Mifflin, 1986.

Beatty, Patricia. *Lupita Mañana.* Morrow, 1981.

Bloor, Edward. *Tangerine.* Harcourt Brace, 1997.

Blume, Judy. *Are You There God? It's Me, Margaret.* Macmillan, 1970.

———. *Freckle Juice.* Illus. Sonia O. Lisker. Four Winds, 1971.

———. *Tales of a Fourth Grade Nothing.* Dutton, 1972.

———. *The Pain and the Great One.* Illus. Irene Trivas. Bradbury, 1974.

———. *Superfudge.* Dutton, 1980.

———. *Iggie's House.* Simon & Schuster, 1982.

———. *It's Not the End of the World.* Simon & Schuster, 1982.

———. *Fudge-a-Mania.* Dutton, 1990.

Broome, Errol. *Tangles.* Illus. Ann James. Knopf, 1993.

Bunting, Eve. *The Wednesday Surprise.* Illus. Donald Carrick. Clarion, 1989.

———. *The Wall.* Illus. Ronald Himler. Houghton Mifflin, 1990.

———. *A Perfect Father's Day.* Illus. Susan Meddaugh. Houghton Mifflin, 1991.

———. *The Hideout.* Harcourt Brace, 1991.

———. *Fly Away Home.* Illus. Ronald Himler. Clarion, 1991.

———. *Coffin on a Case.* HarperCollins, 1992.

———. *The In-Between Days.* HarperCollins, 1994.

———. *Smoky Night.* Illus. David Diaz. Harcourt, 1994.

Buss, Fran Leeper. *Journey of the Sparrows.* Dutton, 1991.

Byars, Betsy. *The Summer of the Swans.* Viking Penguin, 1970.

———. *Wanted . . . Mud Blossom.* Delacorte, 1991.

Cleary, Beverly. *Ramona and Her Father.* Illus. Alan Tiegreen. Avon, 1975.

———. *Ramona Quimby, Age 8.* Illus. Alan Tiegreen. Avon, 1981.

———. *Dear Mr. Henshaw.* Illus. Paul O. Zelinsky. Morrow, 1983.

———. *Ramona's World.* Illus. Alan Tiegreen. Morrow, 1999.

Coman, Carolyn. *Tell Me Everything.* Farrar, Straus & Giroux, 1993.

Creech, Sharon. *Absolutely Normal Chaos.* HarperCollins, 1990.

———. *Walk Two Moons.* HarperCollins, 1994.

Curtis, Jamie Lee. *Tell Me Again about the Night I Was Born.* Illus. Laura Cornell. HarperCollins, 1994.

Danziger, Paula. *Amber Brown Is Not a Crayon.* Putnam's, 1994.

DeClements, Barthe. *Nothing's Fair in Fifth Grade.* Viking Penguin, 1981.

dePaola, Tomie. *Nana Upstairs & Nana Downstairs.* Putnam, 1973.

———. *Oliver Button Is a Sissy.* Harcourt Brace Jovanovich, 1979.

———. *Now One Foot, Now the Other.* Putnam, 1981.

———. *Tom.* Putnam, 1993.

Drucker, Malka. *Grandma's Latkes.* Illus. Eve Chwast. Harcourt Brace, 1992.

Duffey, Betsy. *How to Be Cool in the Third Grade.* Illus. Janet Wilson. Viking Penguin, 1993.

Fox, Paula. *Monkey Island.* Orchard, 1991.

George, Jean Craighead. *Julie of the Wolves.* HarperCollins, 1972.

———. *The Talking Earth.* HarperCollins, 1983.

———. *Julie.* HarperCollins, 1994.

———. *The Cry of the Crows.* Harper, 1988.

Giff, Patricia Reilly. *Adios, Anna.* Illus. DyAnne DiSalvo-Ryan. Bantam Doubleday Dell, 1995.

Girard, Linda Walvoord. *Alex, the Kid with AIDS.* Illus. Blanche Sims. Albert Whitman, 1991.

Greenfield, Eloise. *She Come Bringing Me That Little Baby Girl.* Illus. John Steptoe. Harper, 1974.

Grimes, Nikki. *Growin'.* Dial, 1977.

Hamilton, Virginia. *The House of Dies Drear.* Simon & Schuster, 1970.

Hansen, Joyce. *Yellow Bird and Me.* Clarion, 1991.

Henkes, Kevin. *Two Under Par.* Greenwillow, 1987.

Heo, Yumi. *One Afternoon.* Orchard, 1994.

Hermes, Patricia. *You Shouldn't Have to Say Good-bye.* Harcourt Brace Jovanovich, 1982.

Hesse, Karen. *Sable.* Holt, 1994.

Hoffman, Mary. *Amazing Grace.* Illus. Caroline Binch. Dial, 1991.

Houston, Gloria. *My Brother Joey Died.* Sunny Brook, 1982.

Johnson, Angela. *Tell Me a Story, Mama.* Illus. David Soman. Orchard, 1989.

Kesselman, Wendy. *Emma.* Illus. Barbara Cooney. Doubleday, 1980.

Kinsey-Warnock, Natalie. *Wilderness Cat.* Illus. Mark Graham. Cobblehill, 1992.

Komaiko, Leah. *Annie Bananie Moves to Barry Avenue.* Illus. Abby Carter. Delacorte, 1996.

Konigsburg, E. L. *From the Mixed-up Files of Mrs. Basil E. Frankweiler.* Atheneum, 1967.

———. *The View from Saturday.* Atheneum, 1996.

Larson, Kirby. *Second-Grade Pig Pals.* Illus. Nancy Poydar. Holiday House, 1994.

Levine, Betty. *Gift Horse.* Illus. Joseph A. Smith. Greenwillow, 1996.

Lifton, Betty Jean. *Tell Me a Real Adoption Story.* Illus. Claire A. Nivola. Knopf, 1994.

Luger, Harriet Mandelay. *Bye, Bye, Bali Kai.* Browndeer Press, 1996.

MacLachlan, Patricia. *Mama One, Mama Two.* Illus. Ruth Lercher Bornstein. Harper & Row, 1982.

———. *Journey.* Delacorte, 1991.

———. *Baby.* Delacorte, 1995.

Mathis, Sharon Bell. *Sidewalk Story.* Viking Penguin, 1971.

———. *The Hundred Penny Box.* Illus. Leo D. Dillon & Diane Dillon. Viking Penguin, 1975.

McDaniel, Lurlene. *Mother Help Me Live.* Bantam, 1992.

McKay, Lawrence. *Journey Home.* Illus. Dom Lee & Keunhee Lee. Lee & Low, 1998.

Mead, Alice. *Junebug.* Farrar, Straus & Giroux, 1995.

Miller, Dorothy Reynolds. *The Clearing: A Mystery.* Atheneum, 1996.

Mohr, Nicholasa. *Felita.* Dial, 1979.

———. *Going Home.* Dial, 1986.

Myers, Walter Dean. *Scorpions.* HarperCollins, 1988.

———. *Somewhere in the Darkness.* Scholastic, 1992.

Namioka, Lensey. *Yang the Youngest and His Terrible Ear.* Little, Brown, 1992.

Naylor, Phyllis Reynolds. *To Walk the Sky Path.* Dell, 1973.

———. *Night Cry.* Atheneum, 1984.

———. *Shiloh.* Atheneum, 1991.

Nez, Redwing T. *Forbidden Talent.* Northland, 1995.

Nixon, Joan Lowery. *A Candidate for Murder.* Delacorte, 1991.

———. *Search for the Shadowman.* Delacorte, 1996.

Nodar, Carmen Santiago. *Abuelita's Paradise.* Illus. Diane Paterson. Albert Whitman, 1992.

Park, Barbara. *Mick Harte Was Here.* Knopf, 1993.

Paterson, Katherine. *Bridge to Terabithia.* HarperCollins, 1977.

———. *The Great Gilly Hopkins.* HarperCollins, 1978.

———. *Come Sing, Jimmy Jo.* Dutton, 1985.

———. *Park's Quest.* Dutton, 1988.

———. *Flip-Flop Girl.* Dutton, 1994.

Paulsen, Gary. *Dogsong.* Simon & Schuster, 1985.

———. *Hatchet.* Viking Penguin, 1987.

———. *The Voyage of the Frog.* Orchard, 1989.

———. *The Monument.* Delacorte, 1991.

———. *The River.* Delacorte, 1991.

———. *The Haymeadow.* Delacorte, 1992.

———. *Brian's Winter.* Delacorte, 1996.

———. *Puppies, Dogs, and Blue Northers: Reflections on Being Raised by a Pack of Sled Dogs.* Illus. Ruth Wright Paulsen. Harcourt Brace, 1996.

———. *The Schernoff Discoveries.* Bantam, 1997.

———. *My Life in Dog Years.* Illus. Ruth Wright Paulsen. Bantam Doubleday Dell, 1998.

Peterson, Jeanne Whitehouse. *I Have a Sister, My Sister Is Deaf.* Harper & Row, 1977.

Raskin, Ellen. *The Westing Game.* Dutton, 1978.

Roberts, Willo Davis. *Megan's Island.* Atheneum, 1988.

———. *The Absolutely True Story . . . How I Visited Yellowstone Park with the Terrible Rupes.* Atheneum, 1994.

Robinson, Barbara. *The Best Christmas Pageant Ever.* Harper & Row, 1972.

Rockwell, Thomas. *How to Eat Fried Worms.* Franklin Watts, 1973.

Rodowsky, Colby. *Hannah in Between.* Farrar, Straus & Giroux, 1994.

Rylant, Cynthia. *Missing May.* Orchard, 1992.

Sachar, Louis. *Sixth Grade Secrets.* Scholastic, 1992.

———. *Holes.* Farrar, Straus & Giroux, 1998.

Say, Allen. *The Lost Lake.* Houghton Mifflin, 1989.

Shreve, Susan. *Lucy Forever and Miss Rosetree, Shrinks.* Holt, 1987.

Slote, Alfred. *Finding Buck McHenry.* HarperCollins, 1991.

Snyder, Zilpha Keatley. *The Egypt Game.* Atheneum, 1967.

Sobol, Donald J. *Encyclopedia Brown, Boy Detective.* Lodestar, 1963.

———. *Encyclopedia Brown and the Case of the Slippery Salamander.* Delacorte, 1999.

Spinelli, Jerry. *Maniac Magee.* Little, Brown, 1990.

———. *Fourth Grade Rats.* Scholastic, 1991.

———. *Wringer.* HarperCollins, 1997.

Viorst, Judith. *The Tenth Good Thing about Barney.* Illus. Erik Blegvad. Macmillan, 1971.

———. *Alexander and the Terrible, Horrible, No Good, Very Bad Day.* Illus. Ray Cruz. Atheneum, 1972.

———. *Alexander, Who's Not (Do you hear me? I mean it!) Going to Move.* Illus. Robin Preiss Glasser. Atheneum, 1995.

Voigt, Cynthia. *A Solitary Blue.* Atheneum, 1983.

Waber, Bernard. *Ira Sleeps Over.* Houghton Mifflin, 1972.

———. *Ira Says Goodbye.* Houghton Mifflin, 1988.

Wasson, Valentina P. *The Chosen Baby.* Illus. Glo Coalson. HarperCollins, 1977.

Wilhelm, Hans. *I'll Always Love You.* Crown, 1985.

Williams, Sherley Anne. *Working Cotton.* Illus. Carole Byard. Harcourt Brace, 1992.

Williams, Vera B. *A Chair for My Mother.* Greenwillow, 1982.

Wojciechowska, Maia. *Shadow of a Bull.* Troll, 1964.

Wyeth, Sharon Dennis. *Always My Dad.* Illus. Raul Colon. Knopf, 1995.

Yep, Laurence. *Thief of Hearts.* HarperCollins, 1995.

Zolotow, Charlotte. *William's Doll.* Harper, 1972.

KEY TERMS

 Explore the E-Glossary at **www.ablongman.com/anderson**

bibliotherapy (p. 205)

contemporary realistic fiction (p. 203)

grand conversation (p. 214)

mystery story (p. 219)

reluctant reader (p. 215)

survival story (p. 216)

social reality theme (p. 204)

socioemotional therapy (p. 208)

Ruthie plays the Heavenly angel.
The Year of the Perfect Christmas Tree: An Appalachian Story Written by Gloria Houston and illustrated by Barbara Cooney.

Historical Fiction

Realistic fiction in a real-world setting in the historical past, with events that are partly historical but largely imaginative

As a student, I was never very good at history. It was sooooooo boring! When I discovered historical fiction books, however, I realized that history is not boring. It was the way I was taught history that was boring—listening to classmates slowly read the textbook out loud, one paragraph at a time, and having to memorize names and dates that meant nothing to me. But when I read about real and realistic people within the context of a good story set in past times, history came alive and was not only interesting but also often exciting. Because quality historical fiction presents an accurate portrayal of the historical period depicted, it can be woven into the study of history and can improve children's knowledge and attitudes toward the subject.

Evaluating Historical Fiction

The following questions can guide you as you select historical fiction books.

- Is the story interesting to elementary children?
- Is the setting integral to the story?
- Are there sufficient references to historical events, people, and other clues to allow the reader to place the story in the appropriate historical framework?
- Are the characters believable?
- Is the language authentic for the period?
- Is the setting authentic in every detail?
- Are illustrations authentic for the period?
- Has the author avoided any contradictions with real history?
- Are differing points of view on the issues of the time acknowledged?
- After reading the book, do readers believe they know a time or place better?

Characteristics of Historical Fiction

The major difference between historical fiction and contemporary fiction is the time setting. Both genres can have the same place setting, but they differ in terms of *when* the story takes place. For the purpose of this textbook, **historical fiction** settings include any period from prehistory through 1964, when the Civil Rights Act was passed. Contemporary fiction settings include from 1964 to the present day. As I mentioned in Chapter 8, this dividing line is arbitrary, and not all literature specialists agree on it. I selected 1964 because laws, attitudes, and opportunities concerning minorities in the United States were very different before that year; this fact needs to be kept in mind when we read and evaluate historical fiction.

Literary Element	Historical Fiction	Contemporary Fiction
Time setting	Before and including 1964	After 1964
Place setting	Anywhere on earth	Anywhere on earth
Characters	Realistic people who may be fictional, based on real people, or real historical people	Realistic people, nearly always fictional
Tone	Most often serious	Serious or light
Themes	Frontier life, war, nostalgia, adventure/survival, racial oppression, social issues of the time	Family, friendship, humor, adventure/survival, mystery, modern social reality, personal issues

FIGURE 9.1   Comparison of Historical and Contemporary Fiction

The characters in historical fiction are believable, realistic people whose dialogue reflects the historical period. Main characters are usually fictional. Other characters can be real historical people, but they generally have supporting roles or are only mentioned in passing. For example, it would be difficult to write a book set during the Civil War without mentioning President Lincoln, General Grant, or General Lee. However, it is important for readers to keep in mind that although good historical fiction books are consistent with actual historical evidence, they are *not* history.

Historical fiction stories reflect real-life milieus of past times. Their themes include the basic conflicts of human existence: good and evil, love and hate, peace and war. Plots often deal with events such as war, death, and racial oppression; because of this, authors most frequently write historical fiction with a serious tone. Figure 9.1 compares the characteristics of historical and contemporary fiction.

Biographical Fiction

When authors base their stories on events that happened to real people, the books are called **biographical fiction.** These books are largely fictional because nearly all the dialogue is fabricated, and the author embellishes the story to fill in unknown details and to make it more interesting. For example, Carol Ryrie Brink based *Caddie Woodlawn* (1935) on the life of her grandmother, Caddie Woodhouse. In the introduction, Brink wrote,

> All of the names in the book, except one, are changed a little bit. The names are partly true, partly made up, just as the facts of the book are mainly true but have sometimes been slightly changed to make them fit better into the story. (p. vi)

Brink spent much time listening to her grandmother's stories about growing up on the Wisconsin frontier in the 1860s. However, not all authors of biographical fiction are fortunate enough to have a primary source for their information. Authors who did not know their ancestors must rely on stories handed down through the generations. Even family stories that are handed down by word of mouth tend to become legends, which makes it difficult to separate truth from fiction. There are often gaps of important information in the stories, and—lacking a primary source—the author must research and think of interesting ways to fill in the gaps and weave it all into a good story. One book based on a handed-down story is *Mountain Valor* (1994) by Gloria Houston. The author wrote in the endnote:

> *Mountain Valor* is based on a true event. Valor was Matilda Houston. As an adolescent, she rescued her family's livestock when marauders took them during the Civil War. Exactly how she completed her mission is not known. The story of this very courageous young woman has been a part of the folklore of Avery County, North Carolina, for four generations, yet no written documentation . . . exists. (p. 237)

In a personal communication (November 13, 1999), Houston said she researched the period extensively in order to create probable methods for Valor to make the trek across the mountains to bring her family's livestock home and save her family from starvation.

Other biographical fiction books are based on stories told to an author by someone outside the family. This makes the writing all the more challenging, because the author has no family resources to provide ideas and details to fill in the gaps. One such book is *Sounder* (1969) by William H. Armstrong, which is based on a story told to the author by the person who is the main character in the book, the young African American son of a sharecropper. The author does not name the characters. Only the much-loved family dog, Sounder—a mixture of Georgia redbone hound and bulldog—is named. The absence of names and of a specific setting for the story may have been the author's device to universalize the book's theme of injustice to the poor.

 ## Literature Activity: **Determining Time Setting**

When settings in books are vague, as in *Sounder,* you can help children sharpen their observation skills by thinking like detectives. Because the family members in the story are sharecroppers, they may have lived in the Deep South—possibly in Georgia (because of the dog's breed). But *when* did the story take place? Here are the clues:

1. The author heard the story fifty years before writing the book (author's note).
2. The book was published in 1969 (copyright page).
3. The sharecropper's son was an older man, perhaps 60 years old, when he told the story (author's note).
4. The story took place when the man was a young boy, perhaps 12 years old (story).

What year, approximately, did the story take place? ■

In some biographical fiction books, authors write about their own childhoods, as in the series by Laura Ingalls Wilder that started with *Little House in the Big Woods* (1932). This book is based on events in Wilder's early childhood, some sixty years prior to its publication. The author was the primary source of information and could glean any needed details from her siblings and family artifacts—letters, diaries, Bibles, and so on. Because of this, the book is most accurate in its depiction of the time period. I am often asked why Wilder's books are considered fiction rather than autobiography. The answer is that in her series Wilder freely recreated dialogue and filled in any gaps in her memory with fictional details. She also changed the order of events and compressed events; for example, she took incidents that happened over a period of several years and narrated them as if they all happened in one year.

There is a fine line between biographical fiction and fictionalized biography, which you will read about in Chapter 10. To determine whether a book is considered fiction or biography, it is best to find out in which genre the author and publisher categorize it. A good indicator of genre is the section of the library in which the book is shelved. Historical fiction is found in the J and E sections with all the other fiction, whereas biography is found in the J900 section. Also, most hardcover books and some paperback books will state the genre near the bottom of the copyright page.

Books that were written as contemporary fiction many years ago and are still in print are also considered historical. One classic example is *Little Women* by Louisa May Alcott, which is set during the Civil War (1861–1865). The book was published in 1868, so Alcott wrote about her own time period; however, the setting is historical for today's readers. Always keep in mind that my 1964 dividing line between historical and contemporary is arbitrary. Therefore, when a book published prior to 1964 has a setting that is incidental to the story, it may still be considered contemporary fiction if there is nothing in the story that points to a specific historical period. An example is *The Snowy Day* by Ezra Jack Keats (1962), in which a young African American boy living in an inner city plays all day in the snow, much the way children today do.

Researching Historical Fiction

Historical fiction is one of the most difficult genres to write and illustrate because most often authors and illustrators are depicting a time period prior to their birth. This requires careful research and travel to the place setting of the book. Authors also must research the language of the period so that dialogue will be appropriate to the time, representing vocabulary and figures of speech common to people of the setting. You read in Chapter 7 about problems with authenticity that can occur when an author does not do adequate research. There are similar results when illustrators do not conduct adequate research.

One of my favorite books is *But No Candy* (1992) written by Gloria Houston and illustrated by Lloyd Bloom. Even though Houston was born and raised and has lived most of her life in western North Carolina, where her books are set, she conducts research for each book, using sources of primary material such as the Appalachian

Cultural Center, the Rural Life Museum, and local historians. Imagine her surprise when *But No Candy*, which is set during World War II, was published with anachronistic illustrations! In several illustrations, including the book cover, the characters are shown using a kerosene lamp. In a personal interview, Houston exclaimed, "I never used a kerosene lamp in my life until I was in a hurricane in Florida. My region of North Carolina had electricity in the 1940s, although some rural areas did not."

In addition, the main character Lee and her little brother are illustrated wearing black canvas shoes with rubber soles that look much like Converse All Stars. In the 1940s children did not wear canvas shoes with rubber soles. For one thing, rubber was reserved for military use during World War II, and canvas shoes did not become popular with children until several years after the war. Needless to say, the author and her fans are looking forward to a new edition of the book with new illustrations.

In contrast, Houston's *The Year of the Perfect Christmas Tree* (1988) was illustrated by two-time Caldecott Award winner Barbara Cooney. This book is set in the same region of North Carolina, but during World War I. In preparation for writing the book, Houston conducted research using the sources previously listed as well as the Tweetsie Railroad, Inc., Grandfather Mountain, Inc., and Rogers Whitener (columnist for "Folk Ways and Folk Speech"). She also met with local cabin restorers and photographers. Barbara Cooney traveled with the author to the town of Spruce Pine and toured the school, church, cabins, and train station that appear in the illustrations. Cooney worked ceaselessly for six days making notes, sketches, and photographs that she later used for her paintings. She returned to her home in New England armed with dozens of photographs loaned to her by Hugh Morton, a noted photographer of the area, to provide further authenticity. As examples of Cooney's authentic details, the Spruce Pine Church scenes include a period wood-burning stove (complete with the manufacturer's name, "Acme Champion") and the old church pews, which were discovered in the church basement during her visit. It is easy to see why the talented Barbara Cooney is one of the most respected illustrators of historical fiction.

 ## Responding to Literature

Writing Biographical Fiction

Read a biographical fiction book. Then ask a grandparent or other older relative to tell something interesting he or she did as a child. Write a story about the account, adding fictionalized details and dialogue.

Scott O'Dell Award

The Scott O'Dell Award is a special award given to honor historical fiction books of high literary quality. The award is given annually to a U.S. citizen who has published a distinguished children's historical fiction book with a New World (i.e., North American) setting. The award, established by the noted children's novelist Scott O'Dell, is administered by the Advisory Committee of the Bulletin of the Center for Children's Books. The first award was given in 1984 to Elizabeth George Speare for *The Sign of the Beaver* (1983), which is set in the Maine wilderness in 1768. This and other award-winning books that are geared for elementary schoolchildren are included in this chapter.

Periods Depicted in Historical Fiction

Ancient Times

T. A. Dyer's *A Time of His Own* (1990) is the story of Shutok, a lame boy from a very primitive nomadic tribe. He is abandoned by his clan because he slows down their search for bison. Together, Shutok and an escaped slave girl from another tribe struggle to survive the cruel winter weather, and they must kill a jaguar that invades their cave. When the clan returns in the spring, they are in awe of Shutok and his pelt, realizing he has strength and worth despite his disability.

Children who are fascinated by stories of the Egyptian boy king Tutankhamen will surely enjoy reading Eloise Jarvis McGraw's *The Golden Goblet* (1961). Ranofer, a young Egyptian boy, longs to become a master goldsmith like his father. However, after his father dies, Ranofer's evil half brother Gebu makes him labor in his stone works. When Ranofer finds a magnificently ornate golden goblet among Gebu's belongings, he knows his brother is a grave robber—a crime punishable by death. Ranofer risks his own life to reveal this wicked crime.

The Bronze Bow by Elizabeth George Speare (1961) is set in Galilee in the time of Jesus. Daniel Bar Jamin is a young Jewish rebel who is consumed by hate of the Romans who cruelly killed his parents. Daniel fights to drive the Romans out of Israel, but he is gradually won over to the gentle teachings of Jesus and learns that love, not hate, is the source of strength.

Medieval Times

The House of Wisdom (1999), by Florence Parry Heide and Judith Heide Gilliland, is set in ninth-century Baghdad, then the center of a vast empire and the seat of knowledge and learning. The House of Wisdom is a school, a repository of all the known learned books, and a translation bureau. It attracts thousands of scholars from around the Islamic world who gather to read, exchange ideas, and translate the dusty manuscripts that arrive by camel and ship from all over the world. The protagonist, Ishaq (a real historical person), is the son of a translator, and he longs for adventure. When he travels the world to buy books for the caliph, his greatest find is a previously unknown book by Aristotle. Ishaq devotes his life to the philosopher's works and becomes a brilliant scholar.

Katherine Paterson has written several good books set in feudal Japan, two of which are appropriate for intermediate-grade children. *The Sign of the Chrysanthemum* (1973) is set in the twelfth century during the civil wars between the Genki and Heike clans. This story is about a 13-year-old Japanese boy, Muna, who searches for his father, knowing only that he is a samurai warrior with a chrysanthemum tattoo on his arm. Muna travels to the capital city, Kyoto, and works as a servant to the great swordsmith Fukuji while he continues his quest.

Of Nightingales That Weep (Paterson 1974) takes place during the same era. Takiko is the vain daughter of a samurai. After her warrior father dies in battle, her mother remarries a strange and ugly country potter, whom Takiko fears and despises. Takiko's comfortable home life is ripped apart, but her beauty and musical talent win her a place at the imperial court. There she finds herself torn between opposing warrior clans that struggle for control of Japan during the Gempi Wars.

Several good novels for intermediate-grade children are set in medieval Britain and Europe. The backdrop for *Adam of the Road* (1942) by Elizabeth Janet Gray is England in the year 1294. Eleven-year-old Adam and his father are minstrels. When Adam goes looking for his stolen red spaniel, Nick, he gets separated from his father. Adam travels the roads alone, searching the fairs and market towns for both his father and his beloved dog.

Marguerite de Angeli's *The Door in the Wall* (1949) is the story of Robin, the son of Sir John de Buerford. After his father leaves him in the care of servants, Robin falls ill and his legs become paralyzed. When the servants flee, fearing the plague, Robin is alone and helpless. Brother Luke finds him and takes him to the hospice of St. Mark's, where he is lovingly cared for and taught how to walk with crutches. His dreams of becoming a knight are shattered. However, when the great castle of Lindsay is in danger, it is Robin who ingeniously saves the townspeople.

In *The Midwife's Apprentice* (1995) by Karen Cushman, a homeless, nameless girl is taken in as a servant by a hot-tempered, snaggletoothed midwife. Eventually, the girl cleans herself up, takes the name Alyce—and, by secretly watching the midwife work, learns to deliver calves and babies. She finds a useful and contented place in the world of fourteenth-century England.

Joseph Bruchac is a prolific writer who is of Abenaki Indian descent. The setting for his acclaimed book, *Children of the Longhouse* (1996), is in the late 1400s in the homeland of the five Nations of the Iroquois, which encompassed what is present-day New York State. In this book, Ohkwa'ri, an 11-year-old Mohawk boy, and his twin sister must deal with a hostile gang of older boys after Ohkwa'ri reveals to the elders the boys' plan to raid a small village of Anen:taks, people with whom the Mohawks had made peace. The boys seek revenge by trying to hurt Ohkwa'ri during the brutal villagewide game of *Tekwaarathon* (lacrosse).

Colonial Times in America

The vast majority of historical fiction written for American children is set in the United States. The time line in Figure 9.2 will help you place events and eras of United States history as you read about the books set in these periods. Although not all authors supply an exact time setting for their books, I have arranged books discussed in the following sections in chronological order as near as possible.

Michael Dorris, a Modoc Indian, wrote a much acclaimed book set in this time. *Morning Girl* (1992) is the charming but thought-provoking story of a 12-year-old

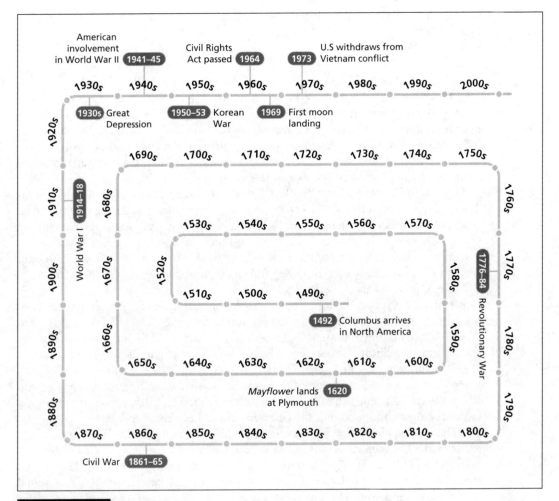

FIGURE 9.2 American History Time Line

Taino Indian, Morning Girl, and her younger brother, Star Boy. In alternating chapters the two children narrate rich descriptions of their lives on a Bahamian island in 1492. At the end of the book, Morning Girl witnesses the arrival of the first Europeans.

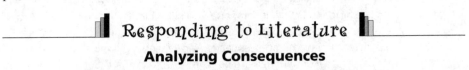

Responding to Literature

Analyzing Consequences

When Columbus landed in the New World, he described the inhabitants as simple, primitive people. What do you read in *Morning Girl* that would run counter to Columbus's evaluation of these Native Americans? Through the eyes of Morning Girl or Star Boy, cite examples of why you think the lives of the Taino people will improve or decline following the arrival of the Europeans.

The Cherokee had lived in the Blue Ridge Mountains for hundreds of years before Europeans first saw them in 1539. In *Itse Selu: Cherokee Harvest Festival* (1994), Daniel Pennington recreates a typical Green Corn Festival prior to the European invasion of the Cherokee homelands. In the story Little Wolf watches anxiously as his family and other villagers prepare to celebrate the corn harvest with a feast. Readers will find authentic accounts of the lifestyle, the harvest feast, a traditional folktale, and the sacred corn dance in this book.

Elizabeth George Speare's *The Witch of Blackbird Pond* (1958) is the story of Kit Tyler, a high-spirited teenage girl who has grown up in the shimmering Caribbean islands. In 1687 after her parents die, Kit sails to her new home with relatives in the bleak, cold Connecticut colony. There she is lonely and feels suppressed by the narrow-minded ways of the stern Puritan community. Kit befriends a lonely old Quaker woman who lives on Blackbird Pond, and she is subsequently accused of witchcraft.

The Spinner's Daughter (Littlesugar 1994) is the story of young Elspeth, whose father died of fever on the long voyage from England to the Puritan colony in Connecticut. She and her mother work very hard, growing flax and spinning it into thread. When an Indian boy shows Elspeth how to make a doll out of cornhusks, she shows the other children. Soon they all have dolls, but the parents burn them because "Puritan children have no time for play." However, the children make more dolls, so when Judge Samuel Sewall comes to town, the villagers ask him to punish Elspeth. When she tells the judge all the work she has completed that day, he says that her only fault is being a child, and that the children should keep their dolls.

The city of New York is an exciting place to be in 1734. In *The Printer's Apprentice* (1995), Stephen Krensky has woven the tale of 10-year-old Gus Croft, apprentice to publisher William Bradford. Gus closely follows the sensational arrest and trial of Peter Zenger, publisher of the *New York Weekly Journal*, who has been jailed for printing scandalous opinions about His Majesty's Governor Cosby. Gus questions whether the governor should be able to imprison publishers who print unwelcome information and why the colonists let him get away with it. Gus becomes entangled in the political arena and in the historic legal case that laid the foundation for freedom of the press.

 ## Literature Activity: **Separating Fact and Fiction**

In reading historical fiction, it is important to help children sort the history from the fiction. Before you start reading a book, make a chart with the two headings: "Historical Fact" and "Fiction." As each new character appears, help readers determine whether he or she is a real historical person (consult reference books if necessary) or a fictional creation. Place the characters' names under the appropriate heading. Similarly, as major parts of the plot unfold, determine which events are historical fact and which are fiction. Information about the setting may also be added. How would you classify the following from *The Printer's Apprentice*?

1. Gus Croft
2. William Bradford
3. Zachariah Bennett
4. Peter Zenger
5. Governor Cosby
6. Andrew Hamilton
7. Squire Wilson
8. Anne (the bookbinder's daughter)
9. Zenger published the *New York Weekly Journal.*
10. Zenger was arrested and tried for libel.
11. Bradford and Gus traveled to Philadelphia.
12. Cosby disbarred Zenger's lawyers before the trial.
13. Wilson was sprayed by the fire engine.
14. Gus watched the trial from the window.
15. Bradford attended Zenger's funeral.
16. New York was once named Nieuw Amsterdam.
17. Forks were new eating utensils in 1734. ■

Adventurous Americans left the relative safety and comfort of the cities and moved westward even in the colonial era, beginning the lengthy process often romanticized as "How the West was won." To the original inhabitants of the land, however, the advancing frontier represented how the West was *lost.*

 Responding to Literature

Examining Points of View

Most older works of historical fiction, such as Walter D. Edmonds's *The Matchlock Gun* (1941/1998, Paper Star), reflect the Colonial era from only the European American point of view, a point of view that changed little before the civil rights era. This book was based on a real event, which is tragic because it is a prime example of brutal racism.

　　The setting of *The Matchlock Gun* is 1757, a time when the French and Indians represent serious threats to the pioneers of the British colonies. When young Edward's father is away and his mother is chased by five Indians, Edward fires an old matchlock gun, killing three men and wounding another, who is later killed by his father. Edward is later commended because he killed more Indians than his father and companions.

　　Share this book with your children as an example of a one-sided point of view of historical fiction. Lead a discussion on what the Indians' point of view might have been as they tried to prevent white people from taking their ancestral homelands.

　　A more positive book is *The Sign of the Beaver* by Elizabeth George Speare (1983). In 1768, 12-year-old Matt is left in a cabin in the Maine wilderness while his father goes to fetch his mother and sister. When the father does not return as planned, Matt struggles to survive. One day he is attacked by swarming bees—and then rescued by an Indian chief and his grandson, Attean. As the boys come to know each other, Attean learns to speak some English, and Matt becomes a skilled hunter. When many months pass with no sign of Matt's family, Attean asks Matt to join the Beaver tribe and move north with them. Matt struggles with the idea of abandoning hope and moving on to a new life with his Indian friends.

Revolutionary Era

Wartime is a popular setting for both children's and adult historical fiction. One of the most unusual books of the Revolutionary period is Gary Paulsen's *The Rifle* (1995). The book is the history of a magnificently crafted rifle that was made in 1768 by a gunsmith named Cornish McManus, who lived near Philadelphia. The accuracy of the rifle makes it a masterpiece, and after John Byam purchases it, he becomes a legendary sharpshooter in the American Revolutionary War. When Byam succumbs to dysentery, the rifle is passed on, but never again fired. The second half of the book traces the history of the rifle through episodic stories of who owns it and how it changes hands over the next 200 years. Since the death of John Byam, no one has ever checked to see if the rifle was loaded. The tragic final episode, set in the present day, reveals that the gun is loaded.

Esther Forbes's *Johnny Tremain* (1943) is a novel of a 14-year-old apprentice silversmith who chronicles the beginnings of the Revolution in the American colonies. Johnny is gravely injured while working with molten silver, and his disability prevents him from continuing his apprenticeship. The historic events of Boston in 1773 are presented through Johnny's point of view, and his courageous involvement in the American Revolution makes an exciting adventure story that is both sad and inspiring.

Early Thunder (1987) by Jean Fritz is set in Salem, Massachusetts, in 1774. Before the Revolutionary War erupts, 14-year-old Daniel West begins to reexamine his loyalty to the king of England as the conflict between Tories and Patriots increasingly divides the townspeople. Finally, David changes his allegiance from Tory to Whig and joins the Patriots.

Scott O'Dell's *Sarah Bishop* (1980) is based on a true story of one girl's strength and courage during the American Revolution. Sarah's family lives on Long Island, and they have split loyalties during the War for Independence. Her father is a British Loyalist, and her brother is a Patriot. When they both die as a result of the war, Sarah is arrested by British soldiers on false pretense. She escapes to the Connecticut wilderness, where she lives in a cave and fiercely fights for survival.

Avi's *The Fighting Ground* (1984) is a tale of 13-year-old Jonathan, who dreams of fighting in the Revolution. Almost by accident, he is recruited into a fighting unit. When he is taken prisoner, he experiences the reality of war. Later, Jonathan experiences inner turmoil as he struggles to understand his feelings about killing.

Early Frontier Era

Although many adventures took place on the American frontier, the early nineteenth century also saw adventures on the high seas. One amazing survival story, *The Castaway* (1983) by Arthur Roth, is based on the true story of a young sailor, the only survivor of a shipwreck. In 1812 the young man is cast up on a tiny rock reef that is nothing more than a jumbled pile of sea-washed boulders in the southern Pacific Ocean. His only possessions are the tattered clothes he wears, a pocket clasp knife, and one wooden oar. Amazingly, the young man survives for three years by killing the slow-moving seals who occasionally visit the reef. His only companion is a friendly penguin.

The Stowaway (1995) by Kristiana Gregory is based on a historic event in 1818 at Monterey Bay settlement in California. Eleven-year-old Carlito and his family are loyal to Spain, as are most Californians. When the Argentine pirate Hippolyte de Bouchard attacks the settlement, Carlito witnesses the death of his father and vows revenge. In an attempt to sabotage the pirates' ship, Carlito sneaks on board. He is quickly discovered and enslaved by the cruel captain. He finds a friend in fellow stowaway Billy Bumpus, who came aboard searching for his imprisoned father. As the pirates terrorize the missions along the California coast, Carlito suffers their filthy living conditions and brutal savagery.

Tales of early settlement on the American frontier in the early 1800s have both adventure themes and themes of everyday family life. In a picture book format that children of all ages can enjoy, Donald Hall's *Ox-Cart Man* (1979) describes a year in the life of a pioneer family. Barbara Cooney's exquisite illustrations depict how each member of the family works hard all year. Each October the father takes whatever they grow or make but do not use to the Portsmouth Market in an oxcart. After he sells all the goods, including the cart and the ox, he buys the things they are unable to make and returns home with the treasures.

Yonder by Tony Johnston (1988) has a similar theme. The text, written in free verse, illuminates a family's history for three generations. The beautiful plum tree the first settler planted outside their house is shown changing and growing in each passing season—like the lives of the people in this three-generation farm family.

Sarah, Plain and Tall (1985) by Patricia MacLachlan has a warm family theme, and in fact it is based on the author's family history. When Anna and Caleb's widowed father, Jacob, places a newspaper advertisement for a wife and mother, Sarah Wheaton answers. She travels from Maine to their Midwestern prairie home to meet them. Though Sarah falls in love with the family, she misses her seaside home. Jacob, Anna, and Caleb anxiously await her decision, and at the end of the book, a wedding is planned. The sequel, *Skylark* (1994), opens the summer after Jacob and Sarah are married. When a devastating drought brings threats of dangerous wildfires and thirst-crazed coyotes, Sarah takes Anna and Caleb to stay with her aunts in Maine, leaving Jacob behind to take care of the farm. Only letters connect them until just before school starts, when Jacob appears in Maine. They are all joyful to hear the family will have a new baby in the spring.

A Gathering of Days: A New England Girl's Journal, 1830–32 (1979) by Joan W. Blos is the story of 14-year-old Catherine Cabot Hill, told through the journal Catherine keeps over the last two years she lives on the family farm, starting in 1830. She records daily events in her small New Hampshire town, as well as the major events of her life: her father's remarriage and the death of her best friend. Catherine comes of age in a time of loss and change.

What the Dickens! (1991) by Jane Louise Curry is filled with adventure and interesting information about the folks who made their living plying a canal in barges and other horse-drawn craft. The father of 11-year-old twins, Cherry and Sam Dobbs, runs a boat on the Juniata Canal in Pennsylvania. During Charles Dickens's 1842 tour of the United States, the twins learn of a Harrisburg bookseller's plan to steal the manuscript Dickens is working on. The twins set out to foil the scoundrels, and there is a chase conducted mostly on the family's freighter and other boats on the canal.

In her inimitable style, Katherine Paterson presents a compelling story of one girl's determination to reunite her family in *Lyddie* (1991). In 1843 Lyddie Worthen's father abandons his impoverished family on their Vermont farm. Her mother sends her brother and sisters to live with others and hires Lyddie out to earn money to pay her father's debts. Eventually Lyddie goes to Lowell, Massachusetts, to work in the textile mills; she is determined to earn enough money to buy back their old homestead and reunite her family.

Gary Paulsen's *Mr. Tucket* (1994) is an adventure story set on the western frontier in 1848. Fourteen-year-old Francis Tucket is heading west on the Oregon Trail, traveling with his family by wagon train. He receives a rifle for his birthday, but when he lags behind to practice shooting, he is captured by Pawnees. A mysterious one-armed trapper named Mr. Grimes helps Francis escape and shows him how to survive the winter by living off the land.

Also set in 1848 is Bruce Clements's *I Tell a Lie Every So Often* (1974). In this rare humorous historical fiction story, two brothers travel 500 miles up the Missouri by riverboat, mule, and wagon. Fourteen-year-old Henry and his brother Clayton take this unnecessary odyssey because of a lie Henry told about talking to someone who had seen a red-haired girl living with the Indians in the Dakota Territory. Henry's family think the girl might be his cousin, who disappeared nine years before, and they insist the boys look for her. Henry's homespun humor, as he interprets the actions of the bigoted and pretentious characters, makes for fun reading, but it also causes the reader to pause and ponder the treatment of Native Americans in Missouri during the pioneer era.

Eleanor Coerr's *Chang's Paper Pony* (1988), written especially for beginning readers, is a story set in San Francisco during the 1850 Gold Rush. Chang, the grandson of a Chinese immigrant, wants a pony more than anything, but his grandfather cannot afford it. The miners make fun of the way Chang looks and talks, but his friend Big Pete takes him panning for gold. Chang is unsuccessful in finding gold nuggets—but when he sweeps Big Pete's cabin, he collects so much gold dust that Pete buys him a pony.

Fred Gipson's *Old Yeller* (1956) takes place in the Texas hill country in the 1860s. An ugly yellow dog is taken in by Travis and his family and becomes a beloved pet. While protecting the family from a rabid bear, the dog is infected, and the mother must kill him.

Native Americans. Although the 1800s were an exciting and venturesome era for the European and European American pioneers, the frontier era was a time of loss and unwanted change for Native Americans, who were continually forced to move westward as the new Americans usurped their ancestral homelands. Scott O'Dell, for whom the O'Dell Award for historical fiction is named, wrote two interesting books set in this era.

Island of the Blue Dolphins (1960) is O'Dell's first book about Karana, an Indian girl living on a rocky island far off the coast of California. Aleuts working for a Russian sea captain invade the island and kill most of the men. In 1835, when the rest of the tribe is evacuated, 12-year-old Karana is left behind, searching for her missing young brother. After her brother is killed by wild dogs, Karana must lay aside the taboos of her people to survive. She makes weapons, finds food, and fights her enemies, the wild dogs. Eventually she tames one of the dogs, and he and his pups serve as her only companions for the eighteen years she lives on the island.

Zia (O'Dell 1976) is narrated by the 14-year-old niece of Karana. Zia and her brother Mando live at the Santa Barbara mission in California, and when they find an eighteen-foot boat washed ashore, they attempt the sixty-mile trip to the island where Karana was left behind. They are unsuccessful, but they do convince people at the mission to search for her. Eventually Karana is rescued from the island and brought to the mission in 1853; however, no one at the mission speaks her language. The padres will not allow Karana's dog, Rontu-Aru, in the dormitory, so she sleeps in the courtyard with him. Later she moves to a cave near the beach and rescues injured animals.

Nancy M. Armstrong's *Navajo Long Walk* (1994) is set in Arizona in 1864. After the U.S. Cavalry burn the crops and drive away livestock, the Navajos realize they must go to Fort Sumner or face starvation. Along with thousands of others, young Kee and his family are forced out of their ancestral home by soldiers, and they march 300 miles east to the government camp in southeast New Mexico. Many die along the way from starvation and exposure; once in the camp, many more die from inadequate food, disease, and homesickness. Four years later—after the near devastation of the Navajo culture—Kee and his people are allowed to return home to what eventually becomes the Navajo reservation.

Slavery. Children need to understand one of the most gruesome elements of U.S. history—the institution of slavery. Paula Fox's *The Slave Dancer* (1973) gives a horrific but realistic picture of the ghastly transport of Africans to the slave market. In 1840 13-year-old Jessie Bollier is kidnapped off the New Orleans docks and dumped aboard *The Moonlight,* a slave ship bound for Africa to pick up human cargo. On the trip back, Jessie is forced to play his fife during the exercise periods that will maintain the slaves' muscles. Many of the Africans die during the frightful sea voyage. After four months of hazardous sailing with a degraded crew, the ship is wrecked, and Jessie and a young African boy are the only ones to survive.

There are several excellent books set in the 1850s, the era before slavery was abolished by President Lincoln. These stories tell of the **abolitionists**, the brave Americans who opposed slavery. Many of the abolitionists operated the **Underground Railroad,** which was neither a railroad nor underground. Rather, it was a secret cooperative network that aided fugitive slaves in reaching sanctuary in the free states or in Canada. It was called a railroad because it had passengers (escaped slaves), conductors (people who led the passengers north), stations (homes of abolitionists who hid them), and stationmasters (leaders of the abolitionists).

Freedom Crossing (1980) by Margaret Goff Clark is the story of a 15-year-old girl who is divided in her beliefs about slavery. Following her mother's death, Laura Eastman spends four years in Virginia with an aunt and uncle who are slave owners. After her father remarries, Laura returns home to the family farm in western New York State. She soon learns that their home is a stopover on the Underground Railroad; her father and brother are helping escaped slaves cross the river to Canada. Laura knows that anyone who helps a runaway slave is breaking the law—but when she meets Martin Paige, a 12-year-old slave who would rather die than be sent back, she begins to understand the abolitionists' views.

For beginning readers, F. N. Monjo's *The Drinking Gourd* (1970), set in 1851, tells of a young boy's courage in saving a family of escaped slaves. When Tommy discovers a man and woman and their two children in the barn, his father explains about the Underground Railroad. Little Jeff tells how his family found their way north by following the "drinking gourd," their name for the Big Dipper constellation, which points to the North Star—the guide to Canada and freedom. Later, a U.S. marshal sees Tommy sitting in a wagon full of hay that is covering the fugitives. Tommy's quick thinking and a "righteous lie" divert the marshal's attention and allow his father to take the black family to safety.

Gloria Houston's *Bright Freedom's Song* (1998) opens in 1853 in North Carolina's Blue Ridge Mountains. Fourteen-year-old Bright Freedom Cameron discovers that her parents are providing a safe house on the Underground Railroad for fugitive slaves they call "bundles." Her father reveals that he too is a fugitive: He was forced off a farm in Scotland, kidnapped, tricked into signing indenture papers, and ultimately driven to flee from a slaveholder who treated black and white people with equal brutality. Bright comes to understand something of the conditions and convictions that led to the Underground Railroad's formation, and when Pa falls ill, she and Marcus—a former slave who fled bondage with her father—transport the bundles to safety, knowing that a grave punishment for both awaits if they are caught.

Katherine Paterson skillfully weaves a mystery in *Jip: His Story* (1996), set in Vermont in 1855. Jip's background is an enigma. Mysteriously abandoned on a roadside when he was about 2 years old, he was taken to the town poor farm to be raised by the other paupers. When the book opens, Jip is practically running the farm, caring for the animals and doing what he can to care for those around him. Jip is the only one who is not afraid of the "lunatic," an old man who must spend much of his life in a locked cage because of the raging madness that periodically overcomes him. Jip comes to love the old man; he also loves his teacher, who shows him genuine concern. When Jip is stalked by a menacing stranger who claims to be a representative of his father, Jip's teacher (who was the protagonist in Paterson's *Lyddie*) tells him what the Quaker abolitionists have discovered of his background and why he must immediately escape.

Civil War Era

Two books set during the Civil War have young females as protagonists. The first is Patricia Beatty's *Who Comes with Cannons?* (1992). Orphaned in 1861, 12-year-old Truth goes to live with her uncle's family in North Carolina. The Civil War breaks out, but Truth and her family, as Quakers, oppose both slavery and war. When a runaway slave seeks refuge on the family's farm, Truth discovers they operate a station of the Underground Railroad. Truth's two cousins are forced into the Confederate Army, and when one of them is captured and imprisoned by the Union Army, Truth goes to Washington via the Underground Railroad to seek a pardon.

Another Civil War heroine is Valor McAimee in *Mountain Valor* (Houston 1994). Valor's father, brothers, and uncle were divided on the issues of the Civil War. The men left to fight on different sides, and 11-year-old Valor, her mother, and her younger cousin Jed must tend the farm. When the farm is robbed by vicious Yankee soldiers, Valor, posing as a boy, infiltrates their camp and manages to recapture and retrieve her family's livestock.

Paul Fleischman's *Bull Run* (1993) is a series of brief vignettes, in which the Civil War's first great battle is recounted from the points of view of sixteen participants. The characters include both Northerners and Southerners, men and women, and black and white people. Each vignette focuses on the life and thoughts of a person who participated in some way in the Battle of Bull Run, including a war-fevered boy, a doctor, a slave woman, a lover of horses, and a black man who is determined to become a soldier.

Few picture books tug at the emotions like *Pink and Say* by Patricia Polacco (1994), a story passed down through generations of the author's family. This is the saga of a remarkable wartime friendship between a young white Union soldier, Sheldon Curtis, and a young black Union soldier, Pinkus Aylee. When Pink finds the 15-year-old white boy left for dead, he tends to Sheldon ("Say") and carries him a great distance to his own home. Pink's mother nurses the boy back to health, but she is later shot by marauders while hiding the boys. Before the boys can rejoin the Union troops, they are both captured by Confederate soldiers and taken to Andersonville Prison. Only one will leave alive.

Charley Skedaddle (1987) by Patricia Beatty is based on real-life Civil War records and memoirs. During the war a 12-year-old New York Bowery boy, Charley Quinn, joins the Union Army as a drummer, but he deserts in Virginia during his first battle. He encounters a hostile old mountain woman, and he learns that fleeing from his first battle doesn't brand him a coward for life.

Across Five Aprils by Irene Hunt (1964) is an unforgettable story of young Jethro Creighton, who grows from a boy to a man when he is left to take care of the family farm in Illinois during the turbulent four years of the Civil War. The book has been acclaimed, both for its historical authenticity and for the warm story it tells of strong family ties.

Carolyn Reeder's *Shades of Gray* (1989) takes place after the Civil War, which has left 12-year-old Will Page an orphan. He is forced to leave his city home and live in the Virginia countryside with his Uncle Jed, who refused to fight for the Confederacy. He considers his uncle a traitor and a coward, but a year spent with his aunt and uncle on their hardscrabble farm helps him understand the courage it took to uphold their pacifist principles.

Post–Civil War Frontier Era

For readers who want comedy and rip-roaring adventure, Kathleen Karr's *Oh, Those Harper Girls!* (1992) is a good read. The setting is west Texas in 1869. Daddy Harper's broken-down ranch falls on hard times, and the bank threatens to foreclose. Harper's six daughters—March, April, May, June, Julie, and Lily—dream up a series of wild schemes to get money to pay off his debts. They try rustling cattle, making moonshine, and robbing a stagecoach. Their subsequent trial earns them national notoriety plus an invitation to reenact the drama on stage in New York.

Laura Ingalls Wilder used the people, places, and stories of her own life to write a series of books loved by generations of children and adults. A long-running television series titled *Little House on the Prairie* (named after one of the books) was closely based on this series of books. The stories are told through Laura's eyes, and the series spans her life from age 4 to the time she is a young wife and mother. In the first book, *Little House in the Big Woods* (1932), it is the 1870s. Wolves, panthers, and bears roam the deep Wisconsin woods, but the Ingalls family is snug in its little log house. Four-year-old Laura lives with her Pa, Ma, and sisters Mary and Carrie. Pioneer life is hard, and the family must grow or catch all their food. Pa makes bullets, hunts, traps, and cures the meat. Ma makes cheese and maple sugar. Life is also exciting when blizzards and wild animals are encountered. The complete list of Wilder's books appears in the bibliography at the end of this chapter.

The Battle of the Little Bighorn in 1876 is told through the eyes of a Cheyenne warrior in Nathaniel Benchley's *Only Earth and Sky Last Forever* (1972). Dark Elk sees his people humiliated and impoverished as the white men's promises are broken one by one. When the white men invade the Black Hills, another promise is broken, and he has no other choice but to join Crazy Horse at the Little Bighorn River to fight for a future for himself and Lashuka, the girl he loves.

More Than Anything Else by Marie Bradby (1995) is a fictionalized account of the early life of Booker T. Washington. In this heartwarming picture book, 9-year-old Booker leaves his cabin before dawn to work all day shoveling salt with his father and brother in the saltworks of West Virginia. Despite the backbreaking labor, there is a sense of freedom, and the boy longs to learn to read. He meets a man reading a newspaper, and the man shows Booker how to write his name, which is the beginning of his education.

The bulk of children's historical fiction books are juvenile novels geared for readers in the intermediate grades. However, there are four picture books with settings in the late 1800s that primary-grade children will enjoy. *The Snow Walker* (Wetterer & Wetterer 1996) is based on a true account of 12-year-old Milton Daubs. Wearing a pair of homemade snowshoes, Milton carries food and medicine between the local stores and his Bronx neighbors when they are snowed in during the great blizzard of 1888. *Tchaikovsky Discovers America* (Kalman 1994) is the tale of a fictional 11-year-old girl, Eugenia, who meets the great composer Peter Ilyich Tchaikovsky during his visit to America in 1891. *Three Names* (MacLachlan 1991) is what a boy calls his dog, who accompanies him each day as he drives a horse-drawn wagon across the prairie road to and from the one-room school house. *Miss Rumphius* (Cooney 1982) tells of the life of Alice Rumphius. She fulfills her dream to travel the world, then settles in a house by the seaside and makes the world more beautiful by sowing lupine seeds as she walks about the countryside.

Two acclaimed books chronicle the Old West. *Shane* (Schaefer 1949) opens in the summer of 1889, when a mysterious man dressed in black rides into the peaceful Wyoming valley occupied by the Starretts, a couple with a young boy. The man is known only as Shane, and he wears no gun. He goes to work for the family and eventually becomes involved in the deadly feud between a powerful cattle rancher and the local homesteaders who are fighting to keep their land. When Mr. Starrett's life is in danger, Shane unpacks and straps on his holster and gun. He goes to town and faces the cattleman's hired gunman. Also by Jack Schaefer is *Old Ramon* (1960), the story of a wise old shepherd. Ramon teaches a young boy—the son of his *patrón*—lessons about survival, bravery, wisdom, and friendship as he shows the boy how to care for a flock of sheep in the harsh Mojave Desert.

In *Stone Fox* (Gardiner 1980), 10-year-old Willy needs to win the big dogsled race in order to pay the back taxes on his grandfather's potato farm in Wyoming. However, he must outrace the huge Indian mountain man Stone Fox and his five beautiful Samoyed dogs, who have won the competition for the past few years. This is a fast-paced adventure story geared for younger readers; however, I warn you that the ending is very sad, as the boy's beloved dog dies.

Two Chinese immigrants, a father and son, are the protagonists in Laurence Yep's *Dragonwings* (1975), which is set in San Francisco in the years preceding and following the great 1906 earthquake that destroyed most of the city. Yep reveals much about the culture and character of the Tang men who have come to the United States to work and support their families in China. With the help of his devoted son and the advice of Orville Wright, Windrider achieves his dream of building and flying a biplane.

World War I Era

An enchanting book for younger children is set in 1918, the year World War I ended. *The Year of the Perfect Christmas Tree* (1988) by Gloria Houston, like the rest of Houston's historical fiction books, is set in the Appalachian area of North Carolina. When Papa is called to war, little Ruthie and her mother must fulfill his obligation of getting the traditional Christmas tree from the top of Grandfather Mountain to the village church for the holiday celebration. On Christmas Eve Ruthie and her mama climb the rocky crags and return with the perfect Christmas tree. Other books by Houston set in this era are *Littlejim* (1990), *Littlejim's Gift* (1994), and *Littlejim's Dreams* (1997).

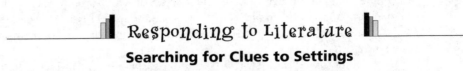

Responding to Literature

Searching for Clues to Settings

Help children sharpen their observation skills. Before you read, ask them to look and listen carefully for clues that will tell them when the story takes place. For example, many readers initially believe that *The Year of the Perfect Christmas Tree* (Houston 1988) is set during World War II.

Following are some of the clues the author and illustrator provide to show the setting is World War I. How is each significant to the setting?

1. "Occasionally an auty-mobile chugged its way through the silence."
2. "Across the ocean the Great War raged. . . ."
3. "The Armistice was signed today! "
4. ". . . every year for more than sixty years, a tiny angel has stood on top. . . ."
5. Illustrations of the schoolroom
6. Illustrations of the soldiers' uniforms
7. Illustrations showing the use of fireplace, oil lamps, and candles for light

---

Great Depression Era

After the collapse of the U.S. stock market in 1929, the country was plunged into a profound economic depression that lasted more than a decade: the **Great Depression era.** At one point about one-quarter of the nation's workforce was unemployed, and jobless workers and their families depended on charity to survive. Chapter 13 contains resources for a thematic unit on the Great Depression.

Uncle Jed's Barbershop (Mitchell 1993) is set in the segregated South. Sarah Jean's beloved Uncle Jed is the only black barber in the area; he dreams of owning his own barbershop, but he spends his savings to pay for an operation to save Sarah Jean's life. Later his savings are wiped out when the bank fails at the beginning of the Depression; but many years later, when he is 79, Uncle Jed finally achieves his dream.

The Larkin family, in *Blue Willow* (1940) by Doris Gates, is representative of people in the Great Depression who survived on a day-to-day basis. Janey's parents own only an old truck and the few pieces of furniture and belongings it carries. The father, a migrant farm worker, travels from town to town to find seasonal work. When the book opens, the family has settled in an abandoned one-room shack on the edge of a cotton farm in the scorching San Joaquin Valley. The father finds work at the farm and pays rent to the dishonest foreman. Janey's dreams are to live in a house that resembles the one on her treasured blue willow plate, and to be able to attend a real school, rather than a workers' camp school.

Karen Hesse's *Out of the Dust* (1997) is a unique novel because it is written as a journal in free verse poetry. It is set in the Dust Bowl, the bleak landscape of the Oklahoma Panhandle in 1934, when a severe drought causes the overfarmed soil to literally blow away. A tragic accident is caused when Billie Jo's father leaves a bucket of kerosene near the stove. Her mother's clothing is ignited; Billie Jo tries to beat out the flames, but her mother dies, and Billie Jo's hands are severely scarred, leaving her unable to play her beloved piano to soothe her anguish. However, the quiet strength she displays in taking care of her grieving father during this time of unspeakable loss is inspiring.

In *Leah's Pony* (Friedrich 1996), a young girl makes the ultimate sacrifice when her parents are unable to pay back the bank loan after their crops fail in the Dust Bowl era. Leah sells her beloved pony to buy back her father's tractor when the bank auctions off their livestock and equipment.

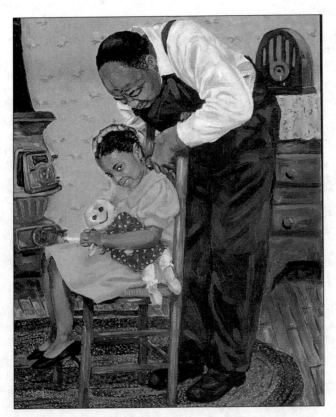

Uncle Jed cuts Sarah Jean's hair. From *Uncle Jed's Barbershop,* written by Margaree King Mitchell and illustrated by James Ransome.

Christopher Paul Curtis's *Bud, Not Buddy* (1999) is a funny yet touching account. After a ghastly (though riotous) evening, 10-year-old Bud (not Buddy) Caldwell is on the run from yet another terrible foster home in 1936 in Flint, Michigan. Bud's mother died when he was six, and he wants to find his father, though his mother never told him who he was. Bud believes she left a clue in the form of a blue flier advertising a jazz show with Herman E. Calloway, bandleader and stand-up bass player for the Dusky Devastators. Bud sets off to track down Calloway, toting his few treasures in a battered old suitcase. He gets into hilarious trouble, such as trying to steal a vampire's car, but he also finds kindness—in the charity food line, at the public library, in a Hooverville squatter camp, and on the road.

Mildred D. Taylor's *Roll of Thunder, Hear My Cry* (1976) is an acclaimed book set in 1933 in the fertile cotton-growing land of northern Mississippi. The story is revealed through the eyes of an 11-year-old African American girl, Cassie Logan, who lives on the family farm with Big Ma (her grandmother); her parents; and brothers Stacey, Christopher-John, and Little Man. The Logans own their land, unlike most of their neighbors (black and white), who are sharecroppers. In order to keep their land during the Depression, the father must work for the railroad in Louisiana, and the mother teaches school. The blacks in the community face night riders and burnings, but the Logans' strong ties to one another and to their land give them the strength to defy racism and hold on to their land and the independence it represents.

At the end of *Roll of Thunder,* readers are left wondering what will happen to Stacey's best friend, T. J., who has been falsely accused of killing a store owner during a break-in committed by two white boys. Mr. Logan's desperate thinking diverts the attention of the lynch mob, and T. J. is taken to jail. In the sequel, *Let the Circle Be Unbroken* (1981), T. J. goes on trial with an all-white jury, and the saga of the Logans and the people in their community continues. Taylor wrote several books about the Logan family. They are, in order of the Logan family's chronology (rather than the order of publication), *The Well* (1995), *The Friendship* (1987), *Mississippi Bridge* (1990), *Song of the Trees* (1975), *Roll of Thunder, Hear My Cry* (1976), *Let the Circle Be Unbroken* (1981), and *The Road to Memphis* (1990).

 ## Responding to Literature
Character Mapping

Sometimes young readers lose interest in books like *Roll of Thunder* because the author introduces and develops several major characters at the beginning of the book and, in so doing, creates a slow buildup to the action in the story. **Character mapping** helps maintain children's attention, as well as helping them keep up with the many characters. It also sets a specific purpose for reading, which will enhance readers' comprehension and enjoyment. After you introduce a book, ask your children to read for information that identifies the major characters by name, relationship, age, physical description, personality traits, and other important qualities. Use this information to build a character map children can refer to while reading. A character map developed from the first five pages of *Roll of Thunder* is provided in Figure 9.3. Readers can complete the map for these characters and add other important characters as they are introduced and developed.

World War II Era

The outbreak of war in Europe at the end of the 1930s resulted in a surge of activity in the U.S. economy as the government expanded the national defense system. America entered World War II in 1941 when the U.S. naval base in Pearl Harbor, Hawaii, was bombed by the Japanese air force. The Great Depression ended, and with so many men enlisted in the military, there was a shortage of workers. During this era, many women entered the workforce for the first time.

A number of good books are set during the United States' four-year involvement in World War II, and I will introduce them according to the age of the protagonist. In *But No Candy* (Houston 1992), Lee is 6 years old when her favorite after-school treat, chocolate Hershey bars, become scarce, as certain foods and other goods are designated for troops overseas. She misses the candy—but most of all she misses her Uncle Ted, who is fighting in Europe.

Name and Relationship	"Big Ma" Logan (Papa's mother)	Papa Logan	Mama Logan	Uncle Hammer (Papa's brother)	Mr. Morrison
Age	Around 65				
Physical Characteristics					
Personality traits Important qualities Role	Takes care of house, works in the field	Works for railroad in Louisiana	Teaches sixth grade, runs the farm	Lives in Chicago	

Name and Relationship	Stacey Logan	Cassie Logan (only sister)	Christopher-John Logan	"Little Man" Logan	T. J. Avery (Stacey's best friend)
Age	12 years old	Around 11	7 years old	6 years old	Around 13
Physical Characteristics			Short and round		Tall and very thin
Personality traits Important qualities Role	Grouchy	Loves the out-doors, dislikes dressy clothes	Cheerful, easy-going, sensitive	Meticulously neat	Failed sixth grade; irritating personality

FIGURE 9.3 Character Map for *Roll of Thunder*

Lois Lowry's *Number the Stars* (1989) is set in Copenhagen in 1943. Ten-year-old Ellen Rosen and her family are in danger, because the Jewish people of Denmark are being removed by the Nazis. Ellen moves in with her best friend, Annemarie Johansen, and pretends to be her sister until she is smuggled out of the country in a daring escape.

In San Diego, 11-year-old Foster is deeply affected by the war in *Foster's War* (Reeder 1998). His older brother is shipped to the Pacific as a gunner on a B-26, and his best friend, Jimmy Osaki, and his family are exiled to an internment camp. Foster's bullying father—an air-raid warden with a cold, harsh attitude—makes life even more difficult.

In *Summer of My German Soldier* (Greene 1973), Patty Bergen turns 12 the summer her small Arkansas hometown becomes the site of a prison camp for German soldiers. Although Patty is Jewish, when she stumbles upon a young German escapee, she begins to see him as a lonely frightened person like herself, not as the enemy. Helping him puts her own freedom at risk. This book is moving, but I must warn you it has a tragic ending.

Katherine Paterson's *Jacob Have I Loved* (1980) is set on a tiny Chesapeake Bay island off the Maryland shore. Louise is envious of and angry with her fair-haired and talented twin, Caroline, whom everyone adores. Caroline leaves the island to study music, but Louise, to help support her family, is compelled to quit school and work alongside her father as a "waterman" when all the young men go to war. Her friendship with the mysterious Captain Wallace helps her fulfill her dreams and leave the island.

Mary Downing Hahn's *Stepping on the Cracks* (1991) is set in 1944 in a small Maryland town. Margaret, a sixth grader whose brother fought and died during the war, and her best friend, Elizabeth, are bullied by Gordy. He grows bolder than ever, and they decide to spy on him. When they discover he is hiding his gentle older brother Stuart, a deserter from the army, they see a new side of Gordy. Slowly they begin to understand Stuart's decision to be a conscientious objector.

Post–World War II Era

A post–World War II novel that will delight younger readers is Bette Bao Lord's *In the Year of the Boar and Jackie Robinson* (1984). In 1947 10-year-old Shirley Temple Wong and her family emigrate from China to Brooklyn. When she first starts at Public School 8, Shirley has no friends, but after earning the friendship of the toughest girl in class, she is included in the playground stickball games. She becomes a loyal fan of the Brooklyn Dodgers and Jackie Robinson.

Ruth White's *Belle Prater's Boy* (1996) is set in the Appalachian town of Coal Station, Virginia, in the 1950s. Belle Prater disappears, and her son, Woodrow—poor and cross-eyed, but brilliant—comes to live with his grandparents. His 12-year-old cousin Gypsy, the town beauty, lives next door and is as curious as the rest of the town about Belle's disappearance. However, Gypsy also ponders the mystery of her own father's death seven years earlier.

Also set in the coal mining area of Virginia is *When I Was Young in the Mountains* (1982) by Cynthia Rylant. In this attractively illustrated picture book, the author relates her memories of spending summers with her grandparents who lived in the mountains.

Civil Rights Movement

In *The Gold Cadillac* (Taylor 1987), Lois and Wilma are proud of their father's brand-new 1950 gold Cadillac. They are excited that the family will be driving in it all the way from Ohio to visit relatives in Mississippi. They cannot understand why their mother is so upset. However, as they travel deeper into the rural South, there are no admiring glances for the shiny new car with the black man behind the wheel—only suspicion and anger. For the first time in their lives, the girls find out what it is like to be afraid because of the color of their skin.

Vaunda Michaeux Nelson's *Mayfield Crossing* (1993) is set in 1960, the year children from Mayfield Crossing must attend school in nearby Parkview when their own school is closed. The Parkview children want nothing to do with the Mayfield students and do not allow them to play on Parkview's new baseball field. Things are especially difficult for 9-year-old Meg and her friends Billie and Sherman, all of whom are black. Meg encounters racial prejudice for the first time. Only baseball appears to be a possibility for drawing the students together.

The sequel, *Beyond Mayfield* (Nelson 1999), is set in the early 1960s. Meg lives in Mayfield Crossing, where blacks and whites live together in harmony, but she still attends school in Parkview, where some of her classmates and teachers are bigots. Lucky, the brother of Meg's white friend Dillon, comes home from the navy, and he decides to go south and join the Freedom Riders. When he is killed, Dillon blames Meg's family for talking him into going, and Meg begins to wonder if they are responsible.

Freedom Songs by Yvette Moore (1991) is narrated by 14-year-old Sheryl. In 1963 she and her family leave their comfortable Brooklyn home for an Easter visit with Sheryl's grandmother in North Carolina. Sheryl enjoys being with the warm extended family, but she experiences segregation for the first time. Her Uncle Pete joins the Freedom Riders, and when she returns to Brooklyn, she organizes a gospel concert fund-raiser to support their cause.

Christopher Paul Curtis's first book, *The Watsons Go to Birmingham—1963* (1995), is something of a paradox. It is *the* funniest children's novel I have ever read, and yet it slowly builds to a dramatic climax that grips readers' hearts. The story is narrated by Kenny, a fourth grader who is different both because he is smart and because he has a lazy eye. As Kenny relates hilarious stories about his middle-class African American family—The Weird Watsons of Flint, Michigan—the characters come alive, and you feel as if you knew them.

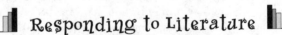

Responding to Literature

Story Mapping

Complete character and story maps *while* you are reading to your children, rather than providing them beforehand. When you ask children to fill in the parts of the map, they are given a purpose for reading, and this results in enhanced comprehension and enjoyment. A story map of *The Watsons*, including full character maps, is provided in Figure 9.4 as an example of mapping a juvenile novel. (If you plan on reading this novel, do not read past the characters' maps until you finish the book!)

A good example of Curtis's creative approach is Kenny's account of what happens when he and his best friend, Rufus, encounter the school bully, Larry Dunn, whom they suspect has stolen Kenny's new leather gloves.

> Larry ran up behind us and said, "This is Friday, y'all, time to do the laundry. Who's gonna be first? Country Corn Flake? Cockeye Kenny?" He didn't wait for us to make up our minds and grabbed me first. He said to Rufus, "If you run away during Cockeye's wash I'ma hunt you down and hurt you bad, boy. This ain't gonna take but a minute so just stick around."
>
> Rufus stood there looking worried. Larry wasn't like other bullies; he wasn't happy taking a handful of snow and smashing it in your face and running off. Larry gave what he called Maytag Washes. With a Maytag Wash you had to go through all of the different cycles that a washing machine did, and even though when Larry gave you a Maytag all of the cycles were exactly the same, each part had a different name and the wash wasn't done until you went through the final spin and had snow in every part of your face.
>
> Ever since Larry got these new leather gloves he was giving *Super* Maytag Washes because he could grind a whole lot more snow in your face for a whole lot longer since his hands weren't getting as cold. Larry was tearing me up, I was crying even before the first rinse cycle was done. . . . (p. 57)

Later, Kenny's 13-year-old brother Byron, who is an even bigger bully, takes the gloves from Larry and gives him a unique punishment. However, Byron's bullying and other misdeeds get him in trouble, both in school and out, so the family takes a trip to Birmingham to visit Grandma Sands, the one person who can put Byron in shape. In 1963 the public schools in Birmingham are undergoing forced integration. In retaliation, a black church—Grandma's church—is bombed. True to historical fact, four girls are killed. The readers' involvement with the Watson family makes this historical crime real and devastating.

Enhancing Curriculum with Historical Fiction

The Watsons Go to Birmingham is an excellent example of how literature can add a human dimension to the historical facts presented in textbooks. That four girls were killed during Sunday school in Birmingham in 1963 was a sad event, but it happened a long time ago to people and families we did not know. However, when readers discover that Kenny's little sister, Joetta, was attending Sunday school at the church that was bombed, they are pulled into the scene. Readers tensely follow Kenny as, in shock, he searches through the rubble and finds a familiar black patent leather shoe. Readers experience the tragic event as if they were there with Kenny and his family.

Setting—Time: Winter 1963

    —Place: Flint, Michigan, and Birmingham, Alabama

Main characters: The Watson family (African American)

Daniel Watson "Dad" 35 years old clowns around	Wilona Watson "Momma" gap in front teeth self-conscious caring mother dislikes Michigan	Byron Watson "By" 13 years old conceited aloof from family mean bad student	Kenneth Watson "Kenny," "Square" fourth grader gullible good natured lazy (crossed) eye smart in school	Joetta Watson "Joey" kindergartner softhearted loves family
⇩	⇩	⇩	⇐	

Grandma Sands Momma's mother tiny and old walks with a cane cackling laugh very strict	Buphead Byron's best friend 14 years old mean bad student	Rufus Fry Kenny's best friend very poor wears ragged clothes skinny talks country	Larry Dunn bully of K–4 mean and tough has mother with a secret no warm clothes poor

Central problem: Byron constantly disobeys his parents and is becoming a real juvenile delinquent.

Goal: Take Byron to Birmingham to live with Grandma Sands.

Events:
1. The family drives to Birmingham and visits with Grandma Sands.
2. Byron saves Kenny from drowning in the whirlpool.
3. The church where Joetta attends Sunday school is bombed.
4. The family returns home, but Kenny is very depressed because of the tragedy.

Resolution: After arriving at Grandma's, Byron begins to show maturity and realizes how much his family means when he nearly loses Kenny and Joetta. Byron becomes a caring big brother by helping Kenny deal with his emotions.

FIGURE 9.4   **Story Map of *The Watsons Go to Birmingham—1963* by Christopher Paul Curtis**

Literature is a fascinating way to transmit the story of the past. After all, history is made up of the stories of people—not words in a textbook. The books introduced in this chapter tell interesting stories about fictional and real people who lived in many places during many times. Reading about the people provides insight into and understanding of problems people encountered in the past, and it can help readers understand why some of those same problems (such as racism) still exist today. Understanding a problem is the first step in overcoming it.

HISTORICAL FICTION BOOKS

Alcott, Louisa May. *Little Women.* Scholastic, 1868/1995.

Armstrong, Nancy M. *Navajo Long Walk.* Roberts Rinehart, 1994.

Armstrong, William. *Sounder.* Illus. James Barkley. HarperCollins, 1969.

Avi. *The Fighting Ground.* Harper & Row, 1984.

Beatty, Patricia. *Charley Skedaddle.* Morrow, 1987.

———. *Who Comes with Cannons?* Morrow, 1992.

Benchley, Nathaniel. *Only Earth and Sky Last Forever.* HarperCollins, 1972.

Blos, Joan W. *A Gathering of Days: A New England Girl's Journal, 1830–32.* Scribner, 1979.

Bradby, Marie. *More Than Anything Else.* Illus. Chris K. Soentiet. Orchard, 1995.

Brink, Carol Ryrie. *Caddie Woodlawn.* Macmillan, 1935.

Bruchac, Joseph. *Children of the Longhouse.* Dial, 1996.

Clark, Margaret Goff. *Freedom Crossing.* Scholastic, 1980.

Clements, Bruce. *I Tell a Lie Every So Often.* Farrar, Straus & Giroux, 1974.

Coerr, Eleanor. *Chang's Paper Pony.* Illus. Deborah Kogan Ray. Harper, 1988.

Cooney, Barbara. *Miss Rumphius.* Viking Penguin, 1982.

Curry, Jane Louise. *What the Dickens!* Puffin, 1991.

Curtis, Christopher Paul. *The Watsons Go to Birmingham—1963.* Delacorte, 1995.

———. *Bud, Not Buddy.* Illus. Trish P. Watts. Delacorte, 1999.

Cushman, Karen. *The Midwife's Apprentice.* Clarion, 1995.

de Angeli, Marguerite. *The Door in the Wall.* Doubleday, 1949.

Dorris, Michael. *Morning Girl.* Hyperion, 1992.

Dyer, T. A. *A Time of His Own.* Houghton Mifflin, 1990.

Fleischman, Paul. *Bull Run.* Harper & Row, 1993.

Forbes, Esther. *Johnny Tremain.* Houghton Mifflin, 1943.

Fox, Paula. *The Slave Dancer.* Bradbury, 1973.

Friedrich, Elizabeth. *Leah's Pony.* Illus. Michael Garland. Boyds Mills, 1996.

Fritz, Jean. *Early Thunder.* Viking Penguin, 1987.

Gardiner, John Reynolds. *Stone Fox.* Crowell, 1980.

Gates, Doris. *Blue Willow.* Viking Penguin, 1940/1999.

Gipson, Fred. *Old Yeller.* Harper, 1956.

Gray, Elizabeth Janet. *Adam of the Road.* Viking, 1942.

Greene, Bette. *Summer of My German Soldier.* Dial, 1973.

Gregory, Kristiana. *The Stowaway.* Scholastic, 1995.

Hahn, Mary Downing. *Stepping on the Cracks.* Clarion, 1991.

Hall, Donald. *Ox-Cart Man.* Illus. Barbara Cooney. Viking Penguin, 1979.

Heide, Florence Parry, & Judith Heide Gilliland. *The House of Wisdom.* Illus. Mary Grandpre. DK, 1999.

Hesse, Karen. *Out of the Dust.* Scholastic, 1997.

Houston, Gloria. *The Year of the Perfect Christmas Tree.* Illus. Barbara Cooney. Dial, 1988.

———. *Littlejim.* Illus. Thomas B. Allen. Philomel, 1990.

———. *But No Candy.* Illus. Lloyd Bloom. Philomel, 1992.

———. *Littlejim's Gift.* Illus. Thomas B. Allen. Philomel, 1994.

———. *Mountain Valor.* Illus. Thomas B. Allen. Philomel, 1994.

———. *Littlejim's Dreams.* Illus. Thomas B. Allen. Harcourt Brace, 1997.

———. *Bright Freedom's Song.* Harcourt Brace, 1998.

Hunt, Irene. *Across Five Aprils.* Follett, 1964.

Johnston, Tony. *Yonder.* Illus. Lloyd Bloom. Dial, 1988.

Kalman, Esther. *Tchaikovsky Discovers America.* Illus. Laura Fernandez & Rick Jacobson. Orchard, 1994.

Karr, Kathleen. *Oh, Those Harper Girls!* Farrar, Straus & Giroux, 1992.

Krensky, Stephen. *The Printer's Apprentice.* Illus. Madeline Sorel. Delacorte, 1995.

Littlesugar, Amy. *The Spinner's Daughter.* Illus. Robert Quackenbush. Pippin, 1994.

Lord, Bette Bao. *In the Year of the Boar and Jackie Robinson.* Harper & Row, 1984.

Lowry, Lois. *Number the Stars.* Houghton Mifflin, 1989.

MacLachlan, Patricia. *Sarah, Plain and Tall.* Harper & Row, 1985.

———. *Three Names.* Illus. Alexander Pertzoff. HarperCollins, 1991.

———. *Skylark.* HarperCollins, 1994.

McGraw, Eloise Jarvis. *The Golden Goblet.* Puffin, 1961.

Mitchell, Margaree King. *Uncle Jed's Barbershop.* Illus. James Ransome. Simon & Schuster, 1993.

Monjo, F. N. *The Drinking Gourd.* Illus. Fred Brenner. Harper & Row, 1970.

Moore, Yvette. *Freedom Songs.* Puffin, 1991.

Nelson, Vaunda Michaeux. *Mayfield Crossing.* Putnam, 1993.

———. *Beyond Mayfield.* Putnam, 1999.

O'Dell, Scott. *Island of the Blue Dolphins.* Houghton Mifflin, 1960.

———. *Zia.* Houghton Mifflin, 1976.

———. *Sarah Bishop.* Houghton Mifflin, 1980.

Paterson, Katherine. *The Sign of the Chrysanthemum.* HarperCollins, 1973.

———. *Of Nightingales That Weep.* Crowell, 1974.

———. *Jacob Have I Loved.* Crowell, 1980.

———. *Lyddie.* Lodestar, 1991.

———. *Jip, His Story.* Lodestar, 1996.

Paulsen, Gary. *Mr. Tucket.* Delacorte, 1994.

———. *The Rifle.* Harcourt Brace, 1995.

Pennington, Daniel. *Itse Selu: Cherokee Harvest Festival.* Illus. Don Stewart. Charlesbridge, 1994.

Polacco, Patricia. *Pink and Say.* Philomel, 1994.

Reeder, Carolyn. *Shades of Gray.* Macmillan, 1989.

———. *Foster's War.* Scholastic, 1998.

Roth, Arthur. *The Castaway.* Scholastic, 1983.

Rylant, Cynthia. *When I Was Young in the Mountains.* Illus. Diane Goode. Dutton, 1982.

Schaefer, Jack. *Shane.* Houghton Mifflin, 1949.

———. *Old Ramon.* Houghton Mifflin, 1960.

Speare, Elizabeth George. *The Witch of Blackbird Pond.* Houghton Mifflin, 1958.

———. *The Bronze Bow.* Houghton Mifflin, 1961.

———. *The Sign of the Beaver.* Houghton Mifflin, 1983.

Taylor, Mildred. *Song of the Trees.* Dial, 1975.

———. *Roll of Thunder, Hear My Cry.* Viking Penguin, 1976.

———. *Let the Circle Be Unbroken.* Viking Penguin, 1981.

———. *The Friendship.* Dial, 1987.

———. *The Gold Cadillac.* Dial, 1987.

———. *The Road to Memphis.* Dial, 1990.

———. *Mississippi Bridge.* Dial, 1990.

———. *The Well.* Dial, 1995.

Wetterer, Margaret K., & Charles M. Wetterer. *The Snow Walker.* Illus. Mary O'Keefe Young. Carolrhoda, 1996.

White, Ruth. *Belle Prater's Boy.* Farrar, Straus & Giroux, 1996.

Wilder, Laura Ingalls. *Little House in the Big Woods.* Illus. Garth Williams. HarperCollins, 1932.

———. *Farmer Boy.* Illus. Garth Williams. HarperCollins, 1933.

———. *Little House on the Prairie.* Illus. Garth Williams. HarperCollins, 1935.

———. *On the Banks of Plum Creek.* Illus. Garth Williams. HarperCollins, 1937.

———. *By the Shores of Silver Lake.* Illus. Garth Williams. HarperCollins, 1939.

————. *The Long Winter.* Illus. Garth Williams. HarperCollins, 1940.

————. *Little Town on the Prairie.* Illus. Garth Williams. HarperCollins, 1941.

————. *These Happy Golden Years.* Illus. Garth Williams. HarperCollins, 1943.

————. *The First Four Years.* Illus. Garth Williams. HarperCollins, 1971.

Yep, Laurence. *Dragonwings.* Harper, 1975.

KEY TERMS

 Explore the E-Glossary at **www.ablongman.com/anderson**

abolitionist (p. 247)
biographical fiction (p. 235)
character mapping (p. 254)

Great Depression era (p. 252)
historical fiction (p. 234)
Underground Railroad (p. 247)

chapter

10

Biography and
Autobiography

This and the next two chapters are devoted to nonfiction. You may recall from Chapter 1 that **nonfiction** includes traditional literature, biography, informational books, and poetry. All the genres of fiction and picture books (Juvenile and Easy sections) make up only 27 percent of a typical library's holdings of children's books. The remaining books are nonfiction, of which informational books make up the bulk. Nonfiction is located in the numbered sections of the library (see Box 1.3).

Biography is one of the most interesting nonfiction genres, because it deals with the lives of interesting people. Most biographies are shelved in the J920 section. (If you are in a public library, make sure you are looking in the J section and not the adult 920 section.) Biographies and autobiographies are shelved together, and the books are arranged in alphabetical order by the *subject's* (not the author's) last name. This is very handy when you are looking for books about an individual, because you will find most of the available biographies about that person together. In some libraries, partial biographies are located in other areas of the 900 section; and brief biographies in picture book format are sometimes located in the E section with other picture books.

Children more easily remember similar words if their derivations are explained. The word **biography** is derived by adding the prefix *bio-,* which means *life,* to *-graphy,* which comes from the Greek for *to write.* A biography, therefore, is a written work about someone's life. Add the prefix *auto-,* meaning *self,* and the word **autobiography** is formed: a work about one's own life. However, unless otherwise stated, when I refer to biographies in this chapter, I am including autobiographies.

Well-written autobiographies often read like a conversation with a familiar friend, as the author draws you into his or her life. They are nearly always written in a narrative style and in the first person. Because children are very familiar with narrative writing (from reading storybooks), autobiographies are especially good for introducing this genre, particularly when children are allowed to select a contemporary person they admire. However, not many people write their own life stories. The vast majority of life stories are written by an author who may or may not have known the person who is the subject of the book. These biographies are typically written from an objective (third-person) point of view, and they are most likely to be written in an expository (informative or explanatory) format.

Because historical fiction can contain some real historical personages, it is important to help children differentiate between it and biography. Explain that if a book has *any* fictional characters, it cannot be biography. It also helps to remind children that historical fiction is shelved in the unnumbered sections (J and E) of the library, whereas biography is in the 900 section (history) of nonfiction.

When working on school assignments, children too often turn to encyclopedias that give only the bare, dry facts. Unfortunately, biographies are often an untapped source of rich and diverse reading. This genre has changed a great deal since most of us were in elementary school. Today many well-written biographies make their subjects come alive. The bibliography at the end of this chapter contains titles of engaging books written on various reading levels. These books encourage readers to identify with the subjects and make a human connection. As each book unfolds, readers can watch an interesting person advance through several stages of life—growing, learning, achieving, and sometimes failing.

As with historical fiction, the writing of exemplary biography requires authors to conduct extensive research, utilizing primary sources where available. A good biographer does not assume young readers have the necessary background knowledge to comprehend and enjoy the book. If the subject lived a long time ago (and to elementary children, that often means any period before they were born), readers need some understanding of the times and places in which the person lived. The author must provide a context for ideas, language, daily life, and the social issues that affected the subject's life.

 ## Responding to Literature

Timelines

After reading an autobiography, construct a timeline of your own life, using strips of poster board. Also add events that you think or hope will happen in your life, such as graduating from college, embarking on a career, getting married, purchasing a house, and having children.

Evaluating Biography

The following questions can guide you as you select biography books.

- Is the book of high literary merit, presenting the subject in an interesting manner?
- Is it rich in factual content that conveys the historical period and geographical place in which the subject lived?
- Is it accurate and authentic, conveying the true nature of the subject?
- Is there evidence of careful research, such as reference notes, bibliographies, maps, or timelines?
- Is there a balance between the subject's achievements and strengths and his or her weaknesses?
- Are any archaic or specialized words explained in the text?
- Is the author qualified to write about this subject?

Reading Biographies for Pleasure

Many children never select biographies for pleasure reading because they view this genre as something to read for a school assignment rather than something to enjoy. However, biographies can be a source of both information and enjoyment, particularly when readers are allowed to select the individuals who interest them.

ATHLETES AND ENTERTAINERS

Youthful readers have youthful interests. They want to read about people such as athletes and entertainers, whose names are familiar to them and whose talents are the current rage—and some of whom may be controversial or unconventional people. Following is a list of books about people who are popular with young readers. (Full information for this and other lists in this chapter can be found in the end-of-chapter bibliography.)

- *Paula Abdul: Straight Up* (Ford 1992)
- *Muhammad Ali* (Duplacey 1999)
- *Backstreet Boys* (Zymet 1999)
- *Joan Baez* (Garza 1991)
- *Sports Great Michael Chang* (Ditchfield 1999)
- *Pride of Puerto Rico: The Life of Roberto Clemente* (Walker 1991)
- *Bill Cosby: Family Man* (Conord 1999)
- *Celine Dion* (Cole 1998)
- *The Story of Walt Disney, Maker of Magical Worlds* (Selden 1989)
- *Gloria Estefan* (Boulais 1998)
- *Lou Gehrig: The Luckiest Man* (Adler 1997)
- *Whoopi Goldberg: Entertainer* (Blue & Naden 1995)
- *Steffi Graf: Tennis Champ* (Brooks 1996)
- *Hammer: 2 Legit 2 Quit* (Saylor-Marchant 1992)
- *Magic Johnson: Champion with a Cause* (Greenberg 1992)
- *Michael Jordan* (Lovitt 1998)
- *Bruce Lee* (Tagliaferro 1999)
- *Madonna* (Claro & Gibbons 1994)
- *Ricky Martin: A Scrapbook in Words and Pictures* (Raso 1999)
- *Rita Moreno* (Suntree 1992)
- *Julia Roberts: Reaching for the Stars* (Wallner 1991)
- *Arnold Schwarzenegger: Larger Than Life* (Doherty & Doherty 1993)
- *Charlie Sheen, Emilio Estevez & Martin Sheen: Star Families* (Press 1995)
- *Will Smith: From Fresh Prince to King of Cool* (Rodriguez 1998)

- *Tallchief: America's Prima Ballerina* (Tallchief & Wells 1999)
- *Jim Thorpe: Athlete of the Century* (Coffey 1994)
- *Denzel Washington* (Hill 1998)
- *El Chino* (Billy Wong) (Say 1990)
- *Kristi Yamaguchi: Female Figure Skating Legends* (Wellman 1998)

AUTHORS AND ILLUSTRATORS

Children who love reading will love to read about their favorite authors and illustrators. Often these books are coming-of-age stories that tell how the individuals were attracted to careers in writing and illustrating. Learning about their lives can provide a deeper understanding of their books. Also, look for introductions to fiction books that have a brief autobiographical statement by the author. These are often the impetus that prompts children to search for a full autobiography.

- *Where the Flame Trees Bloom* (Alma Flor Ada 1994)
- *A Fairy Tale Life: A Story of Hans Christian Andersen* (Burch 1994)
- *Judy Blume* (Wheeler 1996)
- *A Girl from Yamhill: A Memoir* (Beverly Cleary 1988)
- *Michael Dorris* (Weil 1997)
- *Childtimes: A Three-Generation Memoir* (Eloise Greenfield & Lessie Jones Little 1993)
- *Calling the Doves* (Juan Felipe Herrera 1995)
- *I Called It Home* (David Kherdian 1997)
- *I Was a Teenage Professional Wrestler* (Ted Lewin 1993)
- *The Land of Narnia: Brian Sibley Explores the World of C. S. Lewis* (Sibley 1990)
- *Talking to Faith Ringgold* (Ringgold, Freeman, & Roucher 1995)
- *Amy Tan: Author of* **The Joy Luck Club** (Kramer 1996)
- *The Invisible Thread: An Autobiography* (Yoshiko Uchida 1995)
- *Phillis Wheatley: First African-American Poet* (Greene 1995)
- *The Story of Laura Ingalls Wilder, Pioneer Girl* (Stine 1992)
- *The Lost Garden* (Laurence Yep 1996)
- *A Letter from Phoenix Farm* (Jane Yolen 1992)

POLITICAL AND SOCIAL LEADERS

Children also are curious about the people whose names they hear regularly at school and at home. Reading about contemporary political and social leaders will help them better understand the global society in which they live.

- *Corazon Aquino: Journey to Power* (Nadel 1987)
- *Barbara Bush: First Lady of Literacy* (Behrens 1990)
- *George Bush: Power of the President* (Spies 1991)

- *George W. Bush: The Family Business* (Cohen 2000)
- *Jimmy Carter: Beyond the Presidency* (Carrigan 1995)
- *Cesar Chavez* (Schaefer 1998)
- *Richard B. Cheney: A Life of Public Service* (Andrews 2001)
- *Henry Cisneros: Building a Better America* (Bredeson 1995)
- *Bill Clinton* (Kelly 1998)
- *Hillary Rodham Clinton* (Kent 1999)
- *Bill Gates: Software Billionaire* (Forman 1998)
- *Al Gore* (Stefoff 1999)
- *Mikhail Gorbachev* (Butson 1989)
- *Ladonna Harris* (Schwartz 1997)
- *Jesse Jackson: I Am Somebody* (Simon 1997)
- *Aung San Suu Kyi: Standing Up for Democracy in Burma* (Ling & Bunch 1999)
- *Nelson Mandela: Determined to Be Free* (Roberts 1995)
- *Carol Moseley-Braun: Breaking Barriers* (Carrigan 1994)
- *Boris Yeltsin: Man of the People* (Ayer 1992)

LITTLE-KNOWN PEOPLE

Not to be overlooked are biographies about little-known people whose interesting lives present a good story. For example, *My Great Aunt Arizona* (1992) by Gloria Houston is a charming picture book biography about Arizona Houston Hughes, who taught elementary school for fifty-seven years in the Blue Ridge Mountains. *Along the Santa Fe Trail: Marion Russell's Own Story* (Russell & Wadsworth 1993) is an account of Marion Sloan Russell at the age of 7 in 1852, when she, her mother, and her older brother traveled in a wagon train along the Santa Fe Trail.

Types of Biography

Biography is written in diverse formats. Some biographers adhere faithfully to the facts; others add some fictional elements, such as dialogue, to make the book more closely resemble a story. Some books trace the full life of an individual from birth to death; others cover only one period, such as the subject's childhood or most significant life achievement. Some biographies are primarily text, whereas others are in picture book format.

Authentic Biography

Authors who write **authentic biography** are very concerned with accuracy. In their books they carefully distinguish between fact and supposition. They limit information about a person's life to the events that are verifiable. Dialogue is included only if substantiated by reliable personal recollections or historical documents, such as letters and diaries. As part of their research, authors of authentic biography often travel to the places where the subject lived and worked, locating public documents and interviewing people for unpublished information. Authentic biographies are more likely to be written with a balanced perspective, in which the author includes the negative or unfortunate aspects of a person's life as well as the successes.

Jean Fritz provides an honest portrayal of Theodore Roosevelt, twenty-sixth president of the United States, in *Bully for You, Teddy Roosevelt!* (1991). In the book Fritz writes of what happened when Roosevelt's beloved wife, Alice Lee, died shortly after giving birth to their only child—who was also named Alice.

> He believed that anything painful in the past should be left in the past, and of course he had to run to keep ahead of the pain. After the first stages of grief, Teddy never mentioned Alice's name again. He put away her pictures and her letters, and years later, when he wrote his autobiography, he never mentioned that once there had been an Alice Lee in his life. Furthermore, he never told young Alice anything about her mother. Not once. (p. 41)

Another example of an honest portrayal is Doris Faber's *Eleanor Roosevelt: First Lady of the World* (1985). Eleanor Roosevelt was married to Franklin D. Roosevelt (Theodore Roosevelt's cousin), thirty-second president of the United States. Faber attributes Eleanor's lifetime of tireless public work to her husband's lack of discretion.

> [Eleanor] found another reason why she *needed* work. Unpacking Franklin's luggage on his return from a trip, she noticed some letters in a familiar handwriting. Her own pretty secretary, Lucy Mercer, had written them. A glance showed her that these were love letters. To a woman like Eleanor Roosevelt, who had the strictest of moral standards, it was impossible just to forgive Franklin. But when he promised never to see Lucy again, Eleanor coldly said that, for the sake of their children, she would continue living with him. As much as Franklin had hurt her, though, she could not help blaming herself. . . . She simply could not go on day after day—unless she did some work that would make her stop feeling entirely useless. (pp. 30–31)

Authentic biographies can usually be recognized because the text contains little (if any) dialogue, and because a list of information sources is included at the end of the book. An excellent example of authentic biography is *Cleopatra* by Diane Stanley and Peter Vennema (1994). There is no dialogue in the text, and the few quotes were taken from primary sources. Illustrations on the book cover and throughout were exquisitely painted by Stanley in the style of Alexandrian mosaics. Coins with Cleopatra's profile (the only existing examples of her image) were models for the illustrations of the Egyptian queen. The copyright page contains an *acknowledgement* of the specialists in art history and ancient history who advised the authors. Information sources include a *preface* that gives the necessary historical background, a *note on ancient sources* about information obtained in Plutarch's books, and an explanation on why so little information survived about Cleopatra. A two-page spread shows a *map* of Egypt, the Roman Provinces, and surrounding regions in 51 B.C. The text covers the life of Cleopatra from age 18 to 39, when she killed herself, and it is followed by an *epilogue* that explains what happened to Egypt and Cleopatra's children after she died. Also included is a *pronunciation guide* for all the names. At the end of the book is a *reference list* of the eleven books which the authors consulted while writing and illustrating the book.

Another important characteristic of an authentic biography is that it is written by a qualified author. Usually there is a note by or about the author on the inside flaps of the book jacket, or at the beginning or end of the book. After reading the note, ask yourself the following questions to judge the author's qualifications.

- Is there a statement that the author faithfully adhered to facts?
- Is the author well known for writing authentic biographies?
- What is in the author's education or life experience that qualifies her or him to write an authentic biography about the subject?
- Has the author written biographies about others who lived during the same time?
- Did the author know or personally interview the subject?

One of the best-known authors of authentic biography is Jean Fritz, whose humanizing details and amusing tone make her books good reading. Among her many books is a series about founders of the United States—Sam Adams, Benjamin Franklin, John Hancock, Patrick Henry, and Paul Revere. Though her research is scrupulous, she writes with a unique perspective. Her merger of careful research and a strong sense of story with humorous overtones results in both informative and pleasurable reading. Part of Fritz's unique writing style is weaving little-known details about the subject into each book.

The first half of *What's the Big Idea, Ben Franklin?* (Fritz 1976) is devoted to Franklin's childhood, in which the author lays the foundation for the scientific curiosity that led to Franklin's discovery that lightning was electricity. Fritz describes one of his early experiments, performed while he swam in his favorite pond.

> Then he tried lying on his back, holding a kite string, and letting the kite act as a sail and pull him across the pond. This was a great success. There was only one trouble. In those days boys went swimming naked. And if Benjamin didn't want to go home naked, he had to get a friend to carry his clothes to the other side of the pond. (It had to be a good friend because the pond was a mile wide.) (p. 19)

At the end of the book, in a list of notes that are referenced by page number, Fritz adds some interesting details she did not include in the text. For example, she wrote that no one (except Franklin and the woman involved, of course) knew the identity of the mother of his oldest child, William Temple, who went to live with Franklin when he got married. When his son sided with England during the American Revolution, Franklin suffered his greatest disappointment. It is Fritz's illumination of ordinary events that produces a lively interpretation of history, without compromising standards by adding fabricated dialogue and other forms of fictionalization.

Responding to Literature

Analyzing Accuracy

Which is a more accurate source of information: biography or autobiography? Would an autobiography be more accurate, because the author is the primary source of information? Or would a biography be more accurate, because the author is more objective? For example, would former president Richard Nixon's autobiography be more accurate than a biography written by someone not personally associated with him? Give three reasons why you believe autobiography would or would not be more accurate than biography.

In her author's note Megan Stine gives the following information about her subject in *The Story of Malcolm X, Civil Rights Leader* (1994).

In reading and writing about Malcolm X, I have found that there are often different versions of the "truth" about many events in his life. Some of these differences are big, and some are small. In his autobiography, for instance, Malcolm remembers some of the dates incorrectly—probably because the stories he was remembering had all happened so many years before. In other places Malcolm changed the names of people he knew, maybe to protect their privacy. Sometimes Malcolm told the stories from his childhood exactly as they were told to him—regardless of whether he actually thought they were true. Sometimes it is hard to know what is true and what is not. . . . (p. 1)

This passage points out some of the problems with the accuracy of autobiography. Autobiographers may not believe it necessary to research certain data and may rely only on their sometimes faulty memory. Also, autobiographers may omit or change certain information to protect others or to portray themselves more favorably. However, we cannot assume biography is any more accurate than autobiography, because "truth" is subject to interpretation. Biographies about the same subject can have major discrepancies. In comparing Stine's biography of Malcolm X with Arnold Adoff's *Malcolm X* (1970), I found the following major discrepancies:

1. Adoff wrote that Malcolm and his brothers sometimes hunted for rabbit, which they took home for supper (p. 6). However, Stine wrote that Malcolm's mother would not cook or eat pork or rabbit, even when her children were starving (p. 12).

2. Adoff wrote that during the years Malcolm was in prison, he and Elijah Muhammad, the leader of the Nation of Islam, wrote numerous letters to each other (pp. 20, 25). However, Stine wrote that Malcolm and Muhammad exchanged letters only once (p. 41).

3. Adoff wrote that Malcolm married his wife, Betty, after a courtship (p. 32). However, Stine wrote that Malcolm took Betty out one time (to a museum), had her meet with Elijah Muhammad, and then proposed to her over the telephone months later.

4. Adoff wrote that Malcolm and his wife had four daughters (p. 32). Stine wrote that Malcolm and Betty had six daughters, and she listed their names and birth dates (p. 65).

Responding to Literature

Comparing Biographies

Read a historical person's autobiography and one biography (or two authentic biographies) of the person. Take note of any contradictions in the books. What would account for the contradictions? In reference to this activity, explain what is meant by "truth is subject to interpretation."

Fictionalized Biography

Most elementary children prefer fiction to nonfiction. Because of this, many children's biographers write in a narrative style that reads much like a novel, called **fictionalized biography**. This requires the author to provide speculative or imagined scenes and details, which often include **invented dialogue** and **interior monologue**—a device that lets readers know what the subject is thinking. The rationale for fictionalizing biography is that it results in an appealing introduction to a genre that otherwise turns off many children. Adding dialogue contributes to the readers' identification with the subject, and interest increases when readers are sympathetic. Following is an excerpt from *Louis Braille, the Boy Who Invented Books for the Blind* (Davidson 1971):

> Soon [books for the blind] was all Louis could think—or talk—about. And his friends got good and tired of it.
> "Do shut up, Louis," they begged.
> "But it's so important!" Louis tried to explain. "Don't you see? Without books we can never really learn! But just think what we could grow up to be if only we could read. Doctors or lawyers or scientists. Or writers even! *Anything* almost."
> "All right," one of the boys snapped. "We want to read too. Find us a way, if you're so smart."
> "I can't," Louis cried. "I'm blind!" (pp. 35–36)

In this excerpt, the conversation between Louis and his schoolmates was invented by the author to more fully portray Braille's passion for finding a way for blind people to read. Braille's speech is more effective in relating this passion than an expository statement such as "Louis Braille passionately wanted books that blind people could read."

Even autobiographies can be fictionalized. In the introduction to *Homesick: My Own Story* (1982), Jean Fritz wrote:

> Since my childhood feels like a story, I decided to tell it that way, letting the events fall as they would into the shape of a story, lacing them together with fictional bits, adding a piece here and there when memory didn't give me all I needed. I . . . use conversation freely. . . . So although this book takes place within two years . . . the events are drawn from the entire period of my childhood. . . . Strictly speaking, I have to call this book *fiction*, but it does not feel like fiction to me. (p. 7)

Attempting to achieve the emotional engagement of the familiar story-telling format in biography often results in a book of **faction**—a merger of fact and fiction. However, some critics argue that to add *any* element of fiction automatically excludes a book from the category of nonfiction. Nonetheless, you will find numerous books in the children's biography section that are fictionalized in some way. Obviously, fictionalized biography is not as reliable historically, and some authors are even guilty of distorting history with books that read more like legends.

In presenting a dramatic narrative to bring subjects to life through the familiar devices of storytelling, some authors step over the line to *biographical fiction,* fiction that is based on the life of a real person. Recall from the last chapter on historical fiction that in writing biographical fiction, the author uses considerable invention and takes great liberties with the facts about a real person. A prime example is *Amos Fortune, Free Man* (1950), in which Elizabeth Yates invented a story about a former slave, using only his gravestone epitaph and some old legal documents. Yet this book is nearly always shelved in the nonfiction section, because the publisher said it was nonfiction!

Sometimes fictionalized biography and biographical fiction are difficult to differentiate. It is even hard to remember which term is which. It is easier to help children keep the terms straight if you explain that the adjective (first word) is the type, and the noun (second word) is the *genre.*

- Fictionalized *biography* is biography in which the author has included invented elements, such as dialogue (considered nonfiction).
- Biographical *fiction* is a fiction story based on the life of a real person or persons (considered historical fiction).

 Responding to Literature

Comparing a Biography with a Movie

Many motion pictures have been made about historical people, such as Joan of Arc (Christopher 1993). Read a biography about a historical person, and then view a movie on the person's life. Make a Venn diagram (Chapter 11, Figure 11.5) showing the common elements and the differences between the two. From this diagram, determine if the movie is fictionalized biography or biographical fiction. Discuss the information that led to your determination.

Forms of Biography

Biography, like other genres, has several categories: complete, partial, childhood, picture book, and collective biographies.

Complete

Some biographies span the entire life of the subject, from cradle to grave, and are called **complete biographies.** To do justice to their subjects, these books are understandably long and therefore geared for more able readers, such as intermediate-grade children. These are the books most children select or are assigned for biography book reports. Older books often contain only text with no photographs or illustrations. For example, *Invincible Louisa* (Meigs 1933) has 247 pages of small print with no photographs and only one illustration on the book's cover. Cornelia Meigs traces the life of Louisa May Alcott, the author of *Little Women*, from the day she was born in 1832 until 1888, when she died two days after her father. The author covers her life so thoroughly that the reader learns not only about Louisa, but about her parents and sisters as well.

Sometimes, when authors try to write a complete biography for less able readers, the result is a stripped-down version whose briefness does not portray the personality of the subject. When a person's life is reduced to a series of facts that convey no sense of the spirit of the individual, it is no wonder children lose interest in this genre.

Partial

Partial biographies focus on one part or one aspect of a subject's life; this category, of course, includes biographies of living people. Young readers are interested in the childhood and adolescence of admirable people. Often, childhood biographies focus on the influences that led to the subject's achievements later in life. This is particularly interesting if the person had to overcome adversity (such as poverty, a physical impairment, or the early loss of a parent). *Albert Einstein* (1982) by Ibi Lepscky is an interesting childhood biography that focuses on Einstein's unique and inquisitive nature. Readers will be amazed to learn that Einstein, though a genius, did not do well in school—because he was interested only in arithmetic and refused to do his other lessons!

▌CHILDHOOD BIOGRAPHIES AND AUTOBIOGRAPHIES

- *Through My Eyes* (Ruby Bridges 1999)
- *Marie Curie* (Lepscky 1993)
- *Coming Home: From the Life of Langston Hughes* (Cooper 1994)
- *Zora Hurston and the Chinaberry Tree* (Miller 1994)
- *A Girl Named Helen Keller* (Lundell 1995)
- *Young Mozart* (Isadora 1997)
- *My Freedom Trip: A Child's Escape from North Korea* (Frances Park 1998)

Some childhood biographies are sad, because the subject did not live to adulthood. In the fictionalized biography, *Sadako and the Thousand Paper Cranes* (1977), Eleanor Coerr writes about Sadako Sasaki, who died at the age of 12 from leukemia as a result of radiation from the bomb dropped on Hiroshima, Japan. Also very moving is the partial autobiography of a 13-year-old Jewish girl, Anne Frank. She kept a diary for two years while hiding from the Nazis in a secret building annex in

Holland. She and her family were captured and sent to concentration camps, where all but her father perished. Her diary was later found in the annex, and her father published it under the title *Anne Frank: The Diary of a Young Girl* (1952).

Some partial biographies focus on the most important event in a person's life. For example, in *And Then What Happened, Paul Revere?* (1973), Jean Fritz focused on Revere's life as a Patriot and his famous ride to warn the colonists that the British were coming. Little is said about Revere's childhood, and even less about his life after the Revolutionary War.

The Glorious Flight: Across the Channel with Louis Blériot, July 25, 1909 (Provensen & Provensen 1983) also focuses on the most significant part of a person's life. Blériot's fascination with flying machines produced the Blériot XI, which in 1909 became the first heavier-than-air machine to fly the English Channel. In selecting partial biographies, take care to avoid watered-down versions that leave out facts that are essential for a balanced portrayal. When these essential facts are omitted, the reader often sees a distorted view of history.

Picture Book Biography

A fairly new format is **picture book biography**. Some picture book biographies zoom in on a childhood incident of a well-known person, such as *Richard Wright and the Library Card* (Miller 1997), a fictionalized account of an important one-year period (based on his autobiography). During the mid-1920s Wright is working to save money to move north. He convinces a white man to lend him his library card, because blacks cannot check out books. During that year, Wright reads many classics that inspire him to become one of the first great African American authors.

The picture book biographies by Robert Quackenbush are enjoyable reading for elementary children. There is no dialogue in the text; however, Quackenbush keeps a running commentary, often humorous, through the speech bubbles of cartoon characters he illustrates on each two-page spread. For example, in *Once upon a Time!: A Story of the Brothers Grimm* (1999), the book tells of the brothers' fortunate encounter with a genuine storyteller, Frau Viehmann, who "settled for rolls and coffee in exchange for her stories" (p. 22). Underneath the text a cartoon shows Jacob saying in a speech bubble, "Quick! Frau Viehmann is coming! Are there any rolls in the house?" Wilhelm answers, "Will egg rolls do?" Quackenbush is successful in maintaining children's interest through dialogue and humor in his illustrations without compromising the standards of authentic biography in the text.

▌ PICTURE BOOK BIOGRAPHIES

- *Alvin Ailey* (Pinkney 1993)
- *Nothing Is Impossible, Said Nellie Bly* (Carlson 1990)
- *Here a Plant, There a Plant, Everywhere a Plant, Plant: A Story of Luther Burbank* (Quackenbush 1995)
- *The Story of Johnny Appleseed* (Aliki 1987)

- *Aaron Copeland* (Venezia 1995)
- *George Handel* (Venezia 1995)
- *Leonardo da Vinci* (Stanley 1996)
- *Quick, Annie, Give Me a Catchy Line: A Story of Samuel F. B. Morse* (Quackenbush 1999)
- *Picasso* (Venezia 1988)

Collective

Collective biographies examine the lives of several people who are linked by a common thread, such as occupation, ethnicity, or achievement. In collective biographies, photographs or illustrations abound, and brief biographical sketches are provided for each individual. For example, *The Buck Stops Here* (1990) by Alice Provensen devotes one or two pages to each of the presidents through George H. W. Bush. Interesting illustrations with meaningful symbols adorn the pages, and a short description of each president's term with biographical information is located at the back. Sometimes a collective biography such as this will pique a child's interest, and the child will seek a longer biography to read.

▌COLLECTIVE BIOGRAPHIES

- *Extraordinary American Indians* (Avery & Skinner 1992)
- *Extraordinary Asian Pacific Americans* (Sinnott 1993)
- *Extraordinary Black Americans from Colonial to Contemporary Times* (Altman 1994)
- *Extraordinary Hispanic Americans* (Sinnott 1995)
- *Extraordinary Jewish Americans* (Brooks 1998)
- *Famous Mexican Americans* (Morey & Dunn 1989)
- *Lives of the Musicians: Good Times, Bad Times (and What the Neighbors Thought)* (Krull 1993)
- *Lives of the Artists: Masterpieces, Messes (and What the Neighbors Thought)* (Krull 1995)
- *Talking with Artists* (Cummings 1992)
- *Take a Walk in Their Shoes* (famous African Americans) (Turner 1989)

Biography Today is a juvenile periodical that is a fabulous source for collections of brief biographies of contemporary people that are of interest to young readers. Check your school and public library for copies. Recent issues contain a general index, which provides the names of all people who have been featured in the periodical since it was first published in 1992.

Enhancing Curriculum with Biography

Like historical fiction, biography can enliven the study of history by revealing what it was like to live in another time. History is enhanced when books give readers "the chance to reflect on events from one individual viewpoint, to step off the beaten track and into fresh territory" (Wilms 1978, p. 218). When readers closely connect with the subject of a biography, the evocation experience is analogous to walking around in the skin of someone who lived in another place at another time. Biography is unique in its potential to enhance children's understanding of the true significance of past events and of the people involved.

Until recently, U.S. history textbooks omitted the achievements of most minorities and females, but today many good biographies feature these individuals. The following list contains biographies about some African Americans who influenced history.

▌AFRICAN AMERICANS

- *The Story of Frederick Douglass, Voice of Freedom* (Weiner 1992)
- *Martin Luther King, Jr.: Man of Peace* (McKissack & McKissack 1991)
- *Rosa Parks* (Greenfield 1996)
- *The Story of Harriet Tubman, Conductor of the Underground Railroad* (McMullan 1991)
- *The Story of Malcolm X, Civil Rights Leader* (Stine 1994)

Though the elementary curriculum includes the history of Native Americans, in some classrooms this consists of reading the European American version of the first Thanksgiving and making feather headdresses. The following biographies will lend realism to the history of American Indians.

▌NATIVE AMERICANS

- *Black Elk: A Man with a Vision* (Greene 1990)
- *The Life and Death of Crazy Horse* (Freedman 1996)
- *Ishi: The Last of His People* (Collins 2000)
- *Pocahontas and the Strangers* (Bulla 1995)
- *The Story of Sacajawea, Guide to Lewis and Clark* (Rowland 1989)
- *A Boy Called Slow: The True Story of Sitting Bull* (Bruchac 1995)
- *Squanto, First Friend to the Pilgrims* (Dubowski 1990)

In addition to the women who have already been named, the following biographies feature determined, successful women, both historical and contemporary.

▌WOMEN

- *Diana: The People's Princess* (Wood 1998)
- *Lost Star: The Story of Amelia Earhart* (Lauber 1988)
- *Mae Jemison: A Space Biography* (Yannuzzi 1998)
- *Joan of Arc* (Christopher 1993)

Eleanor was the First Lady of the World. From *Eleanor Roosevelt: A Life of Discovery,* written by Russell Freedman.

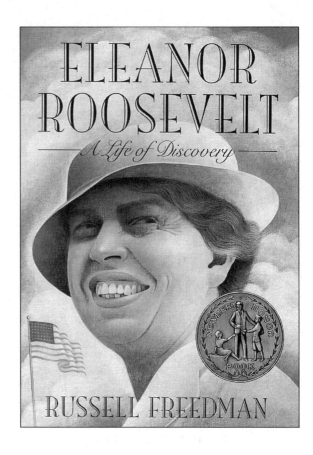

- *Coretta Scott King* (Rhodes 1998)
- *Maya Lin* (Ling 1997)
- *Wilma Mankiller: Principal Chief of the Cherokees* (Schwartz 1994)
- *Antonia Novello: U.S. Surgeon General* (Hawxhurst 1993)
- *Sandra Day O'Connor* (Holland 1997)
- *Sally Ride: A Space Biography* (Kramer 1998)
- *Eleanor Roosevelt: A Life of Discovery* (Freedman 1993)
- *The Secret Soldier: The Story of Deborah Sampson* (McGovern 1975)

Biographies about male historical heroes are abundant, and they bring life to the study of United States history. Some examples follow.

MEN

- *Daniel Boone: Wilderness Pioneer* (Green & Sanford 1997)
- *Lincoln: A Photobiography* (Freedman 1987)

- ■ *Meet Robert E. Lee* (Trow 1969)

- ■ *An American Hero: The True Story of Charles A. Lindbergh* (Denenberg 1998)

- ■ *The Great Little Madison* (James Madison) (Fritz 1989)

- ■ *Franklin Delano Roosevelt* (Freedman 1990)

- ■ *George Washington: First President of the United States* (Greene 1991)

▌▌ BIOGRAPHY BOOKS

Ada, Alma Flor. *Where the Flame Trees Bloom.* Illus. Antonio Martorell. Atheneum, 1994.

Adler, David A. *Lou Gehrig: The Luckiest Man.* Illus. Terry Widener. Gulliver, 1997.

Adoff, Arnold. *Malcolm X.* Illus. John Wilson. HarperCollins, 1970.

Aliki. *The Story of Johnny Appleseed.* Simon & Schuster, 1987.

Altman, Susan. *Extraordinary Black Americans from Colonial to Contemporary Times.* Children's Book Press, 1994.

Andrews, Elaine. *Richard B. Cheney: A Life of Public Service.* Milbrook, 2001.

Avery, Susan, & Linda Skinner. *Extraordinary American Indians.* Children's Book Press, 1992.

Ayer, Eleanor H. *Boris Yeltsin: Man of the People.* Dillon Press, 1992.

Behrens, June. *Barbara Bush: First Lady of Literacy.* Children's Book Press, 1990.

Blue, Rose, & Corinne J. Naden. *Whoopi Goldberg: Entertainer.* Chelsea House, 1995.

Boulais, Sue. *Gloria Estefan.* Mitchell Lane, 1998.

Bredeson, Carmen. *Henry Cisneros: Building a Better America.* Enslow, 1995.

Bridges, Ruby. *Through My Eyes.* Scholastic, 1999.

Brooks, Philip. *Steffi Graf: Tennis Champ.* Children's Book Press, 1996.

——. *Extraordinary Jewish Americans.* Children's Book Press, 1998.

Bruchac, Joseph. *A Boy Called Slow: The True Story of Sitting Bull.* Illus. Rocco Baviera. Philomel, 1995.

Bulla, Clyde Robert. *Pocahontas and the Strangers.* Illus. Peter Burchard. Scholastic, 1995.

Burch, Joann Johansen. *A Fairy Tale Life: A Story of Hans Christian Andersen.* Carolrhoda, 1994.

Butson, Thomas. *Mikhail Gorbachev.* Chelsea House, 1989.

Carlson, Judy. *Nothing Is Impossible, Said Nellie Bly.* Raintree Steck-Vaughn, 1990.

Carrigan, Mellonee. *Carol Moseley-Braun: Breaking Barriers.* Children's Book Press, 1994.

——. *Jimmy Carter: Beyond the Presidency.* Children's Book Press, 1995.

Christopher, Tracy. *Joan of Arc.* Chelsea House, 1993.

Claro, Nicole, & Leeza Gibbons. *Madonna.* Chelsea House, 1994.

Cleary, Beverly. *A Girl from Yamhill: A Memoir.* Morrow, 1988.

Coerr, Eleanor. *Sadako and the Thousand Paper Cranes.* Illus. Ronald Himler. Dell, 1977.

Coffey, Wayne. *Jim Thorpe: Athlete of the Century.* Blackbirch, 1994.

Cohen, Daniel. *George W. Bush: The Family Business.* Millbrook, 2000.

Cole, Melanie. *Celine Dion.* Mitchell Lane, 1998.

Collins, David R. *Ishi: The Last of His People.* Morgan Reynolds, 2000.

Conord, Bruce W. *Bill Cosby: Family Man.* Econo-Clad Books, 1999.

Cooper, Floyd. *Coming Home: From the Life of Langston Hughes.* Philomel, 1994.

Cummings, Pat. *Talking with Artists.* Simon & Schuster, 1992.

Davidson, Margaret. *Louis Braille, the Boy Who Invented Books for the Blind.* Scholastic, 1971.

Denenberg, Barry. *An American Hero: The True Story of Charles A. Lindbergh.* Scholastic, 1998.

Ditchfield, Christin. *Sports Great Michael Chang.* Enslow, 1999.

Doherty, Craig A., & Katherine M. Doherty. *Arnold Schwarzenegger: Larger Than Life.* Walker, 1993.

Dubowski, Cathy. *Squanto, First Friend to the Pilgrims.* Illus. Steven James Petruccio. Parachute Press, 1990.

Duplacey, James. *Muhammad Ali.* Warwick, 1999.

Faber, Doris. *Eleanor Roosevelt: First Lady of the World.* Viking Penguin, 1985.

Ford, M. Thomas. *Paula Abdul: Straight Up.* Dillon Press, 1992.

Forman, Michael. *Bill Gates: Software Billionaire.* Crestwood House, 1998.

Frank, Anne. *Anne Frank: The Diary of a Young Girl.* Doubleday, 1952.

Freedman, Russell. *Lincoln: A Photobiography.* Houghton Mifflin, 1987.

———. *Franklin Delano Roosevelt.* Clarion, 1990.

———. *Eleanor Roosevelt: A Life of Discovery.* Clarion, 1993.

———. *The Life and Death of Crazy Horse.* Illus. Amos Bad Heart Bull. Holiday House, 1996.

Fritz, Jean. *And Then What Happened, Paul Revere?* Illus. Margot Tomes. Putnam & Grosset, 1973.

———. *What's the Big Idea, Ben Franklin?* Illus. Margot Tomes. Putnam & Grosset, 1976.

———. *Homesick: My Own Story.* Putnam's, 1982.

———. *The Great Little Madison* (James Madison). Putnam, 1989.

———. *Bully for You, Teddy Roosevelt!* Illus. Mike Wimmer. Putnam, 1991.

Garza, Hedda. *Joan Baez.* Chelsea House, 1991.

Green, Carl & William R. Sanford. *Daniel Boone: Wilderness Pioneer.* Enslow, 1997.

Greenberg, Keith Elliot. *Magic Johnson: Champion with a Cause.* Lerner, 1992.

Greene, Carol. *Black Elk: A Man with a Vision.* Children's Book Press, 1990.

———. *George Washington: First President of the United States.* Children's Book Press, 1991.

———. *Phillis Wheatley: First African-American Poet.* Children's Book Press, 1995.

Greenfield, Eloise. *Rosa Parks.* Illus. Gil Ashby. HarperCollins, 1996.

Greenfield, Eloise & Lessie Jones Little. *Childtimes: A Three-Generation Memoir.* Illus. Jerry Pinkney. Harper, 1993.

Hawxhurst, Joan C. *Antonia Novello: U.S. Surgeon General.* Millbrook, 1993.

Herrera, Juan Felipe. *Calling the Doves.* Illus. Elly Simmons. Children's Book Press, 1995.

Hill, Anne E. *Denzel Washington.* Chelsea House, 1998.

Holland, Gina. *Sandra Day O'Connor.* Illus. Gary Rees. Raintree Steck-Vaughn, 1997.

Houston, Gloria. *My Great-Aunt Arizona.* Illus. Susan Condie Lamb. HarperCollins, 1992.

Isadora, Rachel. *Young Mozart.* Viking, 1997.

Kelly, Michael. *Bill Clinton.* Chelsea House, 1998.

Kent, Deborah. *Hillary Rodham Clinton.* Children's Book Press, 1999.

Kherdian, David. *I Called It Home.* Blue Crane Books, 1997.

Kramer, Barbara. *Amy Tan: Author of* The Joy Luck Club. Enslow, 1996.

———. *Sally Ride: A Space Biography.* Enslow, 1998.

Krull, Kathleen. *Lives of the Musicians: Good Times, Bad Times (and What the Neighbors Thought).* Harcourt Brace, 1993.

———. *Lives of the Artists: Masterpieces, Messes (and What the Neighbors Thought).* Illus. Kathryn Hewitt. Harcourt Brace, 1995.

Lauber, Patricia. *Lost Star: The Story of Amelia Earhart.* Scholastic, 1988.

Lepscky, Ibi. *Albert Einstein.* Illus. Paolo Cardoni. Barron's Educational, 1982.

———. *Marie Curie.* Illus. Paolo Cardoni. Barron's Educational, 1993.

Lewin, Ted. *I Was a Teenage Professional Wrestler.* Orchard, 1993.

Ling, Bettina. *Maya Lin.* Raintree Steck-Vaughn, 1997.

Ling, Bettina, & Charlotte Bunch. *Aung San Suu Kyi: Standing Up for Democracy in Burma.* Feminist Press, 1999.

Lovitt, Chip. *Michael Jordan.* Scholastic.1998.

Lundell, Margo. *A Girl Named Helen Keller.* Illus. Irene Trivas. Scholastic, 1995.

McGovern, Ann. *The Secret Soldier: The Story of Deborah Sampson.* Illus. Harold Goodwin. Scholastic, 1975.

McKissack, Patricia & Fredrick L. McKissack. *Martin Luther King, Jr.: Man of Peace.* Enslow, 1991.

McMullan, Kate. *The Story of Harriet Tubman, Conductor of the Underground Railroad.* Illus. Steven James Petruccio. Parachute Press, 1991.

Meigs, Cornelia. *Invincible Louisa.* Little, Brown, 1933.

Miller, William. *Zora Hurston and the Chinaberry Tree.* Illus. Cornelius Van Wright & Ying-Hwa Hu. Lee & Low, 1994.

———. *Richard Wright and the Library Card.* Illus. Gregory Christie. Lee & Low, 1997.

Morey, Janet, & Wendy Dunn. *Famous Mexican Americans.* Puffin, 1989.

Nadel, Laurie. *Corazon Aquino: Journey to Power.* Julian Messner, 1987.

Park, Frances & Ginger Park. *My Freedom Trip: A Child's Escape from North Korea.* Illus. Debra Reid Jenkins. Boyds Mills, 1998.

Pinkney, Andrea Davis. *Alvin Ailey.* Illus. Brian Pinkney. Hyperion, 1993.

Press, Skip. *Charlie Sheen, Emilio Estevez & Martin Sheen: Star Families.* Crestwood House, 1995.

Provensen, Alice. *The Buck Stops Here.* HarperCollins, 1990.

Provensen, Alice & Martin Provensen. *The Glorious Flight: Across the Channel with Louis Blériot, July 25, 1909.* Viking, 1983.

Quackenbush, Robert. *Here a Plant, There a Plant, Everywhere a Plant, Plant: A Story of Luther Burbank.* Luther Burbank Home & Gardens, 1995.

———. *Once upon a Time! A Story of the Brothers Grimm.* Robert Quackenbush Studios, 1999.

———. *Quick, Annie, Give Me a Catchy Line: A Story of Samuel F. B. Morse.* Robert Quackenbush Studios, 1999.

Raso, Anne M. *Ricky Martin: A Scrapbook in Words and Pictures.* Dell, 1999.

Rhodes, Lisa Renee. *Coretta Scott King.* Chelsea House, 1998.

Ringgold, Faith, Linda Freeman, & Nancy Roucher. *Talking to Faith Ringgold.* Crown, 1995.

Roberts, Jack L. *Nelson Mandela: Determined to Be Free.* Millbrook, 1995.

Rodriguez, K. S. *Will Smith: From Fresh Prince to King of Cool.* HarperCollins, 1998.

Rowland, Della. *The Story of Sacajawea, Guide to Lewis and Clark.* Illus. Richard Leonard. Parachute Press, 1989.

Russell, Marion, & Ginger Wadsworth. *Along the Santa Fe Trail: Marion Russell's Own Story.* Illus. James Watling. Albert Whitman, 1993.

Say, Allen. *El Chino* (Billy Wong). Houghton Mifflin, 1990.

Saylor-Marchant, Linda. *Hammer: 2 Legit 2 Quit.* Dillon Press, 1992.

Schaefer, Lola M. *Cesar Chavez.* Capstone, 1998.

Schwartz, Melissa. *Wilma Mankiller: Principal Chief of the Cherokees.* Chelsea House, 1994.

Schwartz, Michael. *Ladonna Harris.* Raintree Steck-Vaughn, 1997.

Selden, Bernice. *The Story of Walt Disney, Maker of Magical Worlds.* Parachute Press, 1989.

Sibley, Brian. *The Land of Narnia: Brian Sibley Explores the World of C. S. Lewis.* Illus. Pauline Baynes. HarperCollins, 1990.

Simon, Charnan. *Jesse Jackson: I Am Somebody.* Children's Book Press, 1997.

Sinnott, Susan. *Extraordinary Asian Pacific Americans.* Children's Book Press, 1993.

———. *Extraordinary Hispanic Americans.* Children's Book Press, 1995.

Spies, Karen Bornemann, *George Bush: Power of the President.* Dillon Press, 1991.

Stanley, Diane. *Leonardo da Vinci.* Morrow, 1996.

Stanley, Diane, & Peter Vennema. *Cleopatra.* Illus. Diane Stanley. Morrow, 1994.

Stefoff, Rebecca. *Al Gore.* Millbrook, 1994.

Stine, Megan. *The Story of Laura Ingalls Wilder, Pioneer Girl.* Illus. Marcy Dunn Ramsey. Parachute Press, 1992.

———. *The Story of Malcolm X, Civil Rights Leader.* Parachute Press, 1994.

Suntree, Susan. *Rita Moreno.* Chelsea House, 1992.

Tagliaferro, Linda. *Bruce Lee.* Lerner, 1999.

Tallchief, Marie, & Rosemary Wells. *Tallchief: America's Prima Ballerina.* Illus. Gary Kelley. Viking, 1999.

Trow, George Swift. *Meet Robert E. Lee.* Illus. Ted Lewin. Random House, 1969

Turner, Glennette Tilly. *Take a Walk in Their Shoes.* Illus. Elton C. Fax. Cobblehill, 1989.

Uchida, Yoshiko. *The Invisible Thread: An Autobiography.* Beech Tree, 1995.

Venezia, Mike. *Picasso.* Children's Book Press, 1988.

———. *Aaron Copeland.* Children's Book Press, 1995.

———. *George Handel.* Children's Book Press, 1995.

Walker, Paul Robert. *Pride of Puerto Rico: The Life of Roberto Clemente.* Harcourt Brace, 1991.

Wallner, Rosemary. *Julia Roberts: Reaching for the Stars.* Abdo, 1991.

Weil, Ann. *Michael Dorris.* Raintree Steck-Vaughn, 1997.

Weiner, Eric. *The Story of Frederick Douglass, Voice of Freedom.* Parachute Press, 1992.

Wellman, Sam. *Kristi Yamaguchi: Female Figure Skating Legends.* Chelsea House, 1998.

Wheeler, Jill C. *Judy Blume.* Abdo, 1996.

Wood, Richard. *Diana: The People's Princess.* Raintree, 1998.

Yannuzzi, Della A. *Mae Jemison: A Space Biography.* Enslow, 1998.

Yep, Laurence. *The Lost Garden.* Morrow, 1996.

Yolen, Jane. *A Letter from Phoenix Farm.* Illus. Jason Stemple. Richard C. Owen, 1992.

Zymet, Cathy Alter. *Backstreet Boys.* Chelsea House, 1999.

KEY TERMS

 Explore the E-Glossary at **www.ablongman.com/anderson**

authentic biography (p. 268)
autobiography (p. 264)
biography (p. 264)
collective biography (p. 276)
complete biography (p. 273)
faction (p. 273)

fictionalized biography (p. 272)
interior monologue (p. 272)
invented dialogue (p. 272)
nonfiction (p. 264)
partial biography (p. 274)
picture book biography (p. 275)

Snowflakes come in an endless variety.
A Drop of Water
Written and photographed by Walter Wick.

c h a p t e r

11

Informational
Books

Informational books: Literature whose primary purpose is to inform the reader by providing an in-depth explanation of factual material

000–099 General Works
Computers

100–199 Philosophy and Psychology
Personal improvement

200–299 Religion
Christianity, Islam, Judaism, other religions

300–399 Social Sciences
Family, government, community life, conservation, transportation, law, holidays, costumes, etiquette

400–499 Language
English, other languages

500–599 Natural Sciences and Mathematics
Mathematics, astronomy, physics, chemistry, earth science, dinosaurs, trees, flowers, animals

600–699 Applied Sciences, Useful Arts, and Technology
Medicine, health, diseases, human body, safety, space and aeronautics, gardening, building, pets, sewing, manufacturing, machines, and inventions

700–799 Fine Arts, Sports, and Recreations
Architecture, drawing, handicrafts, painting, music, performing arts, games, sports, photography, hobbies, coins, magic, "how to" books

800–899 Literature

900–999 History, Geography, and Travel
Travel, world history, United States history, geography

The amount of information available to humans doubles every couple of years. Some futurists have predicted that in about two decades, available information will double every two to three months! Consequently, it should be no surprise that **informational books** constitute approximately one-half of the books in most libraries' juvenile collections. Children have inquiring minds and want to learn about themselves and their own world, as well as about things and places they have never seen. Informational books help satisfy this natural inquisitiveness and spark new curiosity.

Like biography, informational books are nonfiction. However, they should not be confused with **textbooks,** which are written on various grade levels and are marketed to school districts (but typically not found in libraries). Whereas textbooks present a breadth of information on a discipline, such as history, informational books present an in-depth look at a particular topic within a discipline, such as the women's rights movement (e.g., *The Day the Women Got the Vote*, Sullivan 1994)—a topic that might be covered in less than a page in a textbook. Also, the genre of informational books does not include **reference books:** dictionaries, encyclopedias, almanacs, atlases, or any other books that are not intended to be read in their entirety. Like the other genres presented in this textbook, informational books are literature and are therefore considered **trade books,** which are primarily marketed to libraries, wholesale booksellers, retail bookstores, and book clubs.

There is an interesting phenomenon in the publishing of nonfiction books that does not exist with fiction: There are two types of publishers. **Institutional publishers** such as Children's Press and Usborne specialize in nonfiction literature books for classrooms and public and school libraries. These publishers primarily produce series rather than individual titles, such as a series of biographies of influential African Americans or a series of books about various Native American tribes. Institutional publishers typically do not attempt to market to bookstores, which are less likely to purchase nonfiction series books. To attract a volume of sales, these books are usually priced lower than other trade books.

In contrast, trade book publishers present a broad range of titles and cater to the more lucrative retail market. Because these publishers pay their authors and illustrators more, "trade books are more likely to be written by an author with more knowledge and experience than the institutional books are" (Patent 1998). Additionally, trade book illustrations are usually of higher quality and are more appealing.

Evaluating Informational Books

The following questions can guide you as you select informational books.

- Is the information accurate and up to date with current research data (with no significant omissions)?
- Is the content organized in a logical sequence to lead the reader from the familiar to the new?
- Is the text clear and interesting, containing appropriate vocabulary for elementary children?
- Is there a glossary with concise definitions of specialized terminology or are terms explained clearly in text?
- Does the author clearly distinguish among fact, theory, and opinion?
- Are both text and illustrations free from stereotypes?
- Is there evidence of careful research, such as bibliography, references, and endnotes?
- Are appropriate reference aids included, such as headings, index, and recommended additional readings?
- Is the visual format uncluttered and appealing with large clear type?
- Are there full-color visual aids, such as photographs, illustrations, maps, charts, graphs, diagrams, original documents, and reproductions of artwork?

- Are the visuals and their captions accurate, and do they clarify and extend the text?

The importance of excellent visual aids cannot be overemphasized. Visual representation of abstract concepts and information outside readers' prior knowledge is essential for children's comprehension and enjoyment of informational books.

Characteristics of Informational Books

Whereas fiction books present stories, informational books present facts and concepts in an in-depth look at a specific topic (or, in younger children's books, a brief overview of a topic). "How-to" books are also included in this genre, for example, how to participate in in-line skating (*On a Roll!* Umansky 1991). In addition to basic information that children might need to include in a school report, informational books contain many interesting details and lesser-known facts.

 ## Responding to Literature

"How-To" Books

From the 700 section of the library, select a book on a sport you want to learn (or learn to play better), such as tennis, golf, basketball, or football. Demonstrate a new technique that you learned from the book.

Unlike fiction, which employs dialogue and narrative language, most informational books utilize **expository language,** the language that is used in textbooks, newspapers, magazines, and nonfiction books. Good informational books are organized with a logical presentation of information, such as simple-to-complex or chronological order. Often, full-color photographs are included to provide authenticity.

When you are selecting informational books, it is important to check copyright dates. Recent books are most likely to contain accurate, up-to-date information. In particular, books on science and technology become outdated quickly. Scientists, researchers, and technologists are constantly making new discoveries, developing new technology, and revealing new facts.

And even in disciplines such as history, knowledge advances and attitudes toward interpreting and reporting information change. Newer books are less likely to contain the racism, sexism, and ageism that characterized some older books—sometimes in the form of omissions, which are often more difficult to detect than blatant bias. According to Tunnell (1992), history-related trade books are "one of the best sources for teaching students history, for they place the human experience in the forefront. In the end, understanding history is indeed a matter of understanding human perspectives" (p. 247).

The Changing Nature of Informational Books

Do you remember the nonfiction books you read as a child? Most likely they were thick, drab books with only a few black and white illustrations. You checked them out only when you had to do a report and knew you could not get away with copying the information out of an encyclopedia.

Modern informational books are colorful and have pleasing, uncluttered designs, often falling within the thirty-two to sixty-four-page range. Many attractive full-color photographs, illustrations, and other graphics adorn the pages. For example, in *Castles* (Delafosse 1993), brightly painted transparent pages, placed between the two-page spreads, show cross sections or reverse views of the colorful illustrations. Also, because informational books are primarily about people, places, events, and ideas, writers increasingly use a narrative framework to convey information—much as I have by writing with the first-person point of view in this textbook.

Informational books may present straightforward information about their subjects, either through a single-subject treatment such as *Lightning!* (Hopping 1999) or in a potpourri such as *Poisonous Creatures* (Andrews 1990). However, some authors treat their subjects, such as the ecology issue, from a particular slant or viewpoint. "Issue books" in science present interesting or relevant phenomena, topics, or trends in relation to developments that pose a threat to our world; an example is *Monteverde: Science and Scientists in a Costa Rican Cloud Forest* (Collard 1997). Rather than trying to persuade readers, exemplary issue books present data directly, so readers can make up their own minds about issues. This can encourage children's belief in their abilities to effect positive change in the world (Collard 1998).

Issue books are not restricted to scientific topics such as the environment. According to Tunnell (1992), "children's trade books present history from varying perspectives and invite discussion that leads to making judgments about issues of morality. The conflicting information found in various trade books can have a positive effect on children's attention, curiosity, and interest" (p. 245).

In order to promote and recognize excellence in the field of nonfiction writing for children, the National Council of Teachers of English established the *Orbis Pictus Award* in 1989. The annual award honors the most outstanding nonfiction (informational and biography) trade books published each year in the United States. The award was named in commemoration of the book *Orbis Pictus* by Johann Comenius, which was first published in 1657 and is considered the first informational book written specifically for children.

Other nonfiction awards include the *Boston Globe/Horn Book Award,* the *Carter B. Woodson Book Award,* the *Children's Book Guild Nonfiction Award,* the *Christopher Awards,* the *Eva L. Gordon Award* for children's science literature, and the *Robert F. Silbert Informational Book Award.* Sometimes an award a book has received will be printed on the book's cover or jacket. In other cases you will need to look at the back cover or on the jacket flaps for a listing of any awards presented to the book's author.

Enhancing Curriculum with Informational Books

Content area textbooks, such as science and social studies, are usually much too difficult for the majority of children in the intended grade level to read independently. This is a result of the books' specialized vocabulary and unfamiliar content, as well as readers' lack of experience reading expository text. Additionally, many textbooks bore children with their dull tones and arid writing. In contrast, the tone of informational books is often exciting, and these books often provide more interesting details and descriptions than textbooks. Children's informational books can supplement and even substitute for traditional textbooks because they strongly support content area learning. Informational books support children's learning across the curriculum. Following are some of the many benefits children can gain from reading informational books:

- Children experience authentic learning as they investigate their own questions and topics of interest.
- Children inquire and solve problems.
- Children see connections and interrelationships among content and concepts.
- Children's critical thinking skills are fostered as they compare and contrast books on the same topic, noting author's various points of view and what information is included (or omitted).
- Children learn about faraway places, past times, and new ideas and concepts.
- Children begin to view the world as changing and evolving.
- Children acquire new vocabulary and broader background knowledge.
- Children develop critical reading skills for comprehending all nonfiction text structures.

Some educators believe that as a result of these benefits, students perform better on standardized tests, which are increasingly used to measure and compare the performance of students, teachers, schools, school districts, and state education systems. Higher standardized test scores can benefit students by increasing their opportunities for placement in advanced classes, scholarships, and entrance to universities. Also, many large companies screen applicants through standardized tests, so a good test-taking ability could result in more career options.

Unlike textbooks, which are written on a single reading level for a particular grade, informational books on many topics are written on a variety of levels, for beginning through advanced readers. "When you have a variety of trade books available, children can select books they are comfortable reading and can focus their attention on learning new content area material" (Freeman & Person 1998, p. xiii). Offering informational books is an important way to help children read independently and acquire and apply knowledge in our ever changing world.

Many educators teach through thematic units that explore a topic in an interconnected way via the various language arts of listening, speaking, reading, writing, viewing, and dramatizing. Instead of organizing instruction around subject areas such as math, science, or geography, a thematic unit is organized around a theme or topic, such as the ocean or mammals. Thematic instruction encourages inquiry through active participation, and it promotes higher-level thinking because it stresses conceptual learning and integration of knowledge. Literature can support the content and concepts targeted in thematic units. Trade books can be read aloud by the teacher or independently by children. Children can consult trade books for reference as they seek answers to questions and investigate topics. The books also serve as models for children's own expository writing across the curriculum.

Many teachers introduce a unit of study by reading aloud from an informational book. This serves to stimulate interest and activate the children's prior knowledge of the topic as well as building schemata for new knowledge. Often this process includes identifying specialized vocabulary to define and post on a bulletin board. It is not necessary to read an entire book to your students. You can choose the sections you think will interest and inform them best. Or you can give a two-minute book talk on each of several books, showing the cover and one or two illustrations and telling students what the book is about. The books can then be placed in the reading center for children to select during reading time. Likewise, children should not be required to finish each book they start. They will find some too difficult or too easy (or too dull). They need an opportunity to browse through several books to find the ones that answer their questions on an appropriate reading level (Grolier 1995).

Contemporary informational books are not only for research and curriculum enhancement. Like other trade books, they are intended for pleasure reading. Their attractive formats, reasonable lengths, and interesting topics are inviting to young readers—but only if children are made aware that these books exist. That is the responsibility of parents, teachers, and librarians. To get you started in selecting informational books for your children, Box 11.1 lists some of the most popular topics along with the Dewey decimal call numbers where books can be found. I suggest you post this list of topics and let children select one or two favorite topics to investigate on their next trip to the library.

Building a Foundation for Content Area Reading

Around the fourth grade, many children who previously had no reading difficulties begin to lag behind in their comprehension of textbooks. This occurs because after third grade, children are increasingly required to engage in independent reading of textbooks and other nonfiction material. If children reach the intermediate grades unfamiliar with both the content of textbooks and the frameworks of expository text, reading difficulties can result (Gillet & Temple 1986). To help protect your children from this pitfall, I suggest you regularly expose them to nonfiction books after they reach first grade.

Nonfiction (expository) text differs vastly from fictional text. All fiction stories follow the highly predictable story structure (characters, setting, problem, goal, events, and resolution). Experienced readers can predict what will happen next in a story based on other stories they have read and even their own life experiences. However, nonfiction is written in a variety of text structures—none of which are very

Box 11.1

Popular Juvenile Nonfiction Topics

Adoption J362.73
Africa J916
Airplanes J629.13
Animals (pets) J636
Animals (wild) J591–599
Arithmetic J510–J513
Armed forces J355
Artists J709, 759, 927.5
Baseball J796.357
Basketball J796.323
Bible stories J220.95
Bigfoot J599.8
Birds J598.2
Black history J325–326
Boats J623.82
Butterflies J595.78
Canada J917.1
Cars J629.2
Cartoons J741.5
Cats J636.8
China J915.1
Civil War J973.73
Coins J737.4
Computers J651.8
Cooking J641.5
Costumes J391
Crime J364
Dancing J793.3
Death J128.5
Dinosaurs J568.1
Disease J610, J616
Divorce J301.428
Dogs J636.7
Drawing J741.4
Drugs J616.863
Egyptians J913.32
Electricity J537
Europe J914
Explorers J910.9, J923.9

Firefighters J363.2, J614.84
Fish J597, J639.34
Fishing J799.1
Flags J929.9
Football J796.332
Foreign languages J400s
Fossils J560
Games J790
GoKart racing J796.76
Government J301
Greece J913.38
Guns J623.44
Gymnastics J796.41
Hamsters J636.9
Health J610.9
Holidays J394.26
Horses J636.1
Human body J612
Insects J595.7
Inventions J608–609
Japan J915.2
Jokes J398.6
Karate J796.815
Kites J796.15
Knights J940.1
Light and sound J534–535
Magic J793.8
Magnets J537–538
Maps J912
Math J510
Mexico J917.2
Monsters J791.4309
Motorcycles J629.227
Mummies J393.0932, J913.32
Musical instruments J781.91
Musicians J780.91, J927.8
Native Americans J970.1
Parties J793
Photography J770

Planets J523.4
Plants J581
Police J363.2
Presidents J923.1
Puppets J791.43
Reproduction J612.6
Revolutionary War J973.3
Riddles J398.6, J793.7
Robots J629.8
Rocks J552
Romans J913.37
Science projects J507.2
Scouting J369.4
Seashells J594
Sharks J597.31
Sign language J419
Slavery J326.973
Snakes J598.12
Soccer J796.334
Solar energy J333.7, J621.87
Songs J784
South America J918
Space shuttle J629.4
Stamps J769.56
Stars J523
States of the U.S. J917.3
Swimming J797.2
Tennis J796.342
Tornadoes J551.55
Trains J385.1, J625.1
Trees J582.16
Trucks J626.22
UFOs J629.134
U.S. history J973
Volcanoes J551.21
Weapons J355
Weather J551.5
Whales J599.5
World War II J940.5

predictable. Text structures can be thought of as organizational patterns for arranging and connecting ideas in expository text (Freeman & Person 1998). When both the text structure and the topic are unfamiliar, children are unable to relate the new knowledge to their existing schemata, and their comprehension is minimal. Children learn story structure by listening to, reading, and writing stories, so it makes sense that they will learn expository text structures by the same means—listening to, reading, and writing expository text. Therefore, it is *critical* for parents and educators to include nonfiction in their reading time with primary-grade children.

Following are descriptions and examples of the six most common **nonfiction text structures.**

1. **Description:** The text describes the topic by listing characteristics, as in *Dinosaurs Alive!* by Dinamation (1992).
2. **Chronology** presents events in the order in which they happened, as in *The Day We Walked on the Moon* by George Sullivan (1990).
3. **Explanation** provides causes, effects, or reasons for various phenomena and events, as in *Earthquakes* by Franklyn M. Branley (1990).
4. **Comparison/contrast:** The author compares and contrasts two things (such as events, concepts, organisms, or phenomena), as in *A Whale Is Not a Fish and Other Animal Mix-Ups* by Melvin Berger (1995).
5. **Definition:** The text gives examples, as in *My Five Senses* by Aliki (1989).
6. **Problem/solution:** The author identifies a problem and its causes, then delineates a solution, as in *Questions and Answers about Bees* by Betty Polisar Reigot (1995).

Graphic Organizers

Graphic organizers help children learn more effectively by letting them categorize information visually. Organizers serve as linkages among topics and subtopics in a book or chapter, and this helps children organize their new knowledge into existing schemata (Grolier 1995). The character and story maps presented in Chapter 9 are graphic organizers for fiction books; similarly, graphic organizers exist for nonfiction.

One of the best graphic organizers for nonfiction is the **KWL chart.** The letters stand for Know, Want to know, and Learned. The KWL activity can be done individually or with the whole class. On the board or chart paper, draw three columns, and label them "What I Know," "What I Want to Know," and "What I Learned." See Figure 11.1 for an example on *Frogs* (Gibbons 1993). The steps are easy to follow:

- First, before reading a nonfiction book, ask children to brainstorm what they already know about the subject, and write the items in the first column, "What I Know."
- Second, ask them to form several questions about the subject, and write these in the second column, "What I Want to Know."
- Third, after reading the book, ask children to tell you the answers to their questions, and write them in the third column, "What I Learned."

FROGS		
What I Know	**What I Want to Know**	**What I Learned**
• They are amphibians. • They live in water. • They swim and hop. • If you touch one, you get warts. [*No, the book did not say this was true.*]	• What do they eat? • How long do they live? • What do baby frogs look like? • Where do frogs go in the winter? • Are toads frogs?	• Tadpoles eat algae, and frogs eat insects and worms. • They live several years. • Tadpoles look like fish and swim underwater. • They hibernate underground • No, toads live on land. • Some frogs have poison glands in their skin. • Snakes, rats, and birds eat frogs.

What Else I Want to Know:

• Can poisonous frogs harm people and pets?

• How do frogs breathe when they hibernate underground?

• What are the different colors of frogs?

FIGURE 11.1   KWL Chart for *Frogs* (Gibbons 1993)

- Next, add additional information children say they learned from the book in the third column, "What I Learned."
- Last, check the items in the first column, "What I Know," to see if there were any misconceptions and make corrections as necessary.
- Extend the activity by asking children to identify and list any questions from the second column, "What I Want to Know," that were not answered in the book. At the bottom add a new section, "What Else I Want to Know," and list new questions they thought of while reading the book. Encourage children to do further reading on the topic to find answers to their new questions.

Examples of other graphic organizers for informational books are depicted in Figures 11.2 through 11.5.

- **Spider maps** (Figure 11.2) are useful for books on a single topic with attributes that can be categorized.
- **Cycle maps** (Figure 11.3) lend themselves to science topics that have a cyclical nature, such as the life cycle.

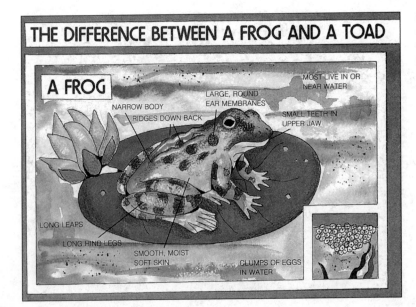

How a frog differs from a toad. From *Frogs,* written and illustrated by Gail Gibbons.

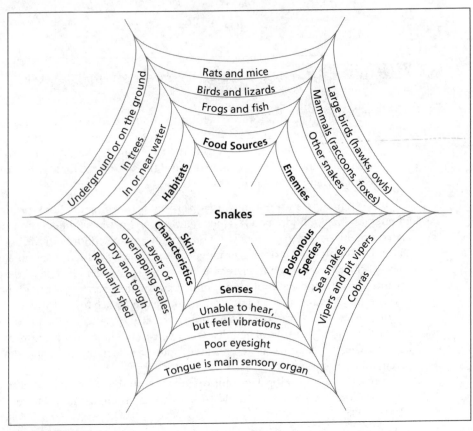

Spider Map for *Take a Look at Snakes* (Maestro 1992)

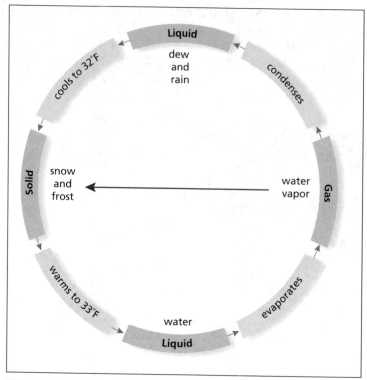

FIGURE 11.3 Cycle Map for *A Drop of Water* (Wick 1997)

- Timelines (Figure 11.4) are helpful for books on historical topics.
- **Venn diagrams** (Figure 11.5) can be used to compare and contrast two things. One circle is devoted to each of the two items. The different attributes are written in the left and right circles, and the shared attributes are written in the center where the two circles overlap.

It is essential to start graphic organizers *before* reading the book (or near the beginning) and have children add to the organizer *during* the reading. Displaying a completed organizer before reading will not actively engage children in the book. Asking children to complete an organizer independently after finishing the book constitutes a test of their memories, rather than a learning experience. However, completing an organizer with children while (and immediately after) reading a book gives them a purpose for listening as they actively anticipate the next bit of information to add to the organizer. Children's comprehension is greatly enhanced when they see the information visually unfold. They do not have to tax their memories in order to see how all the information is interrelated, and they can more easily develop new schemata on the topic.

A teacher may develop a graphic organizer with the whole class or a small group. Once children become comfortable with a strategy such as the KWL, they can com-

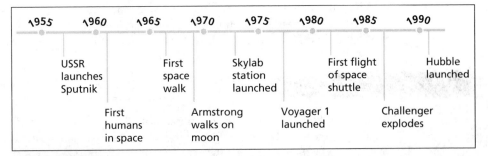

FIGURE 11.4 Timeline of Space Exploration for *The Day We Walked on the Moon* (Sullivan 1990)

plete it individually with their self-selected books. Organizers are also very useful when children are gathering information for writing reports.

In addition to completing graphic organizers, discussion helps children recall, synthesize, and summarize new knowledge. Discussion also assists in the reflection process that needs to accompany the reading of all genres, including informational books. Some sample discussion questions follow:

- What information did you enjoy reading about the most?
- What new information do you plan to share with someone else?
- Which photograph or illustration was the most interesting? Why?

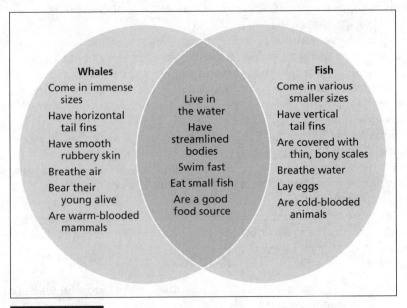

FIGURE 11.5 Venn Diagram for *A Whale Is Not a Fish* (Berger 1995)

- What else would you like to find out about this topic?
- What questions would you like to ask the author?
- What did you learn that can help you in school? Outside of school?

Informational Stories

As I have remarked throughout this textbook, not all literature books fall neatly into one and only one genre. There are many good books, such as *The Great Kapok Tree: A Tale of the Amazon Rain Forest* (Cherry 1990), that inform readers yet have some of the elements of fiction books—for example, characters, dialogue, and fantasy elements. However, the purpose of fiction books is to entertain, rather than to inform readers. Books in which the primary purpose is to inform but which contain some of the entertaining elements of fiction are called **informational stories.**

Informational stories often attract readers who otherwise pass up informational books for storybooks. Informational stories can be very useful for presenting facts and concepts to readers. However, because they are written in the familiar story structure, they will not help less experienced readers make the transition to expository text, but they can serve to introduce younger children to the genre of informational books.

Perhaps the best known informational storybooks are the Magic School Bus series by Joanna Cole. One of my favorites is *The Magic School Bus in the Time of the Dinosaurs* (1994). All the books in this series involve the eccentric Ms. Frizzle, who takes her class of elementary students on field trips in a school bus with fantastic capabilities. It can do things such as transport the students back in time, miniaturize students to the size of microbes, fly in outer space, drill through the core of the earth, and submerge underwater.

Cole's books have three levels of text. First, there is the story narrative, which contains some character dialogue. Second, there are speech bubbles that convey both humor and information through the dialogue of the children. Third, the pages are bordered with notes, charts, and labeled diagrams that convey most of the facts on the book's topic. At the end of each book, the author delineates which parts of the book were fantasy.

The Magic School Bus books were so popular that Scholastic produced an animated TV series based on them. However, following the animation of Cole's books, other authors wrote episodes for the series, and these were later made into books that carry the Magic School Bus logo. I make this distinction because Cole is a well-respected author of traditional informational books (e.g., *How You Were Born*, 1993), and her books in the original Magic School Bus series are superior to the ones written later by the production company's writers. Therefore, look for Cole's name as *author* on the title page.

Following is a list of informational stories children enjoy.

Brown, Laurie Krasny, & Marc Brown. **Dinosaurs to the Rescue! A Guide to Protecting Our Planet.** Joy Street, 1992.

————. *When Dinosaurs Die: A Guide to Understanding Death.* Little, Brown, 1996.

Cherry, Lynne. *The Great Kapok Tree: A Tale of the Amazon Rain Forest.* Harcourt Brace Jovanovich, 1990.

————. *A River Ran Wild: An Environmental History.* Harcourt Brace, 1992.

Cole, Joanna. *The Magic School Bus in the Time of the Dinosaurs.* Illus. Bruce Degen. Scholastic, 1994.

————. *The Magic School Bus and the Electric Field Trip.* Illus. Bruce Degen. Scholastic, 1997.

Cushman, Doug. *Mouse & Mole and the Year-Round Garden.* W. H. Freeman, 1994.

Gelman, Rita Golden. *Body Detectives: A Book about the Five Senses.* Illus. Elroy Freem. Scholastic, 1994.

Gomi, Taro. *Everyone Poops.* Kane/Miller, 1993.

Jones, Kathryn. *Happy Birthday Dr. King!* Illus. Floyd Cooper, 1994.

Leedy, Loreen. *Fraction Action.* Holiday House, 1994.

Pinkney, Andrea Davis. *Seven Candles for Kwanzaa.* Illus. Brian Pinkney. Dial, 1995.

▌ RECOMMENDED INFORMATIONAL BOOKS

GENERAL

- Aliki. *Communication.* Greenwillow, 1993.

- Berger, Gilda. *Celebrate! Stories of the Jewish Holidays.* Illus. Peter Catalanotto. Scholastic, 1998.

- Brimner, Larry Dane. *E-Mail.* Children's Book Press, 1997.

- Cohen, Daniel. *The Alien Files: Conspiracy.* Scholastic, 1998.

- Cone, Molly. *Come Back, Salmon: How a Group of Dedicated Kids Adopted Pigeon Creek and Brought It Back to Life.* Illus. Sidnee Wheelwright. Sierra Club Books, 1992.

- Husain, Shahrukh. *What Do We Know about Islam?* Illus. Celia Hart. Peter Bedrick Books, 1996.

- Osborne, Mary Pope. *One World, Many Religions: The Way We Worship.* Knopf, 1996.

- Schwartz, Cherie Karo. *My Lucky Dreidel: Hanukkah Stories, Songs, Poems, Crafts, Recipes, and Fun for Kids.* Illus. Wendy Edelson and Jonathan Gross. Smithmark, 1994.

MATHEMATICS

- Cushman, Jean. *Do You Wanna Bet? Your Chance to Find Out about Probability.* Illus. Martha Weston. Clarion, 1991.

- Murphy, Stuart J. *A Pair of Socks: Matching.* Illus. Lois Ehlert. HarperCollins, 1996.

- ————. *Give Me Half!* Illus. G. Brian Karas. Harper, 1996.

- ————. *Get Up and Go! Time Lines.* Illus. Diane Greenseid. Harper, 1996.

- Pluckrose, Henry. *Math Counts: Capacity.* Watts, 1994.

- Sachar, Louis. *More Sideways Arithmetic from Wayside School.* Scholastic, 1994.
- Scieszka, Jon. *Math Curse.* Illus. Lane Smith. Viking, 1995.

ANIMALS

- Andrews, Julia L. *Poisonous Creatures.* Trumpet Club, 1990.
- Arnold, Caroline. *Cats: In from the Wild.* Illus. Richard Hewett. Carolrhoda, 1993.
- Berger, Melvin. *A Whale Is Not a Fish and Other Animal Mix-Ups.* Illus. Marshall Peck. Scholastic, 1995.
- Berger, Melvin, & Gilda Berger. *Do Whales Have Belly Buttons? Questions and Answers about Whales and Dolphins.* Illus. Higgins Bond. Scholastic, 1999.
- Bourgoing, Pascale de. *Under the Ground.* Illus. Daniele Bour. Cartwheel, 1990.
- Brandenburg, Jim. *To the Top of the World: Adventures with Arctic Wolves.* Walker, 1993.
- Brooks, Bruce. *Making Sense: Animal Perception and Communication.* Farrar, Straus & Giroux, 1993.
- Cole, Joanna. *My Puppy Is Born.* Illus. Margaret Miller. Morrow, 1991.
- ———. *My New Kitten.* Illus. Margaret Miller. Morrow, 1995.
- Collard, Sneed B. *Animal Dads.* Illus. Steve Jenkins. Houghton Mifflin, 1997.
- Dewey, Jennifer. *Wildlife Rescue: The Work of Dr. Kathleen Ramsey.* Illus. Don MacCarter. Boyds Mill Press, 1994.
- Dinamation. *Dinosaurs Alive!* Campbell Books, 1992.
- Durant, Penny Raife. *Exploring the World of Animals.* Illus. Nancy Woodman. Franklin Watts, 1995.
- Gibbons, Gail. *Frogs.* Holiday House, 1993.
- Goodall, Jane. *With Love: Ten Heartwarming Stories of Chimpanzees in the Wild.* Illus. Alan Marks. North-South Books, 1994.
- Lauber, Patricia. *The News about Dinosaurs.* Simon & Schuster, 1989.
- Maestro, Betsy. *Take a Look at Snakes.* Illus. Giulio Maestro. Scholastic, 1992.
- Maynard, Christopher. *Incredible Little Monsters.* Snapshot, 1994.
- Patent, Dorothy Henshaw. *Dogs: The Wolf Within.* Illus. William Muñoz. Carolrhoda, 1993.
- ———. *Eagles of America.* Illus. William Muñoz. Holiday House, 1995.
- ———. *Why Mammals Have Fur.* Illus. William Muñoz. Cobblehill, 1995.
- Pringle, Laurence P. *Batman: Exploring the World of Bats.* Illus. Merlin Tuttle. Scholastic, 1991.
- ———. *Dolphin Man: Exploring the World of Dolphins.* Illus. Randall S. Wells. Atheneum, 1995.
- ———. *An Extraordinary Life: The Story of a Monarch Butterfly.* Illus. Bob Marstall. Orchard, 1997.
- Reigot, Betty Polisar. *Questions and Answers about Bees.* Scholastic, 1995.

- Smith, Roland. *Journey of the Red Wolf.* Penguin, 1996.

NATURAL SCIENCES

- Allen, Marjorie N., & Shelley Rotner. *Changes.* Silver Burdett Ginn, 1991.
- Armbruster, Ann, & Elizabeth A. Taylor. *Tornadoes.* Franklin Watts, 1989.
- Arnold, Caroline. *El Niño: Stormy Weather for People and Wildlife.* Clarion, 1998.
- Branley, Franklyn M. *Earthquakes.* Illus. Richard Rosenblum. HarperCollins, 1990.
- Collard, Sneed B. *Monteverde: Science and Scientists in a Costa Rican Cloud Forest.* Franklin Watts, 1997.
- Hopping, Lorraine Jean. *Hurricanes!* Illus. Jody Wheeler. Scholastic, 1995.
- ———. *Lightning!* Illus. Jody Wheeler. Scholastic, 1999.
- Landau, Elaine. *Endangered Plants.* First Book, 1992.
- Lasky, Kathryn. *The Most Beautiful Roof in the World: Exploring the Rainforest Canopy.* Illus. Christopher G. Knight. Gulliver, 1997.
- Patent, Dorothy Henshaw. *Fire: Friend or Foe.* Illus. William Muñoz. Clarion, 1998.
- Patent, Dorothy Henshaw. *Biodiversity.* Illus. William Muñoz. Clarion, 1996.
- Rowe, Julian, & Molly Perham. *Amazing Magnets.* Children's Book Press, 1994.
- Schwarz, Alice. *Wind and Weather.* Scholastic, 1994.
- Wick, Walter. *A Drop of Water.* Scholastic, 1997.

APPLIED SCIENCES AND TECHNOLOGY

- Burleigh, Robert. *Flight: The Journey of Charles Lindbergh.* Illus. Mike Wimmer. Philomel, 1991.
- Cobb, Vicki, & Kathy Darling. *Bet You Can! Science Possibilities to Fool You.* Illus. Stella Ormai. Avon, 1989.
- ———. *Wanna Bet? Science Challenges to Fool You.* Illus. Meredith Johnson. Lothrop Lee & Shepard, 1993.
- Haskins, Jim. *Black Eagles: African Americans in Aviation.* Scholastic, 1995.
- Jones, Charlotte Foltz. *Accidents May Happen: Fifty Inventions Discovered by Mistake.* Illus. John O'Brien. Delacorte, 1996.
- Lauber, Patricia. *Seeing Earth from Space.* Orchard, 1990.
- Sullivan, George. *The Day We Walked on the Moon.* Scholastic, 1990.

HEALTH

- Aronson, Virginia. *How to Say No* [to drugs]. Chelsea House, 1999.
- Aliki. *My Five Senses.* HarperCollins, 1989.
- Cole, Joanna. *How You Were Born.* Illus. Margaret Miller. Morrow, 1993.
- Goffe, Toni. *No Smoking.* Child's Play, 1992.
- Haughton, Emma. *A Right to Smoke?* Franklin Watts, 1997.

- Nilsson, Lennart. *How Was I Born?* Illus. Lena Katarina Swanberg. Dell, 1993.
- Pringle, Laurence. *Drinking: A Risky Business.* Morrow, 1997.

SPORTS AND RECREATION

- Macy, Sue. *A Photohistory of American Women in Sports.* Henry Holt, 1996.
- McKissack, Patricia C., & Fredrick McKissack Jr. *Black Diamond: The Story of the Negro Baseball Leagues.* Scholastic, 1994.
- Umansky, Diane L. *On a Roll!* Parachute Press, 1991.
- Wyler, Rose, & Gerald Ames. *Magic Secrets.* Illus. Arthur Dorros. Harper & Row, 1990.

HISTORY AND GEOGRAPHY

- Arnold, Caroline. *The Ancient Cliff Dwellers of Mesa Verde.* Illus. Richard Hewett. Clarion, 1992.
- ————. *Stories in Stone: Rock Art Pictures by Early Americans.* Illus. Richard Hewett. Clarion, 1996.
- Ashabranner, Brent. *Always to Remember: The Story of the Vietnam Veterans Memorial.* Illus. Jennifer Ashabranner. Putnam, 1988.
- Beller, Susan Provost. *Never Were Men So Brave: The Irish Brigade during the Civil War.* Simon & Schuster, 1998.
- Blumberg, Rhoda. *Full Steam Ahead: The Race to Build a Transcontinental Railroad.* National Geographic, 1996.
- Bradley, Catherine. *Life in the Mountains: Animals, People, Plants.* Scholastic, 1991.
- Chang, Ina. *A Separate Battle: Women and the Civil War.* Lodestar, 1991.
- Colman, Penny. *Rosie the Riveter: Women Working on the Home Front in World War II.* Crown, 1995.
- Curlee, Lynn. *Into the Ice: The Story of Arctic Exploration.* Houghton Mifflin, 1998.
- Dash, Joan. *We Shall Not Be Moved: The Women's Factory Strike of 1909.* Scholastic, 1996.
- Delafosse, Claude. *Castles.* Illus. Claude Millet & D. Millet. Cartwheel, 1993.
- ————. *Pyramids.* Illus. Philippe Biard. Cartwheel, 1994.
- Ekoomiak, Normee. *Arctic Memories.* Henry Holt, 1990.
- Feldman, George, & Linda Schmittroth. *Understanding the Holocaust.* UXL, 1998.
- Folsom, Franklin, & Alfonso Ortiz. *Red Power on the Rio Grande: The Native American Revolution.* Council for Indian Education, 1989.
- Freedman, Russell. *Immigrant Kids.* Dutton, 1980.
- ————. *Children of the Wild West.* Clarion, 1983.
- ————. *Buffalo Hunt.* Holiday House, 1988.
- ————. *Kids at Work: Lewis Hine and the Crusade against Child Labor.* Clarion, 1994.
- George, Jean Craighead. *The First Thanksgiving.* Illus. Thomas Locker. Paper Star, 1996.
- Hamanaka, Sheila. *The Journey: Japanese Americans, Racism, and Renewal.* Orchard, 1990.

- Hamilton, Virginia. *Many Thousand Gone: African Americans from Slavery to Freedom.* Illus. Leo D. Dillon & Diane Dillon. Knopf, 1993.
- Hoobler, Dorothy, & Thomas Hoobler. *The Italian American Family Album.* Oxford University Press, 1994.
- Jakobsen, Kathy. *My New York.* Little, Brown, 1993.
- Lamb, Nancy. *One April Morning: Children Remember the Oklahoma City Bombing.* Illus. Floyd Cooper. Lothrop Lee & Shepard, 1996.
- Lester, Julius. *From Slave Ship to Freedom Road.* Illus. Rod Brown. Dial, 1998.
- Levinson, Nancy Smiler. *If You Lived in the Alaska Territory*. Illus. Bryn Barnard. Scholastic, 1998.
- Liestman, Vicki. *Columbus Day.* Illus. Rick Hanson. Carolrhoda, 1991.
- McKissack, Patricia, & Fredrick McKissack. *The Civil Rights Movement in America from 1865 to the Present.* Children's Book Press, 1991.
- ———. *Christmas in the Big House, Christmas in the Quarters.* Illus. John Thompson. Scholastic, 1994.
- Millard, Anne. *Pyramids.* Kingfisher, 1996.
- Murdoch, David. *Tutankhamen: The Life and Death of a Pharaoh.* Illus. Chris Forsey. DK, 1998.
- Murphy, Jim. *Across America on an Emigrant Train.* Clarion, 1993.
- ———. *The Great Fire.* Scholastic, 1995.
- Myers, Walter Dean. *Now Is Your Time: The African-American Struggle for Freedom.* HarperCollins, 1992.
- Peters, Russell. *Regalia: American Indian Dress and Dance.* Illus. Richard Haynes. Sundance, 1994.
- Rosenberg, Maxine B. *Hiding to Survive: Stories of Jewish Children Rescued from the Holocaust.* Clarion, 1994.
- Shalant, Phyllis. *Look What We've Brought You from Mexico.* Illus. Patricia Wynne. Julian Messner, 1992.
- Sneve, Virginia Driving Hawk. *The Sioux: A First Americans Book.* Illus. Ronald Himler. Holiday House, 1993.
- Stanley, Jerry. *Children of the Dust Bowl: The True Story of the School at Weedpatch Camp.* Crown, 1992.
- Stein, R. Conrad. *The Trail of Tears.* Children's Book Press, 1993.
- Sullivan, George. *The Day the Women Got the Vote.* Scholastic, 1994.
- ———. *Facts and Fun about the Presidents.* Scholastic, 1994.
- Swanson, Diane. *Safari beneath the Sea: The Wonder World of the North Pacific Coast.* Sierra Club Books, 1996.
- Wolf, Bernard. *Cuba: After the Revolution.* Dutton, 1999.
- Zeinert, Karen. *The Amistad Slave Revolt and American Abolition.* Linnet, 1977.

KEY TERMS

 Explore the E-Glossary at **www.ablongman.com/anderson**

expository language (p. 286)
graphic organizer (p. 291)
informational book (p. 284)
informational story (p. 296)
institutional publisher (p. 285)
KWL chart (p. 291)

nonfiction text structures (p. 291)
reference book (p. 285)
textbook (p. 284)
trade book (p. 285)
Venn diagram (p. 294)

The Moon of Popping Trees.

Thirteen Moons on Turtle's Back Written by Joseph Bruchac and Jonathan London and illustrated by Thomas Locker.

chapter

12

Poetry and Verse

> *Verse:* A composition having strong rhythm and a rhyming pattern
>
> *Poetry:* Verse in which word images are selected and expressed to create powerful, often beautiful impressions (may or may not rhyme)

Poetry is multifaceted; it can tell a story, describe something in a fresh and novel way, make a comment on humanity, draw a parallel to aspects of your life, or make you laugh. It can also flash a sharp image to your mind, delight your ear, or make you experience strong emotions. Reading poetry allows you to view the world through a new lens. Amazingly, poetry does all this while using far fewer words than any other form of writing. Another unique aspect of poetry is that although most people (above primary grades) will read a book only once, children as well as adults love to hear their favorite poems again and again. Perhaps this is because poets are able to take the feelings that are inside all of us and put them into meaningful words.

For many children the traditional Mother Goose rhymes are their first exposure to verse. Dr. Seuss's rhyming text is also a common introduction to verse for the very young. Note that I did not call these works poetry, for there is an important distinction. Verse is any composition that has a strong rhythm and a rhyming pattern. Because of its uniqueness, poetry is not so easily defined. Indeed, it is a class of text in itself. If a piece of writing is not poetry, it is considered **prose**. All the other genres we have studied so far—fiction and nonfiction—are prose. This classification makes it easy to recognize what is *not* poetry, but it does not define what poetry is. It is difficult to define because it has many forms and can mean something different to each person. Also, drawing the line between verse and poetry is difficult.

Although poetry is verse, certainly not all verse is considered poetry, which is the more sophisticated form of the two. Cullinan (1989) called poetry the distilled language that captures the essence of an idea or experience, appealing to the ear as well as the mind and emotions. In order for poetry to appeal to the ear, you must read it aloud. Beatrice Schenk de Regniers explained,

> To my mind, a poem is not completed until it is read aloud . . . it seems to me that the full power of a poem—the jazzy rhythms, the lyrical cadence, the dance of language, the sheer pleasure of fooling around with sound and meaning—can be fully appreciated only if the poem is read aloud. This would be particularly true for children. (1988, p. xvii)

So, unless you are sitting in class while you read this chapter, I suggest you read each poem aloud as you come to it in order to experience the full effect of the rhythm and rhyme.

Evaluating Poetry and Verse

The following questions can guide you as you select poetry.

- Is the poem appealing to children?
- Is the poem free from didacticism, sentimentality, and patronizing language?
- Does the rhyme scheme sound natural?
- Will children be able to understand and appreciate any figurative language, such as similes and metaphors?
- Does the poem help the listener view the topic in a new way?

Characteristics of Poetry and Verse

Rhythm and Rhyme

Verse must contain **rhythm.** If you are knowledgeable about music, think of rhythm in language as the same as *meter* in music. For the rest of us, rhythm is the pattern of stressed and unstressed syllables in a line that gives poetry its beat or tempo. Read aloud the following limerick line, and listen for the stressed syllables, which are in boldface type. (I divided the two-syllable word.)

There **was** an old **man** from Pe – **ru.**

In the classic limerick, the rhythm is highly structured. Using a dash for unstressed syllables and a slash for stressed syllables, the pattern for this line is

– / – – / – – /

Verses also have a rhyming pattern. Probably everyone knows what rhyme is, although few people know how to define it. Children will tell you it means "words that sound alike." However, the words *two, too,* and *to* sound alike, but are not considered rhymes because each word represents the exact same combination of sounds. These words are **homophones,** words that are pronounced the same but have different meanings, such as *blue* and *blew.*

A **rhyme** is made up of two or more words with the same *ending sounds* (containing at least one vowel sound) but different beginning sounds. In verse, rhymes most frequently appear at the end of lines. The ends of rhyming words need not be spelled alike, as you can see from the following verse.

What is a word that rhymes with blue?
I think it could be either new or canoe.

Now, can you complete this one?

What is a word that rhymes with orange?
I think it could be either _____.

(Not all words have rhymes.)

Sometimes a writer will exercise **poetic license,** which is a deviation from conventional form to achieve a desired effect. In the following example, the writer added some syllables to achieve the rhyme scheme.

There was an old man from Florida,
Whose sight was simply horrid-a.
    While crossing the street,
    He was knocked off his feet.
And now the poor man is no more-ida.

Language

Compare a page of poetry with a page of prose, and you will see there is more white space—areas without print—on a page of poetry. (See "Saucy Little Ocelot" that follows.) The lines do not run flush with the right margin, and there is extra space between groups of lines. Many poets use space creatively. For example, a poet could have only one or two words per line. This is more than a visual effect; it also adds to the meaning of the poem. Additionally, poets use punctuation differently than authors of prose, and this too can enhance the meaning of a poem.

The language of poetry is both condensed and distilled—compacted and purified. The essence of the subject is captured in a few words that cause the reader to recall memories or experience strong reactions. Good poetry contains no extraneous words. Each word contributes to the total effect of the rhythm, rhyme, and message that readers experience. I have heard that the renowned poet, Eve Merriam, once said that a poem is like a can of frozen juice—add three cans of water and you get prose.

Part of the impact of poetry is created by the poet's extensive use of **figurative language** to create imagery in the mind of the reader. Poets use comparisons to vividly describe a thing, emotion, or experience. A **simile** is a comparison of two things that are unlike, and it typically uses the connective words *like* or *as*—for example "hands *as* cold *as* ice" and "legs *like* steel rods." A **metaphor** is a comparison that is implied through analogy by stating that one thing *is* another, for example "her eyes *were* bright diamonds." Images can also be developed through **personification,** which is the representation of animals, ideas, and things as having human qualities, for example, "I heard the wind call my name." These are some of the ways poets use words to create mental images.

Sound patterns make listening to poetry enjoyable. **Alliteration** is the repetition of initial consonant sounds in neighboring words or stressed syllables. Listen for the /s/ sound (spelled with both *s* and *c*) in the title "Sarah Cynthia Sylvia Stout Would Not Take the Garbage Out" (Silverstein 1974b). **Assonance** is the repetition of vowel sounds within words. Listen for the short /o/ sound in the title "Saucy Little Ocelot" (Prelutsky 1982). Prelutsky repeats this sound throughout the poem. His use of assonance, alliteration, rhyme, and a fast tempo make listening to this poem enjoyable. (I recommend you practice reading it aloud a few times before reading it to a group of children.)

[handwritten: — striped t. — wildcat]

Saucy Little Ocelot

Saucy little ocelot *[handwritten: — repition of words]*
    ocelot
        ocelot
You like to turn and toss a lot
    toss a lot
        ocelot
You often fret and fuss a lot
    fuss a lot
        ocelot
Speckled, spotted
    polka-dotted
Saucy little ocelot

[handwritten: ✓ sound / ✓ technique / ✓ well crafted / ✓ funny]

Saucy little ocelot
    ocelot
        ocelot
You're often mean and cross a lot
    cross a lot
        ocelot
You want to be the boss a lot
    boss a lot
        ocelot
Bossy, brassy
    cross and sassy
Saucy little ocelot

Forms of Poetry

Poetry appears in clearly discernible forms that are determined by their **stanzas,** groups of lines in a poem with an identifiable pattern of rhyme or rhythm (or both). Some forms that are commonly found in books of poetry for children follow.

Narrative poems tell a story, usually with setting, characters, events, and climax. Because of this, they are most frequently long poems. One common rhyming scheme for a stanza is A B C B, with each letter representing a line of poetry; lines represented by the same letters rhyme. In the following two stanzas from the beginning of *The Night before Christmas* attributed to Clement C. Moore (1849), lines two and four rhyme.

'Twas the night before Christmas,   A
    when all through the house   B
Not a creature was stirring,   C
    not even a mouse.   B

[handwritten: Pattern]

The stockings were hung   A
    by the chimney with care,   B
In hopes that St. Nicholas   C
    soon would be there.   B

Books
Splash
Flicker Flash

The fun is looking
at the visuals
good to read alone.

The snake lay coiled like a lasso, waiting to loop some unsuspecting prey.

FIGURE 12.1 Concrete Poem

Limericks are humorous five-line verses with a rhyming scheme of A A B B A. They are thought to have originated in the city of Limerick, Ireland, and were first popularized in print by Edward Lear in *A Book of Nonsense* (1846). Limericks are highly structured, typically with a syllable count of 8, 8, 6, 6, 8. Count the syllables in each line of the verse that follows.

There was an old man from Peru	A
Who dreamed he was eating his shoe.	A
He awoke in the night	B
In a terrible fright	B
And found it was perfectly true!	A

Pattern

In **concrete poems,** words are arranged to form a pictorial representation of the subject. Concrete poems are not written in stanzas, and they may or may not rhyme. They are fun to read but challenging to write, because the poet must select a subject that can easily be made into a recognizable shape. See Figure 12.1 for an example.

Lyric poems focus on a single experience, describing the feeling of a moment. They come in a multitude of stanza forms. Much contemporary poetry for children is lyrical. A good example is the following poem by Oliver Herford (Rogasky 1994, p. 12).

I Heard a Bird Sing
I heard a bird sing
In the dark of December
A magical thing
And sweet to remember:
"We are nearer to Spring
Than we were in September,"
I heard a bird sing
In the dark of December.

 Literature Activity: **Pattern Verse**

On each two-page spread of Nancy Van Laan's *A Mouse Is in My House* (1990), a young boy likens himself to different animals. Children can extend this book by selecting an additional animal and using Van Laan's scheme.

A mouse is in my house,
and it's small, gray, and furry
There's a mouse in my house,
and it acts like me.

It climbs and it wriggles
as it nibbles and it giggles.
There's a mouse in my house,
only I can see.

1 A _____ is in my house,	(name of animal)
2 and it's _____, _____, and _____.	(three adjectives)
3 There's a _____ in my house,	(animal in line 1)
4 and it acts like me.	
5 It _____ and it _____	(two present-tense verbs)
6 as it _____ and it _____.	(two present-tense verbs; rhymes with line 5)
7 There's a _____ in my house,	(animal in line 1)
8 only I can see. ■	

If you have helped children write poetry, you know they often concentrate on rhyme and give little attention to meter or conveying a message. What they end up with is not poetry at all, but silly verses that are not very cohesive. For example, once I asked children to write a poem about their pet or another favorite animal. One girl wrote the following verse.

I had a dog
whose name was Spot.
Once he ran around the tree all day,
and he got very, very hot.

Well, it has two rhyming words, but the meter is uneven and the message is nonexistent, especially in view of the fact that the girl had a cat named Muffin but could not think of anything to rhyme with that name.

Removing the necessity of rhyme allows poets more freedom in capturing beautiful or interesting messages in their words.

Free verse can be either rhymed or unrhymed. It is called "free" because it has irregular rhythmic patterns and line lengths. Poets who write in this style aim to recreate the free rhythms of natural speech. The following poem by Langston Hughes (1994, p. 6) is written in free verse.

April Rain Song
Let the rain kiss you.
Let the rain beat upon your head with silver liquid drops.
Let the rain sing you a lullaby.

The rain makes still pools on the sidewalk.
The rain makes running pools in the gutter.

The rain plays a little sleep-song on our roof at night—
And I love the rain.

Karen Hesse used free verse to write her acclaimed novel, *Out of the Dust* (1997). Each poem is a journal entry by the protagonist, who narrates a moving story of loss and hope during the Great Depression in the Oklahoma Dust Bowl.

Almost Rain
It almost rained Saturday.
The clouds hung low over the farm.
The air felt thick.
It smelled like rain.
In town,
the sidewalks
got damp.
That was all.
November 1934 (p. 88)

Haiku is a Japanese form of poetry that consists of seventeen syllables arranged in three lines of five, seven, and five syllables. In the true Japanese style, the subject is something in nature. However, many American haiku are about other subjects. The following haiku is by Mary Ann Hoberman (de Regniers 1988, p. 129).

Fireflies
Fireflies at twilight
In search of one another
Twinkle off and on.

 Literature Activity: **Poem Mobiles**

Select a favorite poem that consists of three to five stanzas. After writing the poem on construction paper, cut the stanzas apart and suspend them from a mobile made of a coat hanger and yarn. Stanzas should be hung at the appropriate length, so they can be read in order from top to bottom. Add illustrations of the poem, and suspend the mobile from the ceiling. ■

Poetry in Our Culture

After you graduated from traditional nursery rhymes, did you have the opportunity to read any of the classics of children's poetry? Several generations of children and adults have enjoyed the timeless poetry in the following list. If you missed these books as a child, I encourage you to read them now, so you can select classic poems for your children to enjoy.

- Robert Browning's *The Pied Piper of Hamelin* (1842/1999)
- Clement C. Moore's [attributed] *The Night Before Christmas* (1849/1999) (See Box 12.1)

Box 12.1

An Accusation of Literary Fraud

Don Foster, an English professor and scholar of authorial attribution at Vassar College, rocked the literary world in 2000 with his announcement that Henry Livingston Jr. wrote the beloved poem, "The Night Before Christmas"—*not* Clement C. Moore, who took credit for the poem some 150 years ago. Foster published this conclusion as part of his book, *Author Unknown: On the Trail of Anonymous*, in which he recounted his early work as a literary sleuth who identified well-known authors of works that had been published anonymously. Foster also recounted his work in "literary forensics," describing his assistance to numerous police forces and even the FBI on high-profile crimes whose evidence included an anonymous piece of writing, such as a ransom note.

"The Night Before Christmas," which is one of the most widely read poems in the world, has been credited with creating the American image of Santa Claus and shaping the modern celebration of Christmas in the United States. It was first published anonymously in 1823 as "An Account of a Visit from St. Nicholas" in *The Troy Sentinel*. In those days publishing in newspapers was considered beneath an educated gentleman (especially something like a "frivolous" poem). Therefore, it was not unusual for gentlemen who wished to publish in a newspaper to ask that their names be withheld.

After Livingston's death, "A Visit" was reprinted throughout the country and gained great popularity. In 1844 Clement C. Moore took credit for the poem and included it in a collection of his typical solemn verses. Livingston's family pointed out the error, but their protests were ignored for many decades.

Responding to a plea from one of Livingston's descendents, Foster conducted a thorough analysis of the famous poem and determined its tone and style are starkly at odds with the body of Moore's other poems, which have a moralizing and pious tone. Foster described Moore as something of a Grinch—a stern parent whose other works often focused on the annoying noise of children, and whose interpretation of Christmas included castigating naughty children. Additionally, Moore was staunchly against tobacco, but in "A Visit," St. Nicholas enjoys a pipe.

Perhaps Moore's biggest blunder occurred while he was writing out the poem by hand. Following an error introduced in a later printing of the poem, Moore misstated the names of Santa's last two reindeer. Instead of writing the original poem's names of "Dunder" and "Blixem" (which are Dutch-American words for thunder and lightening), he wrote the names as "Donder" and "Blitzen," which have stuck to this day.

Armed with a litany of stylistic evidence, Foster concluded that "A Visit" closely matches the views and verse of Henry Livingston Jr., a gentleman-poet of Dutch descent (thus the Dutch reindeer names). Every Christmas, Livingston wrote verses with the distinctive anapestic meter (accenting every third syllable), which is employed in the famous poem. Additionally, his works include mention of Lapland reindeer and images of chariots being pulled through the sky by flying horses or goats.

For more information about Don Foster's evidence, read "Literary Sleuth Casts Doubt on the Authorship of an Iconic Christmas Poem" by David D. Kirkpatrick in the October 26, 2000, issue of *The New York Times* (accessible through the LEXIS-NEXIS Academic Universe database at large libraries).

- Henry Wadsworth Longfellow's *Paul Revere's Ride* (1863/1996)
- Kate Greenaway's *Under the Window* (1879/1985)
- Robert Louis Stevenson's *A Child's Garden of Verses* (1885/1999)
- Alfred Noyes's *The Highwayman* (1906/1999)
- A. A. Milne's *When We Were Very Young* (1924/1988) and *Now We Are Six* (1927/1988)

Poetry is an integral part of our culture, and we can hear and read it in places other than books of poetry. For example, have you considered that most songs are poetry set to music? In Peter Spier's *The Star-Spangled Banner* (1973), you can thoughtfully read the words of this beautiful poem. For children (and adults) who do not know what the words mean, Spier's detailed, colorful illustrations bring them to life.

And the rocket's red glare,
    the bombs bursting in air,
Gave proof through the night
    that our flag was still there.

Some ancient scripture is poetry and may have originally been sung. *The Song of Three Holy Children* (Baynes 1986) is from the Apocrypha. This joyous hymn of praise was sung by Shadrach, Meshach, and Abednego, young Jewish captives in Babylon who refused to worship King Nebuchadnezzar's idol.

O ye Children of Men, bless the Lord:
    praise him, and magnify him for ever.
O let Israel bless the Lord:
    praise him, and magnify him for ever.

Speeches can also be poetic. Perhaps the most beautiful and powerful poetic speech is that of Dr. Martin Luther King Jr., given in Washington, D.C., on August 28, 1963, to an interracial crowd of more than 250,000 people. Scholastic's edition of this speech, titled *I Have a Dream* (1997), is illustrated by fifteen artists who have won the Coretta Scott King Award or Honor—among them Ashley Bryan, Floyd Cooper, Leo and Diane Dillon, Jan Spivey Gilchrist, Brian Pinkney, James Ransome, and Kathleen Atkins Wilson. Throughout his speech, King conveyed strong imagery with his use of metaphors and figures of speech.

NCTE Award for Excellence in Poetry for Children

In 1977 the National Council of Teachers of English (NCTE) established an award titled Excellence in Poetry for Children. The award was given annually from 1977 to 1982, and since 1982 has been given every three years, to honor the lifetime contribution to children's poetry of a living U.S. poet. Winners include Arnold Adoff, John Ciardi, Barbara Juster Esbensen, Eloise Greenfield, X. J. Kennedy, Karla Kuskin, Myra Cohn Livingston, David McCord, Eve Merriam, Lilian Moore, and Valerie Worth.

The spirits of Equality and Justice accompany Dr. King. From *I Have a Dream,* written by Dr. Martin Luther King, Jr., and illustrated by Leo and Diane Dillon.

Developing Love (or Hate) for Poetry

Most young children love poetry. Even when they are too young to understand the words, they will listen to nursery rhymes because they delight in the sounds and rhythm. Often children will reread favorite poems until they have memorized them. With a little encouragement, young children begin to create their own poems. However, by the middle grades, many children begin to lose interest in poetry or even develop a strong dislike for it. Why does this happen?

Ways to Teach Kids to Hate Poetry

For several years I have asked my adult students if they developed a dislike for poetry as they grew older. Those who said they did supplied me with the following prescription for turning children off poetry:

- Read children sentimental poems that you think are wonderful.

- Make them all memorize the same poem, and then make each kid recite it in front of the class.
- Assign the children to write poems, and then make each child read his or her poem to the entire class.
- Assign the kids to write poems, grade them, and display *all* of them on the bulletin board.
- Tediously analyze the scheme of each poem read.
- Discuss a poem until everyone in the class gets the same meaning as you.
- Spend a whole month teaching haiku.

Did any of you experience these teaching methods when you were a child? I did, and it had the same effect on me as it did on some of my students; so I hope you do *not* follow any of these negative examples.

Ways to Encourage Kids to Love Poetry

Here are several ways to ensure that children continue to love poetry as they get older.

- Keep in mind that children have different tastes in poetry, and allow them to help you select the poems to share with the class. (Generally, avoid overly sentimental or abstract poems, which appeal more to adults.)
- Ask children to recite favorite poems that they have memorized. (Even then, they should be allowed to have the poem written on a card in case they get nervous and forget.)
- Encourage volunteers to share poetry they have written, and post poems only with children's permission.
- Ask children to respond to poetry, but avoid picking each line apart, which kills the listener's enjoyment.
- Occasionally analyze a component of a poem to demonstrate the poet's techniques, but avoid analyzing each stanza of each poem, which becomes drudgery.
- Allow listeners to express their own interpretations because a poem will mean something a little different to each listener.
- Share poetry regularly in small measures. Brief daily or weekly experiences with poetry are preferable to a monthlong unit, which makes children weary of the topic.
- Keep a variety of poetry books available at all times.

Have you ever thought of encouraging reluctant readers to read poetry? It is an excellent genre for children who have limited reading ability, or who simply do not like to read. The minimal amount of print on each page of poetry is not as overwhelming as a page of prose. Poet Janet S. Wong explains that "when they look at a poem of mine, a short poem, they see all that white space around it, and it's not intimidating. It doesn't scare them. They look at it and say, 'That's only ten lines. I can read that' " (Yokota & Sanderson 2000, p. 58). Wong tells of a thirteen-year-old girl who read one of her books of poetry in an hour. The girl's grandmother said it was the first time she had ever read a whole book.

In selecting poems for all children, look for those that involve a universal experience or message, written both on the emotional level and on the intellectual level of the listeners. As for the forms of poetry, children often say they prefer poems that rhyme; in particular, they like limericks, narrative poems, and lyric poems that are funny or about familiar experiences. It has been my experience that their least popular forms of poetry are unrhymed poems and haiku, as well as poems that are overly sentimental or abstract.

A list of books that children might enjoy follows.

LIMERICKS

- Ciardi, John. *The Hopeful Trout and Other Limericks.* Illus. Susan Meddaugh. Houghton Mifflin, 1992.
- Jacobs, Frank (ed.). *Loony Limericks.* Dover, 1999.
- Kennedy, X. J. *Uncle Switch: Loony Limericks.* Illus. John O'Brien. Simon & Schuster, 1997.
- Lear, Edward. *A Book of Nonsense.* Everyman's Library, 1846/1992.
- Lobel, Arnold. *The Book of Pigericks.* Harper, 1983.
- Livingston, Myra Cohn (ed.). *Lots of Limericks.* Illus. Rebecca Perry. Simon & Schuster, 1991.

NARRATIVE POETRY

- Baylor, Byrd. *The Table Where Rich People Sit.* Illus. Peter Parnall. Scribner, 1994.
- Browning, Robert. *The Pied Piper of Hamelin.* Illus. Bud Peen. Harry N. Abrams, 1842/1999.
- Clifton, Lucille. *Everett Anderson's Goodbye.* Illus. Ann Grifalconi. Henry Holt, 1989.
- Denarski, Diane Taylor. *Ozark Story-Poems.* August House, 1981.
- Harrison, Michael (ed.). *The Oxford Book of Story Poems.* Oxford University Press, 1990.
- Hesse, Karen. *Out of the Dust.* Scholastic, 1997.
- Kurtz, Jane. *River Friendly, River Wild.* Illus. Neil Brennan. Simon & Schuster, 2000.
- Longfellow, Henry Wadsworth. *Paul Revere's Ride.* Illus. Ted Rand. Puffin, 1983/1996.
- Moore, Clement C. [attributed] *The Night before Christmas.* Illus. Ted Rand. North-South Books, 1849/1999.
- Noyes, Alfred. *The Highwayman.* Illus. Charles Keeping. Oxford University Press, 1906/1999.

HUMOROUS POETRY AND VERSE

- Cole, William (ed.). *Poem Stew.* Illus. Karen Ann Weinhaus. Harper & Row, 1981.
- Dakos, Kalli. *If You're Not Here, Please Raise Your Hand.* Illus. G. Brian Karas. Simon & Schuster, 1990.
- ———. *Don't Read This Book, Whatever You Do!* Illus. G. Brian Karas. Simon & Schuster, 1993.

- Hopkins, Lee Bennett (ed.). ***Good Books, Good Times!*** Illus. Harvey Stevenson. Harper-Collins, 1990.
- Larrick, Nancy (ed.). ***Piping Down the Valleys Wild: A Merry Mix of Verse for All Ages.*** Illus. Ellen Raskin. Yearling, 1999
- Lear, Edward. ***The Owl and the Pussy-Cat.*** Illus. Ian Beck. Atheneum, 1996.
- Lee, Dennis. ***Dinosaur Dinner (with a Slice of Alligator Pie).*** Illus. Debbie Tilley. Alfred A. Knopf, 1997.
- Lesynski, Loris. ***Dirty Dog Boogie.*** Annick, 1999.
- Most, Bernard. ***Four & Twenty Dinosaurs.*** HarperCollins, 1990.
- Nash, Ogden. ***The Adventures of Isabel.*** Illus. James Marshall. Little, Brown, 1994.
- Prelutsky, Jack. ***The Sheriff of Rottenshot.*** Illus. Victoria Chess. Greenwillow, 1982.
- ———. ***The New Kid on the Block.*** Illus. James Stevenson. Greenwillow, 1984.
- ———. ***Something Big Has Been Here.*** Illus. James Stevenson. Greenwillow, 1990.
- ———. ***The Dragons Are Singing Tonight.*** Illus. Peter Sis. Greenwillow, 1993.
- ———. ***The Gargoyle on the Roof.*** Illus. Peter Sis. Greenwillow, 1999.
- Shields, Carol Diggory. ***Lunch Money and Other Poems about School.*** Illus. Paul Meisel. Dutton, 1995.
- Shortsleeve, Kevin. ***13 Monsters Who Should Be Avoided.*** Illus. Michael Austin. Peachtree, 1998.
- Silverstein, Shel. ***A Light in the Attic.*** Harper & Row, 1974a.
- ———. ***Where the Sidewalk Ends.*** HarperCollins, 1974b.
- ———. ***A Giraffe and a Half.*** HarperCollins, 1975.
- ———. ***Falling Up.*** HarperCollins, 1996.

Surely one of the best loved authors of humorous verse for children is the versatile Shel Silverstein—poet, author, illustrator, and song lyricist. His poems have been described as "mischievous and charmingly tasteless." Some adults believe his work is unsuitable for children, claiming much of it is risqué or presents poor role models. However, this has not prevented children of several generations from reading his books and loving the way he makes them laugh. I find his work clever and uproariously funny. Read the poem that follows—which I selected because it has been attacked by some parents and educators—and make your own judgment.

> **They've Put a Brassiere on the Camel**
> They've put a brassiere on the camel,
> She wasn't dressed proper, you know.
> They've put a brassiere on the camel
> So that her humps wouldn't show.
> And they're making other respectable plans,
> They're even insisting the pigs should wear pants,
> They'll dress up the ducks if we give them the chance
> Since they've put a brassiere on the camel.

They've put a brassiere on the camel,
They claim she's more decent this way.
They've put a brassiere on the camel,
The camel had nothing to say.
They squeezed her into it, I'll never know how,
They say that she looks more respectable now,
Lord knows what they've got in mind for the cow,
Since they've put a brassiere on the camel. (Silverstein 1974a, p. 166)

 ## Responding to Literature

Evaluating Poetry

Read one of the poems for which Shel Silverstein's books have been banned from some schools, such as "Prayer of the Selfish Child" (1974a, p. 15) or "Something Missing" (1974a, p. 26). What do you think parents might find objectionable about the poem? How do you think children might react to the poem?

No discussion of humorous verse can be complete without Jack Prelutsky, whose several collections contain a multitude of verses that tickle your funny bone. His work has been well received by children, parents, and educators. The following poem was written after Prelutsky returned from the grocery store; after viewing the packages of boneless chicken, he began wondering where they came from.

Ballad of a Boneless Chicken
I'm a basic boneless chicken,
yes, I have no bones inside,
I'm without a trace of rib cage,
yet I hold myself with pride,
other hens appear offended
by my total lack of bones,
they discuss me impolitely
in derogatory tones.

I am absolutely boneless,
I am boneless through and through,
I have neither neck nor thighbones,
and my back is boneless too,
and I haven't got a wishbone,
not a bone within my breast,
so I rarely care to travel
from the comfort of my nest.

I have feathers fine and fluffy,
I have lovely little wings,
but I lack the superstructure
to support these splendid things.

Since a chicken finds it tricky
to parade on boneless legs,
I stick closely to the hen house,
laying little scrambled eggs. (Prelutsky 1984, pp. 116–117)

TYPES OF POETRY BOOKS

SINGLE-POEM BOOKS

Some books contain only one poem, which may or may not be a narrative poem. The poem may be from a previously published collection, or it may be written specially as the text of a picture book. Often these books are found in the picture book section of the library. The following list contains some recommended single-poem books.

- Adoff, Arnold. *Black Is Brown Is Tan.* Illus. Emily Arnold McCully. HarperCollins, 1973.
- Baylor, Byrd. *Hawk, I'm Your Brother.* Illus. Peter Parnall. Scribner, 1976.
- ———. *The Way to Start a Day.* Illus. Peter Parnall. Scribner, 1978.
- Baynes, Pauline. *The Song of Three Holy Children.* Henry Holt, 1986.
- Carlstrom, Nancy White. *Northern Lullaby.* Illus. Leo D. Dillon & Diane Dillon. Philomel, 1992.
- Frasier, Debra. *On the Day You Were Born.* Harcourt Brace, 1991.
- Hale, Sara Josepha. *Mary Had a Little Lamb.* Illus. Tomie dePaola. Holiday House, 1984.
- Hesse, Karen. *Come on Rain!* Illus. Jon J. Muth. Scholastic, 1999.
- King, Martin Luther Jr. *I Have a Dream.* Illus. Ashley Bryan et al. Scholastic, 1997.
- Lindbergh, Reeve. *Grandfather's Lovesong.* Illus. Rachel Isadora. Viking Penguin, 1993.
- ———. *What Is the Sun?* Illus. Stephen Lambert. Walker, 1994.
- Myers, Walter Dean. *Harlem.* Illus. Christopher Myers. Scholastic, 1997.
- Nash, Ogden. *The Tale of Custard the Dragon.* Illus. Lynn Munsinger. Little, Brown, 1998.
- Oppenheim, Joanne. *Have You Seen Trees?* Illus. Jean Tseng & Mou-sien Tseng. Scholastic, 1995.
- Osofsky, Audrey. *Dreamcatcher.* Illus. Ed Young. Orchard, 1992.
- Spier, Peter. *The Star-Spangled Banner.* Doubleday, 1973.
- Van Laan, Nancy. *A Mouse Is in My House.* Illus. Marjorie Priceman. Knopf, 1990.
- Willard, Nancy. *The Tale I Told Sasha.* Illus. David Christiana. Little, Brown, 1999.

COLLECTIONS OF POETRY

When one poet publishes several poems in one book, it is called a **poetry collection.** The following list contains some recommended poetry collections.

- Adoff, Arnold. *In for Winter, Out for Spring.* Illus. Jerry Pinkney. Harcourt Brace, 1991.
- ———. *Street Music: City Poems.* Illus. Karen Barbour. HarperCollins, 1995.
- ———. *Love Letters.* Illus. Lisa Desimini. Scholastic, 1997.

- ———. *The Basket Counts.* Illus. Michael Weaver. Simon & Schuster, 2000.
- ———. *Touch the Poem.* Illus. Lisa Desimini. Blue Sky Press, 2000.
- Alarcon, Francisco X. *Laughing Tomatoes and Other Spring Poems.* Illus. Maya Christina Gonzalez. Children's Book Press, 1997.
- ———. *From the Bellybutton of the Moon and Other Summer Poems.* Illus. Maya Christina Gonzalez. Children's Book Press, 1999.
- Begay, Shonto. *Navajo: Visions and Voices across the Mesa.* Scholastic, 1995.
- Bruchac, Joseph, & Jonathan London. *Thirteen Moons on Turtle's Back.* Illus. Thomas Locker. Philomel, 1992.
- Bryan, Ashley. *Sing to the Sun.* Harper, 1996.
- dePaola, Tomie. *Songs of the Fog Maiden.* Holiday House, 1979.
- Dunbar, Paul Laurence. *Jump Back, Honey.* Illus. Ashley Bryan et al. Hyperion Books, 1999.
- Esbensen, Barbara Juster. *Words with Wrinkled Knees: Animal Poems.* Boyds Mills, 1998.
- Fleischman, Paul. *Joyful Noise: Poems for Two Voices.* Illus. Eric Beddows. Harper & Row, 1988.
- ———. *Big Talk: Poems for Four Voices.* Illus. Beppe Giacobbe. Candlewick, 2000.
- George, Kristine O'Connell. *The Great Frog Race and Other Poems.* Illus. Kate Kiesler. Clarion, 1997.
- Greenaway, Kate. *Under the Window: Pictures and Rhymes for Children.* Octopus, 1879/1985.
- Greenfield, Eloise. *Honey, I Love and Other Love Poems.* Illus. Diane and Leo Dillon. HarperCollins, 1978.
- ———. *Nathaniel Talking.* Illus. Jan Spivey Gilchrist. Black Butterfly, 1988.
- Grimes, Nikki. *Meet Danitra Brown.* Illus. Floyd Cooper. Lothrop Lee & Shepard, 1994.
- ———. *Aneesa Lee and the Weaver's Gift.* Illus. Ashley Bryan. Lothrop Lee & Shepard, 1999.
- ———. *My Man Blue.* Illus. Jerome Lagarrigue. Dial, 1999.
- ———. *Stepping Out with Grandma Mac.* Simon & Schuster, 2000.
- Harter, Penny. *Shadow Play: Night Haiku.* Illus. Jeffrey Greene. Simon & Schuster, 1994.
- Herrera, Juan Felipe. *Laughing Out Loud, I Fly: Poems in English and Spanish.* Illus. Karen Barbour. HarperCollins, 1999.
- Hughes, Langston. *The Dream Keeper and Other Poems.* Illus. Brian Pinkney. Knopf, 1994.
- ———. *The Block.* Illus. Romare Bearden. Viking, 1995.
- ———. *Carol of the Brown King: Nativity Poems.* Illus. Ashley Bryan. Atheneum, 1998.
- ———. *The Sweet and Sour Animal Book.* Illus. Harlem School of the Arts. Oxford University Press, 1997.
- Katz, Bobbi. *Poems for Small Friends.* Illus. Gyo Fujikawa. Random House, 1989.
- Kennedy, X. J. *Drat These Brats.* Illus. James Watts. Simon & Schuster, 1993.

- ———. *Elympics: Poems.* Illus. Percy Graham. Philomel, 1999.
- Kuskin, Karla. *The Sky Is Always in the Sky.* Illus. Isabelle Dervaux. HarperCollins, 1998.
- Livingston, Myra Cohn. *Flights of Fancy and Other Poems.* Simon & Schuster, 1994.
- Lobel, Arnold. *Whiskers and Rhymes.* Greenwillow, 1987.
- McCord, David. *Every Time I Climb a Tree.* Little, Brown, 1999.
- Merriam, Eve. *Higgle Wiggle: Happy Rhymes.* Illus. Hans Wilhelm. Morrow, 1994.
- ———. *Blackberry Ink.* Illus. Hans Wilhelm. Mulberry, 1994.
- ———. *You Be Good & I'll Be Night: Jump on the Bed Poems.* Illus. Karen Lee Schmidt. Mulberry, 1996.
- Milne, A. A. *When We Were Very Young.* Illus. Ernest H. Shepard. Dutton, 1924/1988.
- ———. *Now We Are Six.* Illus. Ernest H. Shepard. Dutton, 1927/1988.
- Moore, Lilian. *Poems Have Roots: New Poems.* Illus. Tad Hills. Atheneum, 1997.
- Mora, Pat. *Confetti: Poems for Children.* Illus. Enrique O. Sanchez. Lee & Low, 1996.
- ———. *This Big Sky.* Illus. Steve Jenkins. Scholastic, 1998.
- Nash, Ogden. *Ogden Nash's Zoo.* Illus. Etienne Delessert. Stewart Tabori & Chang, 1987.
- O'Neill, Mary. *Hailstones and Halibut Bones.* Illus. John Wallner. Doubleday, 1989.
- Oram, Hiawyn. *Out of the Blue: Poems about Color.* Illus. David McKee. Hyperion, 1993.
- Pomerantz, Charlotte. *Halfway to Your House.* Illus. Gabrielle Vincent. Greenwillow, 1993.
- Quattlebaum, Mary. *A Year on My Street.* Illus. Cat Bowman Smith. Delacorte, 1996.
- Sandburg, Carl. *Poems for Children Nowhere Near Old Enough to Vote.* Illus. Istvan Banyai. Knopf, 1999.
- Shannon, George. *Spring: A Haiku Story.* Illus. Malcah Zeldis. Greenwillow, 1996.
- Shertl, Alice. *I Am the Cat.* Illus. Mark Buehner. Lothrop Lee & Shepard, 1999.
- Soto, Gary. *A Fire in My Hands.* Illus. James M. Cardillo. Scholastic, 1990.
- ———. *Neighborhood Odes.* Illus. David Diaz. Harcourt Brace, 1992.
- ———. *Canto Familiar.* Illus. Annika Nelson. Harcourt Brace, 1995.
- Steig, Jeanne. *Alpha Beta Chowder.* Illus. William Steig. HarperCollins, 1992.
- Stevenson, Robert Louis. *A Child's Garden of Verses.* Illus. Tasha Tudor. Simon & Schuster, 1885/1999.
- Thomas, Joyce Carol. *Brown Honey in Broomwheat Tea.* Illus. Floyd Cooper, HarperCollins, 1993.
- Willard, Nancy. *A Visit to William Blake's Inn.* Illus. Alice Provensen & Martin Provensen. Harcourt Brace, 1981.
- Wong, Janet S. *Good Luck Gold and Other Poems.* Simon & Schuster, 1994.
- ———. *A Suitcase of Seaweed and Other Poems.* Simon & Schuster, 1996.
- ———. *The Rainbow Hand: Poems About Mothers and Children.* Simon & Schuster, 1999.

- ———. *Night Garden: Poems from the World of Dreams.* Illus. Julie Paschkis. Simon & Schuster, 2000.
- Worth, Valerie. *All the Small Poems and Fourteen More.* Illus. Natalie Babbitt. Farrar, Straus & Giroux, 1994.
- Yolen, Jane. *Animal Fare: Poems.* Illus. Janet Street. Harcourt Brace, 1994.
- ———. *O, Jerusalem: Voices of a Sacred City.* Illus. John Thompson. Scholastic, 1996.
- ———. *Sea Watch: A Book of Poetry.* Illus. Ted Lewin. Philomel, 1996.

POETRY ANTHOLOGIES

When someone selects poems by a number of different poets and publishes them in one book, it is called a **poetry anthology.** Often poetry anthologies are themed, with all the poems dealing with a certain topic, such as a season or animals. The person who selects the poems for inclusion in the book is called the **anthologist,** and her or his name appears in the place of an author. Anthologists do more than just pick out some poems for a book. They must carefully select poems that will complement the others and yet are diverse. This becomes even more challenging when the book has a specific theme. Once the poems are selected and permissions to reproduce are obtained, the anthologist must then decide the order in which the poems will appear. Some recommended anthologies follow.

- Adoff, Arnold (ed.). *My Black Me: A Beginning Book of Black Poetry.* Dutton, 1974.
- Alexander, Martha (ed.). *Poems and Prayers for the Very Young.* Illus. Martha Alexander. Random House, 1973.
- de Regniers, Beatrice Schenk (ed.). *Sing a Song of Popcorn: Every Child's Book of Poems.* Illus. Marcia Brown et al. Scholastic, 1988.
- Dunning, Stephen (ed.). *Reflections on a Gift of Watermelon Pickle.* Lothrop Lee & Shepard, 1988.
- Frank, Josette (ed.). *Poems to Read to the Very Young.* Illus. Dagmar Wilson. Random House, 1977.
- Harrison, Michael (ed.). *The Oxford Treasury of Christmas Poems.* Oxford University Press, 1999.
- Harrison, Michael & Christopher Stuart-Clark (eds.). *One Hundred Years of Poetry for Children.* Oxford University Press, 1999.
- Hopkins, Lee Bennett (ed.). *Hand in Hand: An American History Through Poetry.* Illus. Peter M. Fiore. Simon & Schuster, 1994.
- Huang, Tze-Si (ed.). *In the Eyes of the Cat: Japanese Poetry for All Seasons.* Illus. Demi. Henry Holt, 1994.
- Hudson, Wade (ed.). *Pass It On: African-American Poetry for Children.* Illus. Floyd Cooper. Scholastic, 1993.
- Larrick, Nancy (ed.). *Cats Are Cats.* Illus. Ed Young. Philomel, 1988.
- Livingston, Myra Cohn (ed.). *Flights of Fancy and Other Poems.* Simon & Schuster, 1994.
- ———. *Call Down the Moon: Poems of Music.* Simon & Schuster, 1995.

- ———. *Festivals.* Illus. Leonard Everett Fisher. Holiday House, 1996.

- ———. *Cricket Never Does: A Collection of Haiku and Tanka.* Illus. Kees de Kiefte. Simon & Schuster 1997.

- Nye, Naomi Shihab (ed.). *This Same Sky: A Collection of Poems from Around the World.* Simon & Schuster, 1992.

- ———. (ed.). *Salting the Ocean: 100 Poems by Young Poets.* Illus. Ashley Bryan. Greenwillow Books, 2000.

- Phillip, Neil (ed.). *The New Oxford Book of Children's Verse.* Oxford University Press, 1985.

- Prelutsky, Jack (ed.). *The Random House Book of Poetry for Children.* Illus. Arnold Lobel. Random House, 1983.

- ———. *The 20th Century Children's Poetry Treasury.* Illus. Meilo So. Knopf, 1999.

- Rogasky, Barbara (ed.). *Winter Poems.* Illus. Trina Schart Hyman. Scholastic, 1994.

- Taylor, Alice (ed.). *A Child's Treasury of Irish Rhymes.* Illus. Nicola Emoe. Barefoot Books, 1999.

- Yolen, Jane (ed.). *Alphabestiary: Animal Poems from A to Z.* Illus. Allan Eitzen. Boyds Mills, 1995.

- ———. *Mother Earth Father Sky.* Illus. Jennifer Hewitson. Boyds Mills, 1996.

KEY TERMS

 Explore the E-Glossary at **www.ablongman.com/anderson**

alliteration (p. 306)
anthologist (p. 321)
assonance (p. 306)
concrete poem (p. 308)
figurative language (p. 306)
free verse (p. 309)
haiku (p. 310)
homophone (p. 305)
limerick (p. 308)
lyric poem (p. 308)
metaphor (p. 306)
narrative poem (p. 307)

personification (p. 306)
poetic license (p. 306)
poetry (p. 304)
poetry collection (p. 318)
poetry anthology (p. 321)
prose (p. 304)
rhyme (p. 305)
rhythm (p. 305)
simile (p. 306)
stanza (p. 307)
verse (p. 304)
white space (p. 306)

Bud sets out to find his father.

Bud, Not Buddy
Written by
Christopher Paul
Curtis and illustrated
by Trish P. Watts.

BUD, NOT BUDDY

Masters of the New Jazz

HERMAN E. ...WAY

CHRISTOPHER PAUL CURTIS
author of *The Watsons Go to Birmingham—1963*

chapter

13

Tying It Together

If you have been reading children's books along with this textbook, you should now be quite knowledgeable about children's literature. What can you do with your knowledge—besides sharing with others the excitement and beauty of books? I have talked about how historical fiction, biography, and informational books can give a much-needed transfusion to the study of history, and how informational books can be used to teach and learn about virtually every subject. In this final chapter, I demonstrate how to tie together everything you know to use literature in teaching children to read.

Reading Aloud to Children

There is a positive correlation between being read to—both at home and in school—and reading achievement (Anderson, Hiebert, Scott, & Wilkinson 1985). Some of the benefits of reading to children follow:

- It stimulates and broadens children's interest in quality literature in a variety of genres.
- It allows children to experience books that are too difficult for them to read independently.
- It gives children the opportunity to hear excellent literature they might never read for themselves, such as great books with slow beginnings and books above their reading ability.
- It broadens children's background experiences, which builds their schemata.
- It introduces children to a wide range of written language, which helps them expand their vocabulary and their repertoire of sentence patterns.
- It shows children that adults enjoy reading, thereby encouraging reading as a lifetime activity.

I have stressed that children will benefit greatly if their parents read to them daily (or at least several times a week) from the time they are born until they tell you they want to read for themselves (or they want to read to *you*). Unfortunately, many parents do not read to their children. They do not have the time, or they simply do not see the need. Therefore, teachers often must supplement (or substitute for) the reading of parents throughout the elementary school years. I recommend that teachers devote a minimum of fifteen minutes a day to reading aloud from literature. This should be a regular part of the daily curriculum; it should not be used as a reward when the children finish all their work, or omitted as a punishment when they misbehave.

Select books and poems that you like and that you think will appeal to children. Fiction books should generally be fast-paced and contain well-developed characters and generous dialogue. Let children help you select the books to read aloud, making sure that all genres are represented within the school year. When reading to children, let them have a good look at the picture on the page before reading the text. Allowing children to study the illustration *before* listening to the text will encourage them to make mental predictions that will aid their comprehension and enjoyment of the book.

Questioning Guidelines

Asking children questions before, during, and after reading a book or chapter enhances their comprehension (or lets you know when they do not comprehend). Two important guidelines:

- Avoid asking questions that can be answered by *yes* or *no*. They require almost no thinking because the answer is usually phrased in the question. For example:

  Yes or no question: "Do you think Sylvester will ever make wishes with a magic pebble again?"
  Answer: No
  Divergent question: "What do you think Sylvester will do if he ever finds another magic pebble?" Possible answers: Ignore it, bury it, throw it in the lake, tell his parents

- Avoid asking only memory-level questions that can be answered by *who, what, when, where,* and *why.* These literal questions require very little thinking and give you little information about children's comprehension. For example:

  Memory-level question: "What happened when Sylvester saw the lion?"
  Answer: He got scared, so he wished he were a rock.
  Divergent question: "What could Sylvester have done to be safe from the lion?"
  Possible answers: He could wish he could fly away, wish he were invisible, wish he were a bigger lion, wish the lion would not be hungry, or wish the lion fell asleep.

The answers to higher-thinking-level questions will contain the who, what, when, where, and why of the story, but they also require the listener to move beyond the memory level. See Box 13.1 for ideas on phrasing questions that require a variety of thinking skills.

It is not necessary to ask questions in a hierarchy (i.e., from category I through category VII). What is desirable is to ask children questions that require varied thinking. For example, see the questions in Box 13.2.

Listening–Prediction Activity

When you read a fiction book to a group of children for the first time, the type of questions you ask should be different from those you ask when you are reading a nonfiction book or a familiar story. New stories lend themselves well to prediction questions. An excellent activity that will engage children in divergent thinking while they are listening to a new story is the **listening–prediction activity**. This can be done

Box 13.1

Levels of Questioning

I. Memory level

Who is . . . ?
What is . . . ?
Where was . . . ?
What did . . . ?
How many . . . ?
When did . . . ?

II. Translation level

In your own words, tell. . . .
How else might you say . . . ?
Which picture shows . . . ?
Describe. . . .
Tell how. . . .

III. Interpretation level

Compare. . . .
Tell what you think. . . .
Is . . . greater than . . . ?
Why is it called . . . ?
Explain why. . . .
What caused . . . ?
What conclusions have you reached about . . . ?

IV. Application level

When might you . . . ?
Where could you . . . ?
Which would you use if . . . ?
How will this affect . . . ?
Suggest two possible ways to. . . .

V. Analysis level

Why is . . . ?
What evidence is there that . . . ?
In what way might . . . ?
Give some instances in which. . . .
Which of these would . . . ?

VI. Synthesis level

How many ways can you think of to . . . ?
What would happen if . . . ?
Devise a plan to. . . .
How can you explain . . . ?

VII. Evaluation level

Should . . . be permitted to . . . ? Why?
Is . . . accurate? Why do you think this?
Was it wrong/right for . . . ? Why do you think so?
How well did . . . ?
What is the most important . . . ? Why?
What are the chances that . . . ?
Which of the following . . . ?

Source: DeHaven, Edna P. *Teaching and Learning the Language Arts.* Boston: Little, Brown, 1979 (pp. 112–113).

with either a picture book or a chapter in a juvenile novel; however, the book must have a predictable plot that follows the story structure of characters, setting, problem, goal, events, and resolution.

The prediction activity is effective only when the listeners have not previously heard or read the story. Therefore, after selecting a predictable book, the first step is to read the title and show the book cover or first illustration and ask, "Has anyone heard or read this book?" If several of the children are familiar with the book, select an alternate book. If only one or two have heard it, tell them, "Now, I know *you* will

Box 13.2

**Sample Questions for "The Lobster and the Crab"
from *Fables* by Arnold Lobel (1980)**

- Who is getting ready to set sail in his boat? *(memory level)*
- Compare the way the Lobster acted to the way the Crab acted during the storm. *(interpretation level)*
- Describe how the Crab felt when the boat capsized and sank. *(translation level)*
- Why is the Lobster really not afraid of the ocean? *(analysis level)*

- Was it wrong for the Lobster to let the Crab come with him when he knew the boat was full of holes? Why do you think so? *(evaluation level)*
- Suggest a possible way that they might have kept the boat from sinking. *(application level)*
- What would happen if *you* were in a boat that sank? *(synthesis level)*

know all the answers to the questions I am going to ask, so for this story, I want you to zip up your lips, and see if the other children can figure out what you already know." (Usually, those children will attentively—and smugly—listen to hear if the others give appropriate answers.)

After reading the title and showing the book cover or first illustration, engage the children in a discussion to build background schemata for understanding the topic of the story, being sure to introduce any unfamiliar words. Then, ask children to predict what *might* happen in the story. (It is important not to say, "What *will* happen in the story," because that gives kids the idea that this is a "guess-the-right-answer" activity.)

Let children record their predictions in their **literature journals** (special logs they keep to record the books they have read and their responses to the books). You may also want to write a few of their predictions on the board. After recording predictions, read a few pages of the story, and then stop and ask listeners to confirm, reject, or revise their predictions, explaining why they made their choices.

Read a few more pages, and just before something important or interesting happens, ask children to predict what *might* happen next. Ask them to justify their predictions, and listen to determine if they are logical answers. The objective is for children to make plausible predictions based on story structure, on what has happened so far in the story, and on their prior knowledge—not for them to guess the right answer.

Read a page or two until the episode occurs; then ask listeners to confirm or reject their predictions. Repeat the last two steps (no more than three times in one session). After completing the book, ask the children to predict what might happen to the characters if the author wrote a sequel.

Children have much to gain from a prediction activity. It encourages creative divergent thinking and the use of logic, while heightening curiosity and interest in stories (Temple & Gillet 1989). Box 13.3 summarizes the steps of this activity.

Box 13.3

Steps of the Listening–Prediction Activity

1. Select a predictable book children have not heard.
2. Read the title and show the book cover (or first illustration), and engage listeners in a discussion to build background.
3. Ask, "What *might* happen in this story?" Record predictions.
4. Read a few pages, and ask children to confirm, reject, or revise their predictions, explaining why.
5. Read a few more pages, and just before something important or interesting happens,

ask, "What *might* happen next?" Ask listeners to justify their predictions.
6. Read a page or two until the episode is revealed, and then ask children to confirm or reject their predictions.
7. Repeat the last two steps (no more than three times in one session).
8. After completing the book, ask, "If the author writes a sequel, what *might* happen to the characters next?"

Sustained Silent Reading

In addition to listening to you read, children need to engage in **sustained silent reading** (SSR) of literature each day. This practice should start in first grade (perhaps ten minutes a day) and continue through the elementary grades; children may read for at least thirty minutes in the upper grades. This free reading period should be over and above the time allotted to reading instruction. There should be no talking or other interruptions during this time. In some classrooms, even the teacher reads a book during SSR. Children should select their own books, but they may need some guidance and motivating from you. Asking children to complete a reading interest survey such as the one in Figure 13.1 will give you an idea of which genres each one might enjoy.

Readers mentally respond to good literature, both during and following their reading. You can encourage reflections by asking children to tell you their opinions of the books they are reading or to retell their favorite parts. Children can write a few sentences daily in their literature journals to record their thoughts. However, requiring children to answer comprehension questions or to do a book report or worksheet will quickly reduce this activity to drudgery.

Reading Instruction with Trade Books

Basal reading programs with graded sets of textbooks and workbooks are still the most common method of teaching reading in this country. However, many teachers supplement the basals with trade books—and some teachers use only trade books to teach reading. Necessary vocabulary and reading skills are taught with passages from

Name: _____

Directions: Show how you feel about each of the following items by circling the appropriate number. If you are interested only "very little," then circle the number 1. If you are interested "very much," then circle the number 5. If your interest is in between, circle 2, 3, or 4.

I like to read about . . .

		very little ☹		☺		very much ☺
A.	talking animals	1	2	3	4	5
B.	real animals	1	2	3	4	5
C.	art, music, or dance	1	2	3	4	5
D.	boys or girls my age	1	2	3	4	5
E.	funny things	1	2	3	4	5
F.	make-believe characters	1	2	3	4	5
G.	famous people	1	2	3	4	5
H.	history	1	2	3	4	5
I.	magic	1	2	3	4	5
J.	adventure	1	2	3	4	5
K.	mystery	1	2	3	4	5
L.	romance and love	1	2	3	4	5
M.	science	1	2	3	4	5
N.	science fiction and space	1	2	3	4	5
O.	sports	1	2	3	4	5
P.	war and battles	1	2	3	4	5
Q.	folktales and fairy tales	1	2	3	4	5
R.	poems	1	2	3	4	5

FIGURE 13.1   **Reading Interest Survey**

the literature book rather than with workbooks and worksheets. This is a very effective way to teach children to read. Children are more motivated to read real books than to read the excerpts from books or the stories from picture books (minus most of the pictures) that they encounter in basal readers.

Children learn to read by reading—not by completing workbooks, worksheets, board work, and textbook exercises (whether done on paper or on a computer). Money that schools often target for expensive workbooks and duplication of worksheets could be used to buy literature books. The countless hours teachers spend on grading the workbooks and worksheets and preparing board work could be spent on listening to children read and respond in genuine reading experiences. Surely this would be a better investment of both time and money.

When teachers decide to use trade books in lieu of basals, some of their first concerns are, How do I select which books to use? And how do I obtain enough copies? There are many factors to consider in selecting a literature book for reading instruction. Some of the things you should consider in reviewing prospective books are:

- quality of story
- number of pages
- amount and size of print
- difficulty of vocabulary
- sentence complexity
- concept complexity
- sophistication of content
- quality of illustrations
- age of main character

If your school does not have sufficient copies of a single book, that is not a problem. The range of reading abilities and interests in any classroom of children is vast. For example, in a class of thirty third graders, you will most likely have children whose reading abilities range from low first grade through sixth grade. Children's reading interests are just as broad. Therefore, it is often more effective to have six copies each of five different titles. This is the method used in literature circles, in which children decide on the books they will read.

Children sometimes select a book that is too difficult for them (perhaps because they want to be in the same group with a friend). However, they will soon become frustrated with a book that is beyond their reading ability. A quick way for a child to determine whether a book is too difficult is the **five-finger method**, developed by William Powell. When a child is reviewing a book to see if she or he would like to read it, have the child follow these steps:

- Open the book near the center to a page that is full text (no illustrations).
- Read the page to yourself.
- When you come to a word whose meaning you do not know, put up one finger. (Proper nouns, such as names of particular people, places, and things, do not count.)

- At the end of the page, if you have raised five or more fingers, the book is probably too difficult for independent reading.

Children's Oral Reading

As I have reinforced throughout this book, children learn to read by reading. They have very little to gain from listening to other children read aloud who are at or below their own reading level. Most children's oral reading is slow and fairly expressionless, as they are striving to say all the words correctly. This is especially true when they have not been allowed to read the passage silently first, which would have allowed them to decode most of the unfamiliar words. On top of that, many children are required to read material that is far beyond their ability.

The all-time biggest waste of instructional time in schools is when one child reads while the rest of the class (supposedly) listens! Actually, most of the other children will count paragraphs to determine which one they are going to read, so they can spend the rest of the time dreaming and scheming. Some good readers will read ahead in the book to keep from dying of boredom. They will quickly finish the story or chapter and perhaps start the next. In fact, some will even finish the whole book long before the rest of the class. However, if they are called on to read aloud and they do not know what page the teacher is on, they are scolded for not paying attention! They actually get in trouble for *reading* during reading class instead of *listening* to someone else stumble and bumble along! Can you see the ridiculous irony of this?

Individual Oral Reading

The majority of children's reading time should be spent in guided silent reading. However, teachers (but not the whole class) need to listen to each child read orally at least once a week. This can be accomplished in about thirty minutes a day while the rest of the class is reading silently. Divide the class into five groups of about six students each. During the course of a week, meet with one group a day. First guide them in reading several pages silently. Then have the children take turns rereading a paragraph or page orally with the goal of reading fluently and with good expression.

The following week, call individual children to your desk while the other students are reading silently (about six students a day for five minutes each). This is an excellent time to take running records to determine children's progress during the year. During this time ask each child to read the *next* page in the book (one that has not yet been read), so you can assess what strategies the child uses to decode unknown words. You can also determine whether or not children are monitoring their own comprehension by going back to reread a sentence where an error was made that changed the meaning. By alternating each week between the small groups and the individual meetings, you will be able to listen to every child read every week by devoting only thirty minutes a day.

Cunningham (1995) offers six critical guidelines for children's oral reading.

1. *Except when assessing, ALWAYS have a child read a book or passage silently before reading it orally.* Readers comprehend more when they read silently because they can focus on comprehension rather than on saying every word correctly. Beginning readers who have not learned to read silently will benefit when they are allowed to quietly "mumble read" a passage to themselves before reading it orally.

2. *Oral reading should be with a book or passage that is fairly easy.* If readers do not recognize at least 95 percent of the words in a passage, their ability to use context in conjunction with the way an unfamiliar word is spelled (phonics) will dramatically drop because they will make too many errors to make sense of the passage.

3. *Children who are listening should NEVER correct another reader's mistakes!* When they do, it robs the reader of learning to self-correct and monitor her or his own comprehension. Also, children should never be allowed to blurt out a word while a reader is trying to figure it out, because this prevents the reader from using her or his decoding skills. If the reader looks to you for help on an unknown word, ask her or him to reread the beginning of the sentence, skip the unknown word, and read to the end of the sentence or paragraph. Then the child can go back and try to decode the word with the use of context and the way it is spelled. This is known as the **read–skip–read strategy.**

4. *Ignore errors that do not change meaning.* All good readers make small, non-meaning-changing errors when they read aloud. It indicates that their eyes are ahead of their voices. Fluent readers have a well-developed **eye–voice span** (the distance between where our eyes are and where our voice is) of about four or five words. They read by phrases rather than word by word.

5. *When the reader makes a meaning-changing error, WAIT!* To encourage children to develop comprehension monitoring, wait until a reader finishes the sentence (or paragraph) to see if she or he self-corrects after reading the words that follow the error.

6. *If waiting does not work, give sustaining feedback.* If the reader continues, stop her or him and say something like, "That didn't make sense. You read, ...[Read the sentence exactly the way the child did.] Does that word make sense here? What word do you know that makes sense in this sentence and is spelled with these letters?" Always stress that when we are figuring out an unknown word, it must have the right letters *and* make sense.

Group Oral Reading

Repeated oral reading of a selection helps children achieve fluency, and there are several activities that allow all children to participate.

Choral Reading. In choral reading, a group of children read together. In the beginning, you may want to lead the reading until your children learn how to begin and end at the same time—and how to use their soft reading voices, so the teacher next door will not complain. Also, when you lead, you are modeling fluency and good intonation. Choral reading is especially effective with poetry or a favorite rhyming picture book, but it can be used for any situation in which oral reading is called for. Solve the problem of who gets to read the directions in the textbook by letting a row or table group read the directions together. Of course, you will want to ensure that all groups get to read an equal number of times.

Readers Theater. Many fiction books lend themselves well to readers theater. This activity gives children an opportunity to achieve fluency by rereading a piece multiple times until it can be read like a radio play. (See Chapter 6 for a sample script.) The following steps will guide you through this activity.

- In groups of about four, children select a story or a passage from a book. The selection should contain ample dialogue of three or more characters.
- Children select the parts of the characters and the narrator and engage in repeated readings of the passage. First they chorally read the entire piece. Then each practices reading his or her part until all have achieved fluency.
- Children present their piece to the rest of the class. They do not use costumes, scenes, or complex props. Rather, they use the varying tones of their voices and gestures to convey the characters' lines. Simple props found in the school can be used.

Story Theater. A related activity is **story theater,** which involves both reading and dramatizing.

- In groups of about six, children select a story with lots of action. This could be a picture book or a chapter from a juvenile novel.
- Half the group serve as readers, and the other half are mimes and act out the scene.
- Readers practice reading the selection multiple times until they achieve fluency. Concurrently, the mimes prepare their pantomime of the story.
- Groups take turns presenting their stories to the class.
- For the next story theater, the readers and mimes trade places.

Guided Silent Reading

The majority of reading instructional time should be spent in guided silent reading. This can be implemented differently for fiction and nonfiction books.

Reading–Prediction Activity

Just as the prediction activity is an excellent method for guiding children through listening to a new fiction story, it is also an excellent method for guiding children through reading a new fiction story. The procedures of the **reading–prediction activity** are much the same as the listening–prediction activity, except that children read the story instead of listen to it. Because this is a prediction activity, it will not work if children have already been exposed to a story, because their answers will then be based on simple memory recall rather than divergent thinking. Therefore, it is best to use this strategy when introducing the first chapter of a new book. (Thereafter, if children have access to the book, many will read ahead.)

The steps of the reading–prediction activity follow:

1. Distribute the books and tell students to read the title and view the book cover or first illustration. Then ask, "What do you think this book might be about?" Engage students in a discussion to build background for the book, and present any new vocabulary.

2. Ask students, "What might happen in this story?" Have students write predictions in their literature journals and then ask several to share what they have written. Write a few on the board.

3. Ask all students to read silently the first two pages, then stop. Readers who finish first should write in their journals whether they confirm, reject, or need to revise their predictions. They should be encouraged to reread the first two pages and study the illustrations to help make their decisions. When all have finished reading, ask for volunteers to tell you whether they confirmed, rejected, or revised their predictions, and ask them to justify their answers.

4. Have students read a set number of pages and stop and write predictions on what might happen next. Then have them finish reading the section and confirm or reject their predictions. After everyone has finished reading, discuss the predictions and whether they were logical (rather than "correct") based on their own background experiences and what they have read so far. (This step can be completed more than once, as long as you tell students where to stop reading to make a prediction. A sticky note in each book is a good reminder of where to stop.)

5. After completing a book, ask students, "If the author writes a sequel, what do you think might happen to the characters next?"

Directed Reading Activity

Prediction activities are effective only for unfamiliar fiction stories. For other books, I recommend the **directed reading activity** (DRA). It is effective with nonfiction, such as informational books and biography; with fiction books that do not have a full plot (and are therefore unpredictable); and with fiction stories that many of the children are familiar with (for example, when children have read ahead in the book). The directed reading activity has three parts: prereading, guided reading, and postreading.

I. Prereading. Distribute the books and ask children to read the title and view the book cover or first illustration. Ask them, "What do you think you might learn from this book/selection? What information does the book cover (or first illustration) give you about the contents?" Draw children into a discussion about the topic to build background schemata. Be sure to introduce any words you think are unfamiliar.

II. Guided Silent Reading. Children read with better comprehension when they read for a purpose. Therefore, set the purpose for reading each section (two to four pages) by telling the group, "Read this section to find out ———" (something they will read in the section). For example, "Read this section to find out why water holds together in drops." Monitor children while they are reading to be sure they stay on task, and help them with any unfamiliar words. When all children have finished reading the section, ask someone to answer the purpose-setting question, and then ask related comprehension questions. Repeat this process for each section of two to four pages. Readers who finish the section first can write the answer to the purpose-setting questions in their literature journals.

III. Postreading. When all children have finished reading, ask for their reactions. Be accepting of responses, whether they liked or did not like the reading selection; however, ask children to justify their answers. For example, "I liked this book because George made me laugh," or "I didn't like this book because George doesn't talk, and in animal stories the animals are supposed to talk." Next, ask comprehension questions to determine if the children understood what they read. (For fiction books, I recommend you use questions such as the ones in Box 13.1.) It is also appropriate to ask questions after each section of two to four pages during the guided silent reading stage. Regardless of whether the questions are asked during the reading or after the group finishes the selection, children should always be allowed to keep their books open and reinspect the text. Otherwise, you will be checking children's memory rather than their comprehension.

Recall from Chapter 2 that the primary response mode of readers is internal thought. You tap into that by asking for children's reactions after they finish reading. If you also ask them to write an entry in their literature journals, they will have further cause to reflect. By recording their thoughts about a book, children have a source to refer to later when they have read more books and are making comparisons.

Sometimes teachers extend a reading lesson with a writing project. For example, with a fiction book, children could rewrite the ending, write a letter to a story character, write a diary entry in the voice of one of the characters, write another story following the same pattern, or write a readers theater script from an episode.

The steps in the directed reading activity are summarized in Box 13.4.

The directed reading activity can easily be adapted to a **directed listening activity.** In this strategy the teacher, rather than the students, does the reading. This activity would be appropriate when the teacher has selected a nonfiction book, such as an informational book or a biography, to share with the class during the teacher read-aloud time. Figure 13.2 presents a comparison of the four strategies I have described.

Box 13.4

Steps in the Directed Reading Activity

I. Prereading

- Ask children to read the title and view the book cover or first illustration; then ask the following questions:

  "What do you think you might learn from this book/selection?"

  "What information does the book cover (or first illustration) give you about the contents?"

  Build background schemata, and introduce new words.

II. Guided Silent Reading

- Set the purpose for reading each section of two to four pages by saying, "Read this section to find out _____."
- Monitor children while they are reading to ensure they stay on task, and help them with any unfamiliar words.

- When children are finished with the section, ask someone to answer the purpose-setting question, and ask other related comprehension questions as appropriate.
- Repeat this process for each section.

III. Postreading

- Ask for children's reactions to the selection, and have them justify their answers.
- Ask comprehension questions, and allow children to reinspect the text for answers when necessary.
- Conduct literature response activities as appropriate.

Strategy	Type of Text	Children's Task	Type of Questions	Timing of Questions
Listening–Prediction Activity	New fiction	Listen	Prediction	Before something important happens
Reading–Prediction Activity	New fiction	Read	Prediction	Before something important happens
Directed Listening Activity	Nonfiction and familiar fiction	Listen	Comprehension	After something important happens
Directed Reading Activity	Nonfiction and familiar fiction	Read	Comprehension	After something important happens

FIGURE 13.2   Comparison of Reading and Listening Activities

Implementing a Yearlong Literature Program

Teachers who use only trade books to teach reading need a plan for organizing their instruction. Two popular ways are by genres and by thematic units.

Organizing Reading Instruction by Genres

Organizing instruction by genres involves devoting a month to each of the major genres and highlighting one or more authors and illustrators noted for their work in the targeted genre. An example of organizing reading selections by genre and author/illustrator follows.

- *September:* Traditional literature and Leo and Diane Dillon
- *October:* Fantasy and J. K. Rowling
- *November:* Animal fantasy and Arnold Lobel
- *December:* Contemporary fiction and Katherine Paterson
- *January:* Historical fiction and Mildred Taylor
- *February:* Biography and Jean Fritz
- *March:* Informational books and Laurence Pringle
- *April:* Poetry and Francisco Alarcon
- *May:* Multicultural literature and Ed Young

For each genre, it is important to select books on a variety of reading levels, including picture books, juvenile novels, and a few adolescent novels for the gifted readers in your class. Book lists in each of the genre chapters in this textbook cover a range of reading levels. A quick way to find titles for specific authors and illustrators is to look in the Name and Title Index at the end of this book. Your school and public librarians will be able to help you locate the books they own by the featured authors and illustrators.

If you are able to locate multiple copies of a variety of books (for example, six copies each of five titles), **literature circles** are an excellent way to organize this reading program. Recall from Chapter 2 that literature circles are small temporary discussion groups of children who have chosen to read the same book. Children select which of the five books they would like to read first. (If you do not have enough copies for all children to get their first choice, make sure they get it on the next cycle.) Groups meet on a regular schedule, perhaps twice a week. They discuss their reading and bring their literature journals, in which they have kept notes about their reading, to guide their discussion. Discussion topics are initiated by the children, and the responsibility for starting the discussion rotates. Group meetings should consist of open, natural conversations about books. Personal connections are encouraged, and open-ended questions are welcomed. After the teacher has initially explained the process and modeled the students' role, he or she serves as a *facilitator,* not as a group member or instructor.

 Responding to Literature

Book Talks

Book talks are a good way for readers to get others interested in books they really like. Book talks should not be confused with book reports or reviews, which cover an entire book and give away the ending. Rather, book talks cover *no more* than the first half of the book in order to entice others to read it. The following instructions will help children prepare a book talk:

- Select a book you have read that is hilarious, exciting, scary, mysterious, heartrending, or just terrific. (It can be fiction, nonfiction, or poetry.)
- Prepare a two- to three-minute talk, but do not memorize anything.
- Write the main characters' names, the setting, and notes about the first half of the book on a sticky note inside the back cover for reference in case you forget.
- Stand up, face your audience, and state the title and author, showing the book cover.
- Speak clearly and with enthusiasm; conveying admiration for the book gets others interested in reading it. Talk to your group about the book—but only enough to entice them.
- Last, read a paragraph or half page of something that is especially interesting, funny, or exciting, and show a couple of your favorite illustrations.

Organizing Reading Instruction Thematically

Many teachers choose to teach reading through thematic units that focus on one book and draw in other subjects such as language arts and social studies. Instruction is organized around a theme or topic, such as the Civil War, the ocean, the rainforest, or the Great Depression. During the read-aloud period, the teacher shares a book related to the unit. All children read the selected focus novel during the class's reading instruction time. During sustained silent reading and for homework, they also read at least one other novel and one nonfiction book (informational or biography); in addition, they view at least one Internet site. There are five major steps in guiding children through experiencing a novel in a thematic unit.

1. *Select the focus novel and related books.* In addition to selecting the novel that the whole class will read, locate other books with the same theme. Select five to ten titles for each of the following:

- supplemental novels to be read individually
- picture books for enrichment
- informational books to build background
- biographies to supplement background
- internet sites

2. *Introduce the novel.* Provide necessary background to help children comprehend and appreciate the novel, while piquing their interest in the subject.

- Show illustrations and read short excerpts from one or more related informational books.
- Engage students in a discussion to activate prior knowledge.
- Introduce the meanings of important words and concepts.
- Distribute books, and lead students through the *prereading schema-building process* (introduced in Chapter 2).

- Guide children in reading the first section using the reading–prediction activity.

3. *Guide readers in experiencing the novel.* Select one of the resource books for your daily read-aloud session. Children will select from the other resource books or Internet sites for their daily sustained silent reading period and keep notes in their literature journals. For the focus novel, a general guideline is to complete one chapter a day.

- Use the reading–prediction activity or the directed reading activity to guide students in reading the novel silently.
- Students make daily entries into their literature journals to record their predictions and their reactions to what they have read.
- The teacher guides the students in completing a story map and character maps for each of the main characters, and these are posted and added to throughout the unit.

4. *Guide readers in responding to the novel.* There are a variety of highly motivating ways students can respond to the focus novel during and after reading the book. These include:

- grand conversations
- language charts
- dramatization
- webbing
- story boxes

During the unit, students should also be called upon to give book talks on the supplemental books they have read. Notes made in their literature journals can guide them in their presentations.

5. *Guide students in analyzing the novel.* Literature responses named in the preceding step should be continued for at least one day after the children finish the focus novel, giving children an opportunity to develop their internal responses to the story. After that time, the teacher can facilitate a grand conversation in which the students make a final analysis of the book. Some of the things students analyze are a book's content, literary elements, and structural design. Also, comparisons can be made to books previously read.

An innovative way to guide students in analyzing novels in a thematic unit is through **language charts** (Roser, Hoffman, Labbo, & Farest 1995). A language chart is constructed from a large piece of butcher paper that is ruled as a matrix. One axis contains the titles and authors of several books in the unit that a group will read. The second axis is made up of questions, invitations for reflection, and additional prompts for book discussions. After the discussion of each book, the teacher records the children's responses on the chart. However, the chart is "not intended to replace the natural book talk that accompanies and follows book sharing with children; rather, it is intended to focus thinking *after* book conversations have ranged freely" (p. 83).

One of the most valuable functions of the charts is to stimulate children's recall of previously read stories, so they can analyze all the stories, finding connections in the form of similarities and differences. Some other functions of language charts are:

- to make a record of classroom literacy experiences
- to stimulate children's expression of personal responses to literature
- to encourage children to reflect on a literary experience
- to serve as a springboard for other responses to literature (Stoodt, Amspaugh, & Hunt 1996)

In Box 13.5 I have listed resources for a thematic unit on the Great Depression, and a literature chart for this unit is presented in Figure 13.3.

Even if you are teaching reading with conventional basal textbooks, supplemental activities with literature can help children develop specific reading abilities. Box 13.6 is a recommended list of literature activities for developing several essential reading abilities.

I hope those of you who are (or will be) parents read to your children every day. For parents who want to incorporate reading instruction into their daily reading period, Box 13.7 presents a simple and effective routine. Teachers may reproduce this section as a handout for parents if the source citation at the bottom is included.

In addition to books, other media also offer you opportunities to learn about children's literature. In the following section I provide lists of adult periodicals about literature as well as literature-related Internet sites—some of which contain the full text of children's stories that are in the public domain. At the end of this chapter is a list of recommended children's magazines and an annotated bibliography of resources for teaching a thematic unit on the Great Depression.

I have provided addresses for many Internet sites. However, I warn you that some will change or go offline over a period of time. Also, you will not be able to access a site unless you precisely type each character of the address, which can be difficult and time-consuming. Therefore, you may access all the Internet sites in this textbook with direct links through the publisher's companion website to this text at the following address: http://www.ablongman.com/anderson

ADULT PERIODICALS ABOUT CHILDREN'S LITERATURE

Many of the periodicals listed here have the full text of articles available at their websites.

> Note: Typically, it is not necessary to type the "http://" at the beginning of most addresses; likewise, the final "/" can usually be omitted. However, if you receive an error message instead of the desired site, try again using the full address.

- *Book Links: Connecting Books, Libraries, and Classrooms,* 434 West Downer Place, Aurora, IL 60506
  http://www.ala.org/BookLinks/

Box 13.5

Resources for a Thematic Unit on the Great Depression

Full references and annotations appear at the end of this chapter.

Focus Novel

Bud, Not Buddy by Christopher Paul Curtis

Teacher Read-Aloud

Out of the Dust by Karen Hesse

Supplemental Novels

Blue Willow by Doris Gates
Willie Bea and the Time the Martians Landed by Virginia Hamilton
Treasures in the Dust by Tracey Porter
Song of the Trees by Mildred Taylor (short novel for less able readers)
Roll of Thunder, Hear My Cry by Mildred Taylor
Let the Circle Be Unbroken by Mildred Taylor (adolescent novel for advanced readers)

Fiction Picture Books

The Dust Bowl by David Booth
Leah's Pony by Elizabeth Friedrich
A Christmas Star by Linda Oatman High
Potato: A Tale from the Great Depression by Kate Lied
Uncle Jed's Barbershop by Margaree King Mitchell
All for the Better: A Story of El Barrio by Nicholasa Mohr
Angels in the Dust by Margot Theis Raven
Dust for Dinner by Ann Warren Turner

Informational Books

The Dust Bowl: Disaster on the Plains by Tricia Andryszewski
Children of the Dust Days by Karen Mueller Coombs
The Great Depression in American History by David K. Fremon
Black Tuesday: The Stock Market Crash of 1929 by Barbara Silberdick Feinberg
The New Freedom to the New Deal, 1913–1939 by William Loren Katz
Driven from the Land: The Story of the Dust Bowl by Milton Meltzer
We Want Jobs! A Story of the Great Depression by Robert J. Norrell
Children of the Dust Bowl: The True Story of the School at Weedpatch Camp by Jerry Stanley
The Great Depression by R. Conrad Stein
The New Deal by Gail Stewart

Biography

Herbert Hoover by Susan Clinton
Franklin Delano Roosevelt by Russell Freedman
Eleanor Roosevelt: A Life of Discovery by Russell Freedman
Frances Perkins: Champion of the New Deal by Naomi E. Pasachoff

Internet Resources

America from the Great Depression to World War II: Photographs
http://memory.loc.gov/ammem/fsowhome.html

American Life Histories: Voices from the Thirties
http://memory.loc.gov/ammem/wpaintro/wpahome.html

The Great Depression and the New Deal
http://www.bergen.org/AAST/Projects/depression/

The Great Depression Overview
http://www.geocities.com/Athens/Olympus/1545/

New Deal Network
http://newdeal.feri.org/

Voices from the Dust Bowl
http://lcweb2.loc.gov/ammem/afctshtml/tshome.html

Title	Author Illustrator	What hardship did main character face?	How did he or she overcome it?	How did he or she help others in need?	How well did author represent the times?
Bud, Not Buddy	Christopher P. Curtis				
Blue Willow	Doris Gates				
Song of the Trees	Mildred Taylor				
Leah's Pony	Elizabeth Friedrich Michael Garland				
Potato: A Tale from the Great Depression	Kate Lied Lisa Campbell Ernst				
Uncle Jed's Barbershop	Margaree Mitchell James Ransome				
All for the Better: A Story of El Barrio	Nicholasa Mohr Rudy Gutierrez				

FIGURE 13.3 Thematic Language Chart

Box 13.6

Developing Reading Abilities with Literature

Developing listening comprehension (potential for reading comprehension)

Listening–prediction activity
Retelling stories after listening
Summarizing and paraphrasing nonfiction text after listening

Developing reading comprehension

Reading–prediction activity
Story maps, webbing, and other graphic overviews
Retelling a book or passage after reading

Developing sight vocabulary

Reading pattern books
Repeated reading of familiar books
Echo and choral reading with a fluent reader
Shared reading with a partner

Developing fluency

Repeated readings of short passages
Choral reading of poetry with a small group
Practice reading a picture book to read aloud
Readers theater
Story theater

- *Booklist: Books for Youth,* 434 West Downer Place, Aurora, IL 60506
  http://www.ala.org/booklist/v96/002.html

- *The Bulletin for the Center for Children's Books,* University of Illinois Press, BCCB, 1325 South Oak Street, Champaign, IL 61820
  http://www.lis.uiuc.edu/puboff/bccb/subscrip.html

- *Children's Literature,* 7513 Shadywood Road, Bethesda, MD 20817
  http://www.childrenslit.com/home.htm

- *The Horn Book,* 11 Beacon Street, Suite 1000, Boston, MA 02108
  http://www.hbook.com/mag.shtml

- *The Lion and the Unicorn,* The Johns Hopkins University Press, Journals Publishing Division, P.O. Box 19966, Baltimore, MD 21211
  http://muse.jhu.edu/journals/lion_and_the_unicorn/

- *The New York Times Book Review,* to order call 1–800–631–2580
  http://nytimes.com/books/

- *The Reading Teacher,* International Reading Association, PO Box 8139, Newark, DE 19714
  http://www.reading.org/publications/journals/RT/index.html

- *School Library Journal,* P.O. Box 1978, Marion, OH 43305
  http://www.slj.com/

INTERNET SITES ABOUT CHILDREN'S LITERATURE

PUBLISHING COMPANIES

- *Houghton Mifflin:* Information and free resources for parents and teachers, including lessons and educational projects; links to authors
  http://www.eduplace.com/

Box 13.7

Teaching Reading in Thirty Minutes a Night

Would you like to greatly enhance your child's reading ability? If so, are you willing to give up a thirty-minute television show every night and read with your child? The following routine will help your child learn to read to his or her full potential.

Nightly Routine Summary

I. (ten minutes) Read to your child and ask prediction questions (six nights a week) or
Write a **language experience account** (LEA) (one night a week).

II. (fifteen minutes) Listen to your child read without overcorrecting.

III. (five minutes) Reread previously written LEAs (six nights a week) or
Read through the word bank (one night a week).

Part I

Read to your child six nights a week from a book he or she is not able to read independently but can understand when you read it aloud. When reading a book for the first time, ask prediction questions, for example, "From looking at the cover (or first illustration) and listening to the title, what do you think might happen in this story?" After reading a few pages, ask, "What do you think might happen next?" Repeat this question every few pages, and let your child predict what might happen next

in the story. Prediction questions are asked only with new books. After reading a familiar book, ask your child to retell the story as if he or she were telling it to a friend who had never heard it before. Spend about ten minutes reading to your child each session.

On the seventh night, have your child dictate an account of something he or she has experienced, such as a trip to the park, a movie, a favorite television show, a visit from a relative, a family pet, something done with a friend, or something that happened at school. Write each sentence after it is dictated. When your child has finished dictating, read the whole paragraph back, pointing *under* each word as you say it. Next, have your child read it *with* you. Then have your child read it alone. This is called a language experience account, or LEA.

Part II

Listen to your child read from a book that is fairly easy. Do not correct every error your child makes. If an error *does not change* the meaning, ignore it, and let your child continue to read. If the error *does change* the meaning, wait until your child reads to the end of the sentence to see if he or she will go back and self correct. If not, ask your child to stop; then read the sentence exactly the way he or she did. For example, if your child substitutes

---

- *Penguin Putnam:* Information on authors, illustrators, and their books, including pictures and excerpts
  http://www.penguinputnam.com/yreaders/index.htm

- *Random House:* Resource center with teachers' guides, thematic and interdisciplinary indexes, reader's companions, and author and illustrator biographies
  http://www.randomhouse.com/teachers/

- *Simon & Schuster:* New releases and teachers' guides for activities
  http://www.simonsays.com/kids/

the word *green* for the word *great* and does not self-correct by the end of the sentence, say, "Wait a minute. Let me read that sentence to you the way you read it to me: 'Trigger was a green horse.' Does that make sense?" Point to the word missed, and ask your child to think of another word that *would* make sense in the sentence. This will help your child develop use of context clues for decoding unknown words.

When your child is reading and comes to an unknown word, wait at least five seconds to see if he or she can figure it out from the context and the way the word is spelled. (I suggest counting slowly to yourself to resist the urge to blurt it out.) If your child does not say the word correctly after five seconds, say the word and let him or her continue to read. *Avoid saying, "Sound it out"!* This discourages your child from using context to help decode unknown words. If your child is able to sound it out, he or she will do so without your prompting, which actually distracts your child from thinking.

With beginning readers or reluctant readers, use support reading with pattern books or easy-to-read books. Support reading takes three forms:

- **Echo reading:** You read a sentence (or line) while pointing *under* each word. Next, your child reads the same sentence (or line) while pointing.
- **Choral reading:** You and your child read the story together, with you setting the pace and modeling good intonation.
- **Paired reading:** Sit with your child to your right. You read the left-hand pages of the book, and your child reads the right-hand pages. Then switch sides and reread the book.

Spend about fifteen minutes listening to your child read each session.

Part III

Construct a word bank of sight words your child has mastered from books and LEAs. These can be written on index cards and stored alphabetically in a file box. The last five minutes of each session should be spent in rereading LEAs (six nights a week) or reviewing the words in the word bank (one night a week).

If you faithfully devote thirty minutes a night to reading with your child, his or her reading ability can be greatly enhanced. (Or, you can go back to watching *Star Trek*.)

- *Scholastic:* Thousands of lesson plans, classroom activities, and other resources for teachers; favorite book characters and games for children; tips and fun activities for parents to do with their children
  http://www.scholastic.com/index.asp

ORGANIZATIONS

- *American Library Association Literature Sites for Children:* More than 700 colorful sites for children, parents, teachers, and other caregivers
  http://www.ala.org/parentspage/greatsites/

- *American Library Association Resources for Parents, Teens and Kids:* Many links for kids, teens, parents, and other adults; recommended reading and multimedia
  http://www.ala.org/parents/

- *The Children's Book Council:* Links to pages specifically for publishers, booksellers, authors and illustrators, teachers and librarians, and parents
  http://www.cbcbooks.org/

- *International Reading Association:* Home page of a professional association for teachers of reading; many resources for educators
  http://www.reading.org/

- *Internet Public Library Youth Division–Reading Zone:* Provides links to online short stories, some authored by children; links about popular books and authors
  http://www.ipl.org/youth/

- *Reading Is Fundamental:* Develops and delivers children's and family literacy programs that help prepare young children for reading and that motivate school-age children to read
  http://www.rif.org

- *United States Board on Books for Young People:* Encourages the provision of high quality literature for young people throughout the world, and facilitates the international exchange of information about books
  http://www.usbby.org

AUTHORS AND ILLUSTRATORS

Note: Most authors and illustrators have an Internet site, though I list only a few here. To locate another author, key in the following generic address: www.firstandlastname.com (using the full name of the author or illustrator you are looking for). If that does not work, do an Internet search and key in "firstname lastname".

- *Hans Christian Andersen:* Biographical information plus links to the full text of more than one hundred of Andersen's original tales and stories
  http://www.math.technion.ac.il/~rl/Andersen/#list

- *Judy Blume:* Biographical information and photographs; answers to children's most common questions; discussion of Blume's experiences with censors; information on all her books
  http://www.judyblume.com/

- *Jan Brett:* Links to over 1,200 pages of artwork and activities for children designed by Brett
  http://www.janbrett.com/index_ccs-page.html

- *Eric Carle:* Information about Carle and his books along with answers to frequently asked questions, idea exchange bulletin board, and new publications
  http://www.eric-carle.com/

- *Children's Literature Authors and Illustrators:* Links to websites of numerous authors and illustrators, primarily biographical information
  http://web.nwe.ufl.edu/~jbrown/chauth.html

- *The Children's Literature Web Guide on Authors and Illustrators:* Links to sites on numerous authors and illustrators, including personal websites and sites maintained by fans and scholars
  http://www.acs.ucalgary.ca/~dkbrown/authors.html

- *Virginia Hamilton:* Explores the author's world with her family history, photos, awards, publications, and new releases
  http://virginiahamilton.com/

- *Brian Jacques:* Information about the author of the Redwall Abby series and the characters in the fifteen books
  http://www.redwall.org/dave/jacques.html

- *Beatrix Potter:* Kids' Corner features eight of Potter's books with all illustrations, two of which have audio clips
  http://www.education.wisc.edu/ccbc/pcstats.htm

- *J. K. Rowling:* Interview with the author and background information for the Harry Potter books, including games and discussion guides
  http://www.scholastic.com/harrypotter

- *Dr. Seuss:* Games, Cat in the Hat chat, contests, and Dr. Seuss books and CD-ROMs
  http://www.randomhouse.com/seussville/

- *Jon Scieszka and Lane Smith:* Information about this zany author–illustrator team and some of their books; interactive games
  http://www.chucklebait.com/

- *Audrey Wood:* Activities with Audrey Wood; how picture books are written and illustrated
  http://audreywood.com/

OTHER

Note: Amazon.com is not just for buying books! It is the most powerful search tool available for information on children's books, because nearly every book in print can be searched through this site. You can search for books appropriate for a particular age group, using keywords of title, author, or subject. A colorful picture of the book cover is shown for most books, and I find this as helpful as the summaries and reviews.

- *Amazon.com Children's Books:* World's largest online bookstore; view book covers and read summaries and reviews of nearly all books in print
  http://www.amazon.com/exec/obidos/tg/browse/-/4/

- *Advanced Book Exchange:* World's largest network of independent booksellers to order obscure, used, and out-of-print books
  http://abebooks.com/

- *Addall.com:* Automatically compares prices among almost all major online bookstores and finds the Internet-wide best offer for any book you want; also searches for used, hard to find, and out-of-print books
  http://www.addall.com

- *Candlelight Stories:* Listen to classic stories, such as the tales collected by the Brothers Grimm and original stories by Hans Christian Andersen, Rudyard Kipling, and some contemporary authors (requires Media Player 6.4 or higher); also contains games, contests, and other activities
  http://www.candlelightstories.com/defaultnew.asp

- *Carol Hurst's Children's Literature Site:* Ideas on using books in the classroom; collections of books and activities about subject areas, themes, and professional topics
  http://www.carolhurst.com/

- *Children's Literature and Language Arts Resources:* Information for teachers, library media professionals, parents, and students on children's literature and language arts
  http://falcon.jmu.edu/~ramseyil/childlit.htm

- *The Children's Literature Web Guide on Awards:* The most comprehensive guide to English-language children's book awards on the Internet
  http://www.acs.ucalgary.ca/~dkbrown/awards.html

- *The Children's Literature Web Guide Homepage:* A list of sites for children, teachers, parents, and librarians, giving them comprehensive information about children's literature
  http://www.acs.ucalgary.ca/~dkbrown/index.html

- *ERIC Resource List on Native American Books:* Bibliographies with recommended grade levels for both fiction and nonfiction books about contemporary Native Americans, contemporary folktales, and the boarding school experience; includes Internet sites
  http://www.ericeece.org/pubs/reslist/native99.html

- *Fairrosa Cyber Library:* The personal collection of Roxanne Hsu Feldman (Hsu Yu-Feng), containing links to many resources including numerous books about dragons
  http://www.dalton.org/libraries/fairrosa/

- *Native American Indian Resources:* Text on Native narratives, traditional stories, Indian books; biographies and pictures of Native authors; link to order books by Native authors
  http://indy4.fdl.cc.mn.us/~isk/mainmenu.html

- *Project Gutenberg:* Provides online full text of literature in the public domain, including the classics of children's literature
  http://www.gutenberg.net/

- *Pilot Search:* A literary search engine with links to sixty literary sites for children
  http://www.pilot-search.com/

- *Publishers Weekly Children's Bestseller List:* Monthly lists of best-selling children's books for picture books, fiction, nonfiction, series, and tie-ins
  http://www.publishersweekly.com/bsl/currentChildrens.asp

- *The Storytelling Ring:* A ring of sites throughout the Internet featuring storytelling resources, organizations, events, and the tellers themselves
  http://www.tiac.net/users/papajoe/ring.htm

- *Vandergrift's Children's Literature Page:* Brief overview of children's literature and the genres with links for further research
  http://www.scils.rutgers.edu/special/kay/childlit.html

- *The Young People's Zone:* Full text of public-domain stories such as Anne of Green Gables, Tom Sawyer, Sherlock Holmes, Bobbsey twins; also text for Robin Hood ballads and favorite fairy tales
  http://www.youngpeopleszone.cjb.net/

CHILDREN'S MAGAZINES

Following are just a few of the more than 150 magazines published for children under age 13. For a comprehensive list see *Magazines for Kids and Teens* (Stoll 1997), offered through the International Reading Association. The title of each magazine is followed by its primary topic, readers' targeted age group, and subscription address.

- *Biography Today:* Contemporary biographies (8–13). Omnigraphics, 615 Griswold, Detroit, MI 48226.

- *Calliope:* World history (8–13), Cobblestone Publishing, 7 School Street, Peterborough, NH 03458.

- *Chickadee:* Science and nature (4–8), 25 Boxwood Lane, Buffalo, NY 14227.

- *Children's Digest:* General interest and fitness (8–12), Children's Better Health Inst., P.O. Box 567, Indianapolis, IN 46206.

- *Cricket:* Fiction and nonfiction (9–13) P.O. Box 7433, Red Oak, IA 51591.

- *Daybreak Star Indian Reader:* Native American history and contemporary tribal lifestyles (9–12), United Indians of All Tribes, 1945 Yale Place East, Seattle, WA 98102.

- *Harambee:* African American experience (7–13), Just Us Books, 356 Glenwood Avenue, East Orange, NJ 07017.

- *Highlights for Children:* General interest (2–12), P.O. Box 269, Columbus, OH 43272.

- *Humpty Dumpty:* General interest and health (4–6), Children's Better Health, P.O. Box 567, Indianapolis, IN 46206.

- *Jack and Jill:* General interest and health (7–10), P.O. Box 10003, Des Moines, IA 50340.

- *Kid City:* General interest and writing (6–10), P.O. Box 2924, Boulder, CO 80322.

- *Kids Discover:* Themed (6–12), 170 Fifth Avenue, 6th Floor, New York, NY 10010.

- *Kids for Saving Earth News:* Environmental issues (7–13), P.O. Box 47247, Plymouth, MN 55447.

- *Ladybug:* General interest (2–6), P.O. Box 7436, Red Oak, IA 51591.

- *National Geographic World:* Natural history and outdoor adventure (8–13), P.O. Box 2330, Washington, D.C. 20013.

- *Plays:* Dramatic material (6–13), Plays Inc., 120 Boylston Street, Boston, MA 02116.

- *Ranger Rick:* Nature and environment (6–12), National Wildlife Federation, 8925 Leesburg Pike, Vienna, VA 22184.

- *Scienceland:* Nature and physical science (5–10), 501 Fifth Avenue, Suite 2108, New York, NY 10017.

- *Skipping Stones:* Cultural diversity and social issues (7–13), P.O. Box 3939, Eugene OR 97403.
- *Soccer JR:* Soccer skills and fitness (8–13), P.O. Box 420442, Palm Coast, FL 32142.
- *Sports Illustrated for Kids:* Sports (8–13), Time Inc., P.O. Box 830609, Birmingham, AL 35282.
- *Stone Soup:* Children's writing and art (6–13) Children's Art Foundation, P.O. Box 83, Santa Cruz, CA 95063.
- *Storyworks:* Literature (9–11), Scholastic Inc., P.O. Box 3710, Jefferson City, MO 65101.
- *Surprises:* Activities for children and parents (5–12), Children's Surprises, P.O. Box 20471, Bloomington, MN 55405.
- *Time for Kids:* Current events (9–12), P.O. Box 30609, Tampa FL 33630.
- *Zillions: The Consumer Reports for Kids:* Consumer education (8–13), Zillions Subscriptions, P.O. Box 51777, Boulder, CO 80321.

BIBLIOGRAPHY FOR UNIT ON THE GREAT DEPRESSION

FICTION NOVELS

- Curtis, Christopher Paul. ***Bud, Not Buddy.*** Delacorte, 1999. After his mother dies, Bud runs away from a terrible foster home in Flint, Michigan, and embarks on a thrill-packed journey in search of the man he believes to be his father—a famous band leader.
- Gates, Doris. ***Blue Willow.*** Illus. Paul Lantz. Viking Penguin, 1940/1999. A homeless family is allowed to stay in a run-down shack and work on the farm while their little girl attends the migrant workers' school.
- Hamilton, Virginia. ***Willie Bea and the Time the Martians Landed.*** Morrow, 1983. In October 1938, on a farm homestead in Ohio, Willie Bea is sad because there is no money for Halloween costumes; however, she is aware her family is more fortunate than many others. In the evening, Willie Bea's family is caught up in the fear and hysteria generated by the famous Orson Welles radio-play broadcast of *War of the Worlds*—a tale of Martians landing on earth.
- Hesse, Karen. ***Out of the Dust.*** Scholastic, 1997. Fourteen-year-old Billie Jo chronicles her life in the Oklahoma Dust Bowl through journal entries written in free-verse poems. The tragic death of her mother and newborn brother and her own physical and mental scars make Billie Jo long to leave Oklahoma.
- Porter, Tracey. ***Treasures in the Dust.*** HarperCollins, 1997. Two 11-year-olds chronicle how they cope with the hardships of the Oklahoma dust storms. Violet's family migrates to California while Annie's stays.
- Taylor, Mildred. ***Song of the Trees.*** Dial, 1975. The Logans, an African American family in Mississippi, struggle against prejudice and poverty to keep their land when a lumber company wants to cut down the treasured giant old trees that surround their home.
- ———. ***Roll of Thunder, Hear My Cry.*** Viking Penguin, 1976. Cassie Logan's family struggles to make the payments on their land. Father goes north to work for the railroad, but when Mother loses her teaching job and the bank calls in the mortgage, Uncle Hammer makes a sacrifice.

- ———. *Let the Circle Be Unbroken.* Viking Penguin, 1981. In 1935, the Logan children watch as their friend T. J. is tried by an all-white jury for a murder he did not commit.

FICTION PICTURE BOOKS

- Booth, David. *The Dust Bowl.* Illus. Karen Reczuch. Kids Can Press, 1997. During a drought, Matthew's grandfather tells him about the Big Dry of the 1930s, when great dust clouds could block out the sun for days.

- Friedrich, Elizabeth. *Leah's Pony.* Illus. Michael Garland. Boyds Mills Press, 1996. When drought turns the family farm to dust, Leah's papa has to put everything they own up for auction. Leah sells her beloved pony to buy the tractor so they can start again.

- High, Linda Oatman. *A Christmas Star.* Illus. Ronald Himler. Holiday House, 1997. On a Depression-era Christmas Eve, a young girl discovers all the presents under the tree at church have been stolen; however, while the service proceeds, Santa stops by and drops off new gifts.

- Lied, Kate. *Potato: A Tale from the Great Depression.* Illus. Lisa Campbell Ernst. National Geographic Society, 1997. After grandfather Clarence loses his job and the bank takes their house, Clarence and his family move to Idaho to harvest potatoes, living in a tent and earning enough money to keep the family together through hard times.

- Mitchell, Margaree King. *Uncle Jed's Barbershop.* Illus. James Ransome. Simon & Schuster, 1993. Sara Jean's beloved Uncle Jed dreams of owning his own barbershop, and after many years and many setbacks, including Depression bank failures, he achieves his goal.

- Mohr, Nicholasa. *All for the Better: A Story of El Barrio.* Illus. Rudy Gutierrez. Raintree, 1992. An 11-year-old Puerto Rican girl, Evelina, is sent to the mainland so her family will be less financially burdened during the Depression.

- Raven, Margot Theis. *Angels in the Dust.* Illus. Roger Essley. Bridgewater, 1997. A 12-year-old girl takes charge of the household after her mother's death, struggling with her father and little sister to save their farm through drought, dust, and fire.

- Turner, Ann Warren. *Dust for Dinner.* Illus. Robert Barrett. HarperCollins, 1995. Jake's family is forced to sell their farm in Oklahoma when all the crops die. They travel to California where the father eventually finds a job.

INFORMATIONAL BOOKS

- Andryszewski, Tricia. *The Dust Bowl: Disaster on the Plains.* Millbrook, 1994. Using photographs and diary excerpts, the author describes the human and natural causes that led to the 1930s environmental disaster known as the Dust Bowl.

- Coombs, Karen Mueller. *Children of the Dust Days.* Carolrhoda, 2000. The book describes through text and photos how the dust and drought of the 1930s impacted every aspect of life—the dark blizzards of dirt, the decimation of crops from grasshoppers, the economic disasters, and the journey to find a better life in California.

- Fremon, David K. *The Great Depression in American History.* Enslow, 1997. The stock market crash, the Dust Bowl, President Roosevelt, and the New Deal are all discussed as part of this analysis of the Great Depression, which ended when World War II erupted.

- Feinberg, Barbara Silberdick. ***Black Tuesday: The Stock Market Crash of 1929.*** Millbrook, 1995. This book chronicles the financial circumstances that contributed to the most disastrous stock market crash in U.S. history and the extensive impact the crash had on the entire country.

- Katz, William Loren. ***The New Freedom to the New Deal, 1913–1939.*** Raintree Steck-Vaughn, 1993. This multicultural history of the United States, from 1913 to 1939, focuses on the experiences of women and minorities.

- Meltzer, Milton. ***Driven from the Land: The Story of the Dust Bowl.*** Benchmark Books, 2000. A renowned author chronicles the migration of Americans during the days of the Dust Bowl.

- Norrell, Robert J. ***We Want Jobs! A Story of the Great Depression.*** Illus. Jan N. Jones. Raintree Steck-Vaughn, 1992. This account of an unemployed steelworker and his family in Pittsburgh describes the events of the economic depression that led to the 1932 march on Washington for jobs.

- Stanley, Jerry. ***Children of the Dust Bowl: The True Story of the School at Weedpatch Camp.*** Crown, 1992. This book chronicles the life of migrant-worker children at a farm-labor camp in Weedpatch, California. When the children were not allowed to attend regular schools, they built their own on a farm.

- Stein, R. Conrad. ***The Great Depression.*** Children's Book Press, 1993. This book provides a description of the 1929 stock market crash and ensuing events that caused the economic depression. It includes descriptions of the New Deal programs that were implemented to restore the economy.

- Stewart, Gail. ***The New Deal.*** New Discovery Books, 1993. This book discusses the events leading up to America's Great Depression and President Roosevelt's plan to rescue the economy with the New Deal.

BIOGRAPHY

- Clinton, Susan. ***Herbert Hoover.*** Children's Book Press, 1988. A biography of Herbert Hoover—a mining engineer and millionaire businessman—who served his country as director of food relief in Europe after World War I, secretary of commerce, and president of the United States during the Depression.

- Freedman, Russell. ***Franklin Delano Roosevelt.*** Clarion, 1990. Photographs and text portray Roosevelt as an active young man who later won political office in spite of his paralysis from polio. His leadership through the Great Depression and World War II are highlighted.

- ———. ***Eleanor Roosevelt: A Life of Discovery.*** Clarion, 1997. Through photographs and text, Eleanor Roosevelt is revealed as a person who genuinely cared about people—a strong advocate of human rights and world peace.

- Pasachoff, Naomi E. ***Frances Perkins: Champion of the New Deal.*** Oxford University Press, 2000. As secretary of labor for twelve years, Perkins was the first female to serve as a presidential cabinet member. She instituted labor reforms such as unemployment insurance, minimum wages, maximum hours, safety regulations, and social security.

▌INTERNET SITES ON THE GREAT DEPRESSION

- *America from the Great Depression to World War II: Photographs:* Extensive Library of Congress collection of both black-and-white and color photos of Americans from the Depression era
  http://memory.loc.gov/ammem/fsowhome.html

- *American Life Histories: Voices from the Thirties:* Library of Congress collection of 2,900 life history manuscripts from the Federal Writers Project Folklore Collection, 1936 to 1940
  http://memory.loc.gov/ammem/wpaintro/wpahome.html

- *The Great Depression and the New Deal:* A historical overview of the Depression and its causes and a comparison of the New Deal with similar social programs that followed
  http://www.bergen.org/AAST/Projects/depression/

- *The Great Depression Overview:* Factual overview, featuring a timeline and biographies of presidents Hoover and Roosevelt (created by high school students as an assignment)
  http://www.geocities.com/Athens/Olympus/1545/

- *New Deal Network:* Online resources for the study of the New Deal projects of the 1930s, including a photograph collection
  http://newdeal.feri.org/

- *Voices from the Dust Bowl:* Library of Congress collection of folk songs, documents, and images detailing the existence of Dust Bowl farmers during the era
  http://lcweb2.loc.gov/ammem/afctshtml/tshome.html

KEY TERMS

 Explore the E-Glossary at **www.ablongman.com/anderson**

choral reading (p. 345)
directed listening activity (p. 335)
directed reading activity (p. 334)
echo reading (p. 345)
eye–voice span (p. 332)
five-finger method (p. 330)
language chart (p. 339)
language experience account (p. 344)

listening-prediction activity (p. 325)
literature journal (p. 327)
paired reading (p. 345)
reading–prediction activity (p. 333)
read–skip–read strategy (p. 332)
sustained silent reading (p. 328)
story theater (p. 333)

References

Alter, Gloria (ed.) (1995). "Touching Magic with Jane Yolen." *Social Studies and the Young Learner* 8(2): 29–32.

American Library Association (2000a). "The 100 Most Frequently Challenged Books of 1990–1999." Chicago, IL. Retrieved June 29, 2000, from the World Wide Web: http://www.ala.org/alaorg/oif/top100bannedbooks.html.

———. (2000b). "Coping with Challenges." Chicago, IL. Retrieved June 23, 2000, from the World Wide Web: http://www.ala.org/alaorg/oif/kidsandlibraries.html.

———. (2000c). *Intellectual Freedom and Censorship Q & A.* Chicago, IL. Retrieved July 10, 2000, from the World Wide Web: http://www.ala.org/alaorg/oif/intellectualfreedomandcensorship.html#ifpoint3

———. (2000d). "Library Bill of Rights." Chicago, IL. Retrieved June 23, 2000, from the World Wide Web: http://www.ala.org/work/freedom/lbr.html.

Andersen, Hans Christian (1855/1975). *The Fairy Tale of My Life: An Autobiography.* New York Paddington Press.

Anderson, Nancy A. (1995). "Developing and Assessing Emergent Literacy through Children's Literature." In M. D. Collins & B. G. Moss (eds.), *Literacy Assessment for Today's Schools* (pp. 227–234). College Reading Association.

———. (1998). *Best-Selling Children's Books: Just What Books Do Children Read?* Paper presented at the International Reading Association Conference, Orlando, FL, May 1998.

Anderson, Richard C., E. H. Hiebert, J. A. Scott, & I. A. G. Wilkinson (1985). *Becoming a Nation of Readers: The Report of the Commission on Reading.* Pittsburgh, PA: National Academy of Science.

Atleo, Marlene, Naomi Caldwell, Barbara Landis, Jean Mendoza, Deborah Miranda, Debbie Reese, & LaVera Rose (1999). "Fiction Posing as Truth: A Critical Review of Ann Rinaldi's *My Heart Is on the Ground: The Diary of Nannie Little Rose, A Sioux Girl.*" *Rethinking Schools* 13 (Summer). Available at http://www.rethinkingschools.org/Archives/13_04/review.htm

Baghban, M. (2000). "Conversations with Yep and Soentpiet: Negotiating Between Cultures." *The Dragon Lode, 18*(2), 41–51.

Beaty, Janice J. (1997). *Building Bridges with Multicultural Picture Books: For Children 3–5.* Upper Saddle River, NJ: Merrill.

Bishop, Rudine Sims (1992). "Multicultural Literature for Children: Making Informed Choices." In Violet J. Harris (ed.), *Teaching Multicultural Literature in Grades K–8.* Norwood, MA: Christopher-Gordon, pp. 37–53.

Blount, R. Howard, Jr., & Martha Venning Webb (undated). *Art Projects Plus.* Instruction Fair – TS Denison.

Boykin, A. W. (1983). "The Academic Performance of Afro-American Children." In J. Spence (ed.), *Achievement and Achievement Motives.* San Francisco: W. H. Freeman.

Brinson, Sabrina A. (1997). "Literature of a Dream: Portrayal of African American Characters before and after the Civil Rights Movement." *The Dragon Lode* 15: 7–10.

Bromley, Karen D'Angelo (1996). *Webbing with Literature: Creating Story Maps with Children's Books* (2nd ed.). Boston: Allyn & Bacon.

Brown, Jean E., & Elaine C. Stephens (1995). *Teaching Young Adult Literature: Sharing the Connection.* Albany, NY: Wadsworth.

Carter, B., & K. Harris (1982). "What Junior High Students Like in Books." *Journal of Reading* 26: 42–46.

Cefali, Leslie (1995). "Alphabet Books Revisited." *Book Links* 5 (July): 36–41.

Chamberlain, Julia, & Dorothy Leal (1999). "Caldecott Medal Books and Readability Levels: Not Just 'Picture Books.' " *The Reading Teacher* 52: 898–901.

Chi, Marilyn Mei-Ying. (1993). "Asserting Asian-American Children's Self and Cultural Identity Through Asian-American Children's Literature." *Social Studies Review,* 32(2): 50–55.

Chisholm, Margaret (1972). "Mother Goose—Elucidated." *Elementary English*: 1141–1144.

Cianciolo, Patricia Jean (1973). "Use Wordless Picture Books to Teach Reading, Visual Literacy and to Study Literature." *Top of the News* (American Library Association) 29 (April): 226–234.

Coffin, Tristram Potter (1999). *Encarta Encyclopedia 99.* Microsoft Corporation.

Colbath, Mary Lou (1971). "Worlds as They Should Be: Middle-earth, Narnia and Prydain." *Elementary English* 48: 937–945.

Collard, Sneed B (1998). "Sharing the Passion of Science." *Book Links* 8 (May): 30–34.

Cooperative Children's Book Center. (2001). *Children's Books by and About People of Color Published in the United States.* Retrieved June 2001 from the World Wide Web: http://www.education.wisc.edu/ccbc/pcstats.htm

Cornett, Claudia E. (1999). *The Arts as Meaning Makers.* Upper Saddle River, NJ: Merrill.

Council for Interracial Books for Children. (1976). "How Children's Books Distort the Asian American Image." *Interracial Books for Children Bulletin,* 7(2), 3–23.

———. (2000). *Criteria for Analyzing Books on Asian Americans.* Retrieved June 2001 from the World Wide Web: http://nisus.sfusd.k12.ca.us/org/tact/analyze.html

Cox, Carole, & Paul Boyd-Batstone (1997). *Crossroads: Literature and Language in Culturally and Linguistically Diverse Classrooms.* Upper Saddle River, NJ: Merrill, 1997.

Cullinan, Bernice E. (1989). *Literature and the Child* (2nd ed.). San Diego: Harcourt Brace Jovanovich.

———. (1992). *Read to Me: Raising Kids Who Love to Read.* New York: Scholastic.

Cunningham, Patricia M. (1995). *Phonics They Use.* New York: HarperCollins.

D'Angelo, Karen (1981). "Wordless Picture Books and the Young Language-Disabled Child." *Teaching Exceptional Children* 4: 34–37.

Day, Frances Ann (1997). *Latina and Latino Voices in Literature for Children and Teenagers.* Portsmouth, NH: Heinemann.

———. (1999). *Multicultural Voices in Contemporary Literature: A Resource for Teachers.* Portsmouth, NH: Heinemann.

Daniels, Harvey (1994). *Literature Circles: Voice and Choice in the Student-Centered Classroom.* York, ME: Stenhouse.

DeCasper, Anthony J., Jean-Pierre Lecanuet, Marie-Claire Busnel, & Carolyn Granier-Deferre (1994). "Fetal Reactions to Recurrent Maternal Speech." *Infant Behavior & Development* 14: 159–164.

Donelson, Kenneth L., & Alleen Pace Nilsen (1997). *Literature for Today's Young Adults* (5th ed.). New York: Longman.

Dreyer, Sharon S. (1989). *The Bookfinder.* Circle Pines, MN: American Guidance Services.

Driscoll, Sally (1999). "Coping with Violence." *Book Links* 9 (September): 17–19.

Evslin, Bernard, Dorothy Evslin, & Ned Hoopes (1966). *The Greek Gods.* New York: Scholastic.

Family Friendly Libraries (2000). "What's Wrong with Harry Potter?" Retrieved June 29, 2000, from the World Wide Web: http://www.fflibraries.org/Book_Reports/HarryPotter/WHATS_WRONG_WITH_HARRY_POTTER.htm

Foster, Donald W. (2000). *Author Unknown: On the Trail of Anonymous.* Henry Holt.

Freeman, Evelyn B., & Diane Goetz Person (1998). *Connecting Informational Children's Books with Content Area Learning.* Boston: Allyn & Bacon.

Gerson, Lani (2000). "Modern China in Fiction." *Book Links* 9 (July): 19–22.

Gillet, Jean Wallace, & Charles Temple (1986). *Understanding Reading Problems: Assessment and Instruction* (2nd ed.). Boston: Scott Foresman.

Glazer, Joan I. (1997). *Introduction to Children's Literature* (2nd ed.). Upper Saddle River, NJ: Merrill.

Goforth, Frances S. (1998). *Literature and the Learner.* Belmont, CA: Wadsworth.

Grindler, Martha C., Beverly D. Stratton, & Michael C. McKenna. (1997). *The Right Book, the Right Time.* Boston: Allyn & Bacon.

Grolier Classroom Publishing (1995). *Using Nonfiction Effectively in Your Classroom.* New York: Children's Press/Franklin Watts/Orchard.

Grover, Eulalie Osgood (1971). Foreword to *Mother Goose.* Northbrook, IL: Hubbard Press.

Groff, Patrick (1974). "Children's Literature versus Wordless 'Books.' " *Top of the News* (American Library Association) 30 (April): 294–303.

Gunning, Thomas G. (1998). *Best Books for Beginning Readers.* Boston: Allyn & Bacon.

Harris, Theodore L., & Richard E. Hodges (eds.) (1995). *The Literacy Dictionary: The Vocabulary of Reading and Writing.* Newark, DE: International Reading Association.

Helton, Sonia M. (1995). "Journal Keeping in Mathematics Class." *Teaching Children Mathematics* 1: 336–340.

Hillman, Judith (1999). *Discovering Children's Literature* (2nd ed.). Upper Saddle River, NJ: Merrill.

Hirsch, Eric Donald, Jr. (1987). *Cultural Literacy: What Every American Needs to Know.* Boston: Houghton Mifflin.

Houston, Gloria (1999). *Literature for Young Readers.* Cullowhee, NC: Western Carolina University.

Huck, Charlotte S., Susan Hepler, Janet Hickman, & Barbara Z. Kiefer (1997). *Children's Literature in the Elementary School* (6th ed.). Madison, WI: Brown & Benchmark.

International Reading Association. (February 2001). "Censorship in the Cyber Age." *Reading Today,* 22–23.

Jalongo, M. (1983). "Bibliotherapy: Literature to Promote Socioemotional Growth" *The Reading Teacher* 36: 796–802.

Jurenka, Nancy E. Allen, & Rosanne J. Blass (1996). *Cultivating a Child's Imagination through Gardening.* Englewood, CO: Teacher Ideas Press.

Klesius, Janell, Kathryn L. Laframboise, & Mary Gaier (1998). "Humorous Literature: Motivation for Reluctant Readers." *Reading Research and Instruction* 37: 253–261.

Kupetz, Barbara N. (1999). "Extended Families." *Book Links* 9 (November): 26–30.

Lawson, Cornelia V. (1972). *Children's Reasons and Motivation for the Selection of Favorite Books.* Doctoral dissertation, University of Arkansas.

Li, Suzanne (2000 July). "Mulan and More: Heroines of Chinese Folklore in Picture Books." *Book Links, 10,* 15–18.

Lukens, Rebecca J. (1999). *A Critical Handbook of Children's Literature* (6th ed.). New York: Longman.

Lynch-Brown, Carol, & Carl M. Tomlinson. (1999). *Essentials of Children's Literature* (3rd ed.). Boston: Allyn & Bacon.

May, Jill P. (1980). "Film Productions of Children's Books: Weston Wood Studios and Disney." *Catholic Library World* 51: 210–214.

Mesmer, Heidi Anne (1998). "Goosebumps: The Appeal of Predictability and Violence." *The New Advocate* 11: 107–118.

Muse, Daphne (ed.) (1997). *The New Press Guide to Multicultural Resources for Young Readers.* New York: New Press.

Nodelman, Perry (1996). *The Pleasures of Children's Literature* (2nd ed.). White Plains, NY: Longman.

Norton, Donna E. (1999). *Through the Eyes of a Child* (5th ed.). Englewood Cliffs, NJ: Merrill.

———. (2001). *Multicultural Children's Literature: Through the Eyes of Many Children.* Upper Saddle River, NJ: Merrill.

O'Bruba, W., & D. Camplese (1983). "Beyond Bibliotherapy." In K. VanderMeulen (ed.), *Reading Horizons: Selected Readings, 2.* Kalamazoo, MI: Western Michigan University.

O'Malley, Judy (1999). "Talking with J. K. Rowling." *Book Links* 9 (July): 32–36.

Ouzts, Dan (1991). "The Emergence of Bibliotherapy as a Discipline." *Reading Horizons* 31: 199–206.

———. (1998). *An Examination of the International Reading Association's Children's Choices, Teachers' Choices, and Young Adults' Choices as Related to Bibliotherapy.* Paper presented at the 42nd annual conference of the College Reading Association, Myrtle Beach, SC, November 1998.

Pasco County Library System (undated). *Dewey Decimal and You: A User's Guide.* Hudson, FL.

Patent, Dorothy Hinshaw (1998). "Science Books for Children: An Endangered Species?" *The Horn Book* 74: 309–314.

Peterson, Gordon Charles. (1971). *A Study of Library Books Selected by Second Grade Boys and Girls in the Iowa City, Iowa Schools.* Doctoral dissertation, University of Iowa.

Pollock, Barbara (ed.) (1992). *Black Authors and Illustrators of Children's Books.* New York: Garland, pp. 85–86.

Pratt, Linda, & Janice J. Beaty (1999). *Transcultural Children's Literature.* Upper Saddle River, NJ: Merrill.

Publishers Weekly (1995a). "All-Time Best-Selling Hardcover Children's Books." In *PW Online Edition.* Retrieved June 18, 2000, from the World Wide Web: http://www.publishersweekly.com/articles/19960205_83599.asp

———. (1995b). "All-Time Best-Selling Paperback Children's Books." In *PW Online Edition.* Retrieved June 18, 2000, from the World Wide Web: http://www.publishersweekly.com/articles/19960205_83601.asp

Radencich, Marguerite Cogorno, & Martha Harrison (1997). "Images of Principals in Children's and Young Adult Literature." *The New Advocate* 10: 335–348.

Rosenblatt, Louise M. (1995). *Literature as Exploration* (5th ed.). New York: Modern Language Association.

Roser, Nancy L., & Miriam G. Martinez (1995). *Book Talk and Beyond: Children and Teachers Respond to Literature.* Newark, DE: International Reading Association.

Roser, Nancy L., James V. Hoffman, Linda D. Labbo, & Cindy Farest (1995). "Language

Charts: A Record of Story Time Talk." In Roser, Nancy L., & Miriam G. Martinez, *Book Talk and Beyond: Children and Teachers Respond to Literature.* Newark, DE: International Reading Association.

Rothlein, Liz, & Anita Meyer Meinbach (1996). *Legacies: Using Children's Literature in the Classroom.* New York: HarperCollins.

Russell, David L. (1997). *Literature for Children: A Short Introduction.* New York: Longman.

Sanacore, J. (1982). "Selecting Controversial Materials: Bringing the Forces Together." *Journal of Reading* 25: 506–511.

Schneider, Jenifer Jasinski, & Roger N. Brindley (1997). "Process Drama: Bringing Literature to Life." *The Florida Reading Quarterly* 34: 14–20.

Schulman, Janet (ed.) (1998). Foreword to *The 20th Century Children's Book Treasury.* New York: Knopf.

Schwartz, Albert V. (1977). "*The Five Chinese Brothers*: Time to Retire." *Interracial Books for Children Bulletin,* 8(3), 3–7.

Siu-Runyan, Yvonne (1999). "1998 Notable Books for a Global Society: A K–12 list." *The Reading Teacher* 52: 498–504.

Smith, Laura J. (1992). *Children's Book Awards International.* Jefferson, NC: McFarland.

Stewig, John Warren (1980). *Children and Literature.* Chicago: Rand McNally.

Stoll, Donald R. (1997). *Magazines for Kids and Teens.* Glassboro, NJ: Educational Press.

Stoodt, Barbara D., Linda B. Amspaugh, & Jane Hunt (1996). *Children's Literature: Discovery for a Lifetime.* Scottsdale, AZ: Gorsuch Scarisbrick.

Sutherland, Zena (1997). *Children and Books* (9th ed.). New York: Longman.

Temple, Charles A., & Jean Wallace Gillet (1989). *Language Arts: Learning Processes and Teaching Practices.* Boston: Little, Brown.

Temple, Charles, Miriam Martinez, Junko Yokota, & Alice Naylor (1998). *Children's Books in Children's Hands: An Introduction to Their Literature.* Boston: Allyn & Bacon.

Tomlinson, Carl M. (1998). *Children's Books from Other Countries.* Lanham, MD: Scarecrow Press.

Tompkins, Gail E., & Lea M. McGee (1993). *Teaching Reading with Literature: Case Studies to Action Plans.* Upper Saddle River, NJ: Merrill.

Tunnell, Michael O. (1992). "Books in the Classroom: Columbus and Historical Perspective." *The Horn Book* 68: 244–248.

Warner, Marina (1991). "The Absent Mother: Women against Women in Old Wives' Tales." *History Today* 41.

Warren, Janet S., Norma Jean Prater, & Diane L. Griswold (1990). "Parental Practices of Reading Aloud to Preschool Children." *Reading Improvement* 27: 41–45.

Whitney, Phyllis A. (1976). *Writing Juvenile Stories and Novels.* Boston: The Writer.

Wilburn, Medicine Hawk (1998). *Buffalo Dreams: Using Native American Creation Legends to Stimulate Writing.* Paper presented at the International Reading Association Conference, Orlando, FL, May 1998.

Wilms, Denise M. (1978). "An Evaluation of Biography." *Booklist* 75: 218–220.

Wynn, Marjorie J. (1996). *Creative Teaching Strategies.* Albany, N.Y.: Delmar.

Yokota, Junko, & Stephanie Sanderson (2000). "Talking with Janet S. Wong." *Book Links* 9 (January): 57–61.

Yolen, Jane. (1973). *Writing Books for Children.* Boston: The Writer.

———. (1981). *Touch Magic: Fantasy, Faerie and Folklore in the Literature of Childhood.* New York: Philomel.

Name and Title Index

Subject Index

Credits

"Reader Response Theory" on pp. 35–37 is printed by permission of Gloria Houston.

Illustration on p. 41 is from *The Voyage of the Frog* by Gary Paulsen. Copyright © 1989. Reprinted by permission of Grolier Publishing Company.

Illustration on p. 44 is from *Ed Emberley's ABC* by Ed Emberley. Copyright © 1978 by Edward R. Emberley. By permission of Little, Brown and Company (Inc.).

Excerpt on p. 56 is reprinted with the permission of Simon & Schuster Books for Young Readers, an imprint of Simon & Schuster Children's Publishing Division from *Chicka Chicka Boom Boom* by Bill Martin, Jr., and John Archambault. Text copyright © 1989 Bill Martin, Jr., and John Archambault.

Excerpt on p. 57 is from *Dr. Seuss's ABC* by Dr. Seuss, ™ & copyright © by Dr. Seuss Enterprises, L. P. 1963, renewed 1981. Used by permission of Random House Children's Books, a division of Random House, Inc.

Excerpt on p. 61 is from *Arctic Fives Arrive* by Elinor J. Pinczes. Text copyright © 1996 by Elinor J. Pinczes. Reprinted by permission of Houghton Mifflin Company. All rights reserved.

Illustration on p. 69 is from *Sing, Pierrot, Sing: A Picture Book in Mime,* copyright © 1983 by Tomie dePaola, reproduced by permission of Harcourt, Inc.

Illustration on p. 74 is by Charles Santore, illustration copyright © 1988 by Charles Santore, from *Aesop's Fables* illustrated by Charles Santore. Used by permission of Crown Children's Books, a division of Random House, Inc.

Illustration on p. 93 is from *Lon Po Po* by Ed Young, copyright © 1989 by Ed Young. Used by permission of Philomel Books, an imprint of Penguin Putnam Books for Young Readers, a division of Penguin Putnam Inc.

Poem on pp. 96–97 is from *Bringing the Rain to Kapiti Plain* by Verna Aardema, illustrated by Beatriz Vidal, copyright © 1981 by Verna Aardema, text. Copyright © 1981 by Beatriz Vidal, illustrations. Used by permission of Dial Books for Young Readers, an imprint of Penguin Putnam Books for Young Readers, a division of Penguin Putnam Inc.

"A Peanut" and "Fuzzy Wuzzy" on p. 105 are from *A Rocket in My Pocket: The Rhymes and Chants of Young Americans,* compiled by Carl Withers.

Copyright © 1948 by Carl Withers. Copyright © 1976 by Samuel H. Halperin. Reprinted by permission of Henry Holt and Company, LLC.

"Censorship" (pp. 108–111) and Box 5.1, "Censorship and *Harry Potter*" (p. 137), are printed by permission of Jenifer Jasinski Schneider.

Illustration on p. 112 is from *Harry Potter and the Sorcerer's Stone,* written by J. K. Rowling, illustrated by Mary Grandpre. *Harry Potter* characters, names, and all related indicia are trademarks of Warner Bros. 2001. Reprinted by permission.

Illustration on p. 129 is by Diane Goode, illustration copyright © 1983 by Random House, Inc., from *Peter Pan* by J. M. Barrie, adapted by Josette Frank, illustrated by Diane Goode. Used by permission of Random House Children's Books, a division of Random House, Inc.

Illustration on p. 148 is from *Frog and Toad Together* by Arnold Lobel. Copyright © 1971, 1972 by Arnold Lobel. Used by permission of HarperCollins Publishers.

Excerpt on p. 153 is from *Rudolph the Red-Nosed Reindeer* by Robert L. May. Copyright © 1939, 1967 by Robert L. May Company. Published by Modern Curriculum Press. Used by permission of Pearson Education, Inc.

Excerpt on p. 155 is from *Frog and Toad Are Friends* by Arnold Lobel. Copyright © 1970 by Arnold Lobel. Used by permission of HarperCollins Publishers.

Illustration on p. 157 is reprinted with the permission of Simon & Schuster Books for Young Readers, an imprint of Simon & Schuster's Children's Publishing Division from *Sylvester and the Magic Pebble* by William Steig. Copyright © 1969 William Steig.

Illustration on p. 171 is from *Navajo: Visions and Voices across the Mesa* by Shonto Begay. Copyright © 1995 by Shonto Begay. Reprinted by permission of Scholastic Inc.

Illustration on p. 176 is from *Felita* by Nicholasa Mohr, illustrated by Ray Cruz, copyright © 1979 by Ray Cruz, illustrations. Used by permission of Dial Books for Young Readers, an imprint of Penguin Putnam Books for Young Readers, a division of Penguin Putnam Inc.

"African American Literature" on pp. 179–181 is printed by permission of Sabrina A. Brinson.